This volume contains the FUSHIGI YÛGI installments from ANIMERICA EXTRA Vol. 2, No. 5 through Vol. 2, No. 10 in their entirety.

STORY & ART BY YÛ WATASE

English Adaptation/Yuji Oniki
Touch-Up Art & Lettering/Bill Spicer
Cover Design/Hidemi Sahara
Layout & Graphics/Carolina Ugalde
Editor/William Flanagan
Managing Editor/Annette Roman

V.P. of Editorial/Hyoe Narita
Publisher/Seiji Horibuchi
V.P. of Sales & Marketing/Rick Bauer

Printed in Canada

Published by Viz Communications, Inc.
P.O. Box 77010, San Francisco, CA 94107

10 9 8 7
First printing, December 1999
Fifth printing, November 2001
Sixth printing, May 2002
Seventh printing, October 2002

FUSHIGI YÛGI GRAPHIC NOVELS TO DATE
VOLUME 1: PRIESTESS
VOLUME 2: ORACLE
VOLUME 3: DISCIPLE
VOLUME 4: BANDIT
VOLUME 5: RIVAL
VOLUME 6: SUMMONER

- get your own vizmail.net email account
- register for the weekly email newsletter
- sign up for your free catalog
- voice 1-800-394-3042   fax 415-384-8936

Get your free Viz Shop-By-Mail catalog!
(800) 394-3042 or fax (415) 348-8936

ANIMERICA EXTRA GRAPHIC NOVEL

fushigi yûgi™

The Mysterious Play
VOL. 2: ORACLE

Story & Art By
YÛ WATASE

CONTENTS

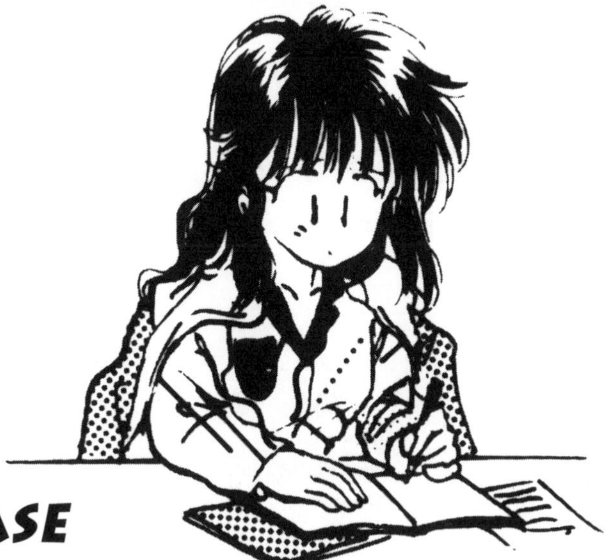

YÛ WATASE

Yû Watase was born on March 5 in a town near Osaka, and she was raised there before moving to Tokyo to follow the dream of creating manga. In the decade since her debut short story, *Pajama de Ojama* ("An Intrusion in Pajamas"), she has produced more than 50 compiled volumes of short stories and continuing series. Her latest series, *Ayashi no Ceres* ("Ominous Ceres"), is currently running in the anthology magazine *Shôjo Comic*. She loves science fiction, fantasy and comedy.

The Universe of the Four Gods is based on ancient China, but Japanese pronunciation of Chinese names differs slightly from their Chinese equivalents. Here is a short glossary of the Japanese pronunciation of the Chinese names in this graphic novel:

CHINESE	JAPANESE	PERSON OR PLACE	MEANING
Tai Yi-Jun	*Tai Itsukun*	*An oracle*	*Preeminent Person*
Daichi-San	*Daikyokuzan*	*A mountain*	*Greatest Mountain*
Lai Lai	*Nyan Nyan*	*A servant*	*Nanny*
Hong-Nan	*Konan*	*Southern Kingdom*	*Crimson South*
Qu-Dong	*Kutô*	*Eastern Kingdom*	*Gathered East*

STORY THUS FAR

Chipper junior high-school girl Miaka is trying to study as hard as she can to get into Jonan High School like her mother wants her to. During a study session in the City Central Library, Miaka and her best friend Yui find a strange book—*The Universe of the Four Gods*. As they start to read, the book draws them physically into its universe, a fantasy version of ancient China! After a short adventure in the world of the book, they return to modern-day Tokyo thinking it was only a dream.

Miaka and her mother get into a terrible argument, and Miaka escapes back into the world of the book. There she finds that she is being offered the role of the book's heroine, the Young Lady of Legends who will be granted a wish and special powers by the god Suzaku. First she must gather all seven Celestial Warriors of Suzaku. Luckily, she has already found the dashing Tamahome, the sophisticated emperor Hotohori, and the beautiful-but-vindictive Nuriko. Now Hotohori has declared that he will make Miaka his empress, which enrages the love-struck Nuriko, and when Miaka confesses her love for Tamahome, he gives her the brush-off. Miaka swoons and collapses.

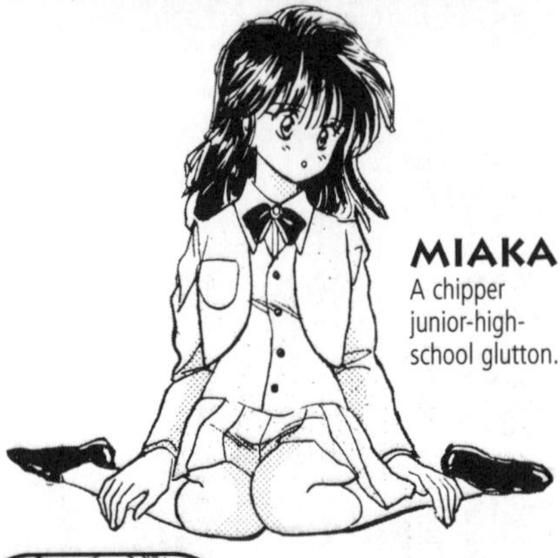

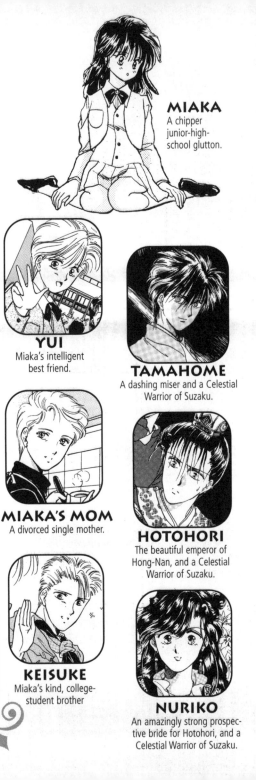

MIAKA
A chipper junior-high-school glutton.

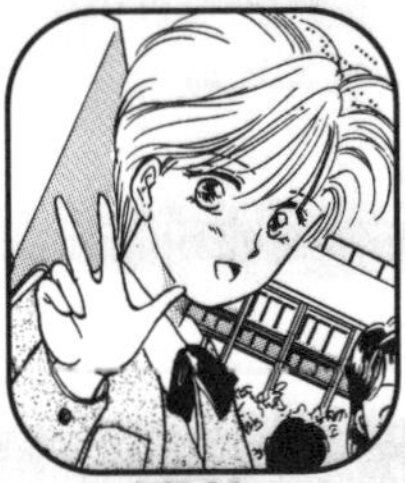

YUI
Miaka's intelligent best friend.

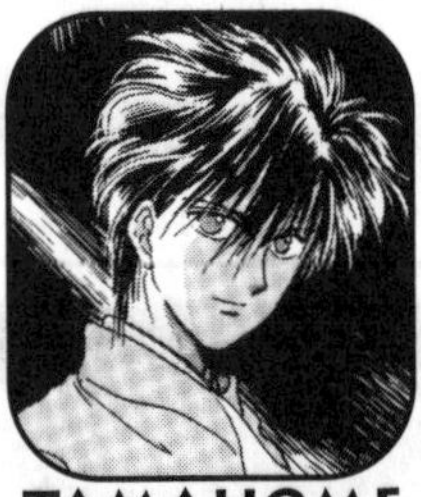

TAMAHOME
A dashing miser and a Celestial Warrior of Suzaku.

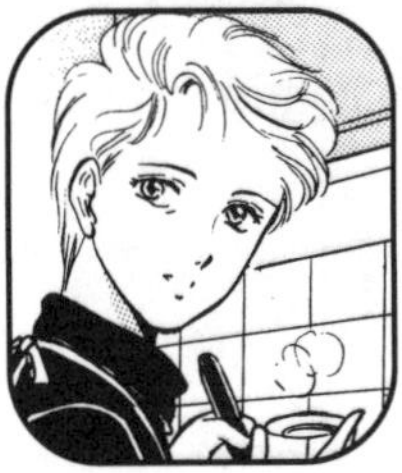

MIAKA'S MOM
A divorced single mother.

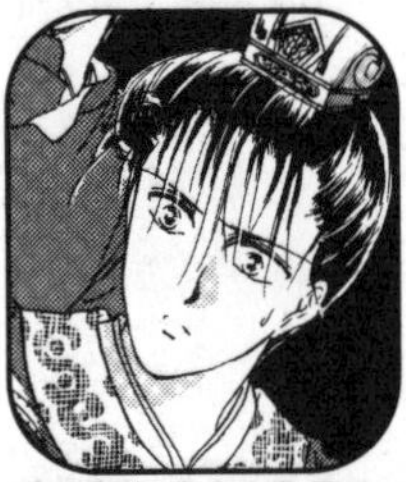

HOTOHORI
The beautiful emperor of Hong-Nan, and a Celestial Warrior of Suzaku.

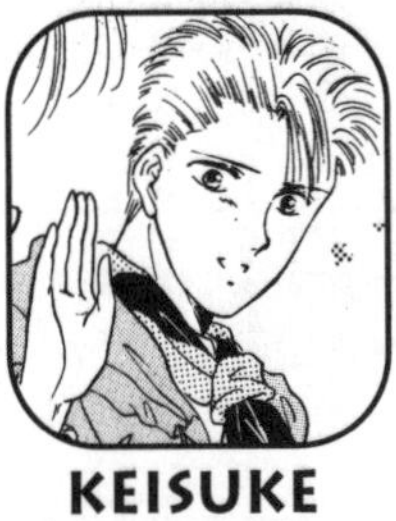

KEISUKE
Miaka's kind, college-student brother

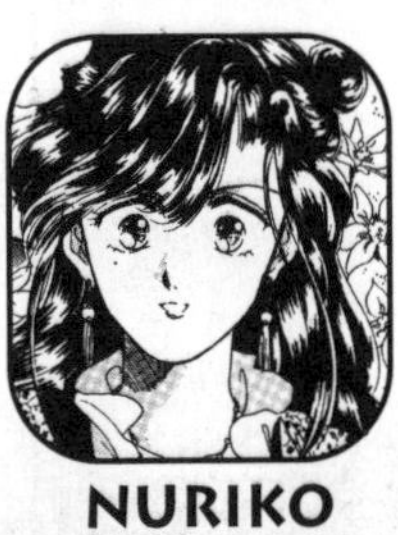

NURIKO
An amazingly strong prospective bride for Hotohori, and a Celestial Warrior of Suzaku.

CHAPTER SEVEN
THE AIMLESS HEART

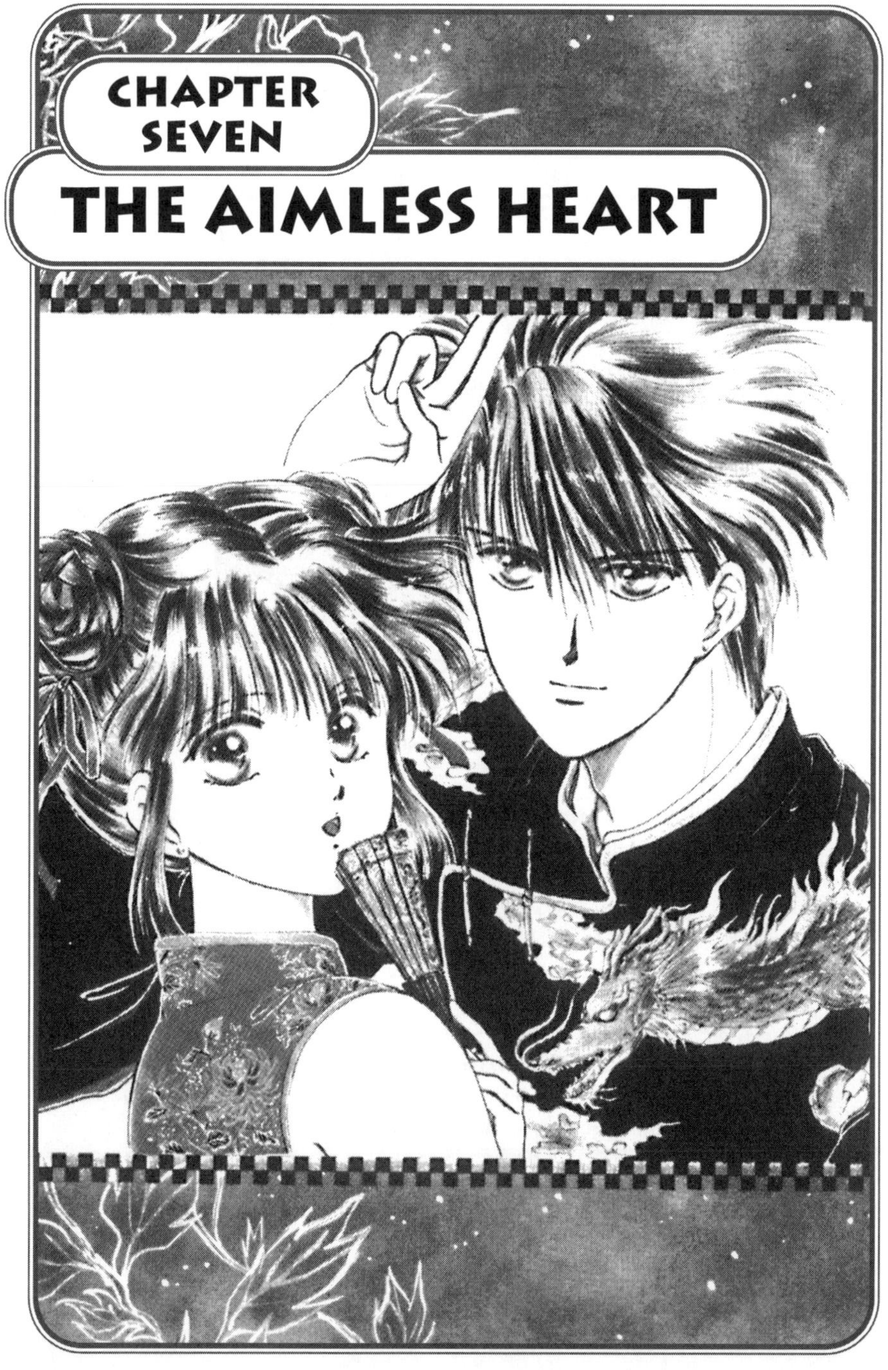

MIAKA YŪKI

夕 城 美 朱

MIAKA

- Born in Tokyo. Age: 15
- Third District Junior High School, 9th Grade, 4th Homeroom, Seat Number 18
- Residing with her mother and her brother (a college student)
- Height: 5' 2", Weight: 106 lb
  Slightly pudgy. (But she manages to avoid getting fat.)
- Hobbies: Reading manga, eating, and baking cookies.
- Personality: Outgoing and optimistic. Amicable with everyone. Tends to be guileless and sentimental. Never suspicious. Naive, but sometimes she surprises adults with an insightful comment. Can be unassuming. Magnanimous and courageous but somewhat unsophisticated. Seems to give the impression she always needs help so she always seems to have someone looking after her. Believes herself to be considerate.

Flower Circle
Seal of Approval

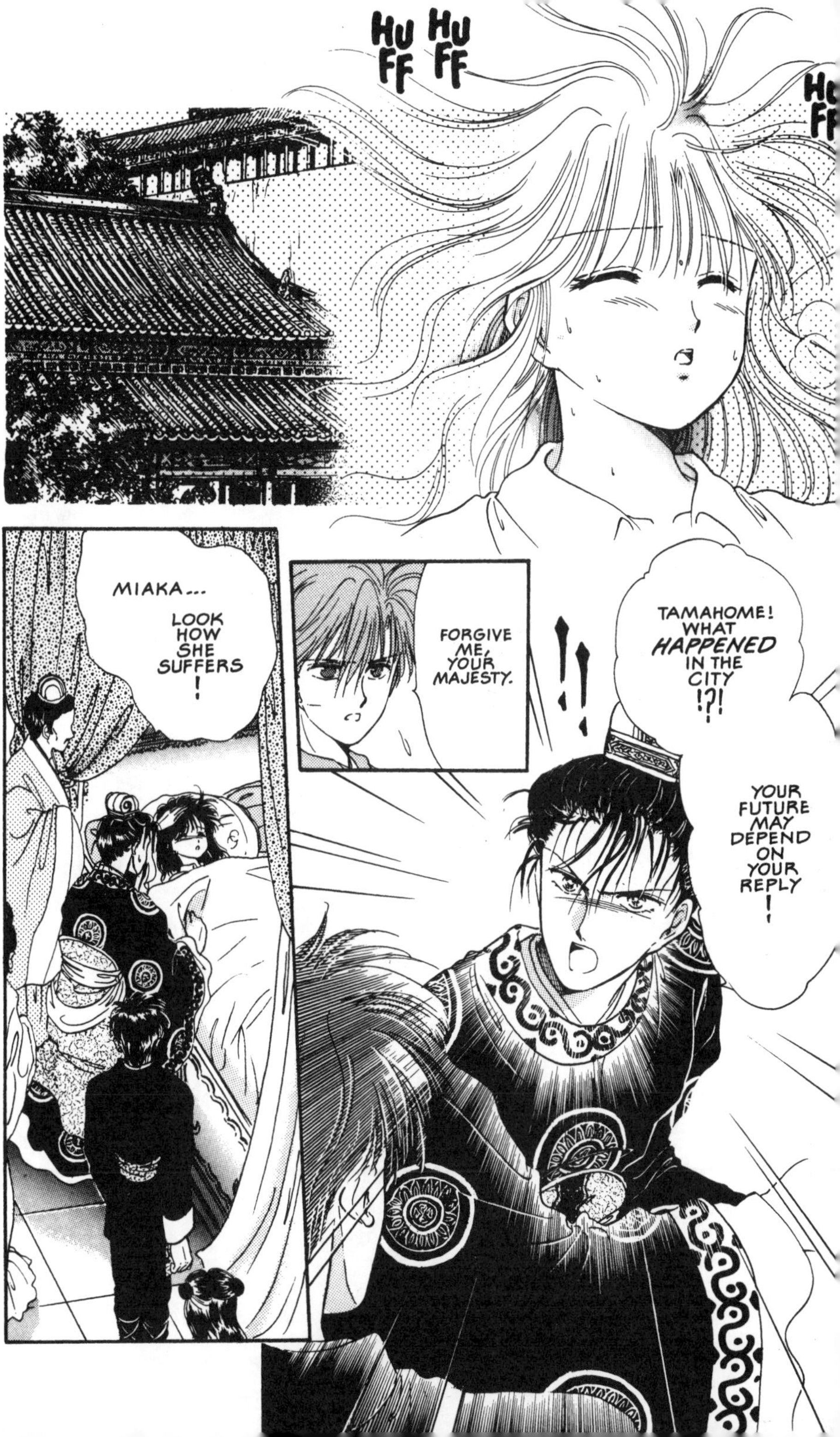
HUFF HUFF
HUFF
MIAKA...
LOOK HOW SHE SUFFERS!
FORGIVE ME, YOUR MAJESTY.
!!
TAMAHOME! WHAT HAPPENED IN THE CITY!?!
YOUR FUTURE MAY DEPEND ON YOUR REPLY!

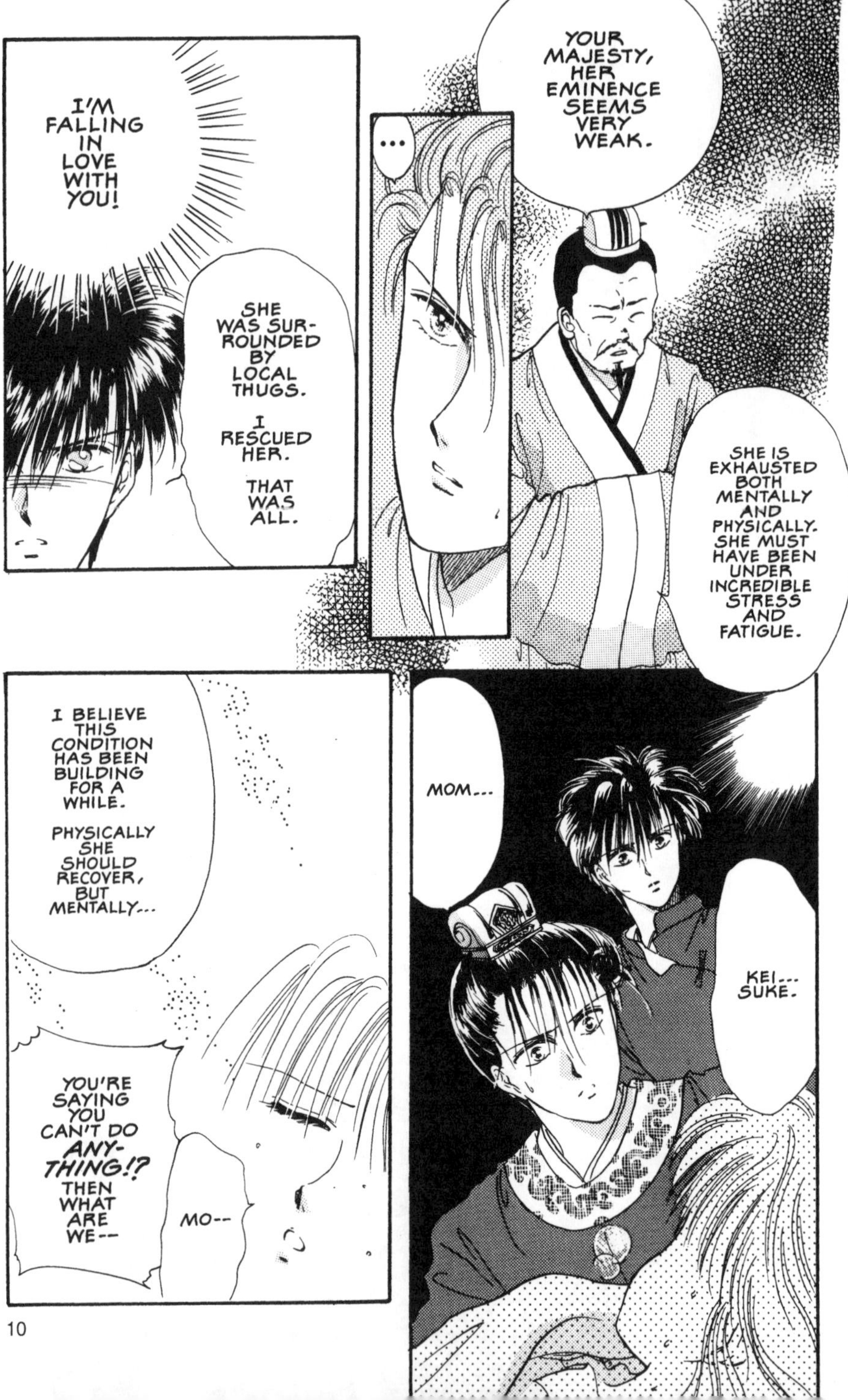
I'M FALLING IN LOVE WITH YOU!
SHE WAS SURROUNDED BY LOCAL THUGS. I RESCUED HER. THAT WAS ALL.
...
YOUR MAJESTY, HER EMINENCE SEEMS VERY WEAK.
SHE IS EXHAUSTED BOTH MENTALLY AND PHYSICALLY. SHE MUST HAVE BEEN UNDER INCREDIBLE STRESS AND FATIGUE.
I BELIEVE THIS CONDITION HAS BEEN BUILDING FOR A WHILE. PHYSICALLY SHE SHOULD RECOVER, BUT MENTALLY...
YOU'RE SAYING YOU CAN'T DO ANYTHING!? THEN WHAT ARE WE--
MO--
MOM...
KEI... SUKE.

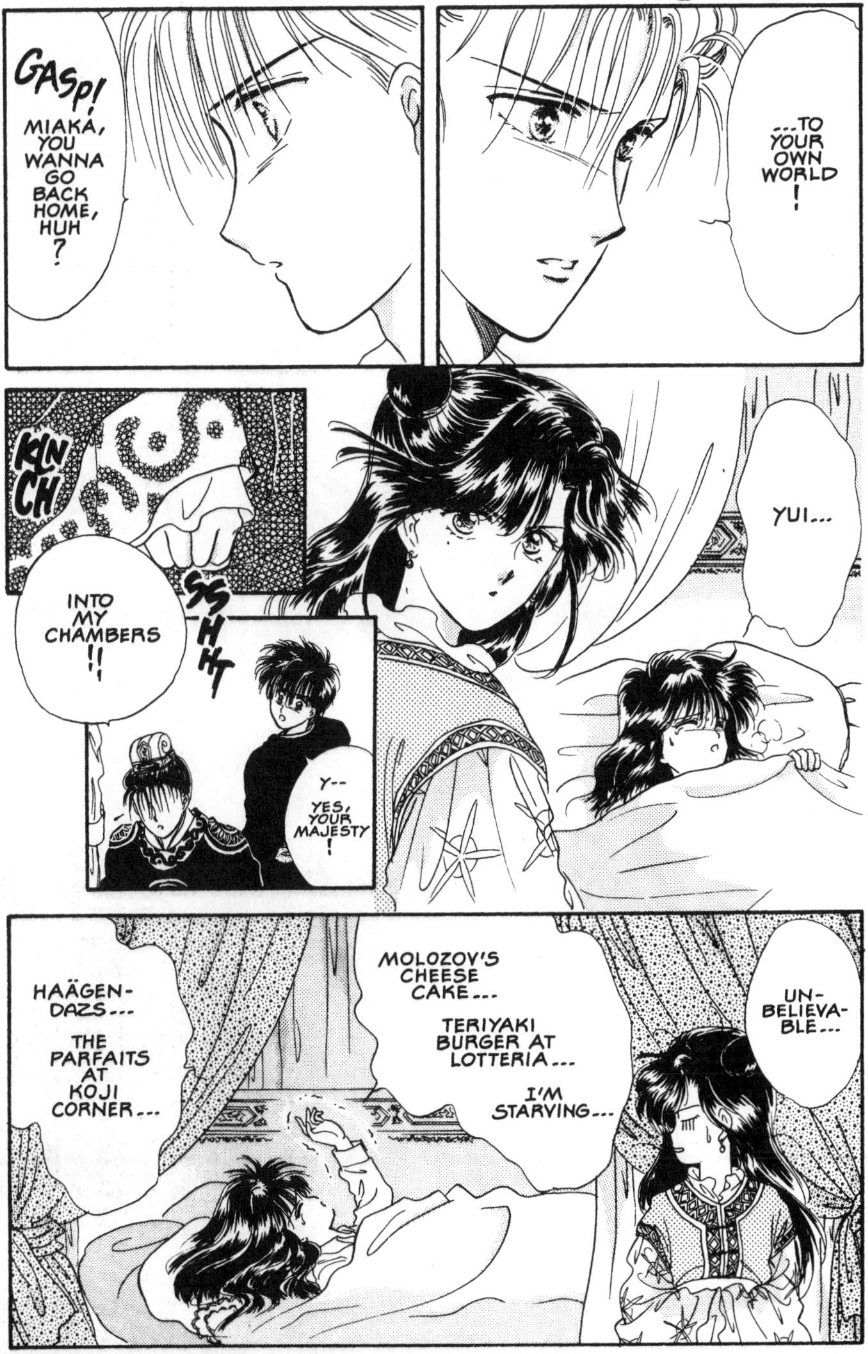
GASP!
MIAKA, YOU WANNA GO BACK HOME, HUH?
...TO YOUR OWN WORLD!
KLNCH
INTO MY CHAMBERS!!
SSHHT
Y-- YES, YOUR MAJESTY!
YUI...
HAÄGEN-DAZS...
THE PARFAITS AT KOJI CORNER...
MOLOZOV'S CHEESE CAKE...
TERIYAKI BURGER AT LOTTERIA...
I'M STARVING...
UN-BELIEVA-BLE...

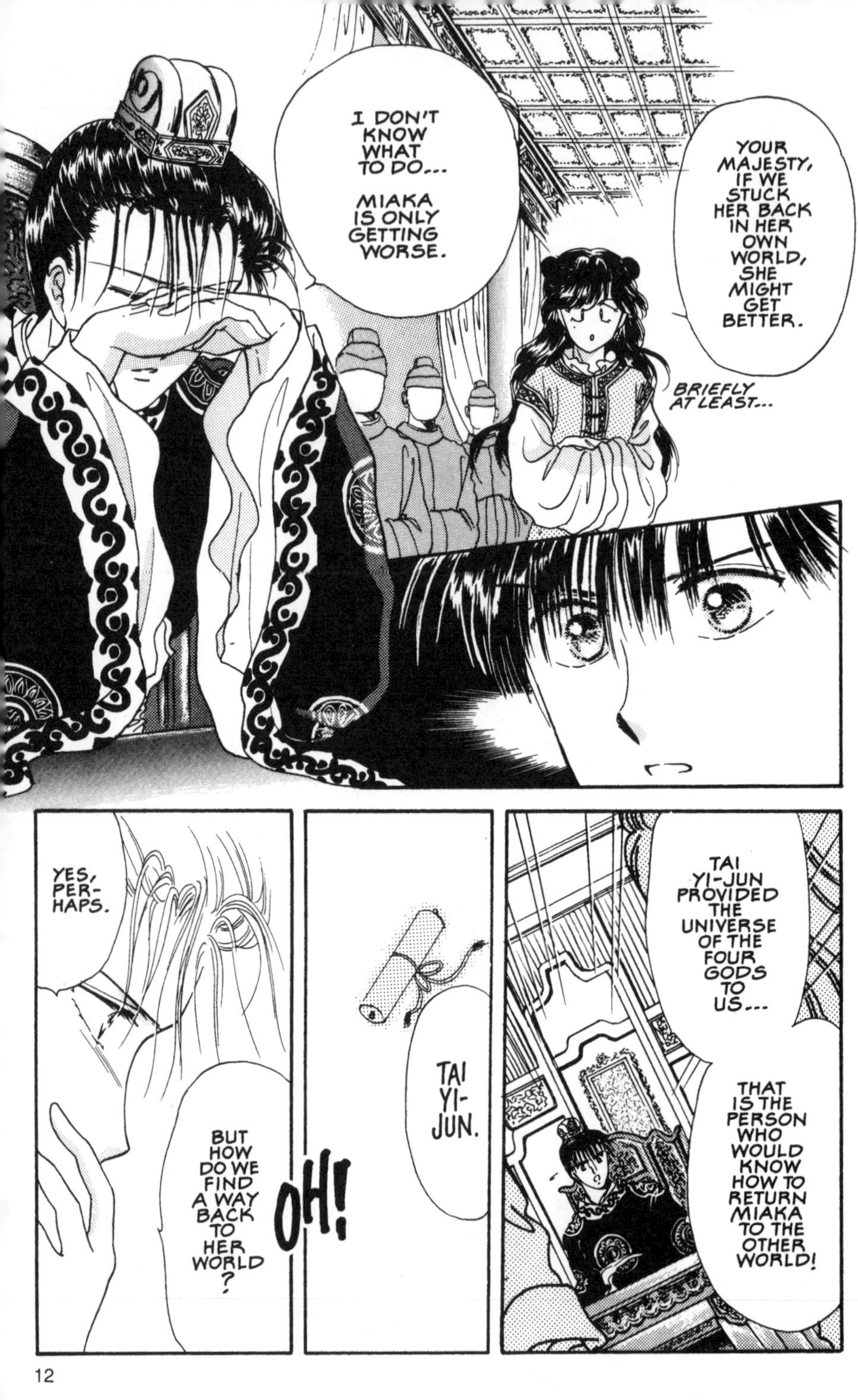

I DON'T KNOW WHAT TO DO... MIAKA IS ONLY GETTING WORSE.
YOUR MAJESTY, IF WE STUCK HER BACK IN HER OWN WORLD, SHE MIGHT GET BETTER.
BRIEFLY AT LEAST...
YES, PERHAPS.
BUT HOW DO WE FIND A WAY BACK TO HER WORLD?
OH!
TAI YI-JUN.
TAI YI-JUN PROVIDED THE UNIVERSE OF THE FOUR GODS TO US...
THAT IS THE PERSON WHO WOULD KNOW HOW TO RETURN MIAKA TO THE OTHER WORLD!

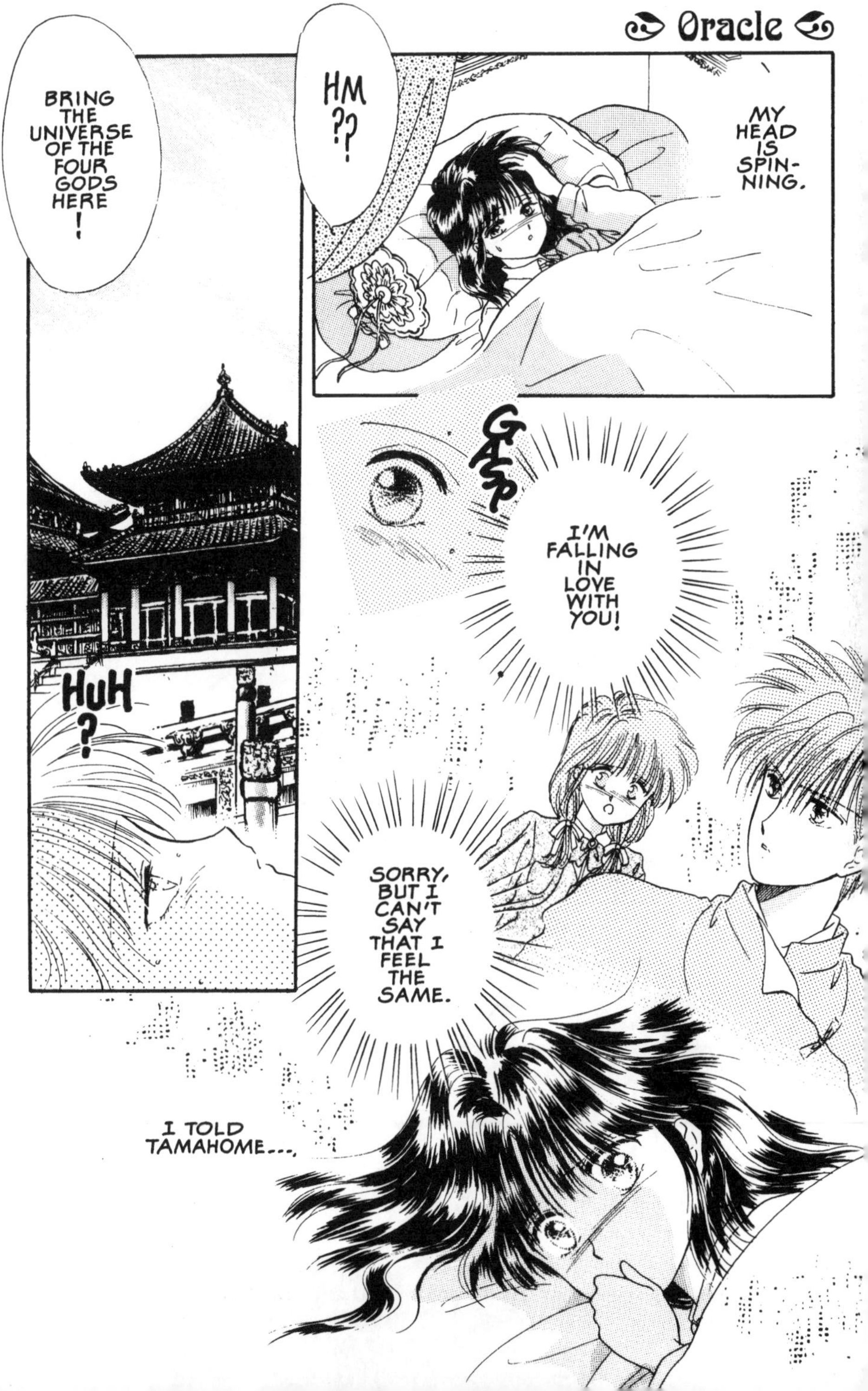
BRING THE UNIVERSE OF THE FOUR GODS HERE !
HUH ?
HM ??
MY HEAD IS SPIN-NING.
GASP
I'M FALLING IN LOVE WITH YOU!
SORRY, BUT I CAN'T SAY THAT I FEEL THE SAME.
I TOLD TAMAHOME...,

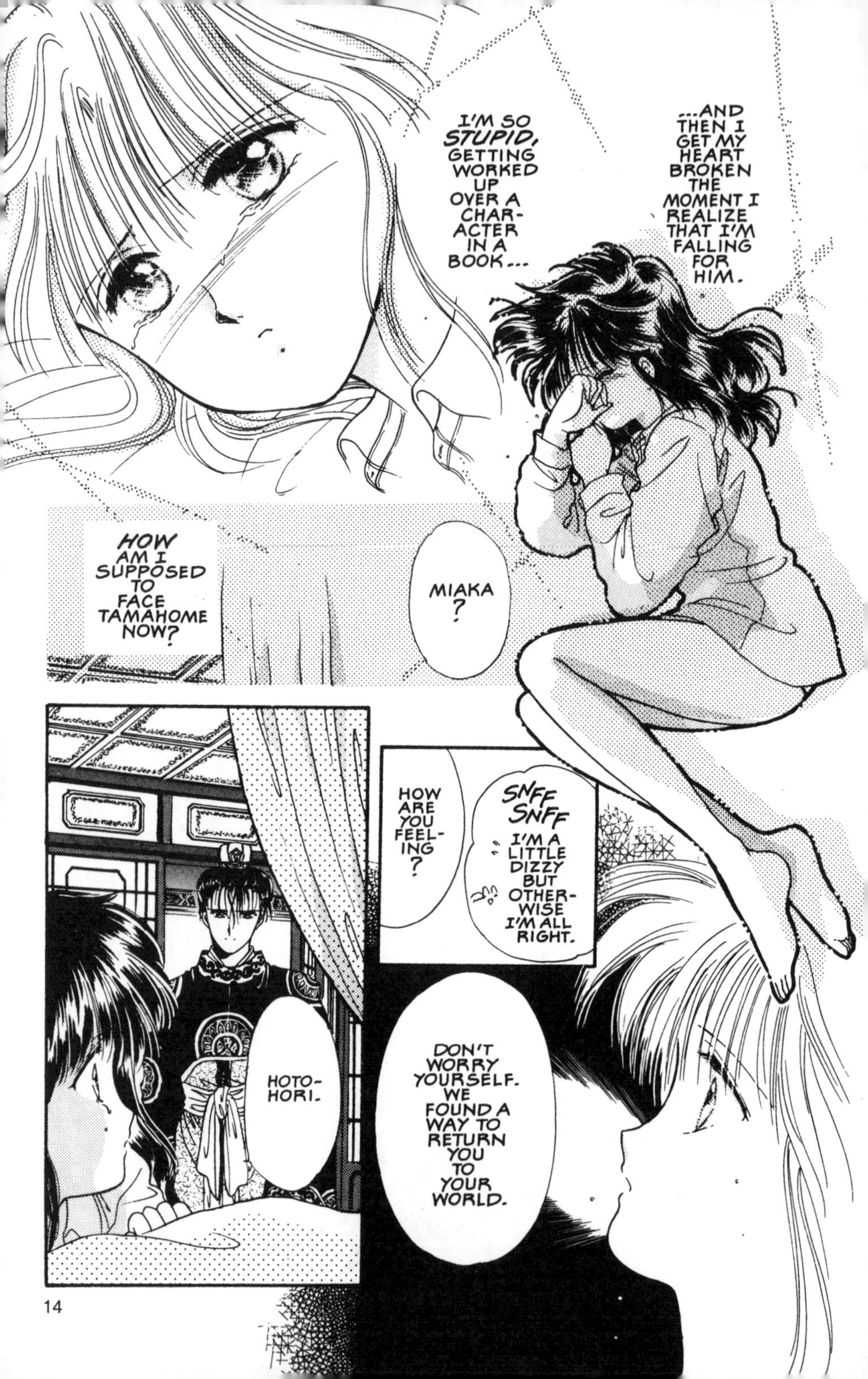
I'M SO STUPID, GETTING WORKED UP OVER A CHARACTER IN A BOOK...
...AND THEN I GET MY HEART BROKEN THE MOMENT I REALIZE THAT I'M FALLING FOR HIM.
HOW AM I SUPPOSED TO FACE TAMAHOME NOW?
MIAKA?
HOTO-HORI.
HOW ARE YOU FEELING?
SNFF SNFF
I'M A LITTLE DIZZY BUT OTHERWISE I'M ALL RIGHT.
DON'T WORRY YOURSELF. WE FOUND A WAY TO RETURN YOU TO YOUR WORLD.

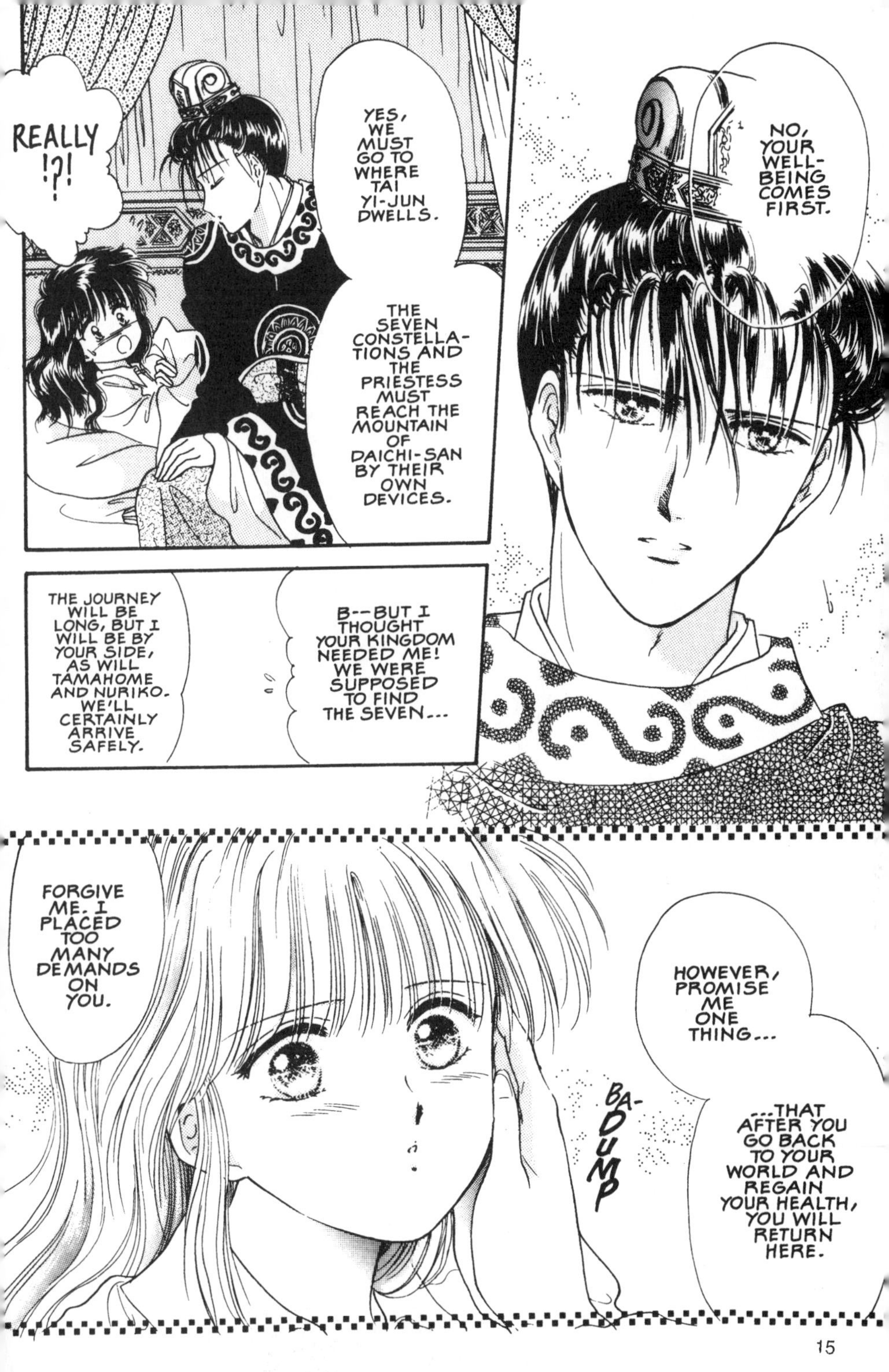
REALLY !?!
YES, WE MUST GO TO WHERE TAI YI-JUN DWELLS.
THE SEVEN CONSTELLATIONS AND THE PRIESTESS MUST REACH THE MOUNTAIN OF DAICHI-SAN BY THEIR OWN DEVICES.
THE JOURNEY WILL BE LONG, BUT I WILL BE BY YOUR SIDE, AS WILL TAMAHOME AND NURIKO. WE'LL CERTAINLY ARRIVE SAFELY.
B--BUT I THOUGHT YOUR KINGDOM NEEDED ME! WE WERE SUPPOSED TO FIND THE SEVEN...
NO, YOUR WELL-BEING COMES FIRST.
FORGIVE ME. I PLACED TOO MANY DEMANDS ON YOU.
HOWEVER, PROMISE ME ONE THING...
BA-DUMP
...THAT AFTER YOU GO BACK TO YOUR WORLD AND REGAIN YOUR HEALTH, YOU WILL RETURN HERE.

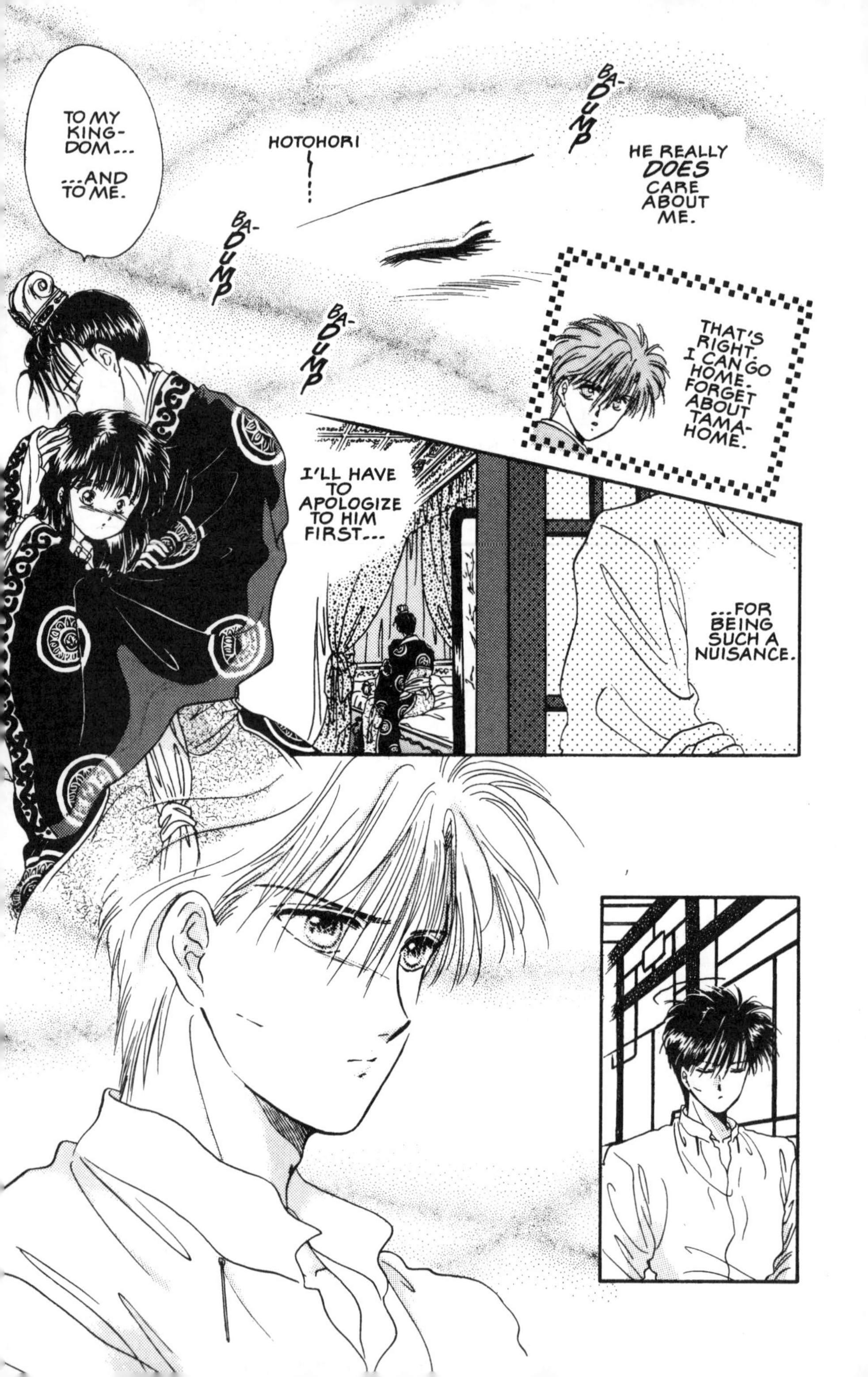

TO MY KING-DOM... ...AND TO ME.
HOTOHORI !!
BA-DOUMP
BA-DOUMP
BA-DOUMP
HE REALLY DOES CARE ABOUT ME.
THAT'S RIGHT. I CAN GO HOME. FORGET ABOUT TAMA-HOME.
I'LL HAVE TO APOLOGIZE TO HIM FIRST...
...FOR BEING SUCH A NUISANCE.

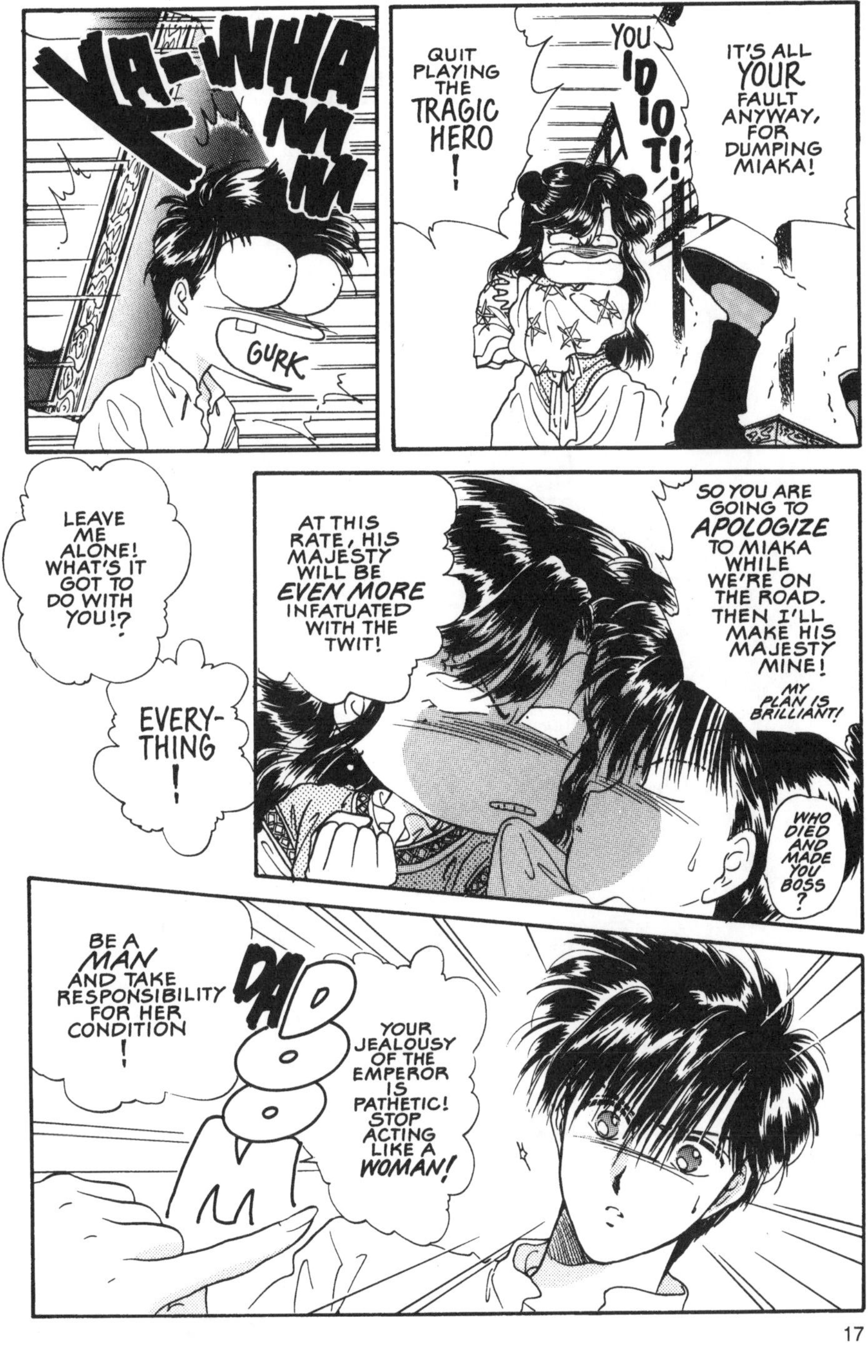
YA-WHAMMM
GURK
QUIT PLAYING THE TRAGIC HERO!
YOU IDIOT!
IT'S ALL YOUR FAULT ANYWAY, FOR DUMPING MIAKA!
LEAVE ME ALONE! WHAT'S IT GOT TO DO WITH YOU!?
EVERYTHING!
AT THIS RATE, HIS MAJESTY WILL BE EVEN MORE INFATUATED WITH THE TWIT!
SO YOU ARE GOING TO APOLOGIZE TO MIAKA WHILE WE'RE ON THE ROAD. THEN I'LL MAKE HIS MAJESTY MINE!
MY PLAN IS BRILLIANT!
WHO DIED AND MADE YOU BOSS?
BE A MAN AND TAKE RESPONSIBILITY FOR HER CONDITION!
DADOOM
YOUR JEALOUSY OF THE EMPEROR IS PATHETIC! STOP ACTING LIKE A WOMAN!

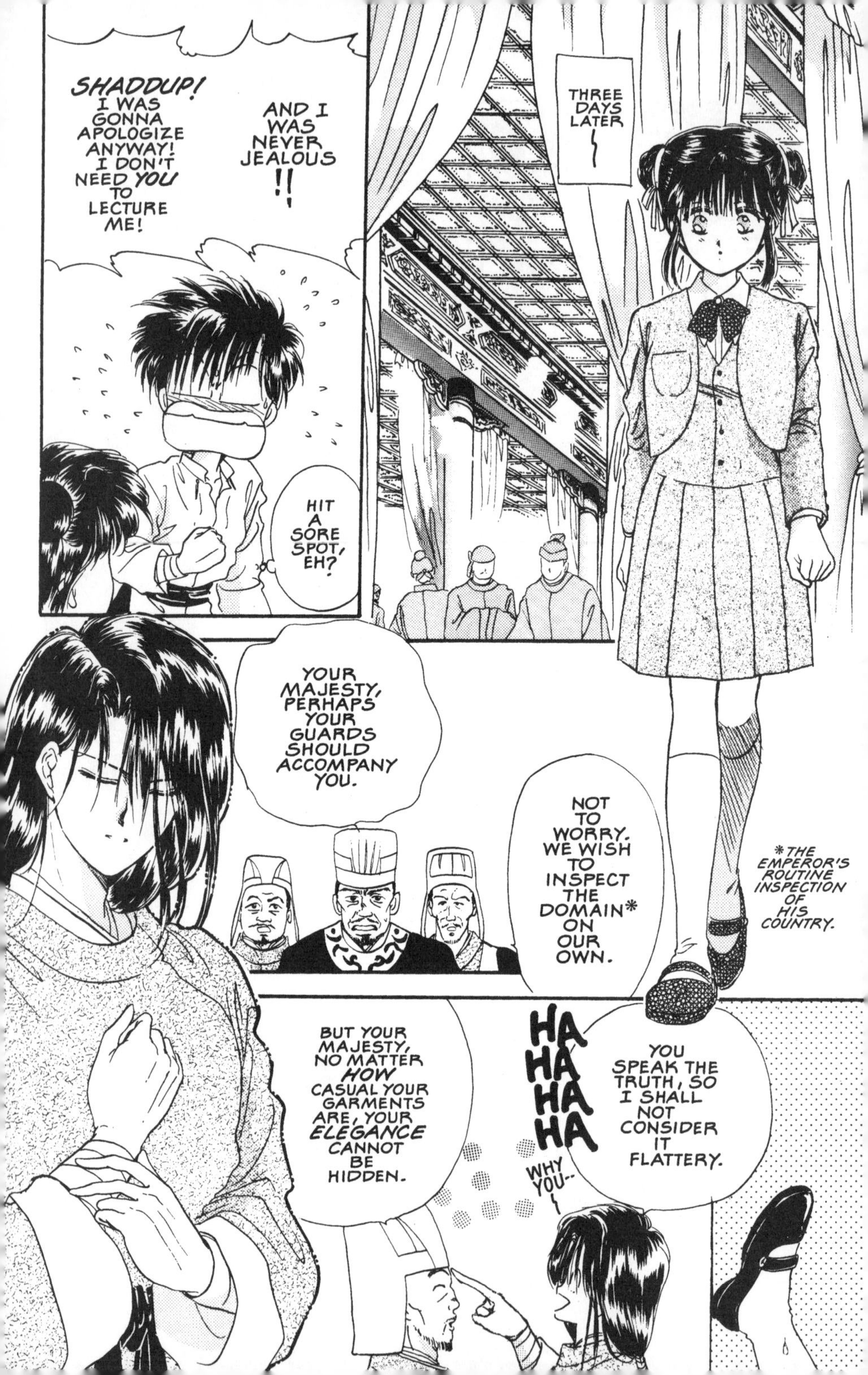
SHADDUP! I WAS GONNA APOLOGIZE ANYWAY! I DON'T NEED YOU TO LECTURE ME!
AND I WAS NEVER JEALOUS !!
HIT A SORE SPOT, EH?
THREE DAYS LATER
YOUR MAJESTY, PERHAPS YOUR GUARDS SHOULD ACCOMPANY YOU.
NOT TO WORRY. WE WISH TO INSPECT THE DOMAIN* ON OUR OWN.
*THE EMPEROR'S ROUTINE INSPECTION OF HIS COUNTRY.
BUT YOUR MAJESTY, NO MATTER HOW CASUAL YOUR GARMENTS ARE, YOUR ELEGANCE CANNOT BE HIDDEN.
HA HA HA HA
YOU SPEAK THE TRUTH, SO I SHALL NOT CONSIDER IT FLATTERY.
WHY YOU--

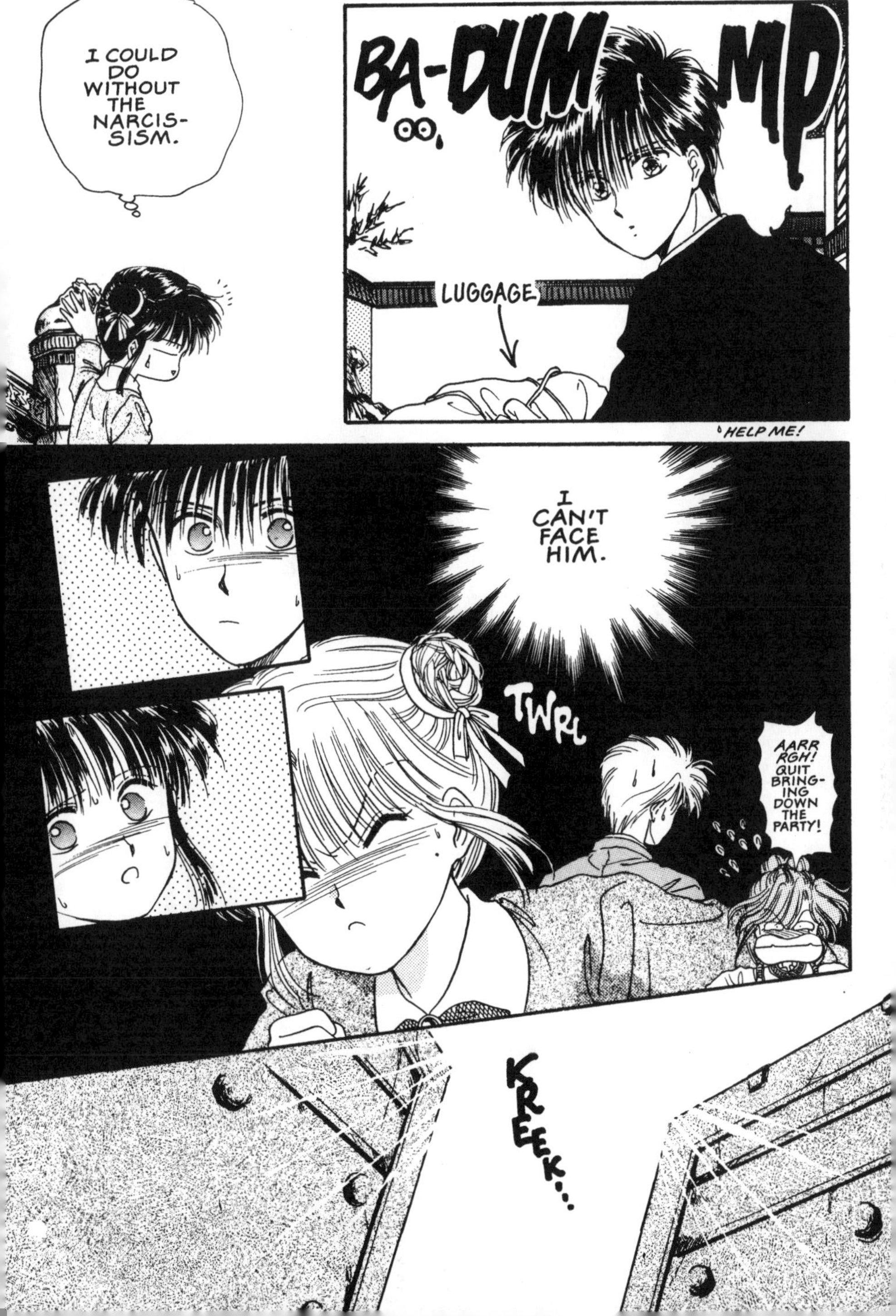
I COULD DO WITHOUT THE NARCISSISM.
BA-DUMP
oo,
LUGGAGE
HELP ME!
I CAN'T FACE HIM.
TWRL
AARRRGH! QUIT BRINGING DOWN THE PARTY!
KREEK...

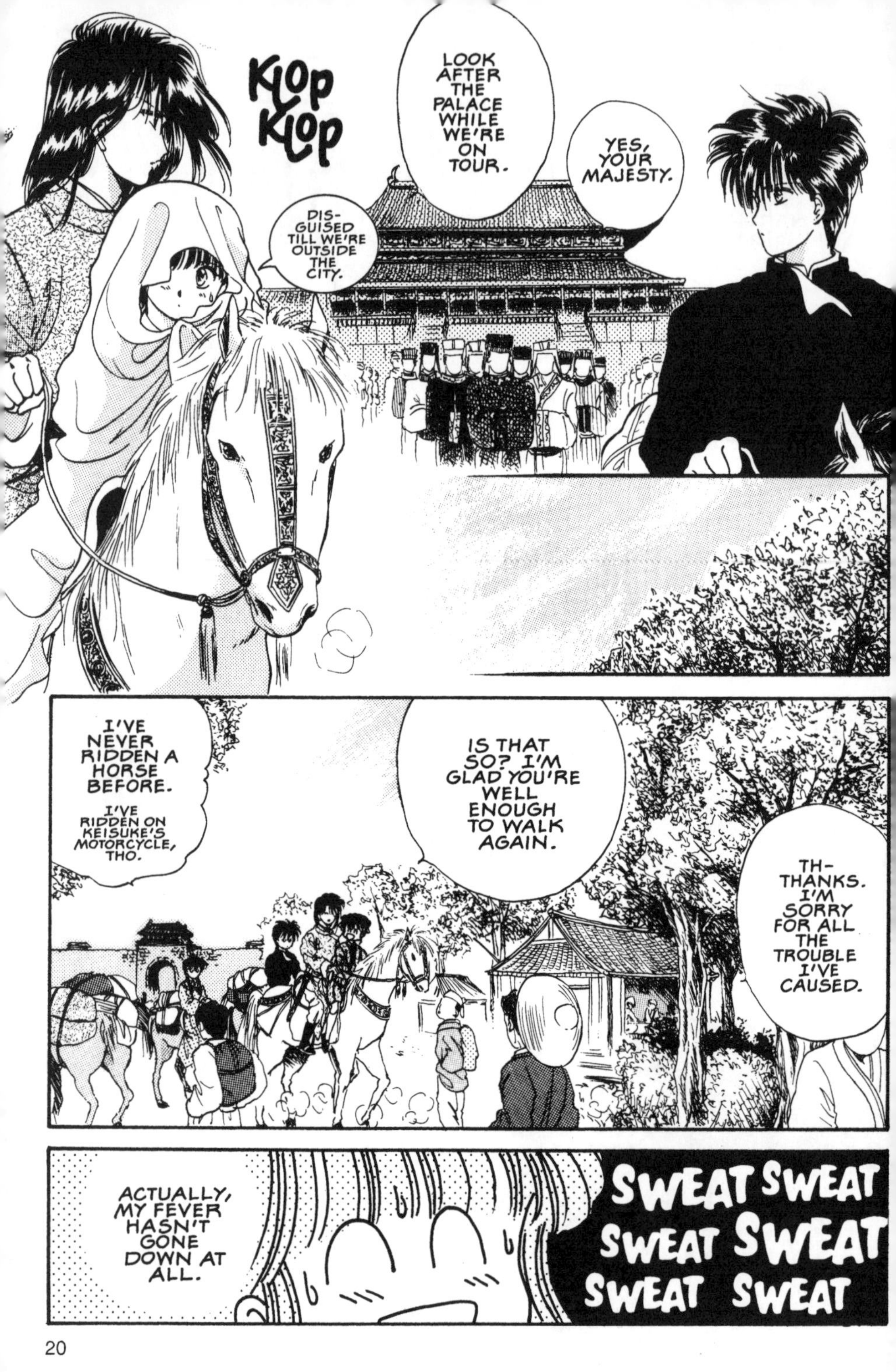
KLOP KLOP
LOOK AFTER THE PALACE WHILE WE'RE ON TOUR.
YES, YOUR MAJESTY.
DIS-GUISED TILL WE'RE OUTSIDE THE CITY.
I'VE NEVER RIDDEN A HORSE BEFORE.
I'VE RIDDEN ON KEISUKE'S MOTORCYCLE, THO.
IS THAT SO? I'M GLAD YOU'RE WELL ENOUGH TO WALK AGAIN.
TH-THANKS. I'M SORRY FOR ALL THE TROUBLE I'VE CAUSED.
ACTUALLY, MY FEVER HASN'T GONE DOWN AT ALL.
SWEAT SWEAT SWEAT SWEAT SWEAT SWEAT

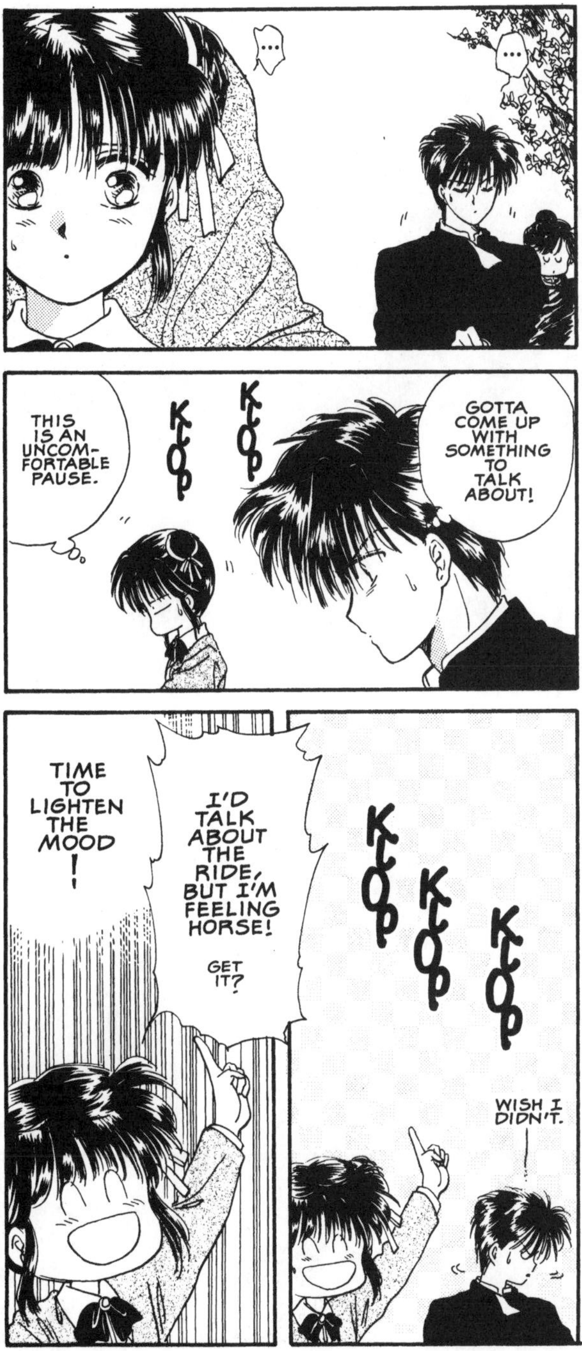
...
...
THIS IS AN UNCOMFORTABLE PAUSE.
KLOP
KLOP
GOTTA COME UP WITH SOMETHING TO TALK ABOUT!
TIME TO LIGHTEN THE MOOD!
I'D TALK ABOUT THE RIDE, BUT I'M FEELING HORSE!
GET IT?
KLOP
KLOP
KLOP
WISH I DIDN'T.

I've been a little tired lately. How are you all doing? I've been writing these chat sections for every chapter, but nowadays nobody else is doing them. I thought of quitting, but they told me, "Your fans buy the books to read the chat sections." So I'm stuck and I gotta write them. Sniff, sniff.

From "Prepubescence" on I've been writing a lot of stuff on manga because I get so many questions from the fans (everybody wants to become a manga artist!), but I've only been a pro for three years. A real veteran manga artist might say that I'm not telling you the right things. I may talk about drawing or other parts of manga but I'm not the artist I want to be yet. And I can't hide my emotions. Whether I'm angry or happy, it always shows right on my face. 😐☺ And that gets me into trouble.

Suddenly my thoughts have come to a halt. I've decided not to think about this stuff anymore. My readers should be priority no. 1! No more long essays on manga.

Besides, I never thought that other artists read these books, but a few other artists told me they did read it!

I was super embarrassed. I gotta apologize for my know-it-all lectures. Everybody around me knows that I really have no self confidence. When this series began, I would look over my drawings and feel sick to my stomach. I'd cry and cry while I continued my work! ☹

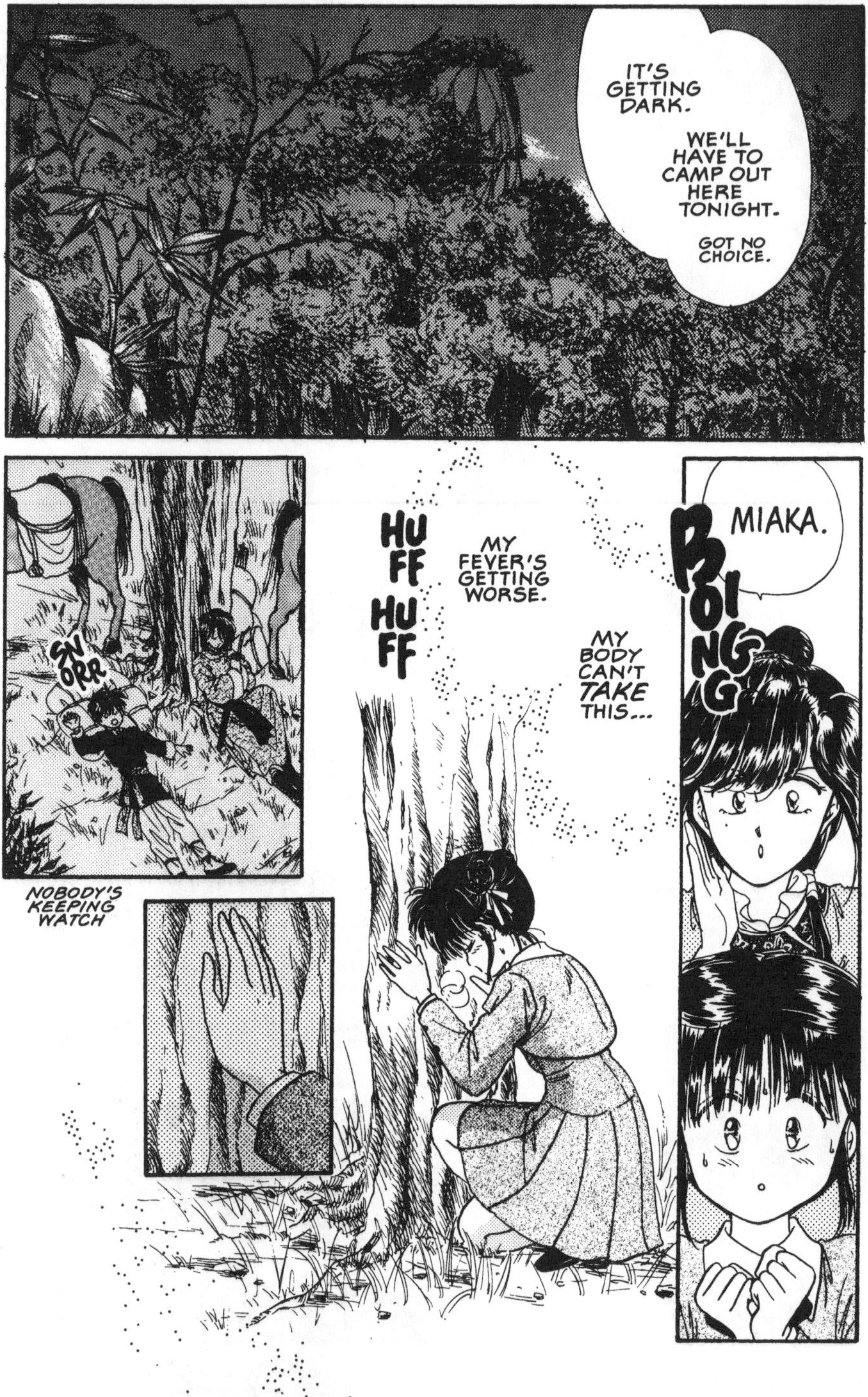
IT'S GETTING DARK.
WE'LL HAVE TO CAMP OUT HERE TONIGHT.
GOT NO CHOICE.
SNORR
NOBODY'S KEEPING WATCH
HUFF HUFF
MY FEVER'S GETTING WORSE.
MY BODY CAN'T TAKE THIS...
MIAKA.
BOINGNG

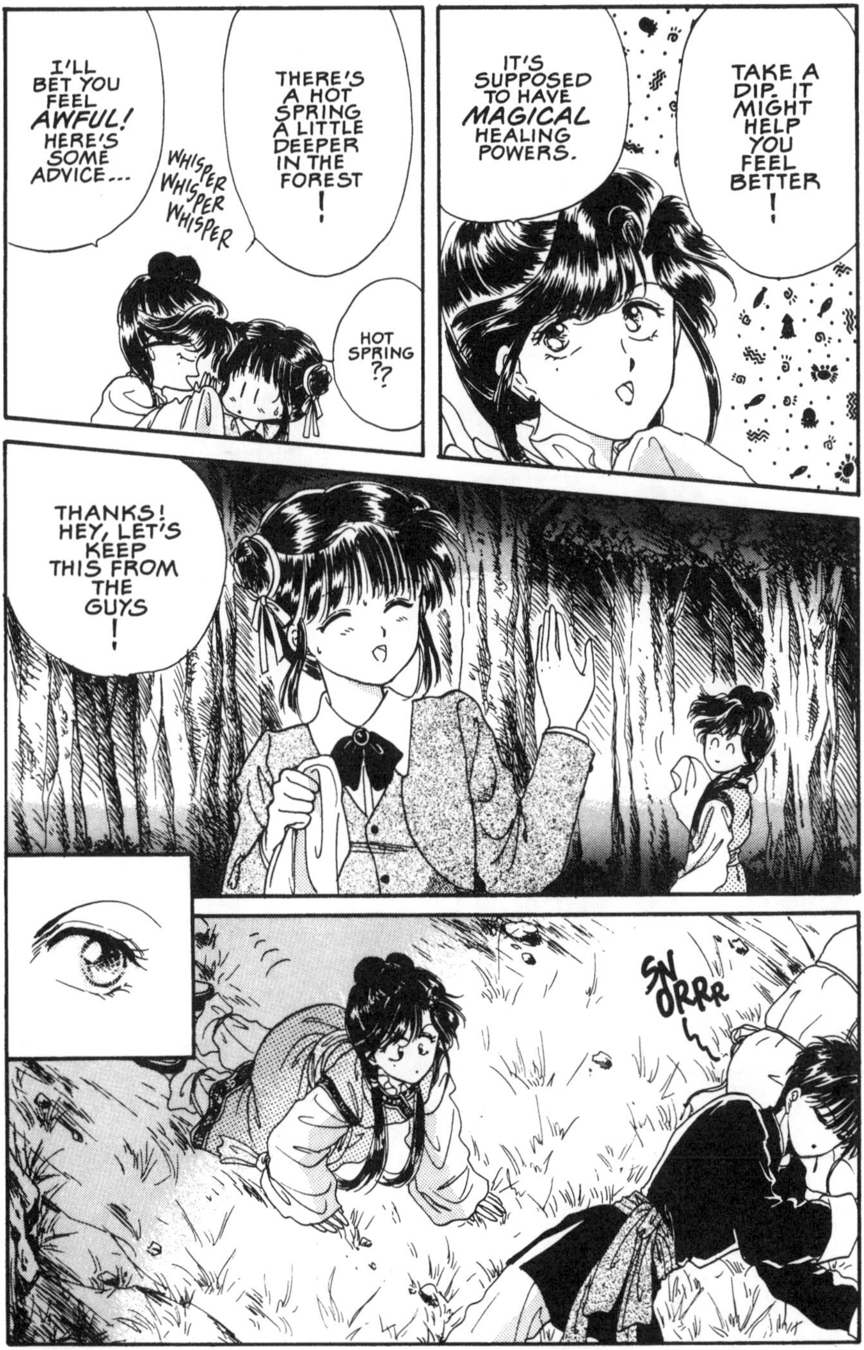
I'LL BET YOU FEEL AWFUL! HERE'S SOME ADVICE...
WHISPER WHISPER WHISPER WHISPER
THERE'S A HOT SPRING A LITTLE DEEPER IN THE FOREST!
HOT SPRING ??
IT'S SUPPOSED TO HAVE MAGICAL HEALING POWERS.
TAKE A DIP. IT MIGHT HELP YOU FEEL BETTER!
THANKS! HEY, LET'S KEEP THIS FROM THE GUYS!
SNORRR

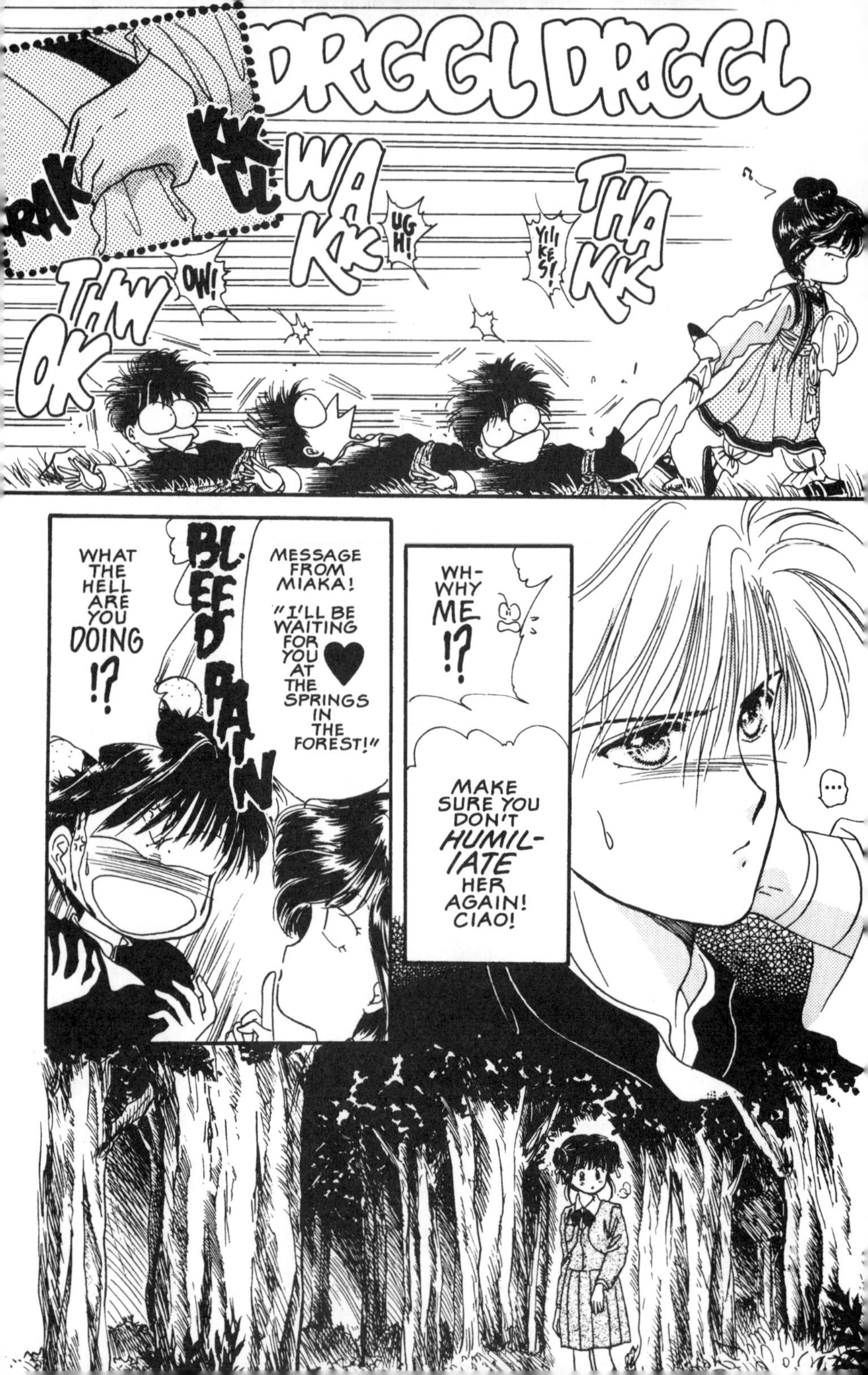
DRGGL DRGGL
RAK
KKKLL
WAKK
UGH!
YIIIKES!
THAKK
THWOK
OW!
WHAT THE HELL ARE YOU DOING !?
BLEED PAIN
MESSAGE FROM MIAKA! "I'LL BE WAITING FOR YOU ♥ AT THE SPRINGS IN THE FOREST!"
WH-WHY ME !?
MAKE SURE YOU DON'T HUMILIATE HER AGAIN! CIAO!
...

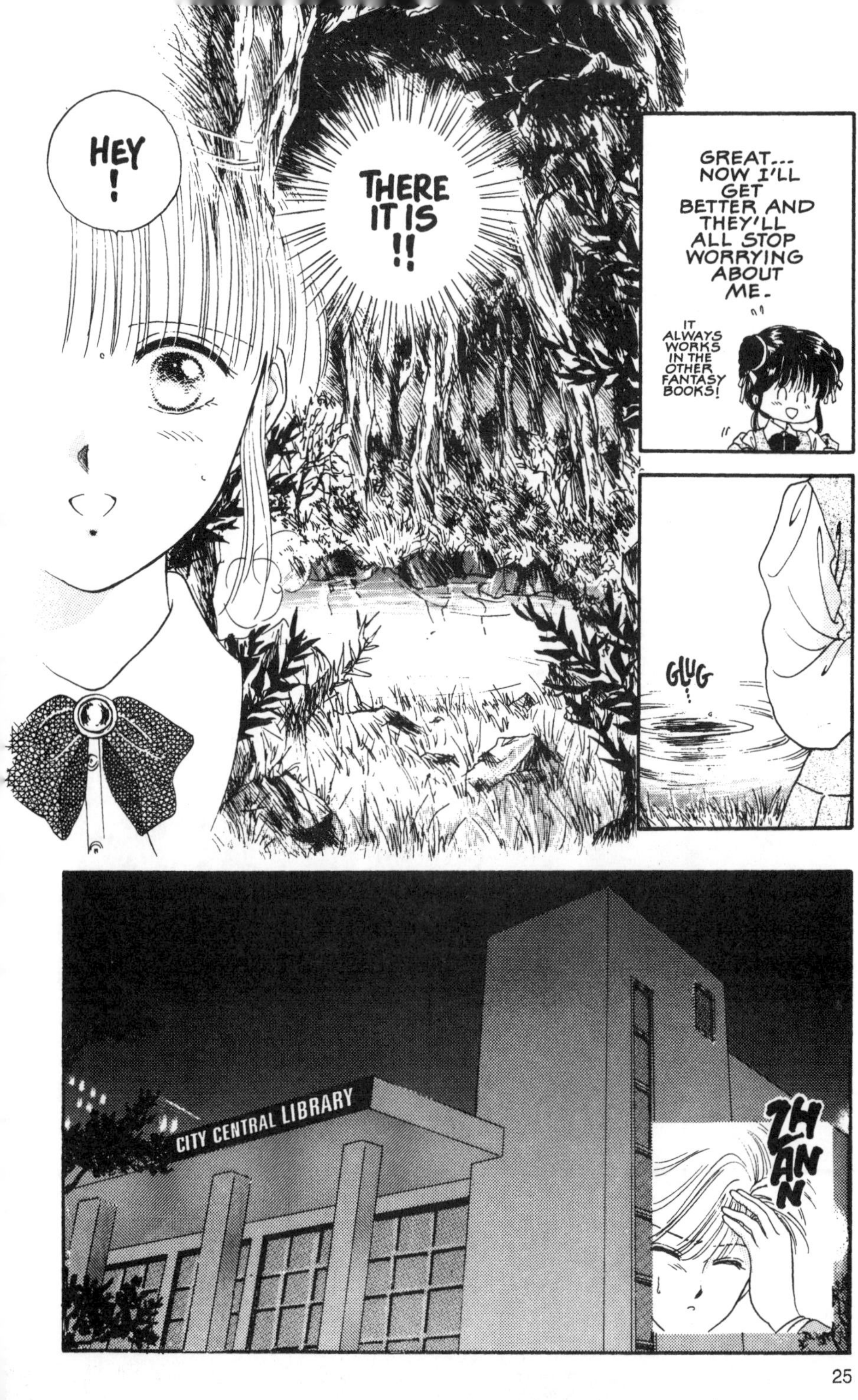
HEY!
THERE IT IS!!
GREAT... NOW I'LL GET BETTER AND THEY'LL ALL STOP WORRYING ABOUT ME.
IT ALWAYS WORKS IN THE OTHER FANTASY BOOKS!
GLUG
CITY CENTRAL LIBRARY
ZHAN

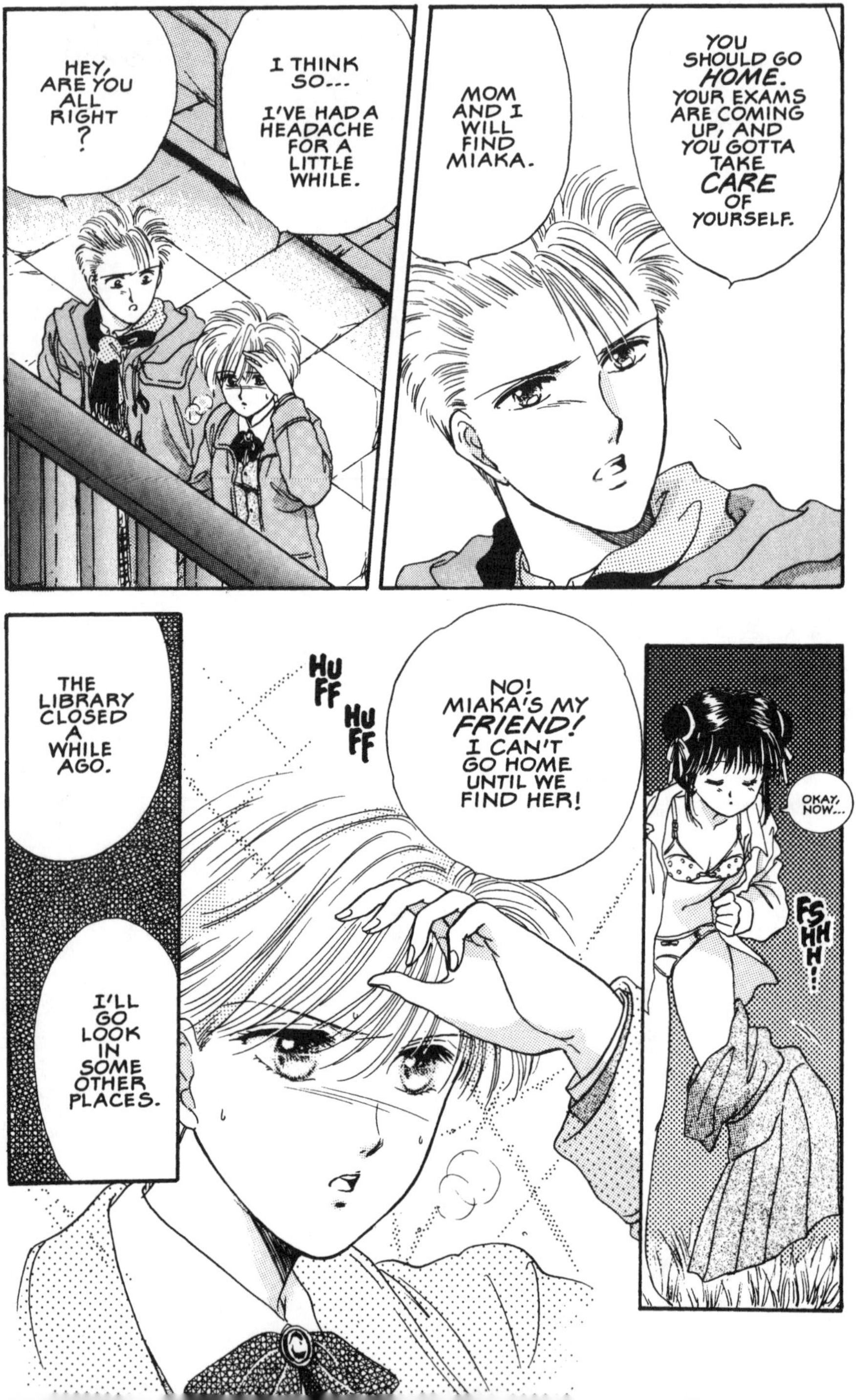
HEY, ARE YOU ALL RIGHT?
I THINK SO... I'VE HAD A HEADACHE FOR A LITTLE WHILE.
MOM AND I WILL FIND MIAKA.
YOU SHOULD GO HOME. YOUR EXAMS ARE COMING UP, AND YOU GOTTA TAKE CARE OF YOURSELF.
THE LIBRARY CLOSED A WHILE AGO.
HUFF HUFF
NO! MIAKA'S MY FRIEND! I CAN'T GO HOME UNTIL WE FIND HER!
I'LL GO LOOK IN SOME OTHER PLACES.
OKAY, NOW...
FSHHH!!

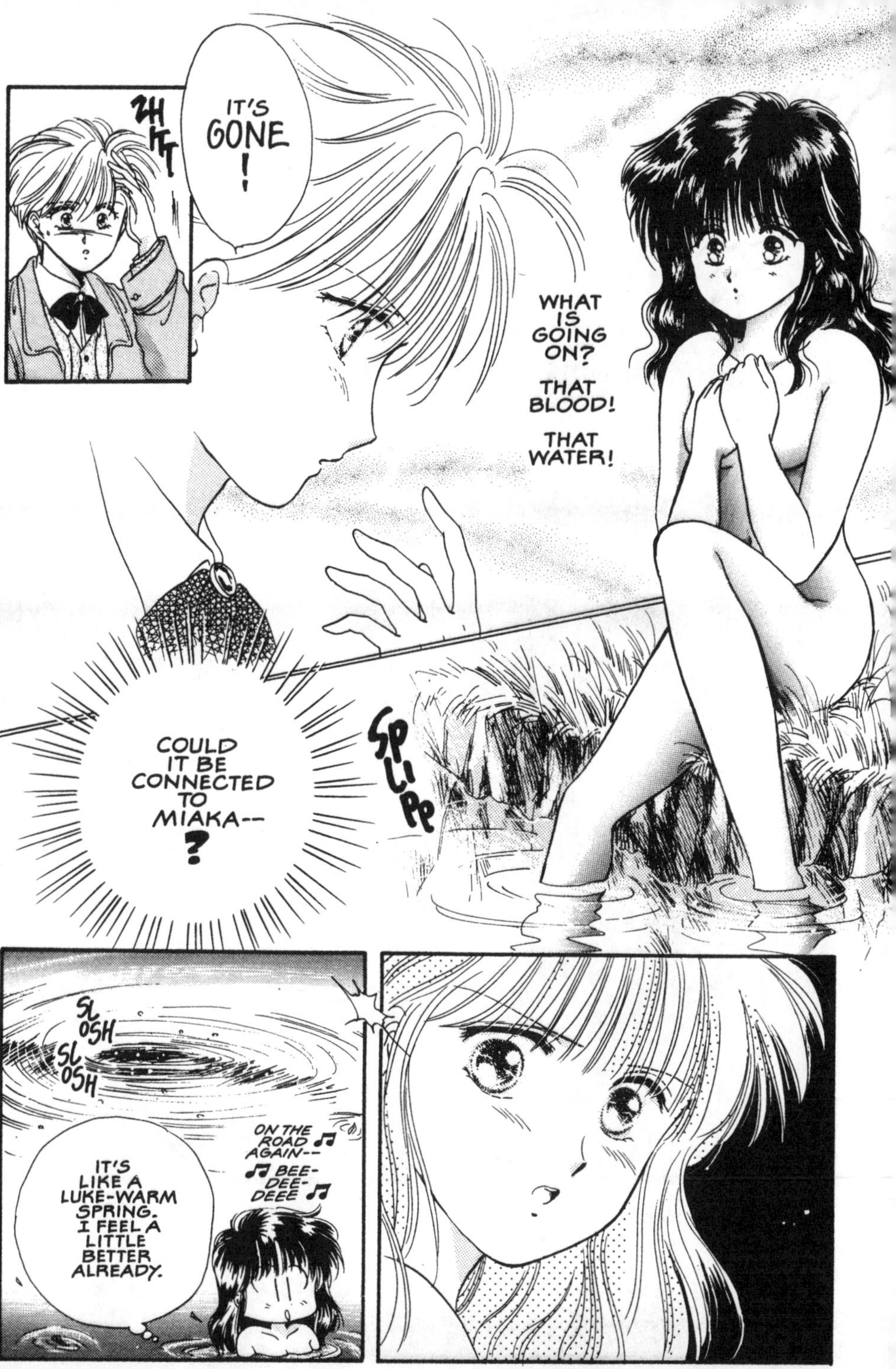
ZHITT
IT'S GONE!
WHAT IS GOING ON?
THAT BLOOD!
THAT WATER!
COULD IT BE CONNECTED TO MIAKA--?
SPLIPP
SLOSH
SLOSH
IT'S LIKE A LUKE-WARM SPRING. I FEEL A LITTLE BETTER ALREADY.
ON THE ROAD AGAIN-- BEE-DEE-DEEE

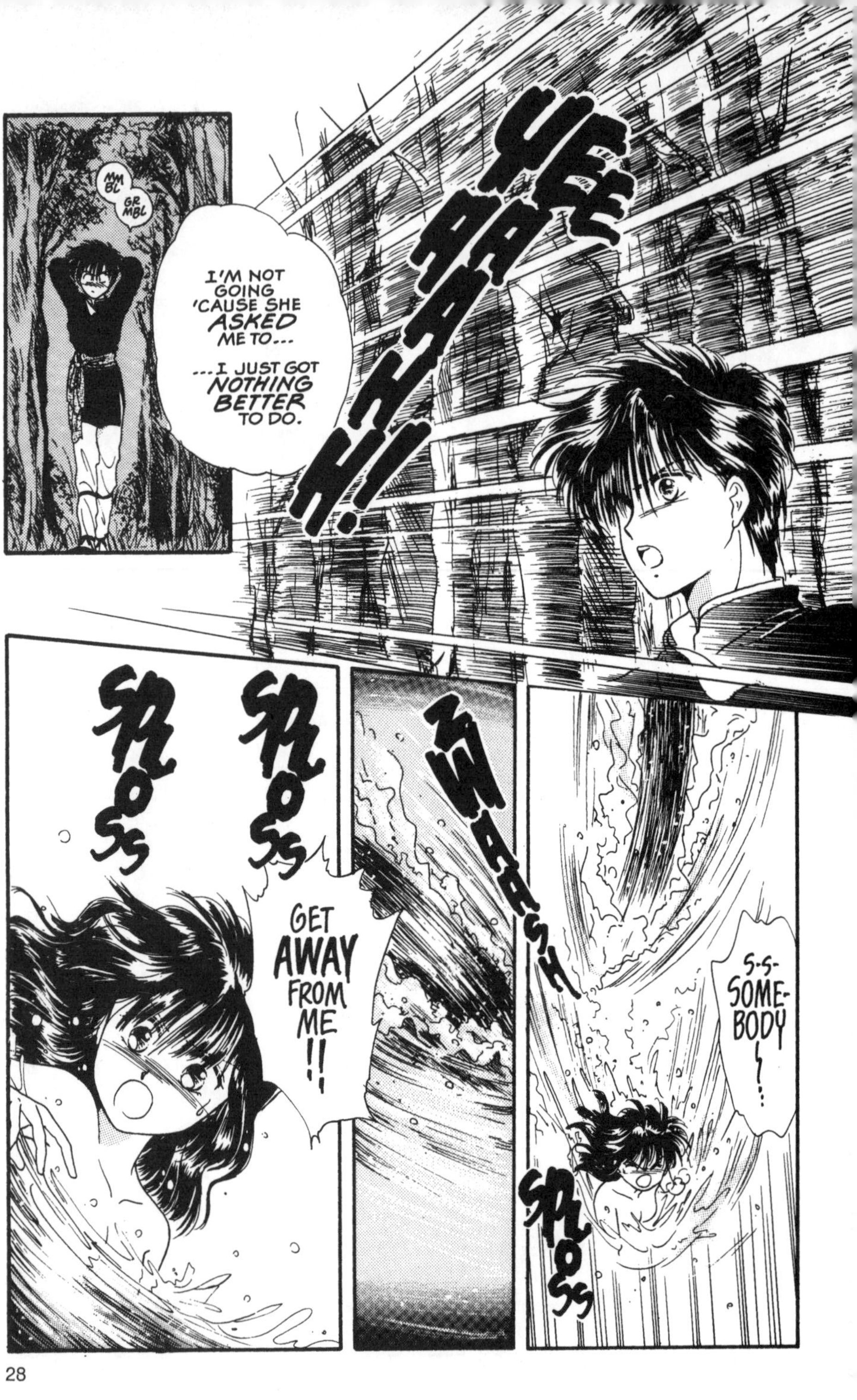

MMBL GRMBL
I'M NOT GOING 'CAUSE SHE ASKED ME TO...
...I JUST GOT NOTHING BETTER TO DO.
WEEAAAHHHH!!
SPLOSSS
SPLOSSS
GET AWAY FROM ME!!
ZWAAASH!
S-S-SOMEBODY...!
SPLOSSS

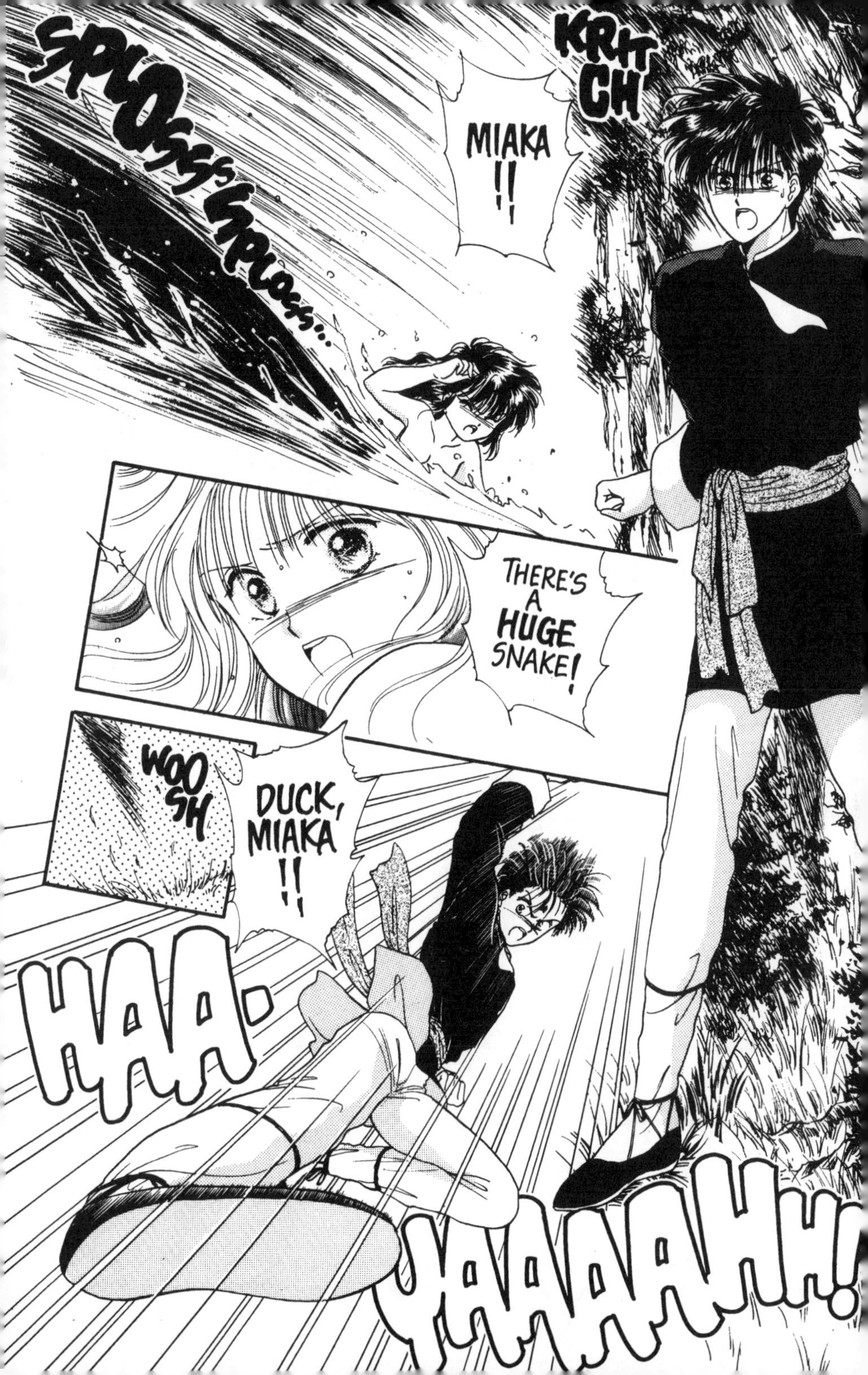
SPLOOSSS SPLOOSSS SPLOOSSS...
KRITCH
MIAKA!!
THERE'S A HUGE SNAKE!
WOOSH
DUCK, MIAKA!!
HAA.
HAAAAAHH!

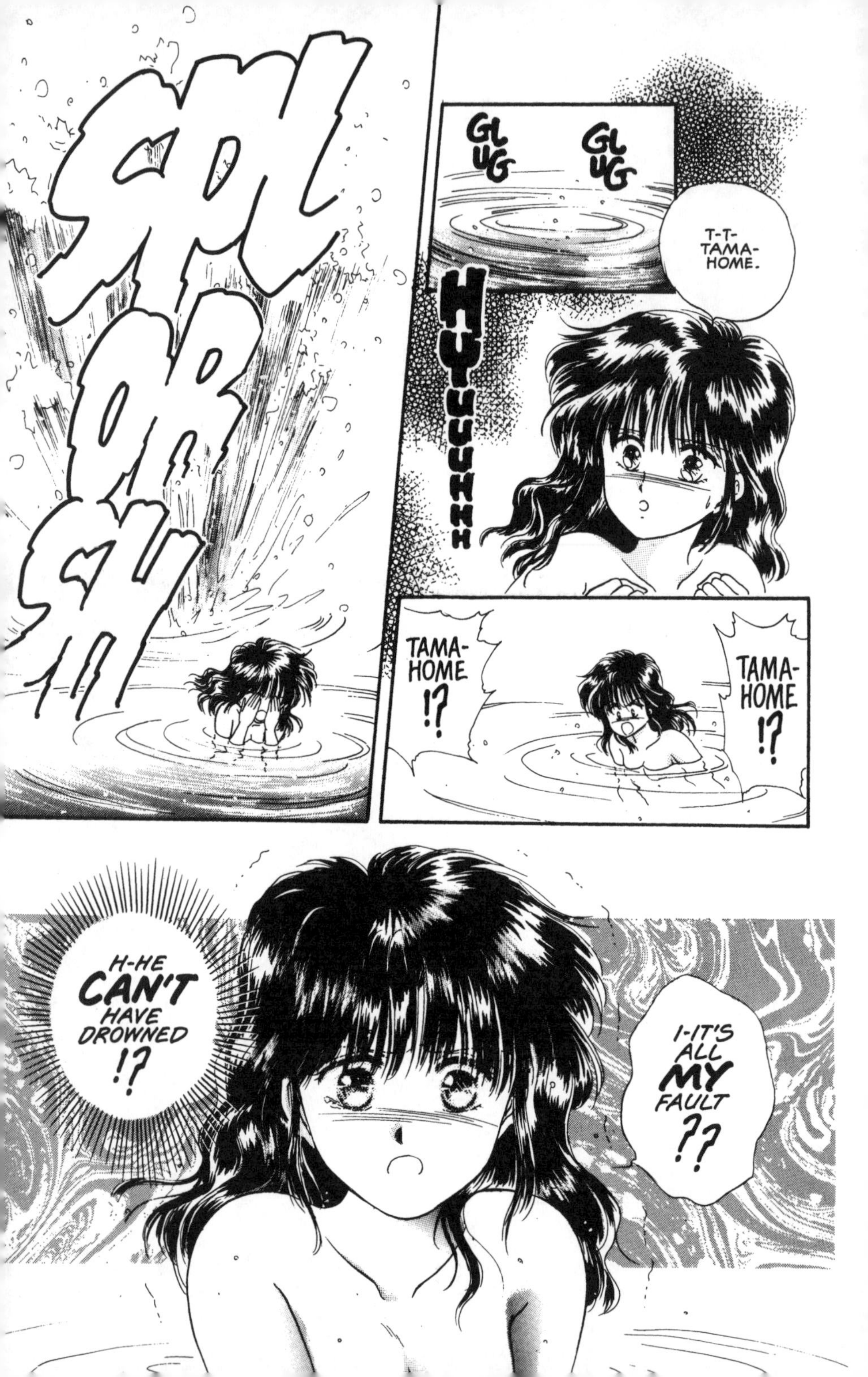
SPLOOSH
GLUG GLUG
T-T-TAMA-HOME.
HUUUUUHHH
TAMA-HOME!?
TAMA-HOME!?
H-HE CAN'T HAVE DROWNED!?
I-IT'S ALL MY FAULT??

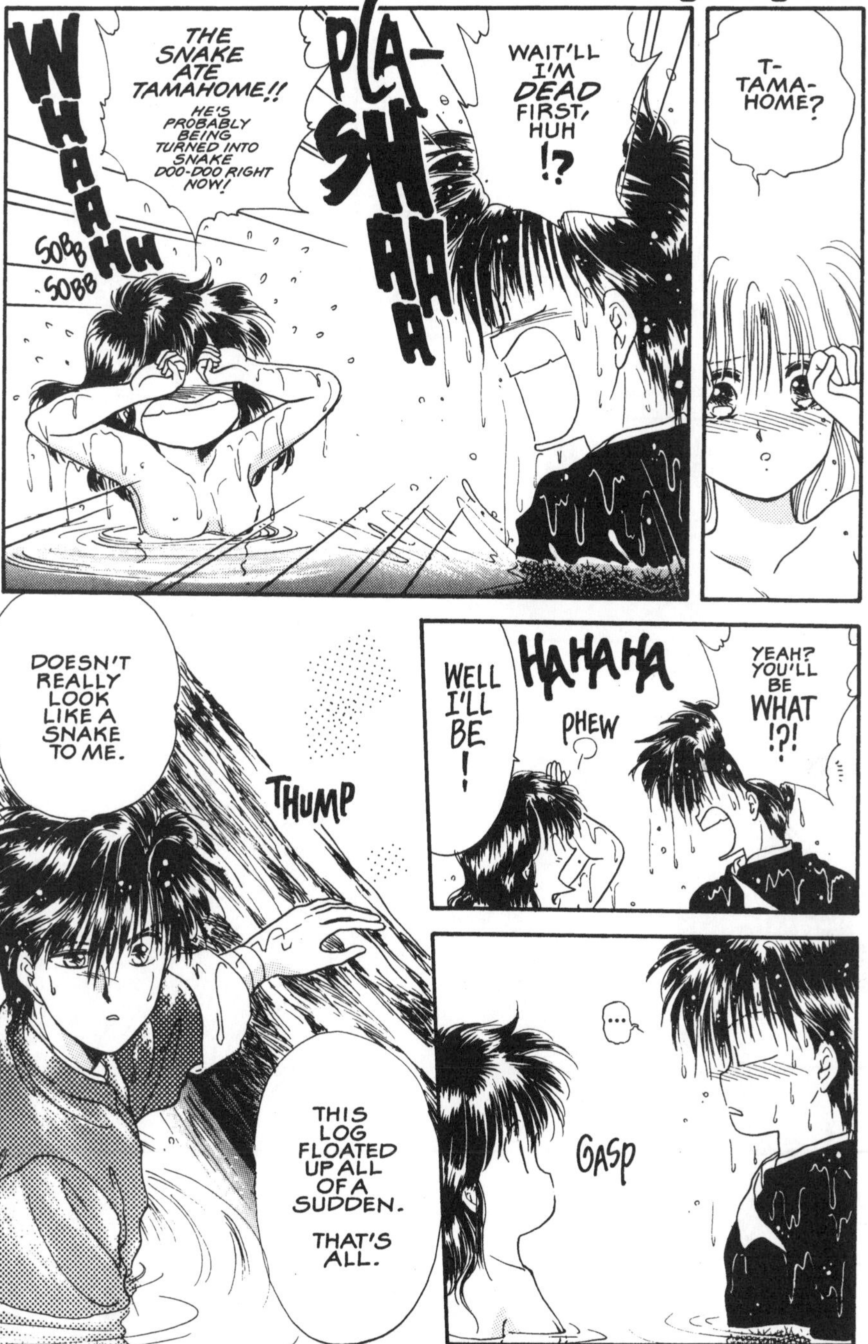
WHAAAHHH
SOBB SOBB
THE SNAKE ATE TAMAHOME!!
HE'S PROBABLY BEING TURNED INTO SNAKE DOO-DOO RIGHT NOW!
PLA-SHHAAA
WAIT'LL I'M DEAD FIRST, HUH!?
T-TAMA-HOME?
DOESN'T REALLY LOOK LIKE A SNAKE TO ME.
THUMP
THIS LOG FLOATED UP ALL OF A SUDDEN.
THAT'S ALL.
WELL I'LL BE!
HAHAHA
PHEW
YEAH? YOU'LL BE WHAT!?!
...
GASP

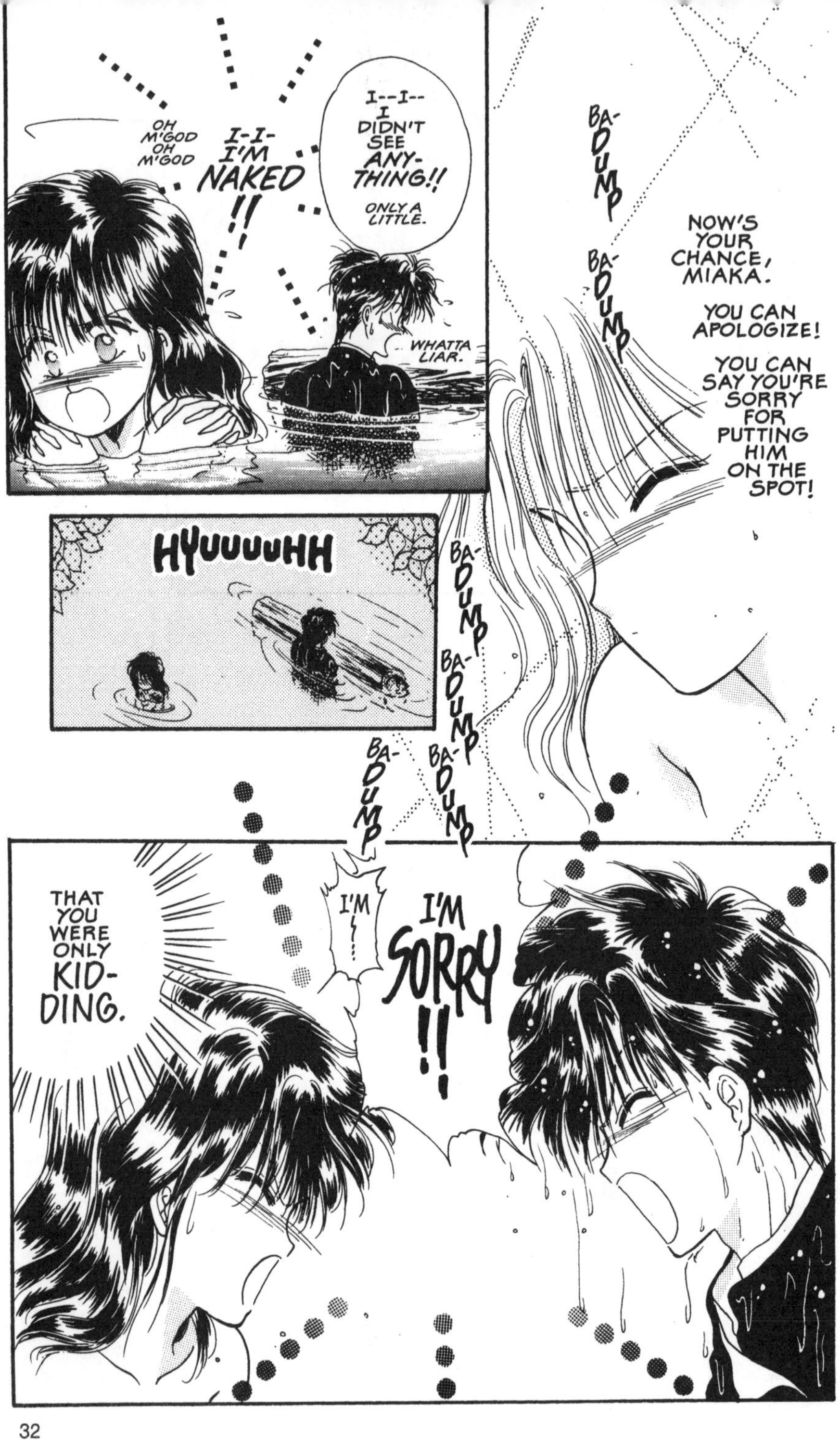
OH M'GOD OH M'GOD
I-I-I'M NAKED!!
I--I-- I DIDN'T SEE ANYTHING!!
ONLY A LITTLE.
WHATTA LIAR.
BA-DUMP
BA-DUMP
NOW'S YOUR CHANCE, MIAKA.
YOU CAN APOLOGIZE!
YOU CAN SAY YOU'RE SORRY FOR PUTTING HIM ON THE SPOT!
HYUUUUHH
BA-DUMP
BA-DUMP
BA-DUMP
BA-DUMP
THAT YOU WERE ONLY KIDDING.
I'M...!
I'M SORRY!!

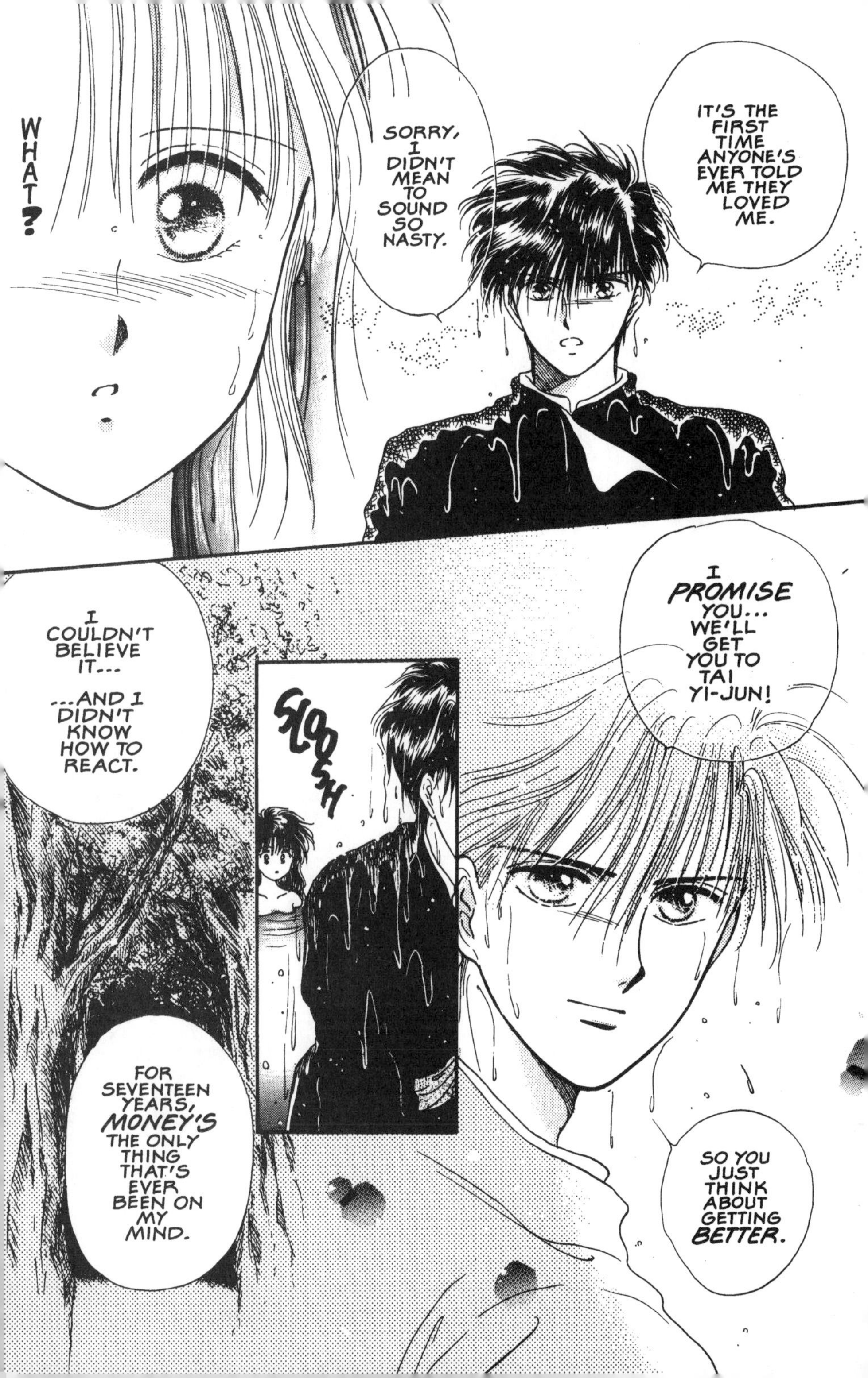
WHAT?
SORRY, I DIDN'T MEAN TO SOUND SO NASTY.
IT'S THE FIRST TIME ANYONE'S EVER TOLD ME THEY LOVED ME.
I COULDN'T BELIEVE IT...
...AND I DIDN'T KNOW HOW TO REACT.
I PROMISE YOU... WE'LL GET YOU TO TAI YI-JUN!
SLOOSH
FOR SEVENTEEN YEARS, MONEY'S THE ONLY THING THAT'S EVER BEEN ON MY MIND.
SO YOU JUST THINK ABOUT GETTING BETTER.

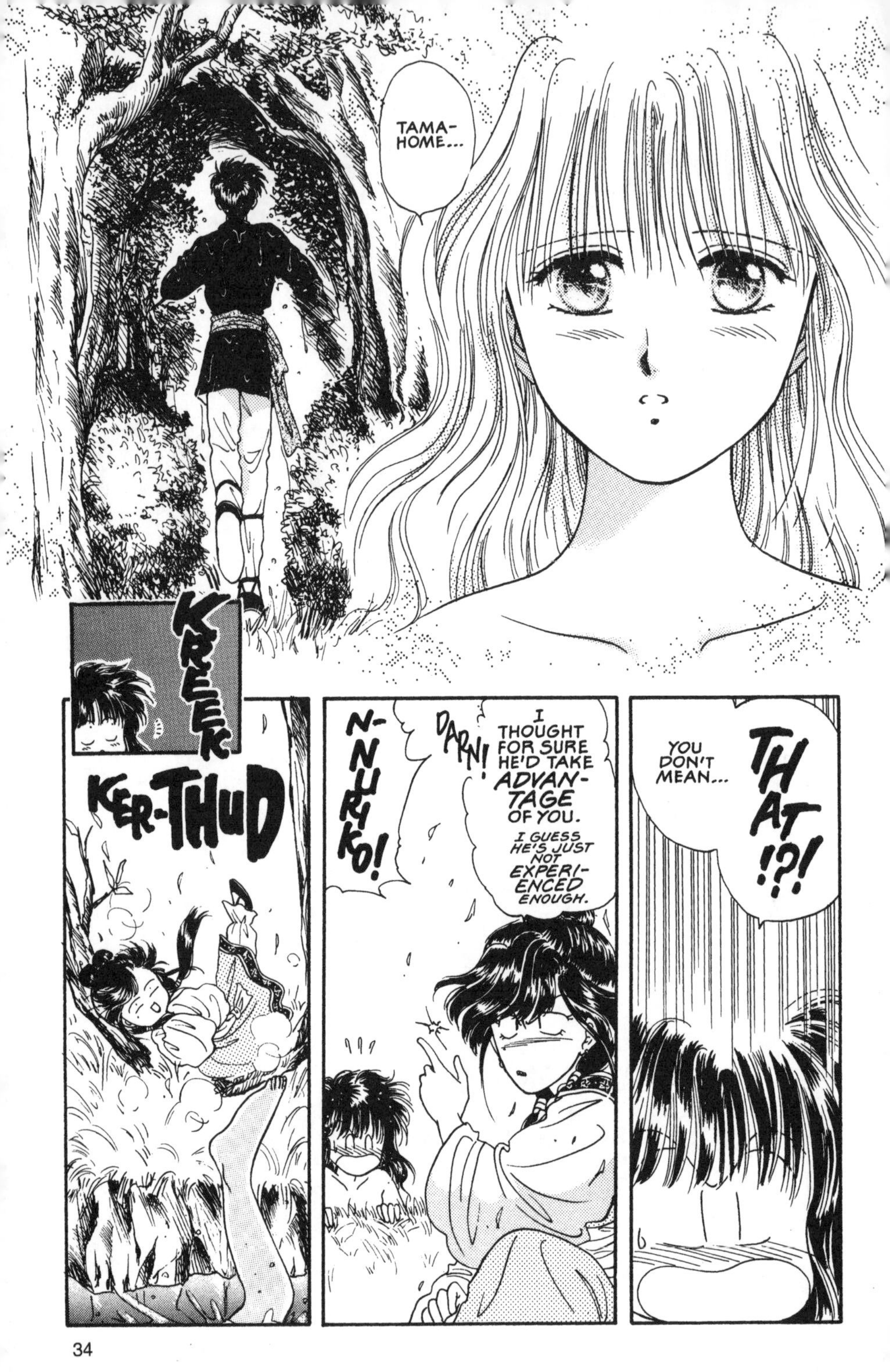
TAMA-HOME...
KREEK
KER-THUD
N-NURIKO!
DARN!
I THOUGHT FOR SURE HE'D TAKE ADVANTAGE OF YOU.
I GUESS HE'S JUST NOT EXPERIENCED ENOUGH.
YOU DON'T MEAN... THAT!?!

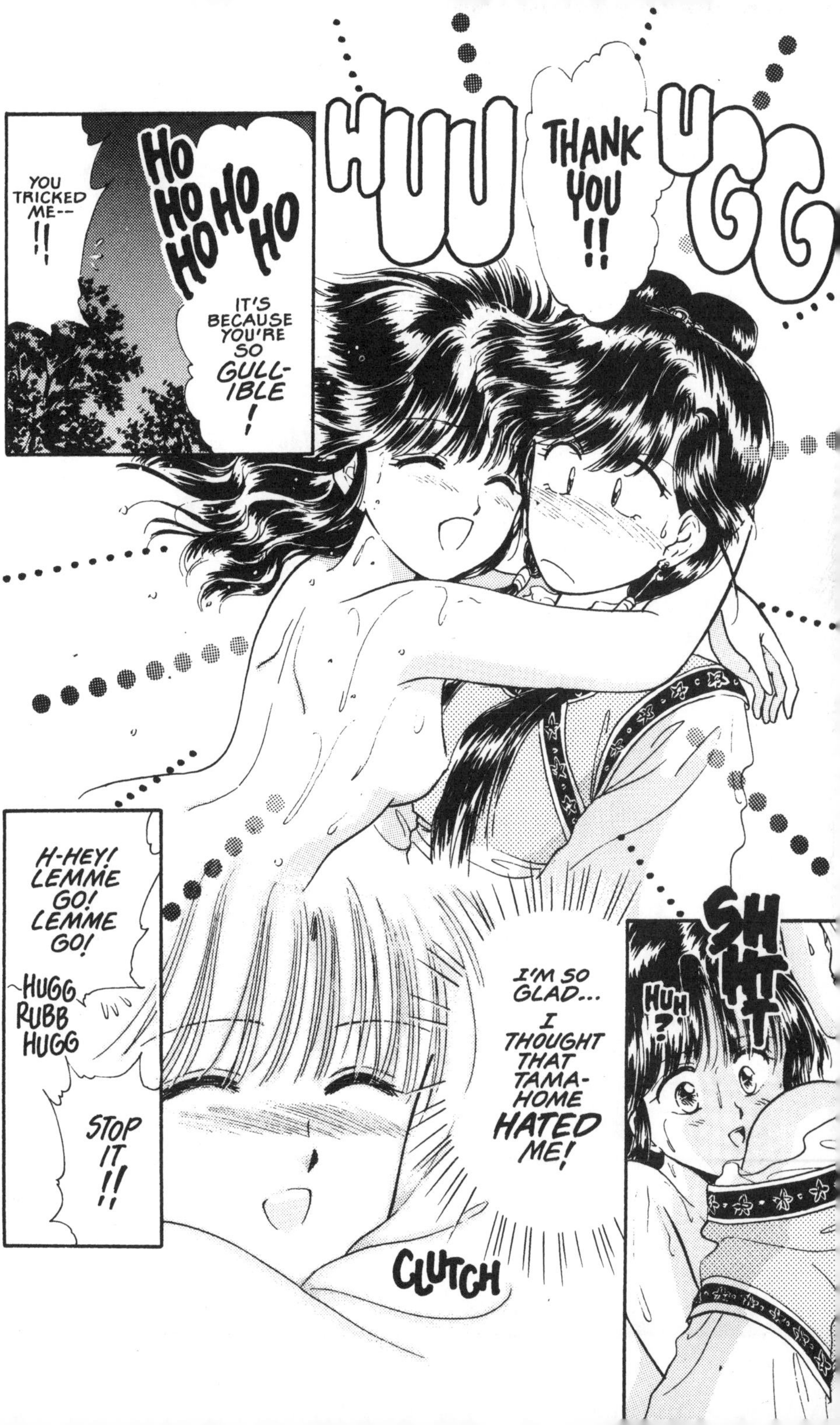
YOU TRICKED ME--!!
HO HO HO HO HO
IT'S BECAUSE YOU'RE SO GULLIBLE!
HUUUGG
THANK YOU!!
H-HEY! LEMME GO! LEMME GO!
HUGG RUBB HUGG
STOP IT!!
I'M SO GLAD... I THOUGHT THAT TAMA-HOME HATED ME!
CLUTCH
HUH?

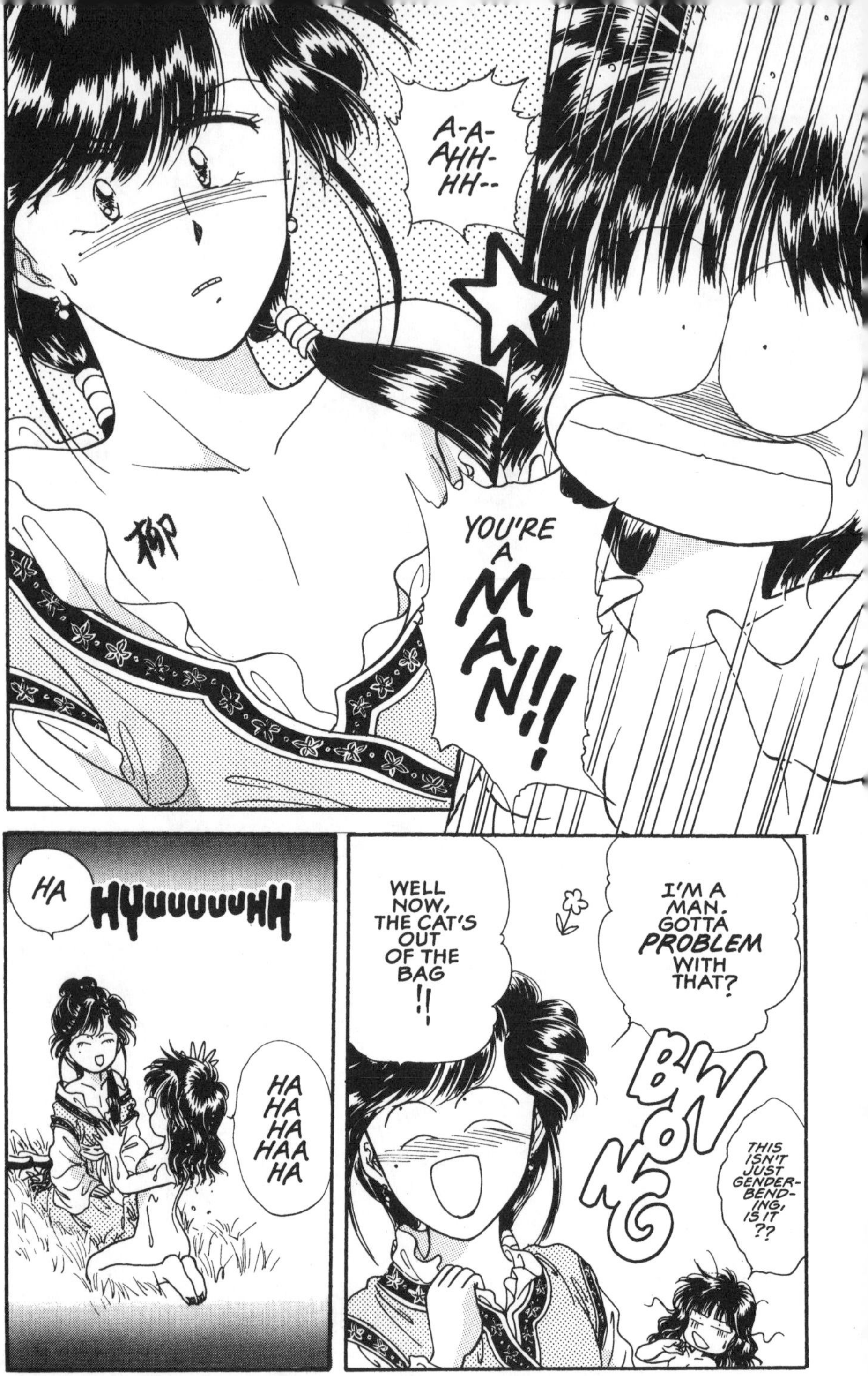
A-A-AHH-HH--
YOU'RE A MAN!!
HA
HYUUUUUUHH
HA HA HA HAA HA
WELL NOW, THE CAT'S OUT OF THE BAG !!
I'M A MAN. GOTTA PROBLEM WITH THAT?
BWONG
THIS ISN'T JUST GENDER-BENDING, IS IT??

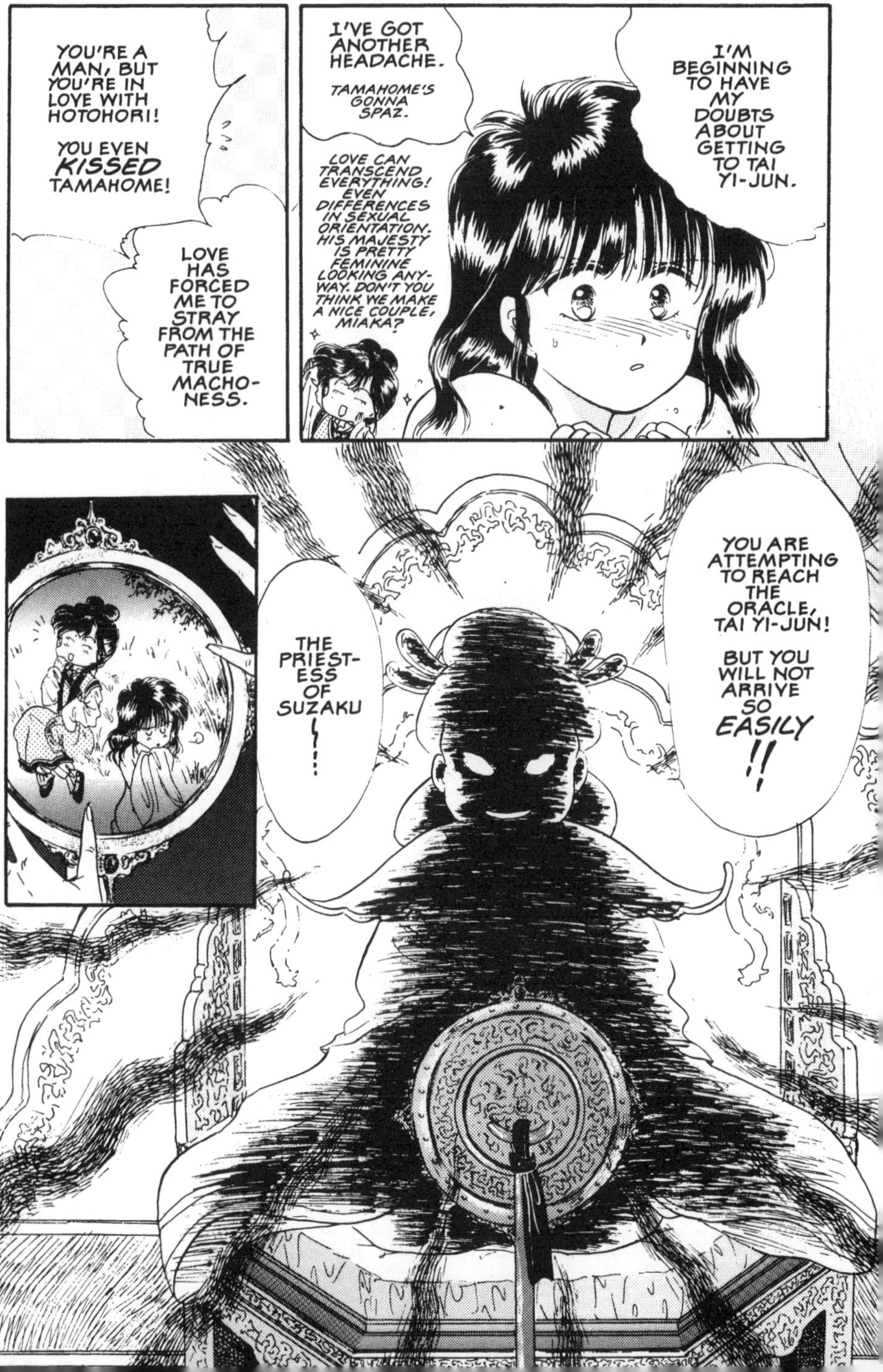
YOU'RE A MAN, BUT YOU'RE IN LOVE WITH HOTOHORI!
YOU EVEN *KISSED* TAMAHOME!
LOVE HAS FORCED ME TO STRAY FROM THE PATH OF TRUE MACHO-NESS.
I'VE GOT ANOTHER HEADACHE.
TAMAHOME'S GONNA SPAZ.
LOVE CAN TRANSCEND EVERYTHING! EVEN DIFFERENCES IN SEXUAL ORIENTATION. HIS MAJESTY IS PRETTY FEMININE LOOKING ANY-WAY. DON'T YOU THINK WE MAKE A NICE COUPLE, MIAKA?
I'M BEGINNING TO HAVE MY DOUBTS ABOUT GETTING TO TAI YI-JUN.
THE PRIEST-ESS OF SUZAKU!!
YOU ARE ATTEMPTING TO REACH THE ORACLE, TAI YI-JUN!
BUT YOU WILL NOT ARRIVE SO *EASILY*!!

Surprise! Some thoughts on the background music of Fushigi Yūgi...

Lately I've been receiving tons of tapes. It makes me so happy! *(Things like "Romancing Saga," "Nadia of the Mysterious Seas," etc.!)* One fan sent me Urusei Yatsura and Ranma (was that really Ranma, it was super dark stuff) material to be set to Fushigi. *(Well done. Thank you.)*

I might also recommend the game music for "Romance of the Three Kingdoms II." Its sound combines state of the art technology with ethnic music. It's totally my thing. I bought it immediately because Mr. Mukodani from Cassiopeia composed it. ♥ I like the first song that sounds Chinese but the 11th song "Chosen no Mai" is pretty too. (Better to listen to it on headphones.) But the 14th song doesn't really work for me. I've been skipping it, sorry Mr. Mukodani!
Also the game music to "Madara." I really like the first song "Ma Da Ra" (reminds me of the image of the Suzaku seven stars), and the 2nd song "Yasuragi no Kimi e" (Comfort in You) reminds me of Miaka. Only 5 songs but that's all right.

Before we began this series, I heard the theme song "Hitomi no Naka no Far Away" (Far Away in Your Eyes) *I think!* from "Five Star Stories," *(I still haven't seen it)* and it gave me an image idea for this manga. A previous assistant copied "Wo Ai Ni" by 135 for me and I fell in love with it! *Another song I love is "Nasuka no Kaze" (The Winds of Nasuka)! The voice of that singer sounds as if Tamahome's singing.*
Also Logic System's "To Gen Kyo" (it's a long story so I won't get into how I got hold of it. Maybe I should return it.) The CD cover was modeled after the mountains of Daichi-san! "Coffee Rumba" is on it. Most of the songs are in Chinese ("Rydeen" is sung in Chinese. The lyrics are incredible!) by a woman with lyrics in English, Chinese, and Japanese. I really like "Shanghai Moonlight" (although I haven't seen much of it). It's got a sad, romantic melody with backing vocals singing "sayonara" in Japanese -- way cool. They're also singing "I love you" in Chinese as well. (The Japanese lyrics remind me of Japanese enka though). The first song is in Chinese, and the 11th song is the controversial "Virtual Reality." There are several instrumentals. Check it out if you can.

This is a little retro but the lyrics to "China Town" and "China Boy" have been used for "Koi wa Passion" (Love is Passion). I don't understand the English lyrics to "Adieu et Fortuna" from "Lodoss Wars," but I like it a lot too. ↳ *(sorry if I'm wrong, I'd like to hear this song on a nice system).*

SO THE LATEST THING IS TECHNO POP, HUH?

Hey, "O", P-Model's really good.

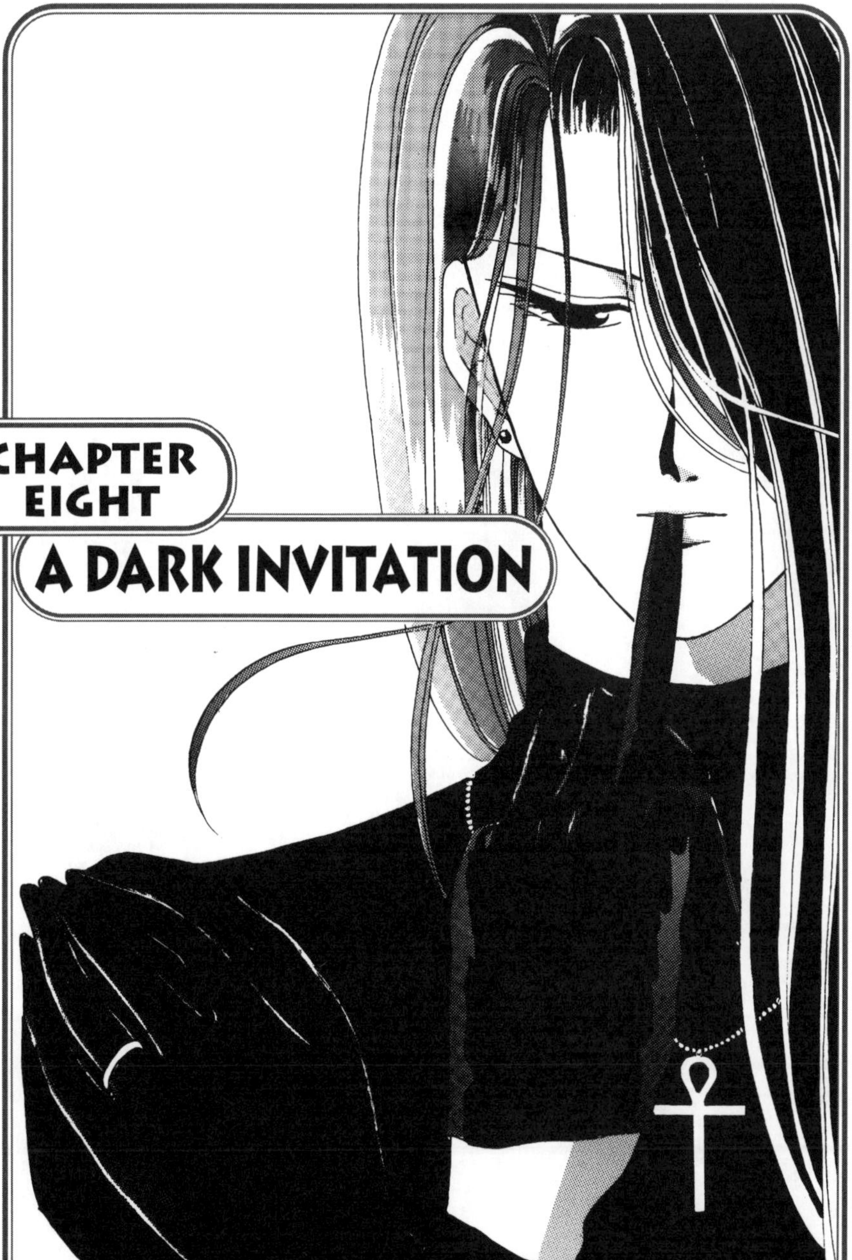
CHAPTER EIGHT
A DARK INVITATION

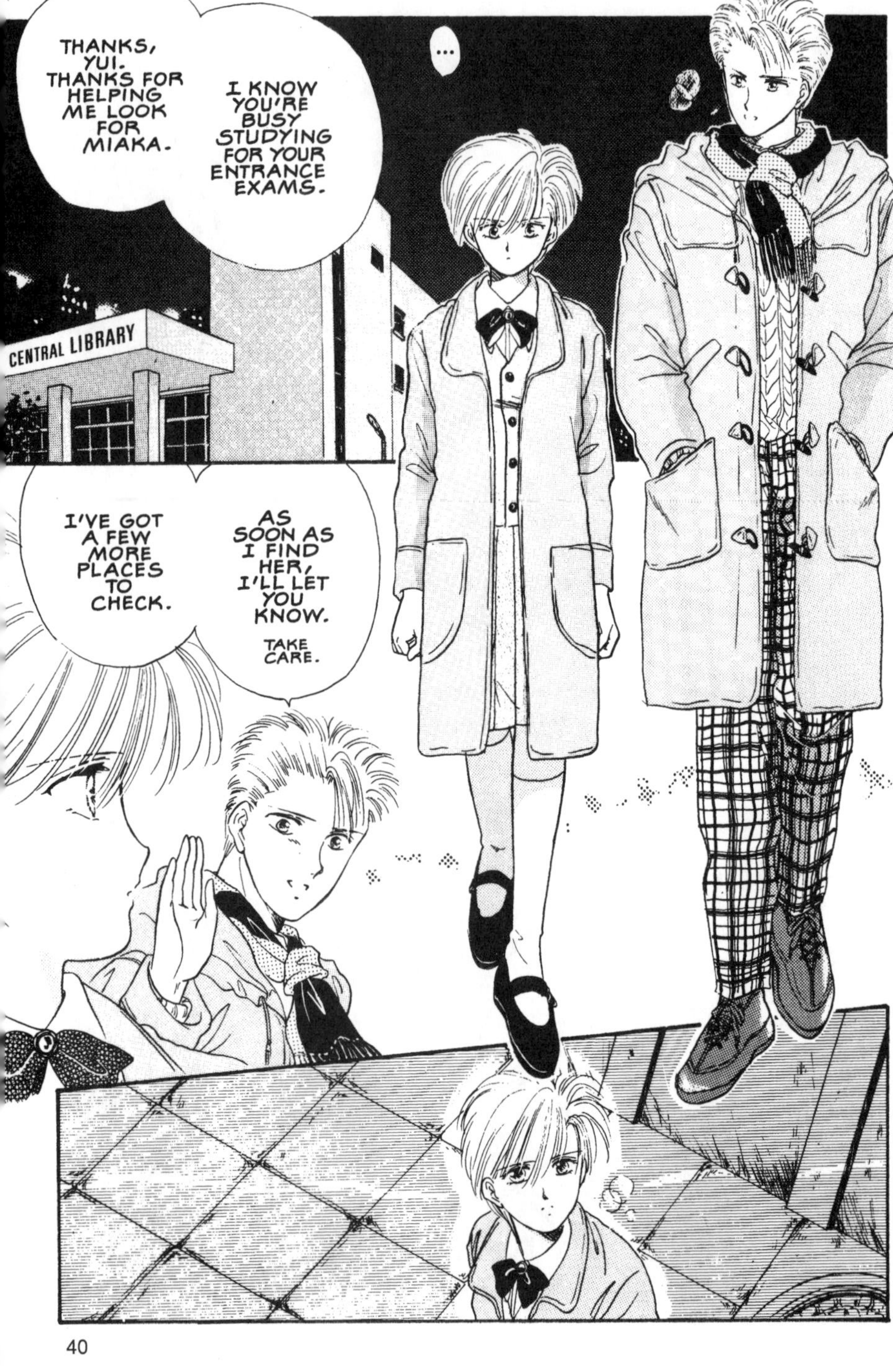
THANKS, YUI. THANKS FOR HELPING ME LOOK FOR MIAKA.
I KNOW YOU'RE BUSY STUDYING FOR YOUR ENTRANCE EXAMS.
...
CENTRAL LIBRARY
I'VE GOT A FEW MORE PLACES TO CHECK.
AS SOON AS I FIND HER, I'LL LET YOU KNOW.
TAKE CARE.

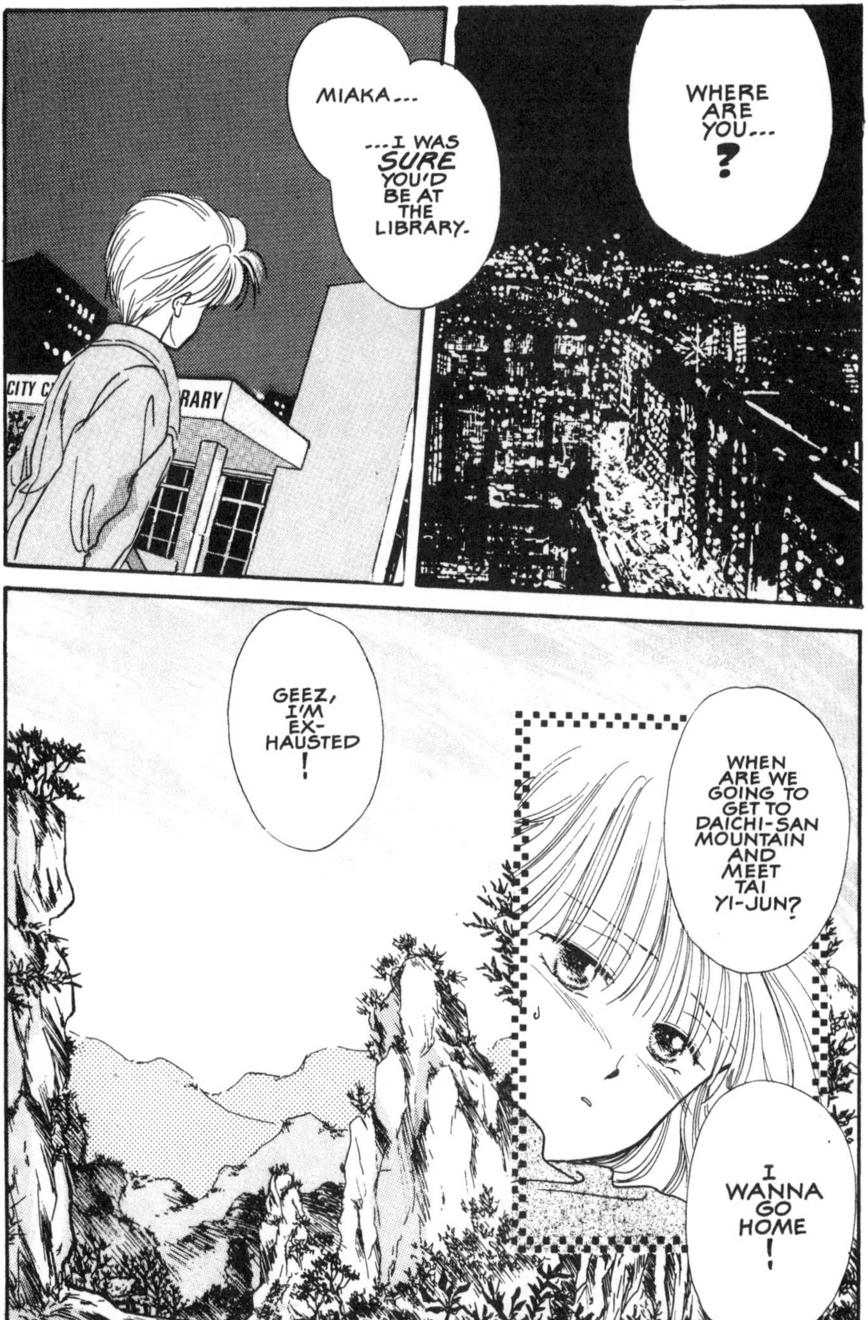
MIAKA...
...I WAS SURE YOU'D BE AT THE LIBRARY.
WHERE ARE YOU...?
GEEZ, I'M EX-HAUSTED!
WHEN ARE WE GOING TO GET TO DAICHI-SAN MOUNTAIN AND MEET TAI YI-JUN?
I WANNA GO HOME!

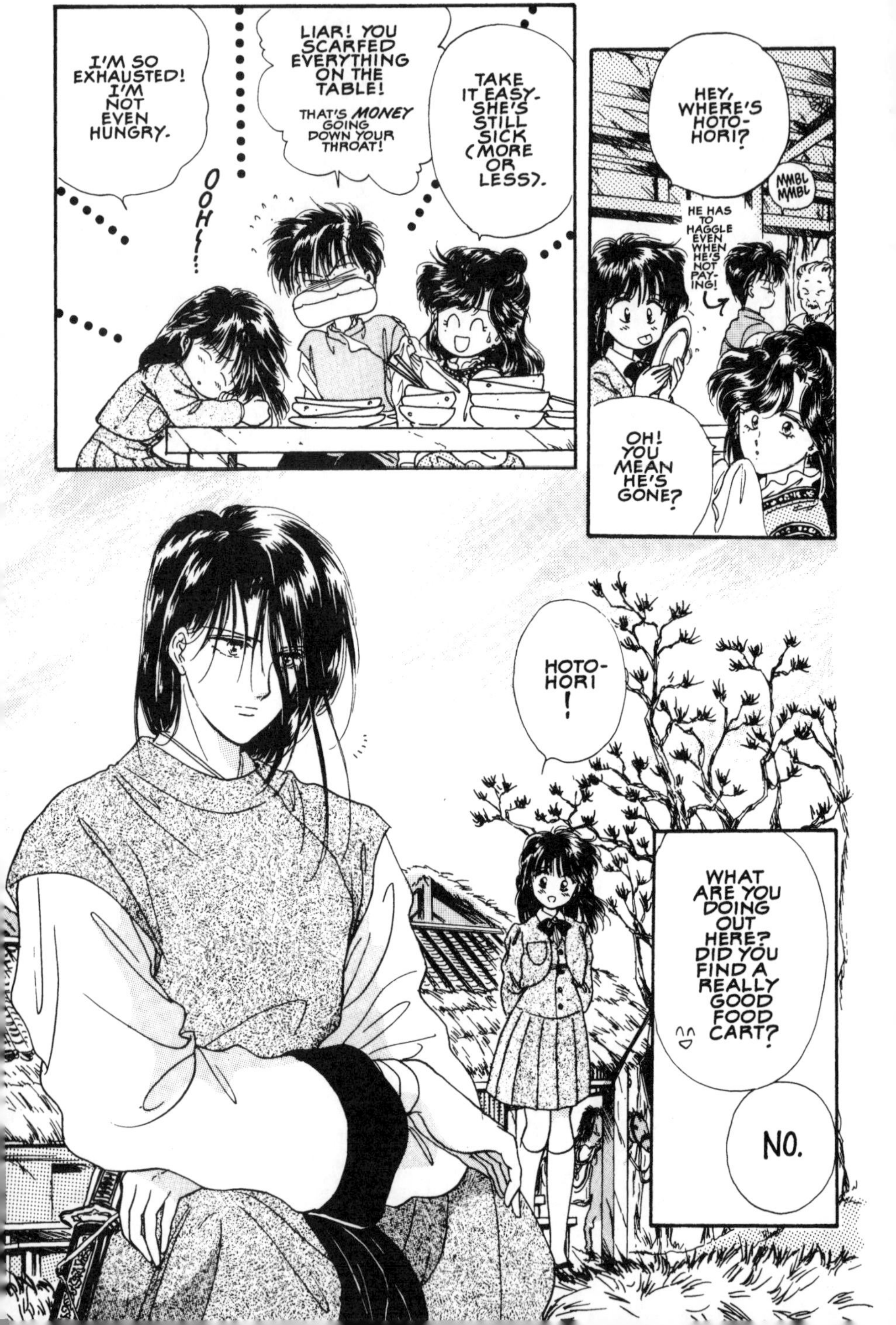
I'M SO EXHAUSTED! I'M NOT EVEN HUNGRY.
OOH!!!
LIAR! YOU SCARFED EVERYTHING ON THE TABLE!
THAT'S MONEY GOING DOWN YOUR THROAT!
TAKE IT EASY- SHE'S STILL SICK (MORE OR LESS).
HEY, WHERE'S HOTO-HORI?
MMBL MMBL
HE HAS TO HAGGLE EVEN WHEN HE'S NOT PAYING!
OH! YOU MEAN HE'S GONE?
HOTO-HORI!
WHAT ARE YOU DOING OUT HERE? DID YOU FIND A REALLY GOOD FOOD CART?
NO.

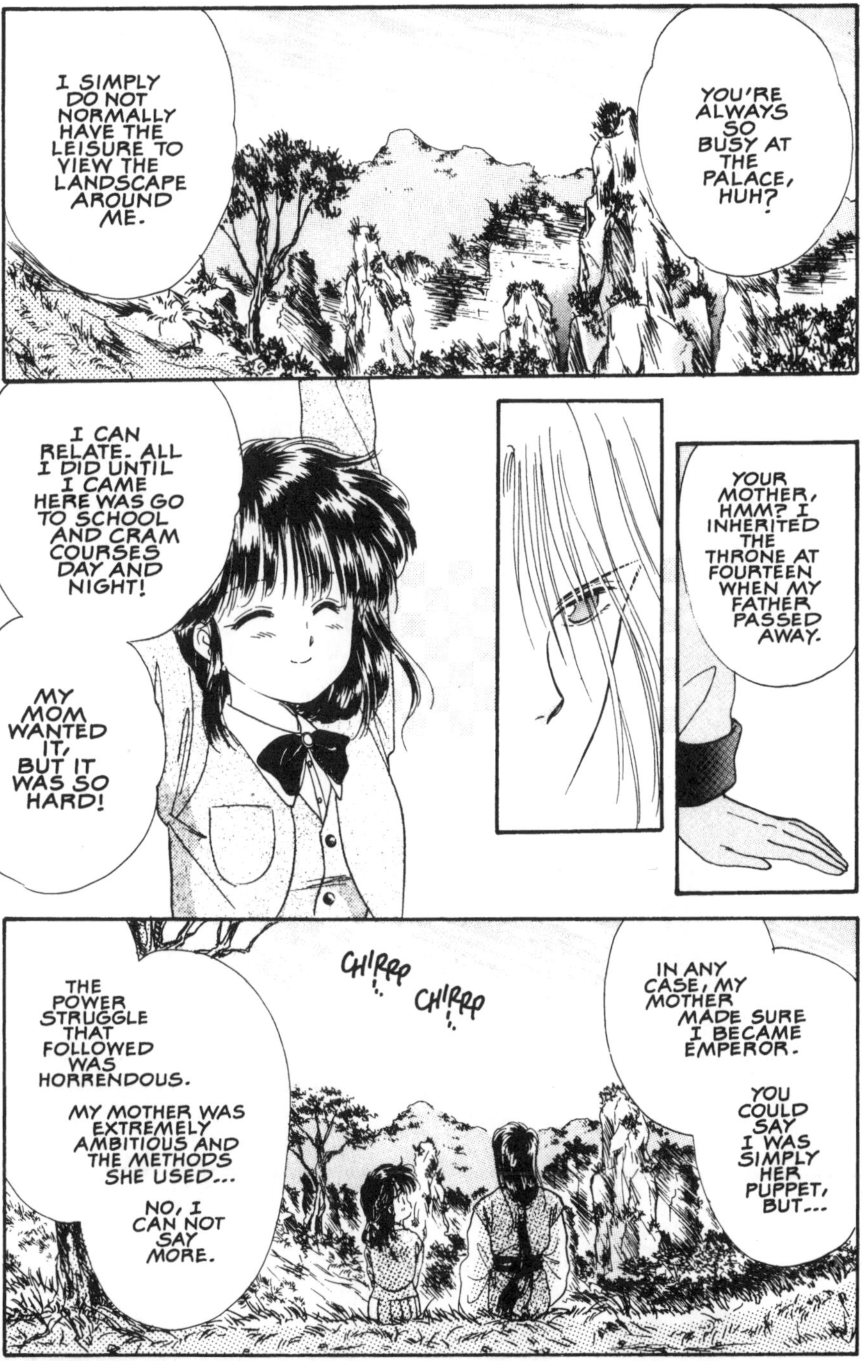
I SIMPLY DO NOT NORMALLY HAVE THE LEISURE TO VIEW THE LANDSCAPE AROUND ME.
YOU'RE ALWAYS SO BUSY AT THE PALACE, HUH?
I CAN RELATE. ALL I DID UNTIL I CAME HERE WAS GO TO SCHOOL AND CRAM COURSES DAY AND NIGHT!
MY MOM WANTED IT, BUT IT WAS SO HARD!
YOUR MOTHER, HMM? I INHERITED THE THRONE AT FOURTEEN WHEN MY FATHER PASSED AWAY.
THE POWER STRUGGLE THAT FOLLOWED WAS HORRENDOUS.
MY MOTHER WAS EXTREMELY AMBITIOUS AND THE METHODS SHE USED...
NO, I CAN NOT SAY MORE.
CHIRRP
CHIRRP
IN ANY CASE, MY MOTHER MADE SURE I BECAME EMPEROR.
YOU COULD SAY I WAS SIMPLY HER PUPPET, BUT...

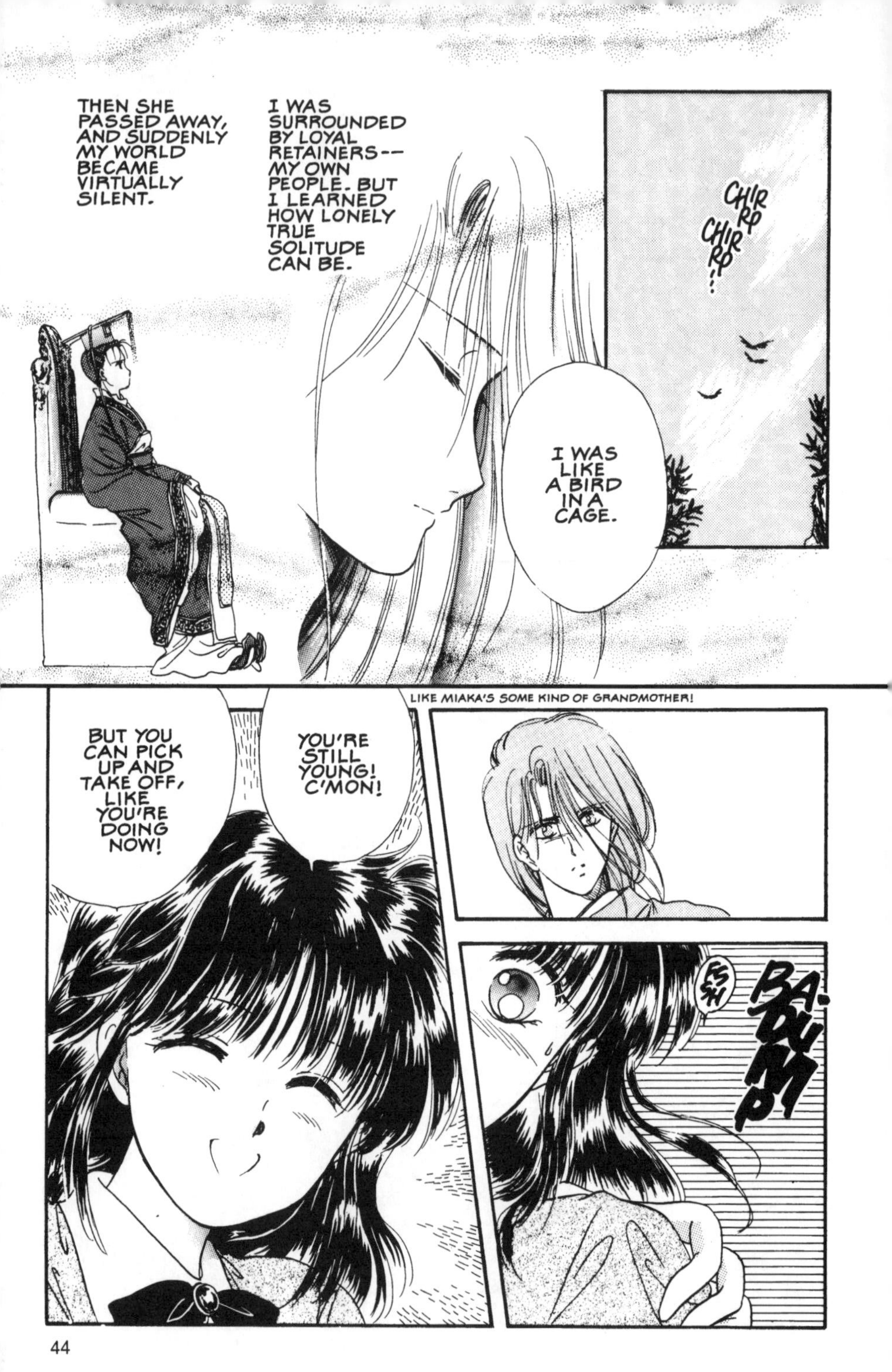
THEN SHE PASSED AWAY, AND SUDDENLY MY WORLD BECAME VIRTUALLY SILENT.
I WAS SURROUNDED BY LOYAL RETAINERS-- MY OWN PEOPLE. BUT I LEARNED HOW LONELY TRUE SOLITUDE CAN BE.
CHIRP CHIRP!!
I WAS LIKE A BIRD IN A CAGE.
BUT YOU CAN PICK UP AND TAKE OFF, LIKE YOU'RE DOING NOW!
YOU'RE STILL YOUNG! C'MON!
LIKE MIAKA'S SOME KIND OF GRANDMOTHER!
BA-DUMP

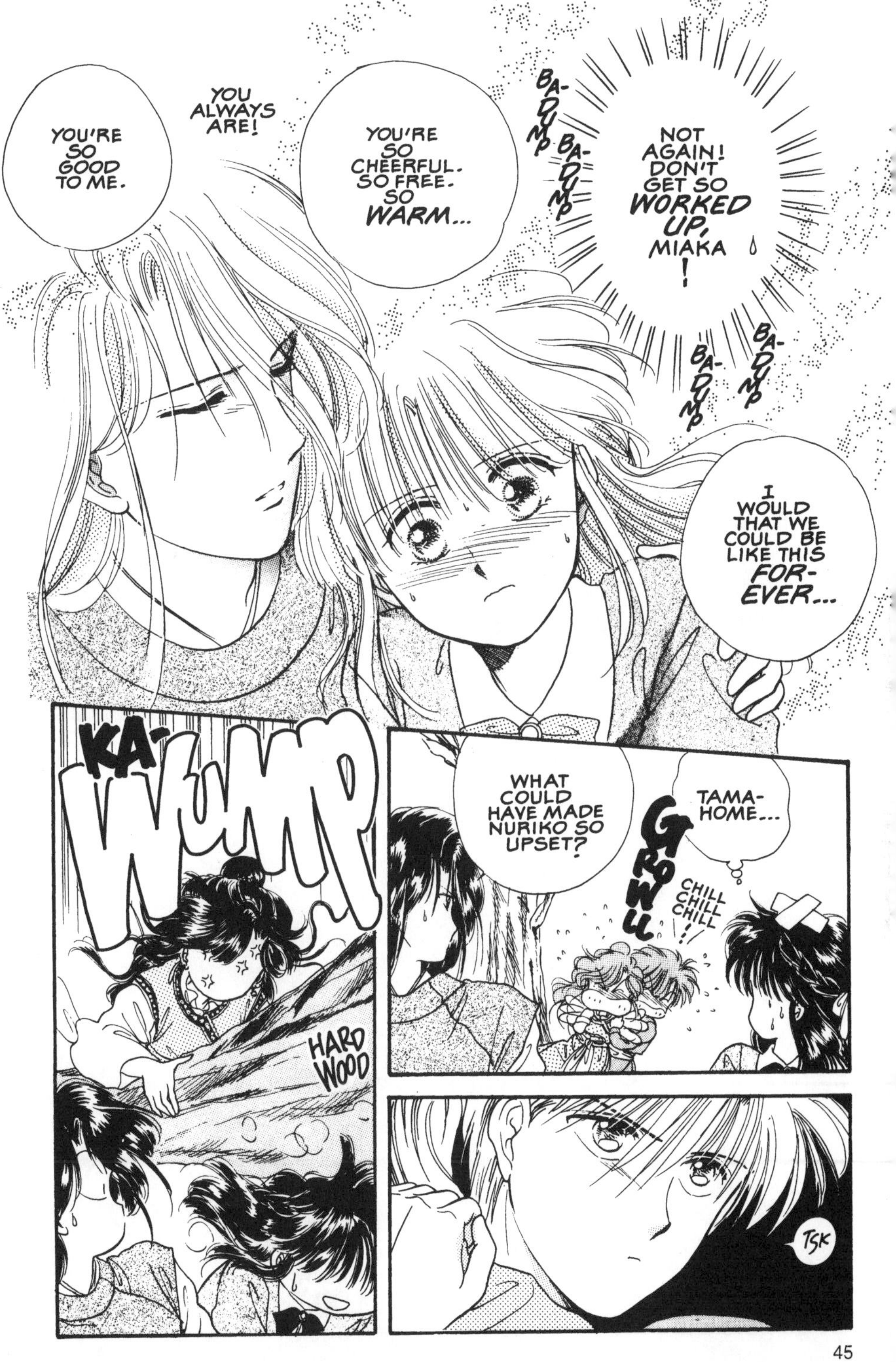
YOU'RE SO GOOD TO ME.
YOU ALWAYS ARE!
YOU'RE SO CHEERFUL. SO FREE. SO WARM...
BA-DUMP
BA-DUMP
NOT AGAIN! DON'T GET SO WORKED UP, MIAKA!
BA-DUMP
BA-DUMP
I WOULD THAT WE COULD BE LIKE THIS FOREVER...
KA-WUMP
HARD WOOD
WHAT COULD HAVE MADE NURIKO SO UPSET?
TAMA-HOME...
GROWL
CHILL CHILL CHILL!!
TSK

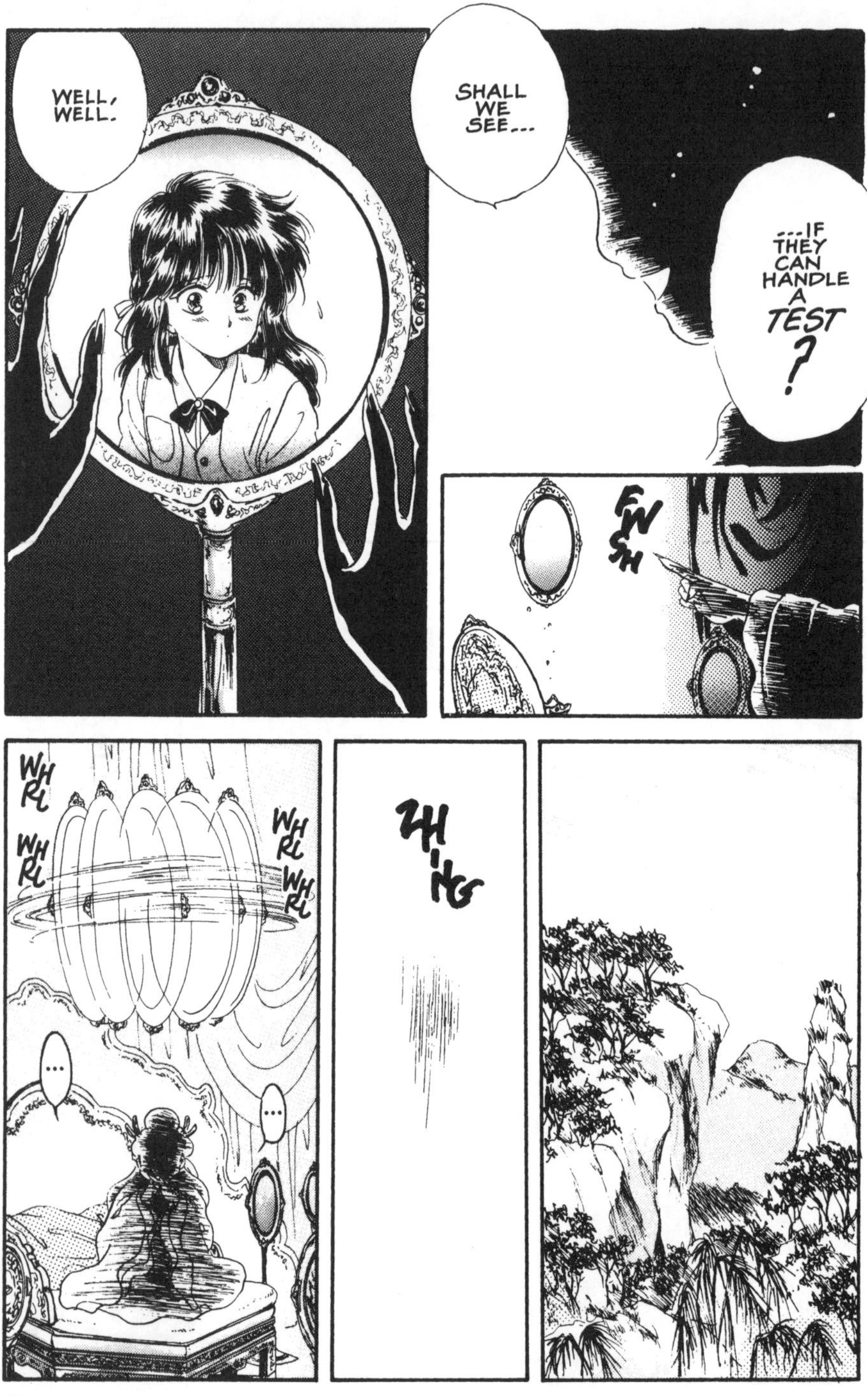
WELL, WELL.
SHALL WE SEE...
...IF THEY CAN HANDLE A TEST?
FWSH
WHRL
WHRL
WHRL
WHRL
...
...
ZHING

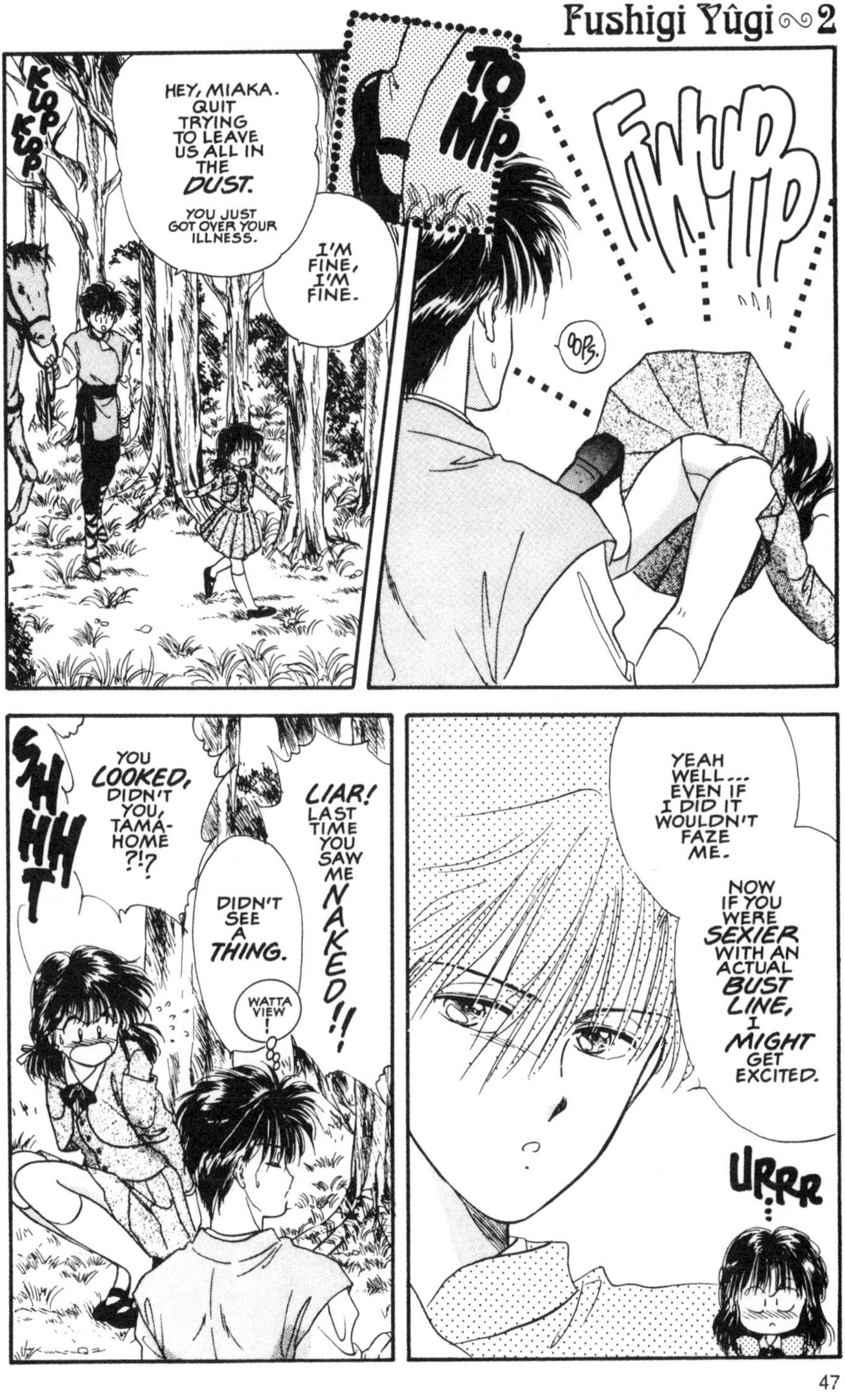
KLOP KLOP
HEY, MIAKA. QUIT TRYING TO LEAVE US ALL IN THE DUST.
YOU JUST GOT OVER YOUR ILLNESS.
I'M FINE, I'M FINE.
TOMP
OOPS.
SHHHT
YOU LOOKED, DIDN'T YOU, TAMAHOME ?!?
DIDN'T SEE A THING.
LIAR! LAST TIME YOU SAW ME NAKED!!
WATTA VIEW!
YEAH WELL... EVEN IF I DID IT WOULDN'T FAZE ME.
NOW IF YOU WERE SEXIER WITH AN ACTUAL BUST LINE, I MIGHT GET EXCITED.
URRR

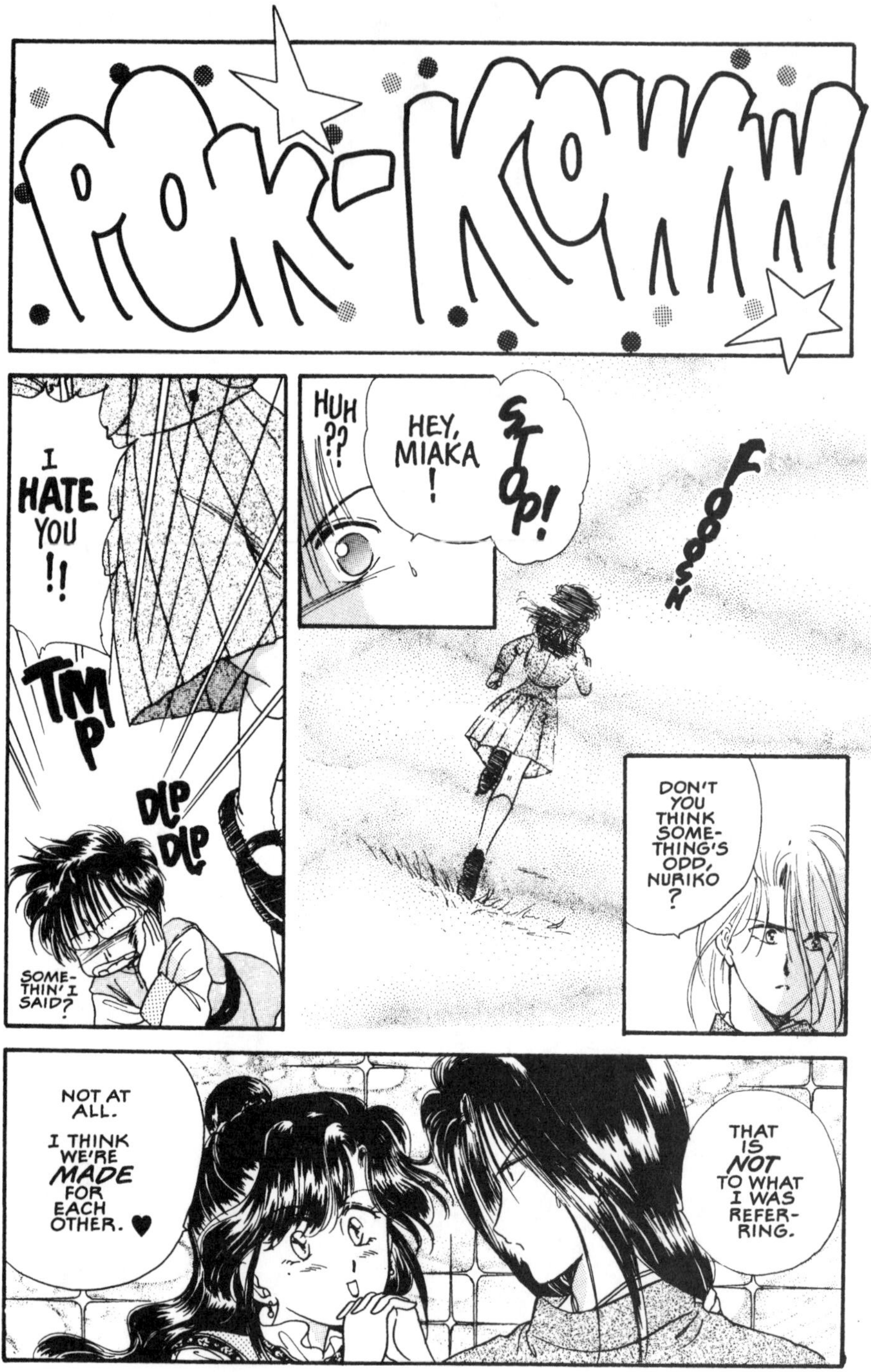
POK-KOWW
I HATE YOU !!
TMP
DLP DLP
SOMETHIN' I SAID?
HUH ??
HEY, MIAKA !
STOP!
FOOOOSH
DON'T YOU THINK SOMETHING'S ODD, NURIKO ?
NOT AT ALL.
I THINK WE'RE *MADE* FOR EACH OTHER. ♥
THAT IS *NOT* TO WHAT I WAS REFERRING.

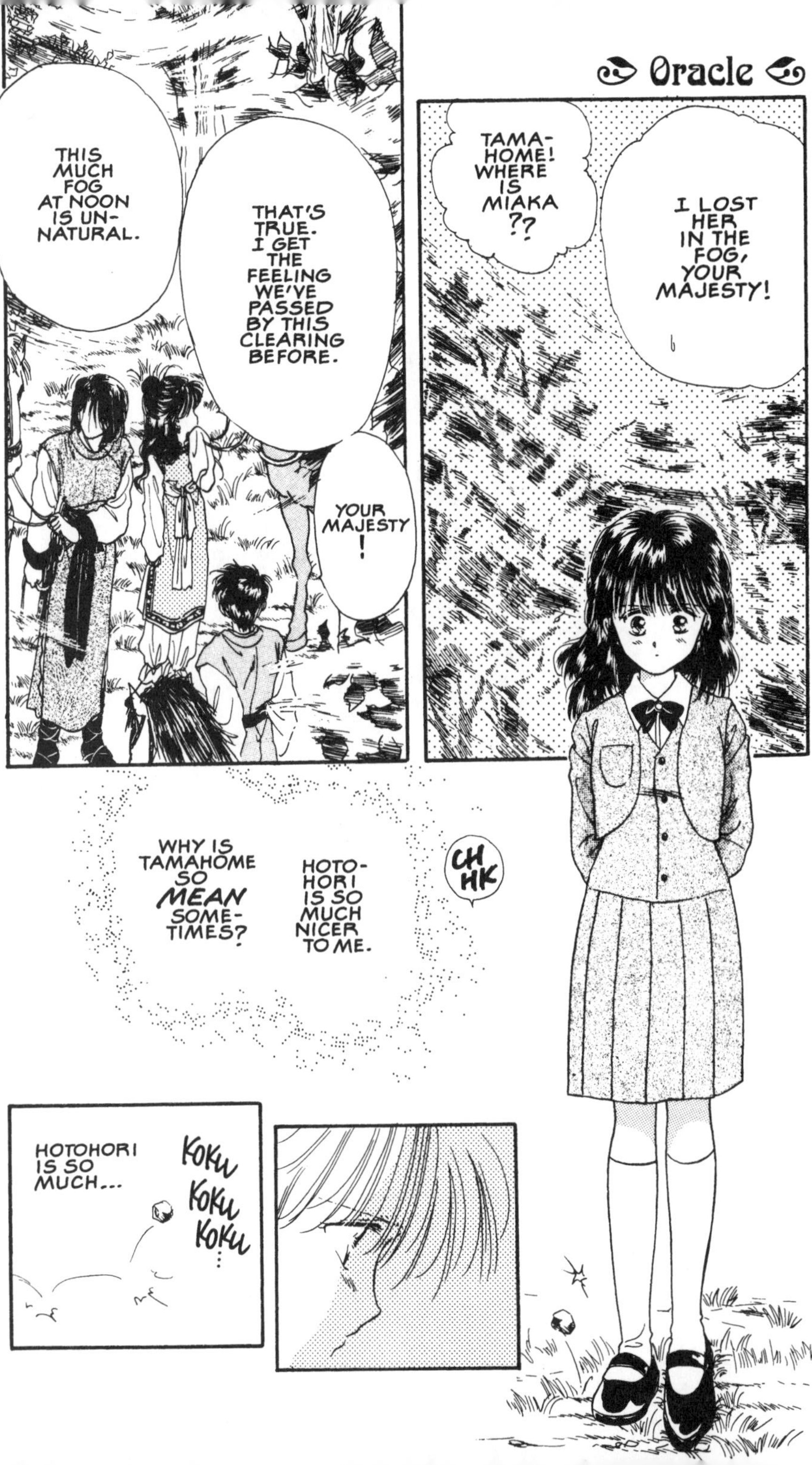
THIS MUCH FOG AT NOON IS UN-NATURAL.
THAT'S TRUE. I GET THE FEELING WE'VE PASSED BY THIS CLEARING BEFORE.
YOUR MAJESTY!
TAMA-HOME! WHERE IS MIAKA??
I LOST HER IN THE FOG, YOUR MAJESTY!
WHY IS TAMAHOME SO MEAN SOMETIMES?
HOTO-HORI IS SO MUCH NICER TO ME.
CH HK
HOTOHORI IS SO MUCH...
KOKU KOKU KOKU...

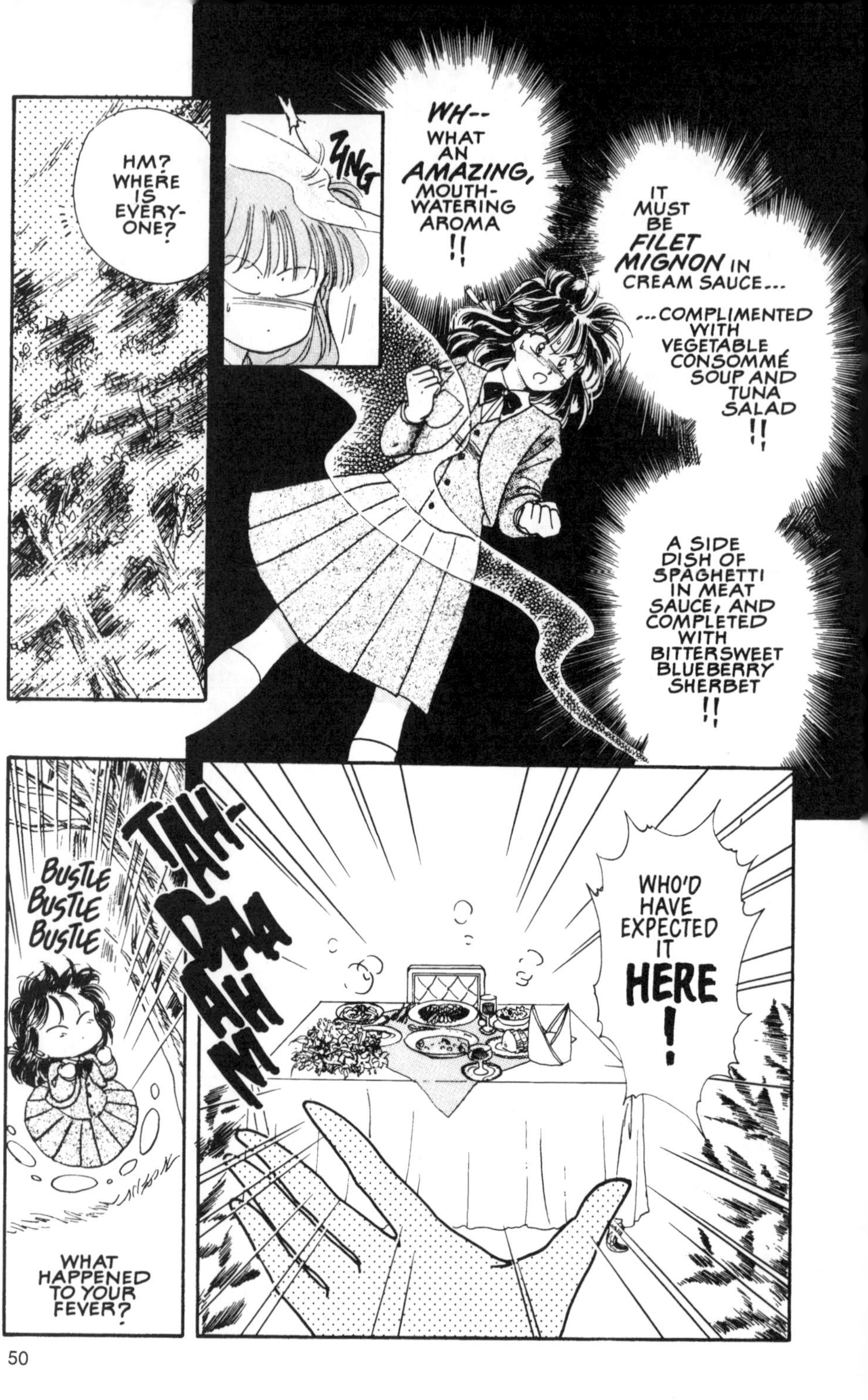
HM? WHERE IS EVERY-ONE?
ZING
WH-- WHAT AN AMAZING, MOUTH-WATERING AROMA !!
IT MUST BE FILET MIGNON IN CREAM SAUCE...
...COMPLIMENTED WITH VEGETABLE CONSOMMÉ SOUP AND TUNA SALAD !!
A SIDE DISH OF SPAGHETTI IN MEAT SAUCE, AND COMPLETED WITH BITTERSWEET BLUEBERRY SHERBET !!
BUSTLE BUSTLE BUSTLE
WHAT HAPPENED TO YOUR FEVER?
TAH-DAA-AHM
WHO'D HAVE EXPECTED IT HERE!

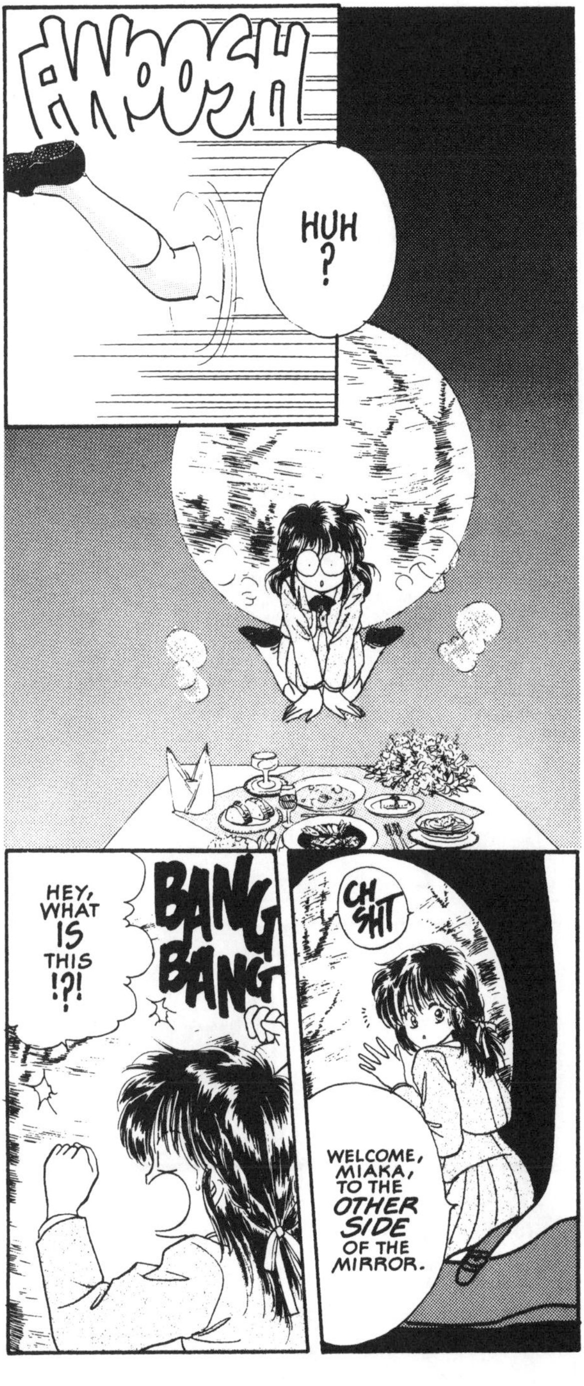
FWOOSH
HUH ?
HEY, WHAT IS THIS !?!
BANG BANG
CH SHT
WELCOME, MIAKA, TO THE *OTHER SIDE* OF THE MIRROR.

When I said that I felt sick, I wasn't being modest or begging for sympathy. So don't say, "Oh no, your work is great!!"
Before starting the series my confidence was at such an all time low that my stomach really began to ache. My editor told me, "Oh that, it's an occupational illness." Even now sometimes when I look at my pages I just want to tear them to shreds. Or when I'm assigned to do some color pages in the weekly magazine I ask, "Are you sure you want me to do them?" Or I end up worrying whether they would even put out the first graphic novel. What is wrong with me? My assistant told me I'm weird. Maybe I put down my characters or my work because I lack confidence. By criticizing it, I can be the first to say, "What is this junk?" That's why your letters mean so much to me. I'm so pathetic... Even when the first graphic novel came out I was more stressed than happy (which has always been the case with my other manga as well).
I would worry that someone would pick it up and say, "What is this junk," and toss it away. So I'm happy to hear that people are reading it. I'm happy about the Fushigi Yûgi CDs as well, but I deal with them the same way. Today is June 30, the day before the release of volume two, so it'll already be out by the time you read this. Ugh, how much longer will this go on?!
Oh yes, thanks to those readers receiving the short "Watase Newsletter" for expressing their gratitude (by fan mail, of course.) The reason why I had "Yû" in small letters was that my full name is often mistaken for a boy's name, so just to avoid any misunderstanding with your parents, I figured we could pretend to be friends (which might end up creating further misunderstandings).

The "Post-Recording Anecdotes" in the CD booklet was supposed to be "Recording Anecdotes." Human error. No one seemed to notice anyway.

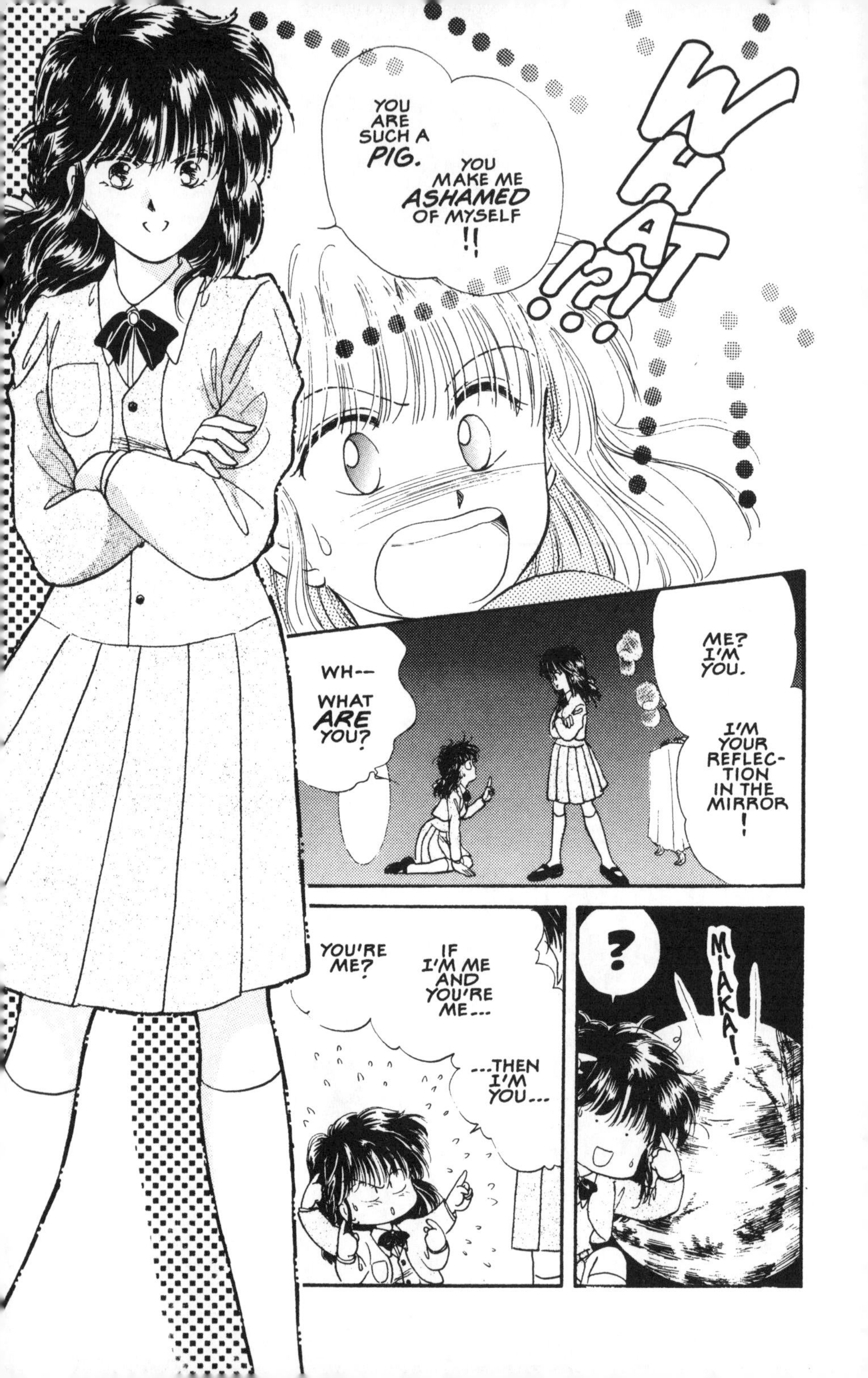
YOU ARE SUCH A PIG. YOU MAKE ME ASHAMED OF MYSELF !!
WHAT !?!
WH-- WHAT ARE YOU?
ME? I'M YOU.
I'M YOUR REFLECTION IN THE MIRROR !
YOU'RE ME?
IF I'M ME AND YOU'RE ME...
...THEN I'M YOU...
?
MIAKA!

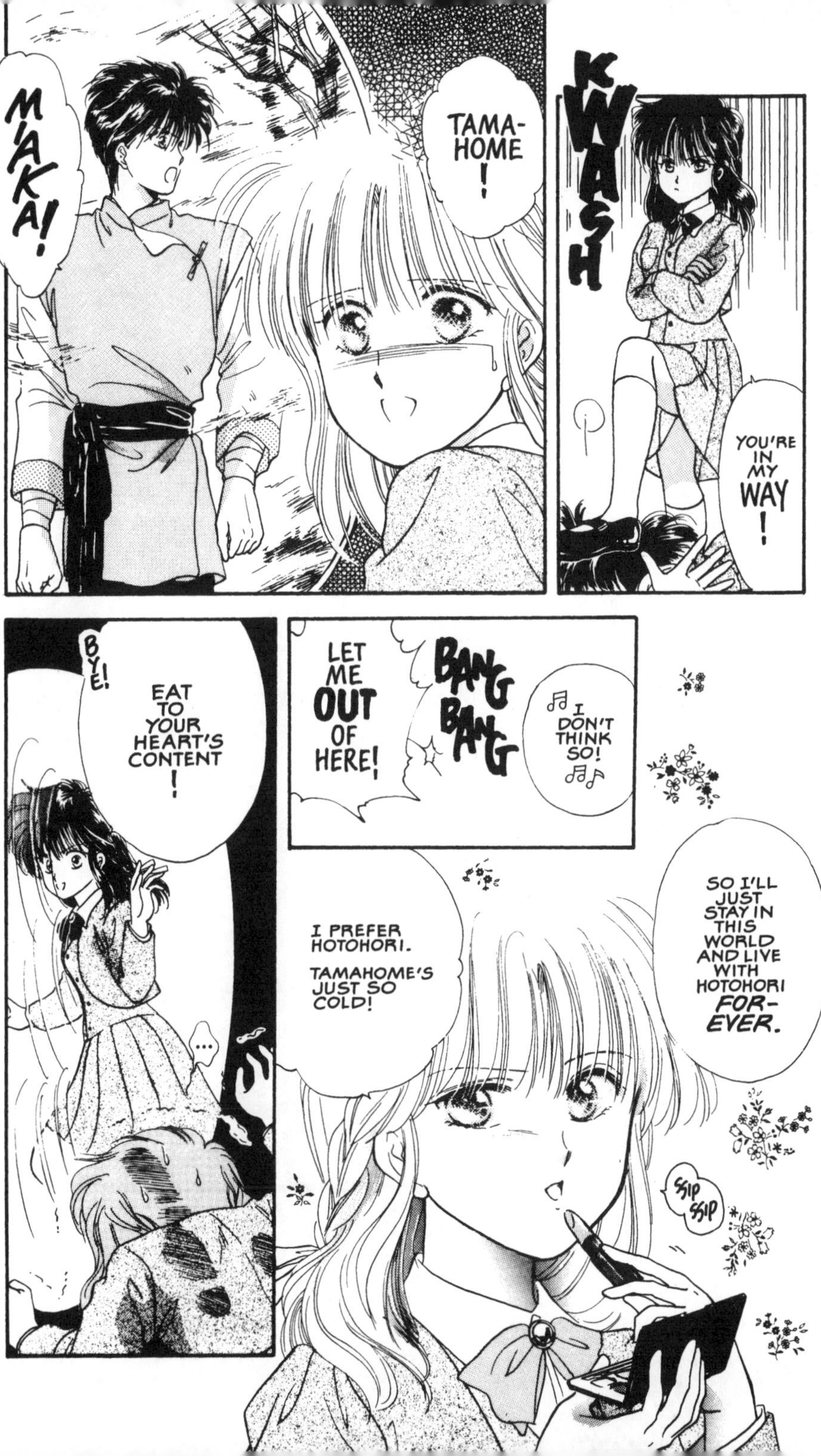

MIAKA!
TAMA-HOME!
KWASH
YOU'RE IN MY WAY!
BYE!
EAT TO YOUR HEART'S CONTENT!
...
LET ME OUT OF HERE!
BANG BANG
I DON'T THINK SO!
I PREFER HOTOHORI.
TAMAHOME'S JUST SO COLD!
SO I'LL JUST STAY IN THIS WORLD AND LIVE WITH HOTOHORI FOREVER.
SSIP SSIP

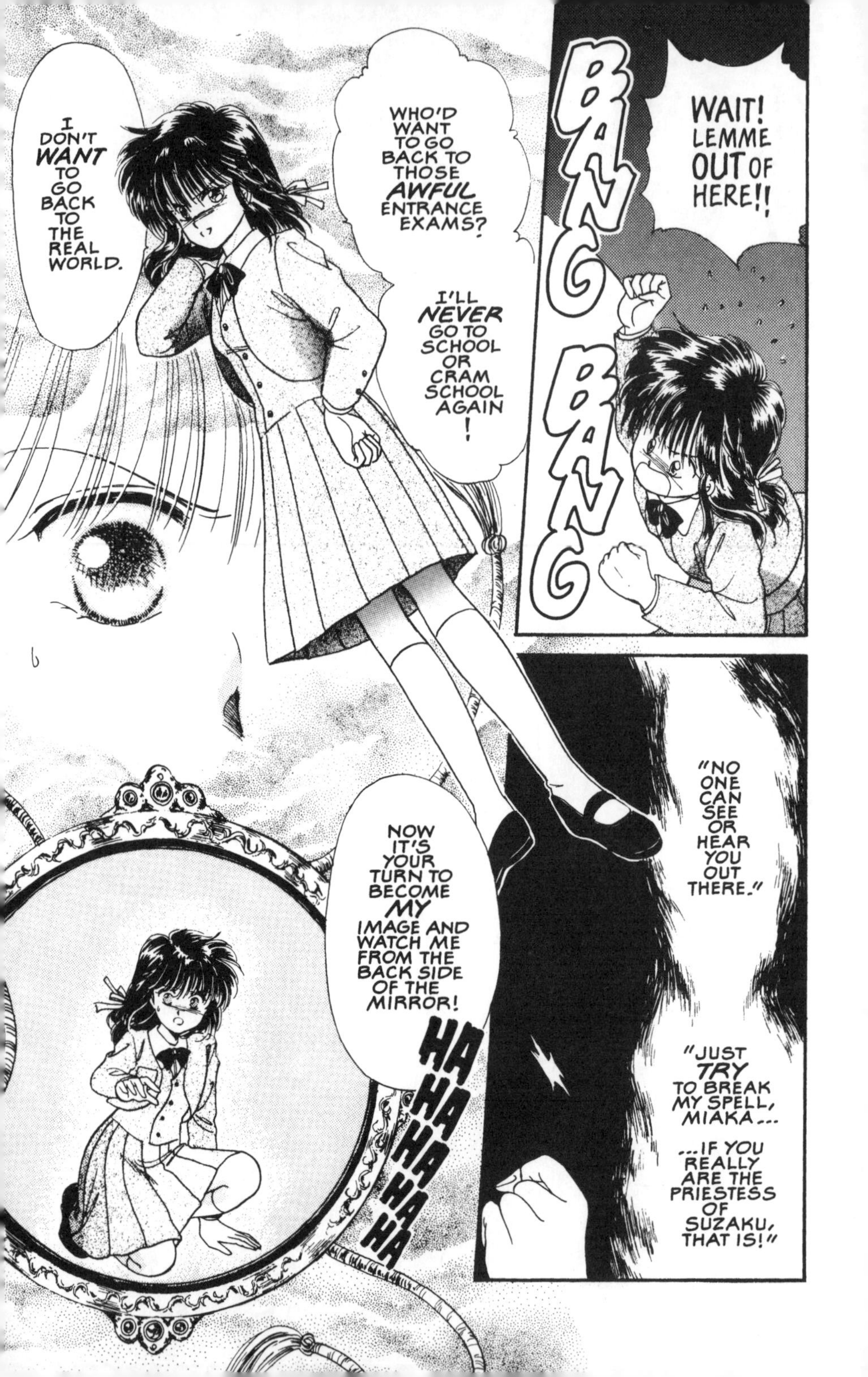

I DON'T WANT TO GO BACK TO THE REAL WORLD.
WHO'D WANT TO GO BACK TO THOSE AWFUL ENTRANCE EXAMS?
I'LL NEVER GO TO SCHOOL OR CRAM SCHOOL AGAIN!
NOW IT'S YOUR TURN TO BECOME MY IMAGE AND WATCH ME FROM THE BACK SIDE OF THE MIRROR!
HAHAHAHAHAHAHA
WAIT! LEMME OUT OF HERE!!
BANG BANG BANG
"NO ONE CAN SEE OR HEAR YOU OUT THERE."
"JUST TRY TO BREAK MY SPELL, MIAKA...
...IF YOU REALLY ARE THE PRIESTESS OF SUZAKU, THAT IS!"

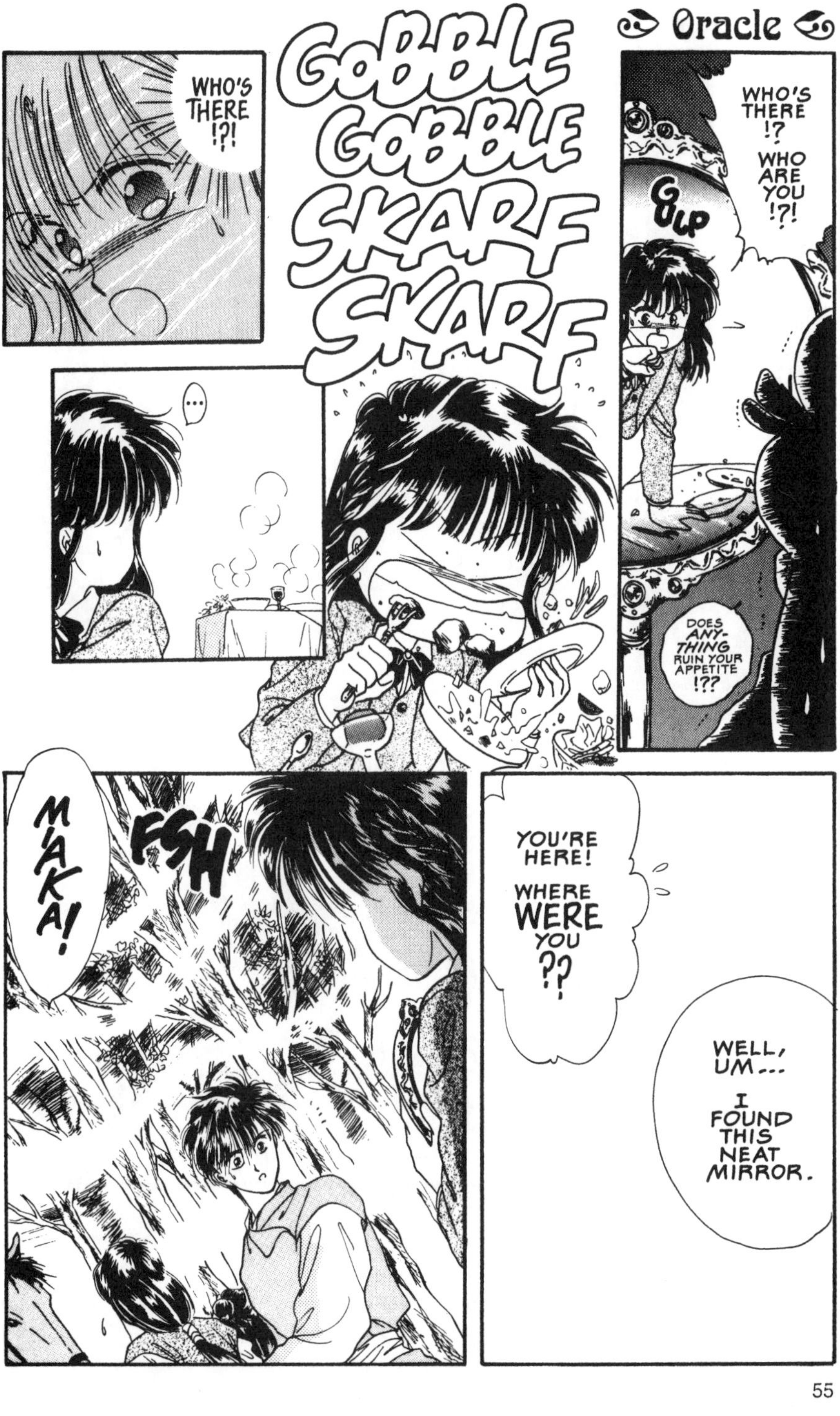
WHO'S THERE !?!
...
GOBBLE GOBBLE SKARF SKARF
GULP
WHO'S THERE !? WHO ARE YOU !?!
DOES ANYTHING RUIN YOUR APPETITE !??
MIAKA!
FSH
YOU'RE HERE! WHERE WERE YOU ??
WELL, UM... I FOUND THIS NEAT MIRROR.

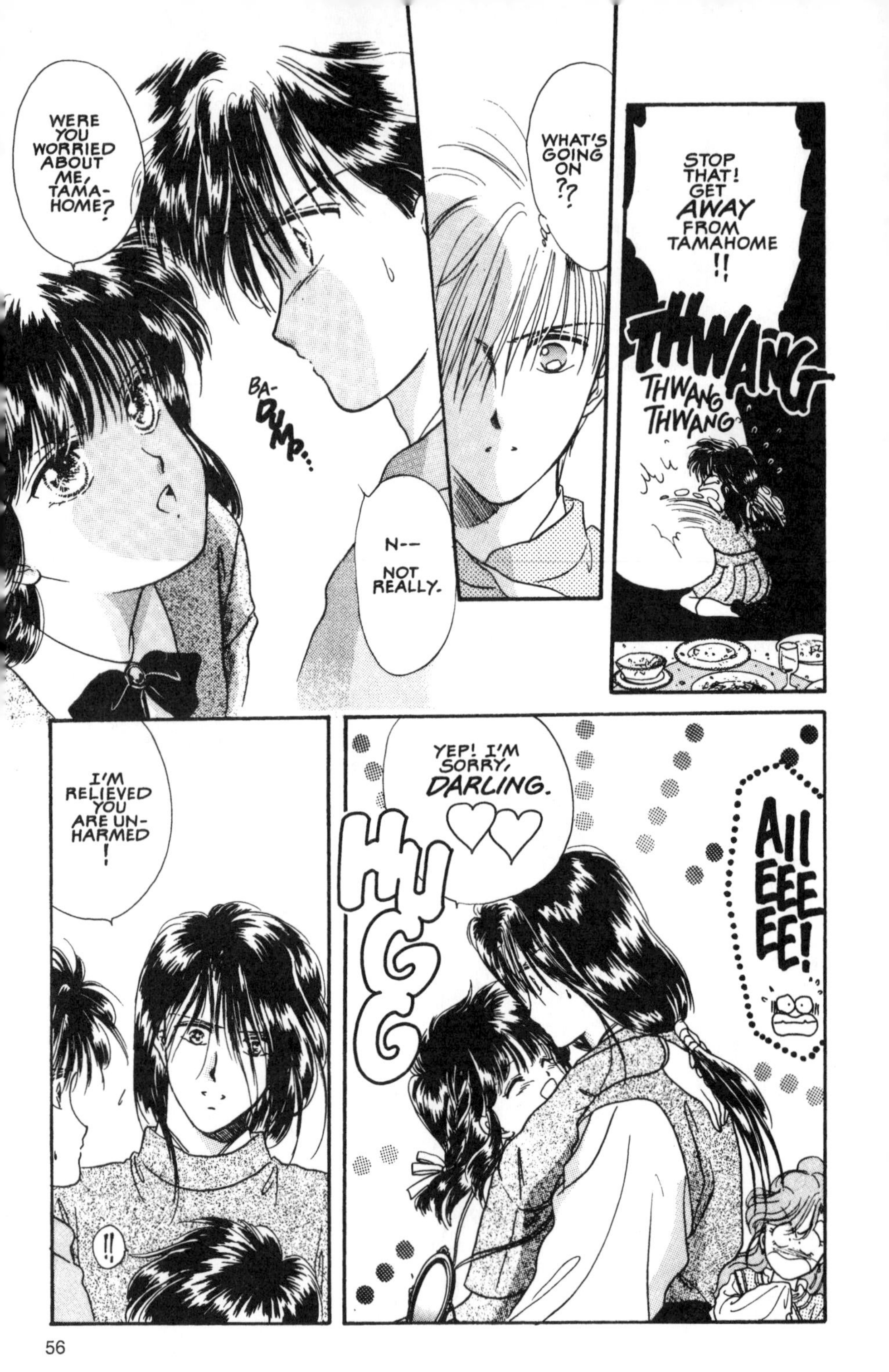
WERE YOU WORRIED ABOUT ME, TAMAHOME?
BA-DUMP...
N-- NOT REALLY.
WHAT'S GOING ON ??
STOP THAT! GET AWAY FROM TAMAHOME !!
THWANG
THWANG THWANG
I'M RELIEVED YOU ARE UNHARMED!
!!
YEP! I'M SORRY, DARLING.
HUG
AIIEEEEEE!

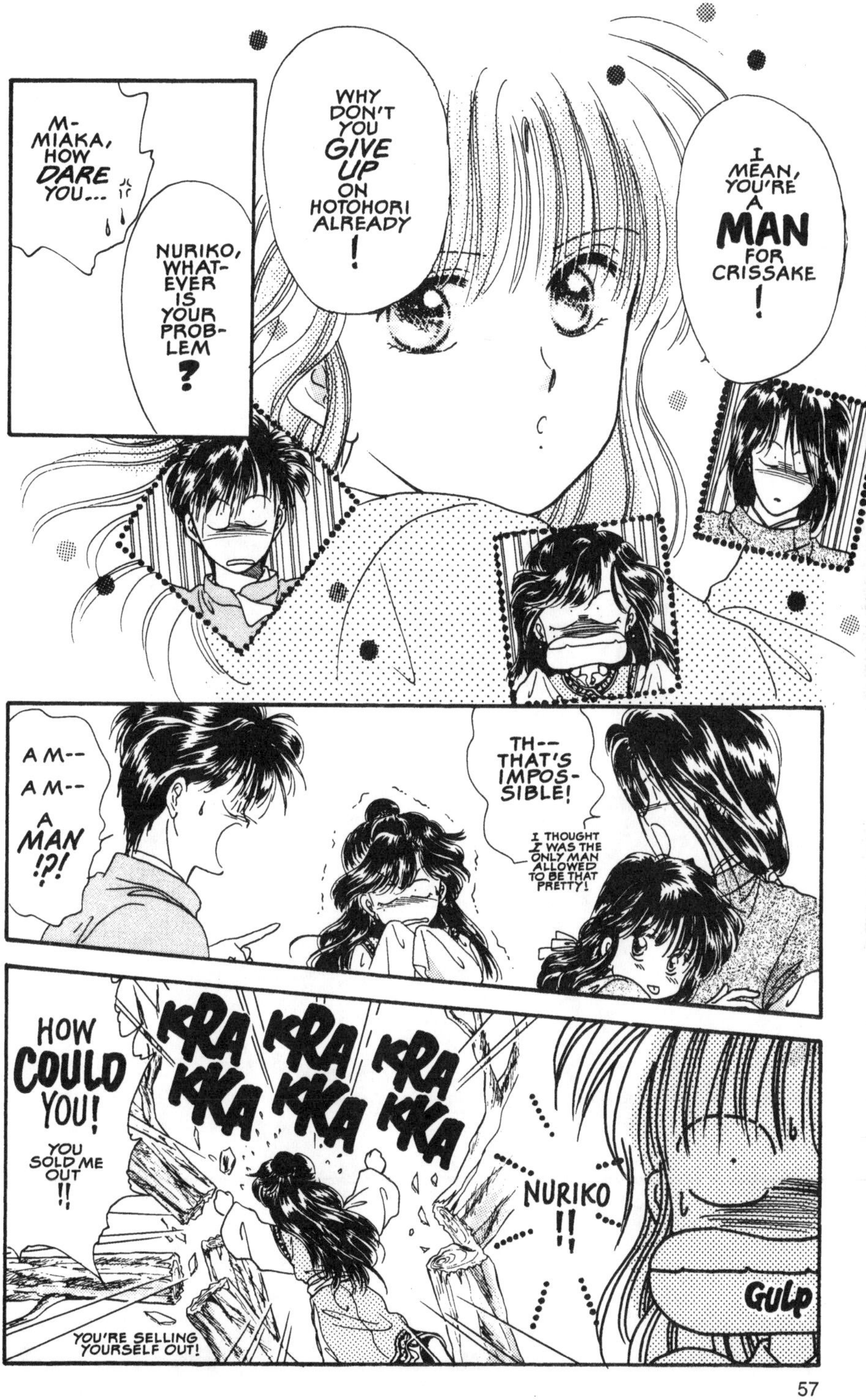
WHY DON'T YOU GIVE UP ON HOTOHORI ALREADY!
I MEAN, YOU'RE A MAN FOR CRISSAKE!
NURIKO, WHATEVER IS YOUR PROBLEM?
M-MIAKA, HOW DARE YOU...
TH-- THAT'S IMPOSSIBLE!
I THOUGHT I WAS THE ONLY MAN ALLOWED TO BE THAT PRETTY!
AM-- AM-- A MAN!?!
NURIKO!!
GULP
KRAKKA KRAKKA KRAKKA
HOW COULD YOU!
YOU SOLD ME OUT!!
YOU'RE SELLING YOURSELF OUT!

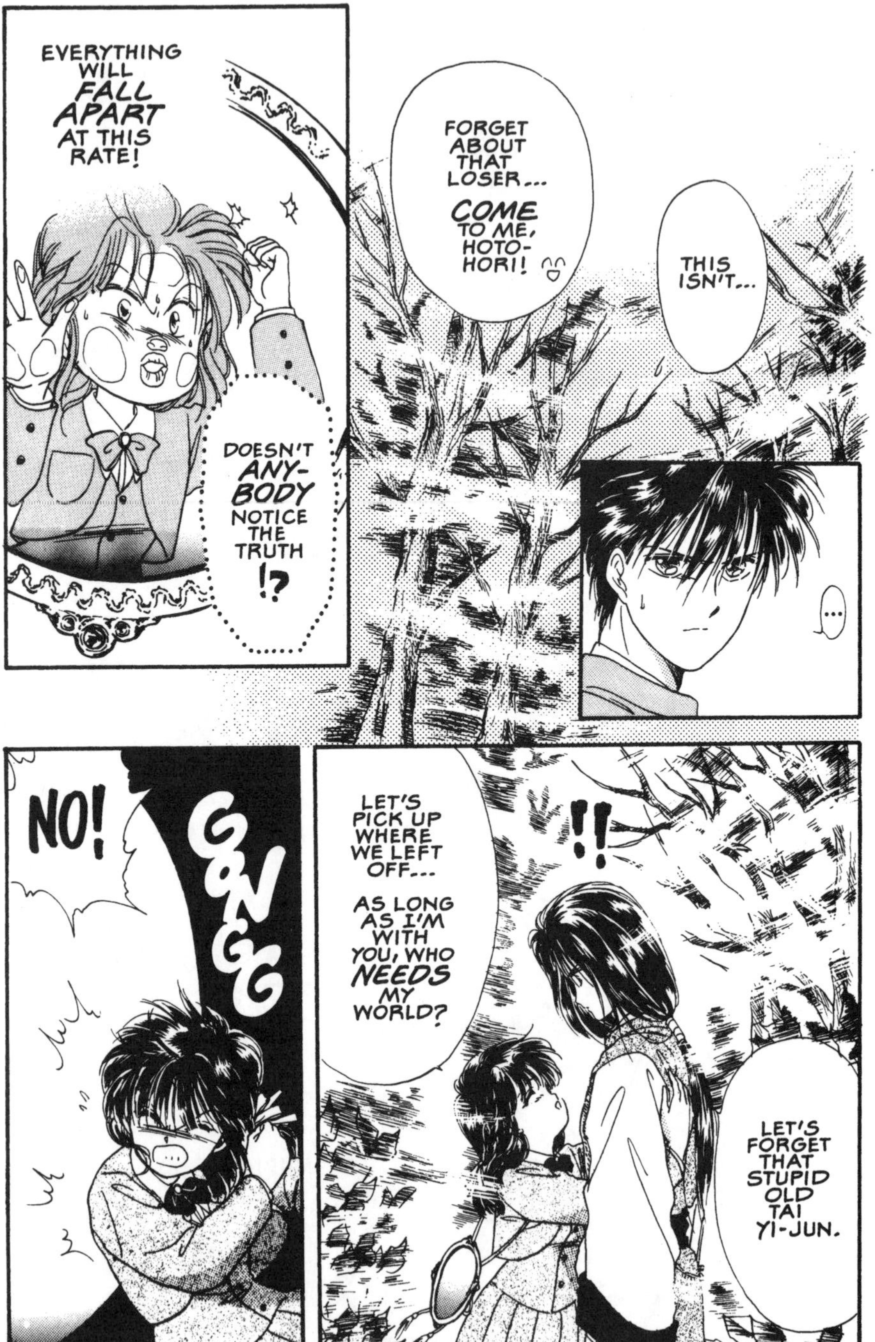
EVERYTHING WILL FALL APART AT THIS RATE!
DOESN'T ANYBODY NOTICE THE TRUTH !?
FORGET ABOUT THAT LOSER... COME TO ME, HOTOHORI!
THIS ISN'T...
...
NO!
GONG
LET'S PICK UP WHERE WE LEFT OFF... AS LONG AS I'M WITH YOU, WHO NEEDS MY WORLD?
!!
LET'S FORGET THAT STUPID OLD TAI YI-JUN.

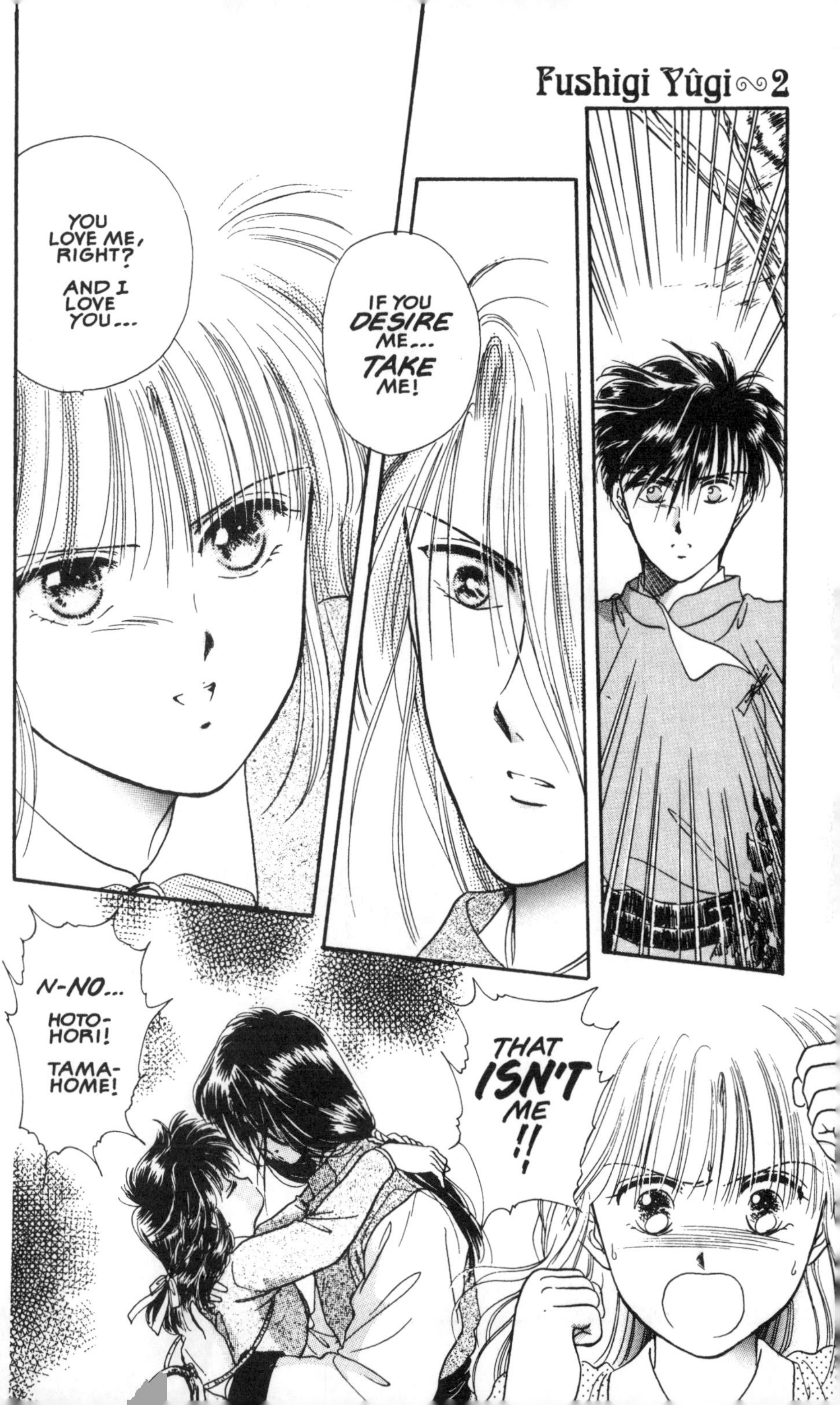
YOU LOVE ME, RIGHT?
AND I LOVE YOU...
IF YOU DESIRE ME... TAKE ME!
N-NO...
HOTO-HORI!
TAMA-HOME!
THAT ISN'T ME!!

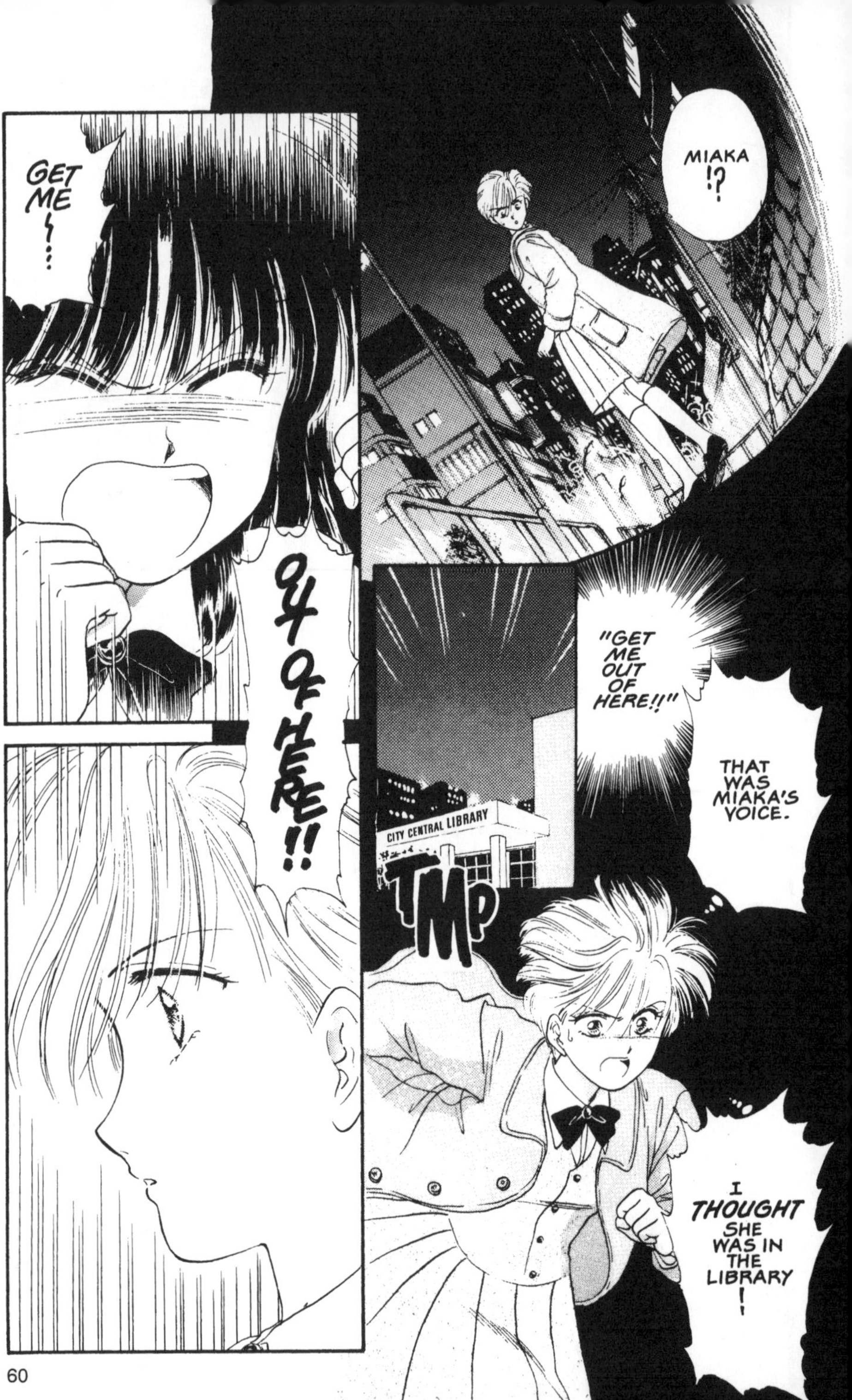
GET ME...
MIAKA!?
OUT OF HERE!!
CITY CENTRAL LIBRARY
"GET ME OUT OF HERE!!"
TMP
THAT WAS MIAKA'S VOICE.
I *THOUGHT* SHE WAS IN THE LIBRARY!

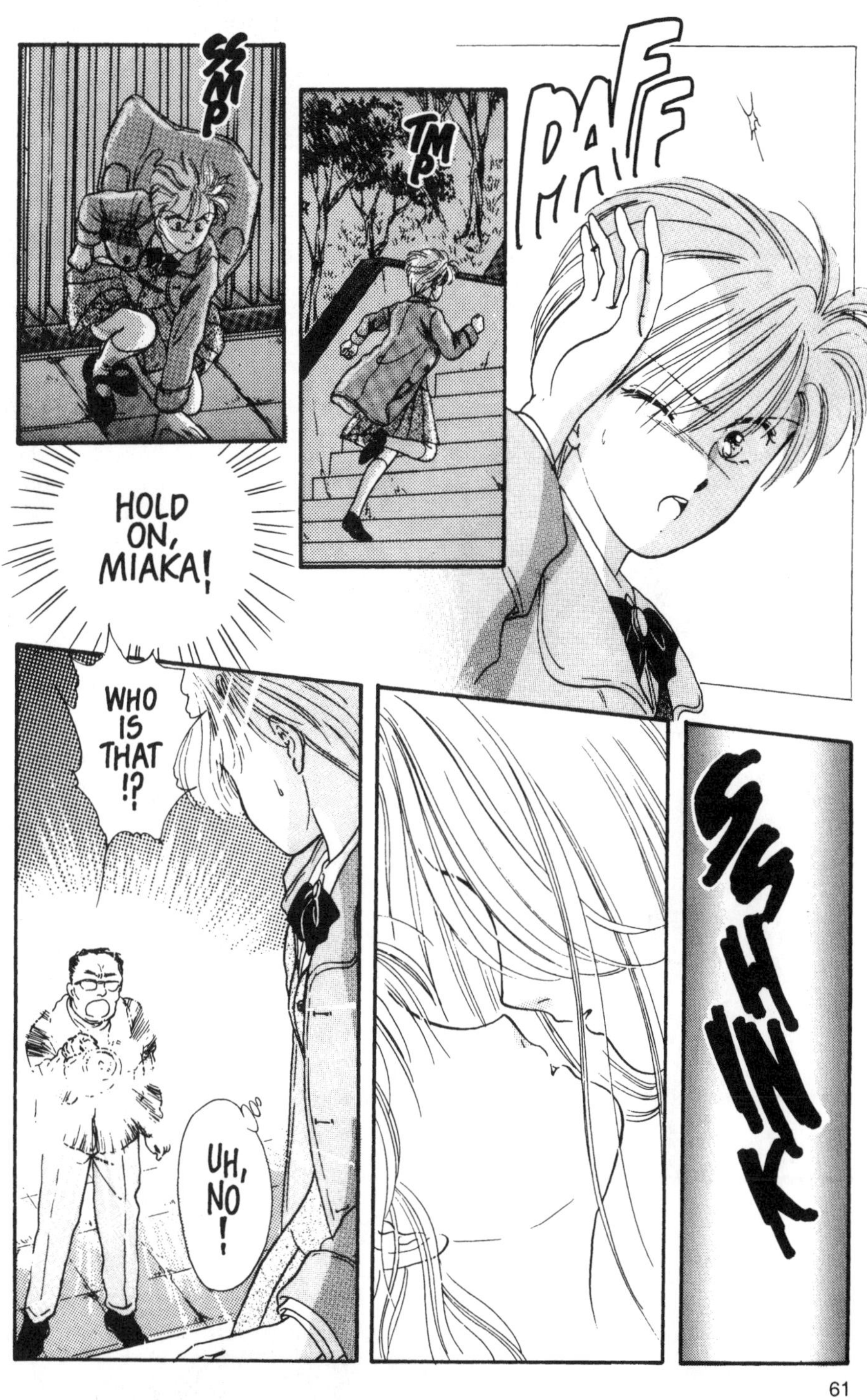
SSMP
TMP
PAFF
HOLD ON, MIAKA!
WHO IS THAT!?
UH, NO!
SSHHNK

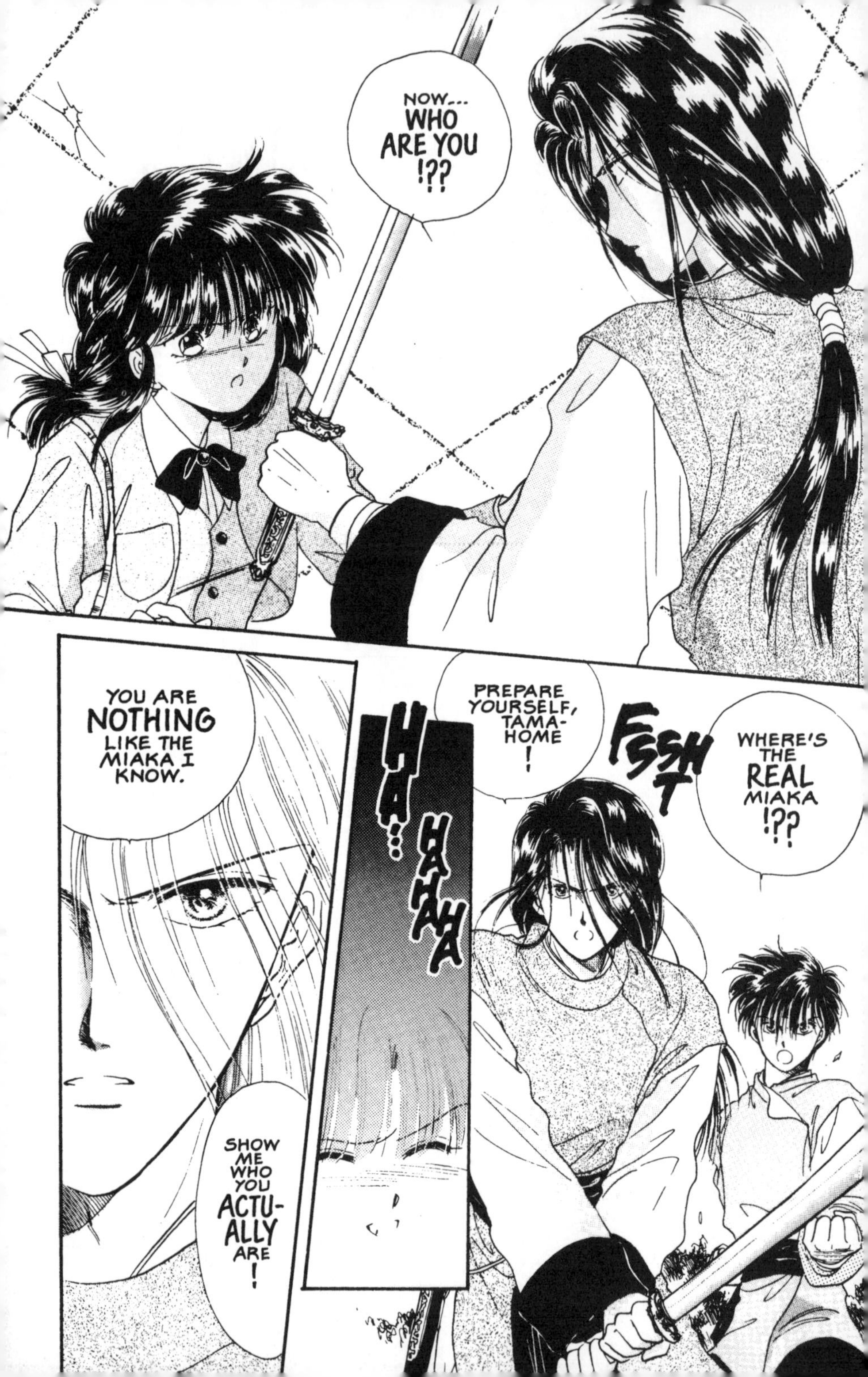
NOW... WHO ARE YOU !??
YOU ARE NOTHING LIKE THE MIAKA I KNOW.
SHOW ME WHO YOU ACTU-ALLY ARE!
HA... HAHAHA
PREPARE YOURSELF, TAMA-HOME!
FSSHT
WHERE'S THE REAL MIAKA !??

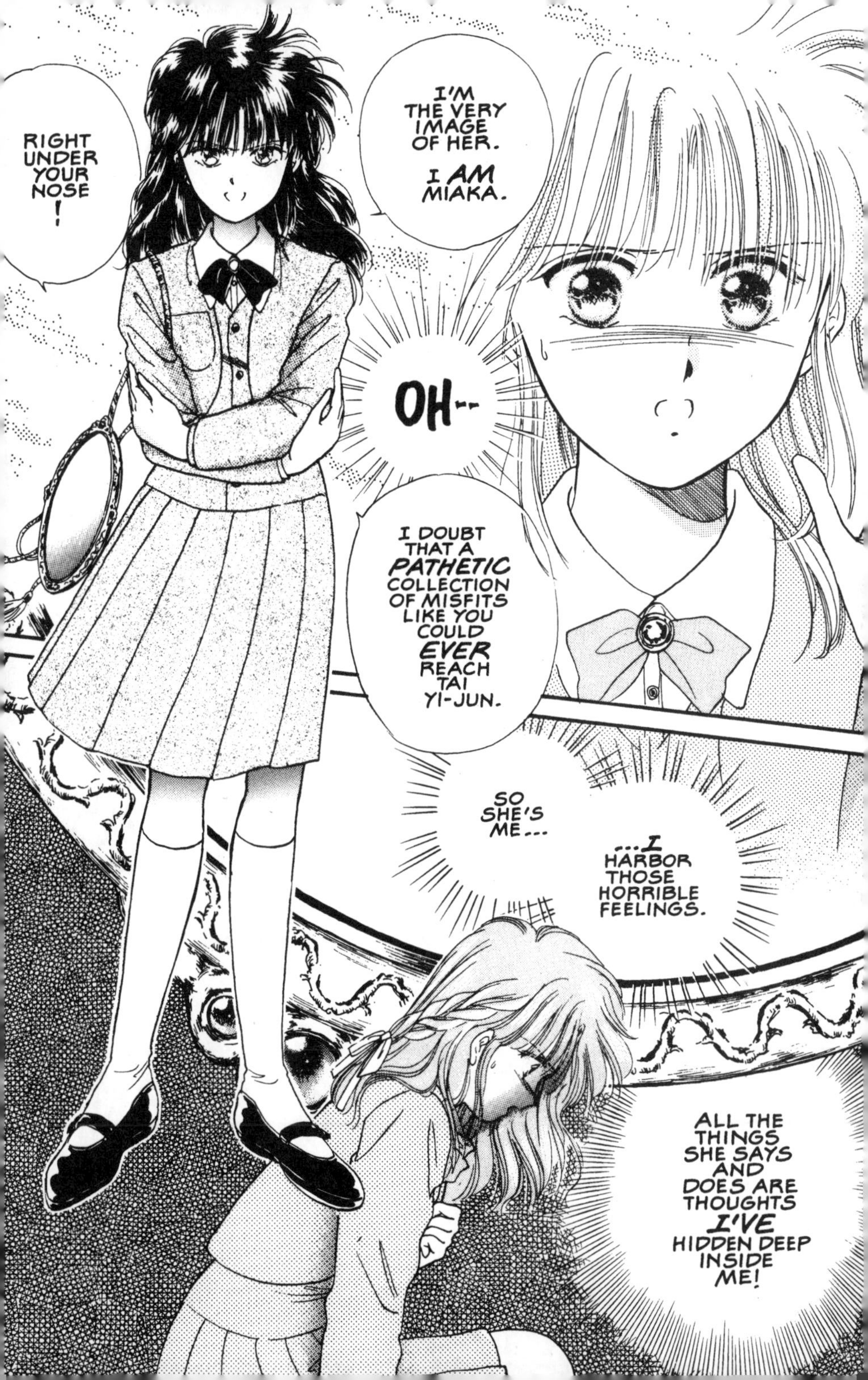
RIGHT UNDER YOUR NOSE!
I'M THE VERY IMAGE OF HER. I AM MIAKA.
OH--
I DOUBT THAT A PATHETIC COLLECTION OF MISFITS LIKE YOU COULD EVER REACH TAI YI-JUN.
SO SHE'S ME...
...I HARBOR THOSE HORRIBLE FEELINGS.
ALL THE THINGS SHE SAYS AND DOES ARE THOUGHTS I'VE HIDDEN DEEP INSIDE ME!

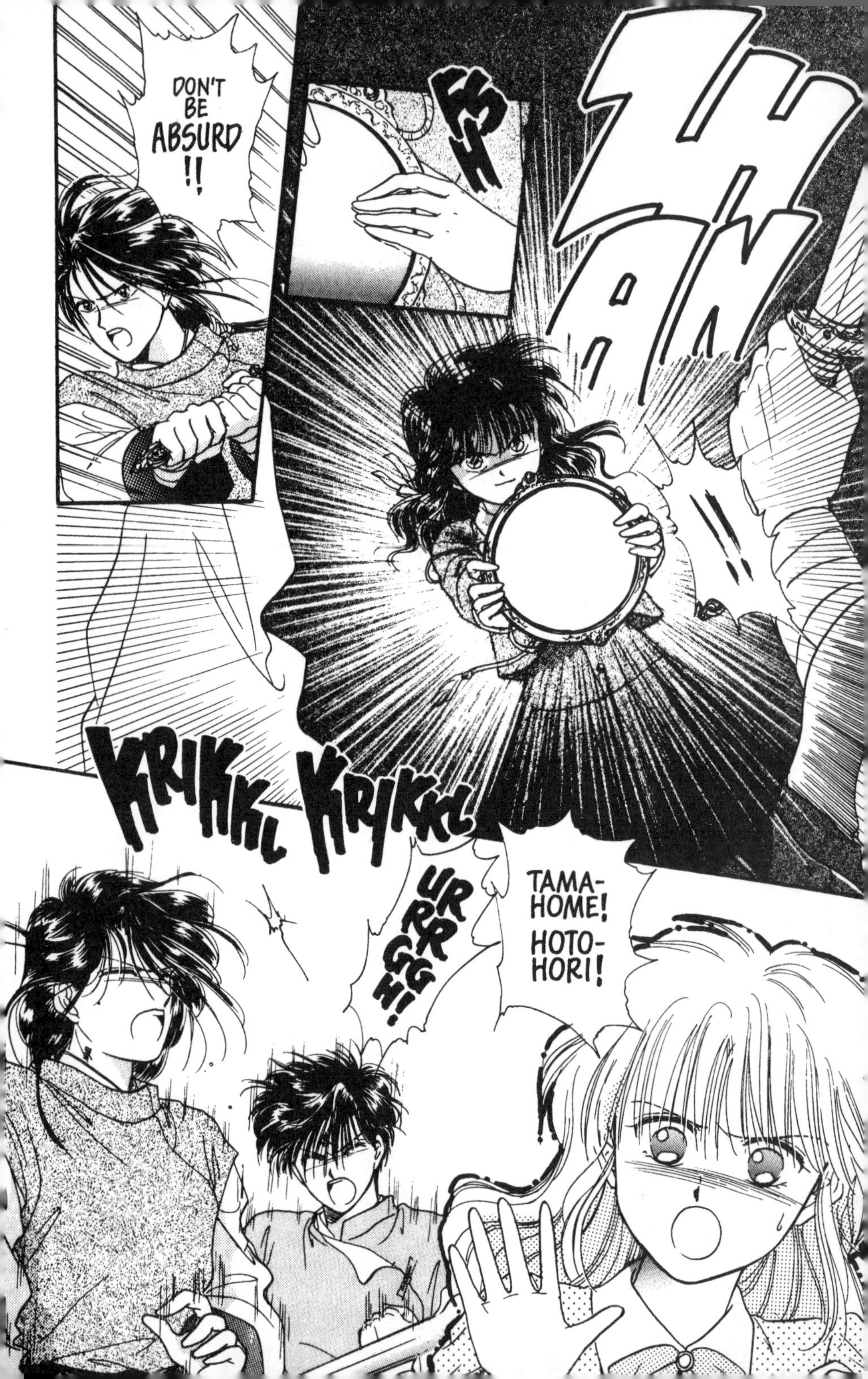
DON'T BE ABSURD !!
FSH
ZHAAN
!!
KRIKKL KRIKKL
URRRGGH!
TAMA-HOME! HOTO-HORI!

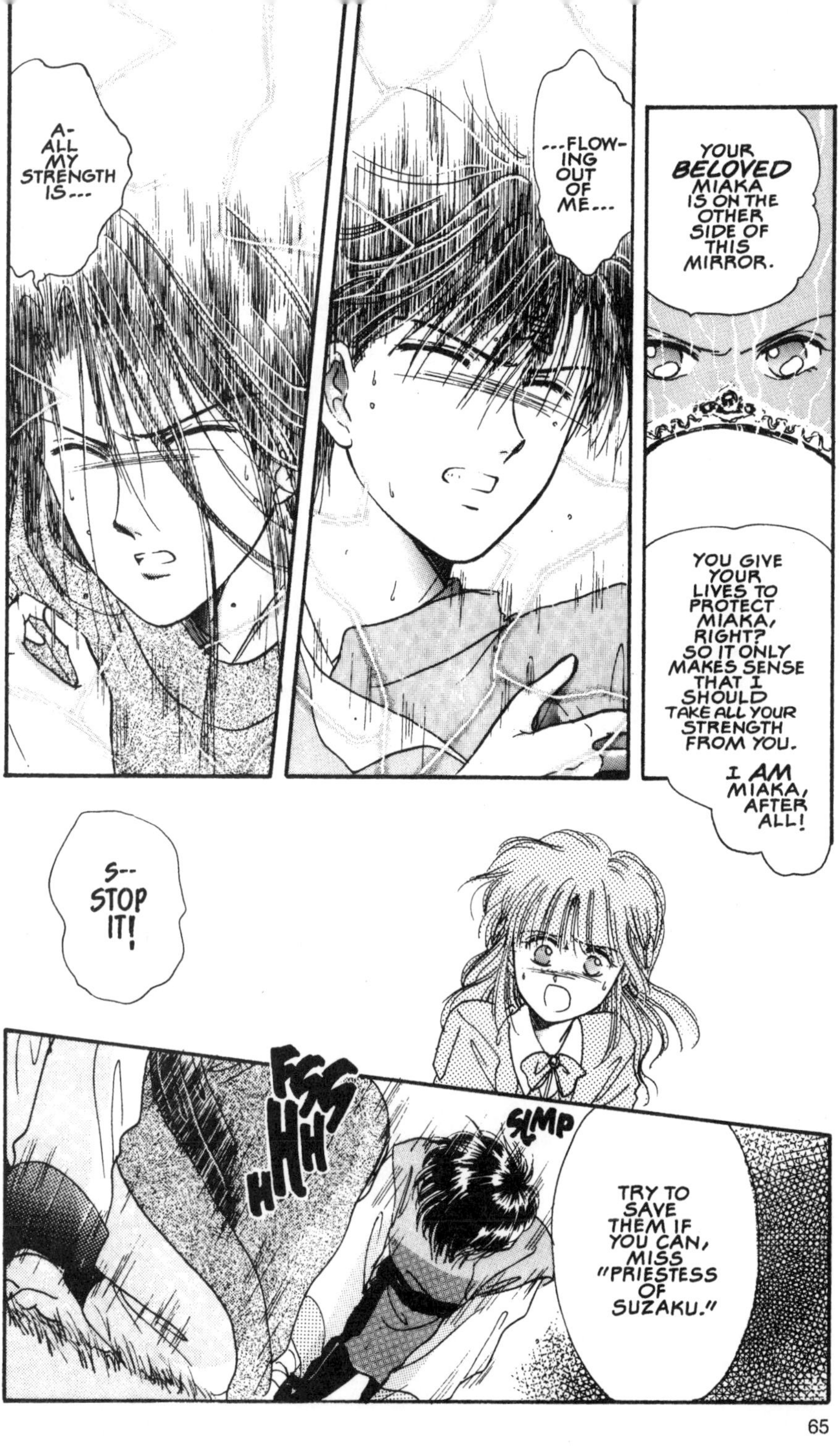
A-ALL MY STRENGTH IS---
---FLOWING OUT OF ME---
YOUR BELOVED MIAKA IS ON THE OTHER SIDE OF THIS MIRROR.
YOU GIVE YOUR LIVES TO PROTECT MIAKA, RIGHT? SO IT ONLY MAKES SENSE THAT I SHOULD TAKE ALL YOUR STRENGTH FROM YOU.
I AM MIAKA, AFTER ALL!
S-- STOP IT!
FSSSHHHH
SLMP
TRY TO SAVE THEM IF YOU CAN, MISS "PRIESTESS OF SUZAKU."

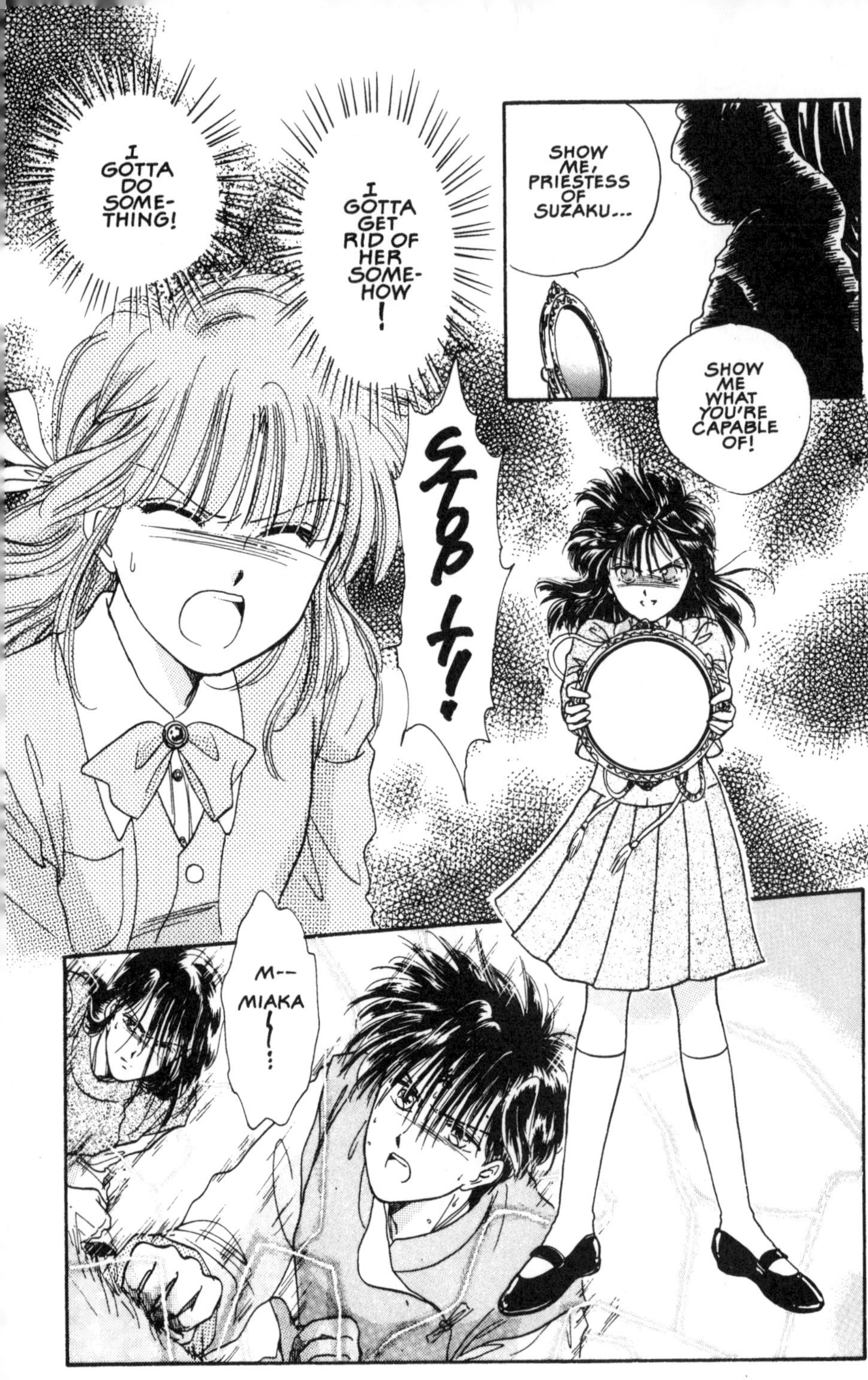
I GOTTA DO SOME-THING!
I GOTTA GET RID OF HER SOME-HOW!
SHOW ME, PRIESTESS OF SUZAKU...
SHOW ME WHAT YOU'RE CAPABLE OF!
M-- MIAKA...!

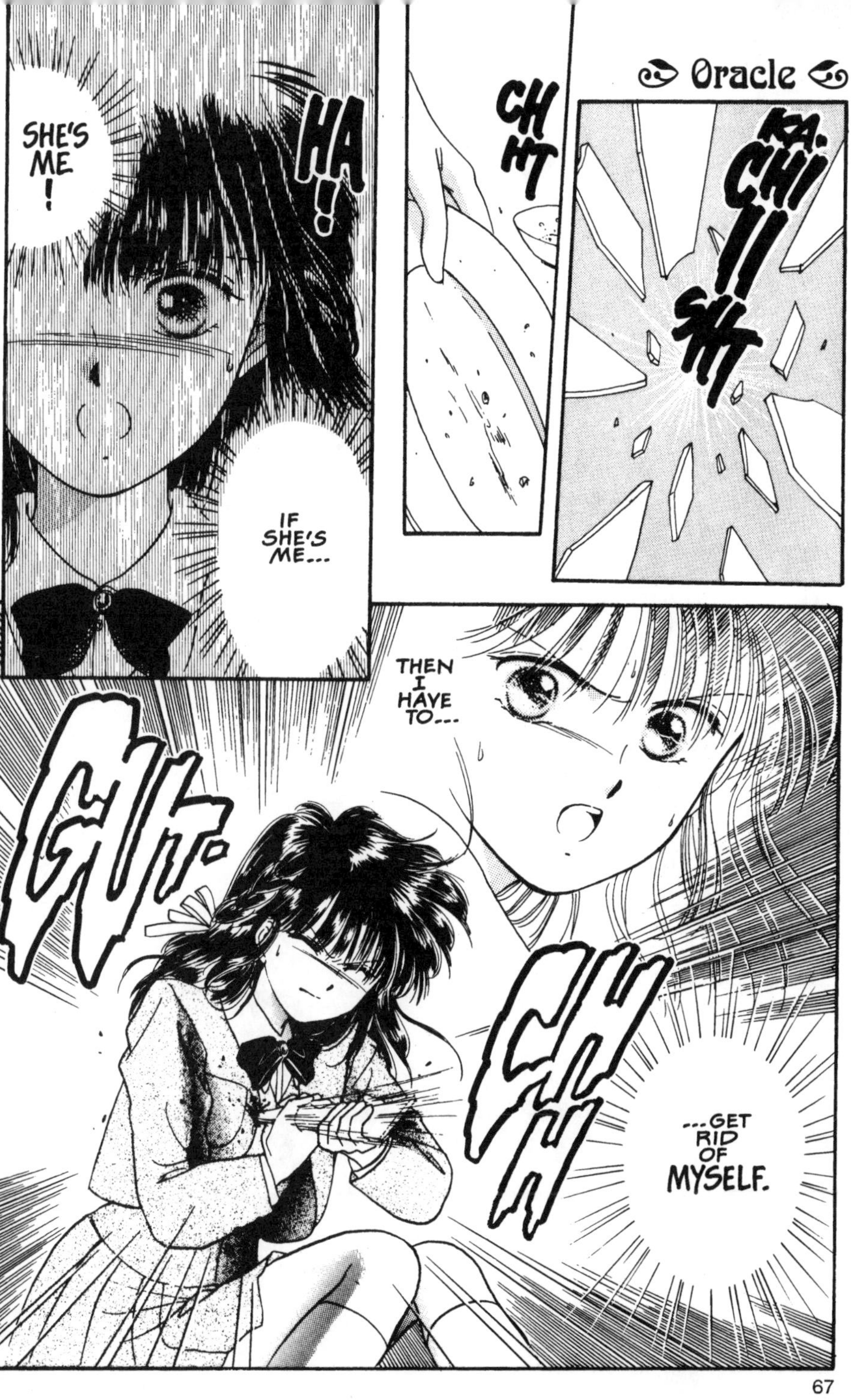
SHE'S ME!
HA!
IF SHE'S ME...
CHHT
KA-CHI I I SHT
THEN I HAVE TO...
GUT.
CHH
...GET RID OF MYSELF.

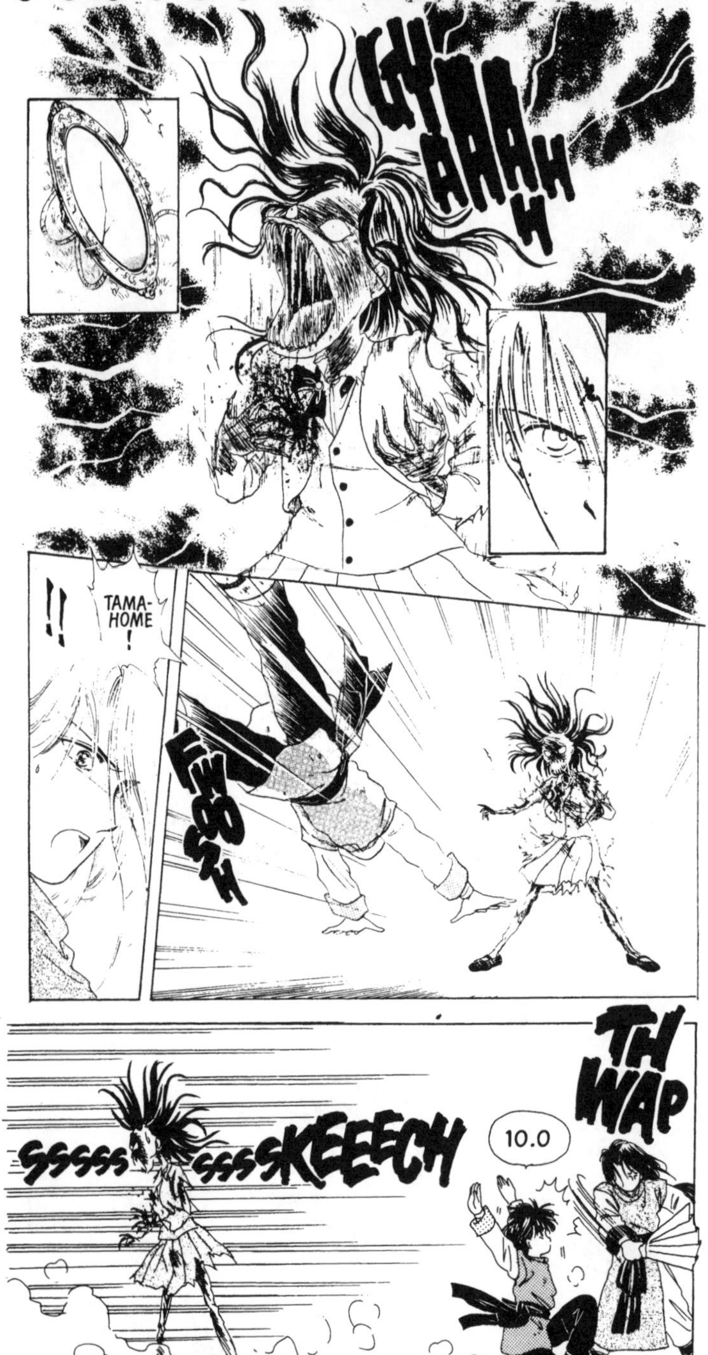
GYAAAAAHHH
!!
TAMA-HOME!
FWOOSH
SSSSSSSSSKEEECH
10.0
THWAP

PARDON THE PARODY

INCREASING YOUR FUSHIGI YŪGI ENJOYMENT BY 100%!

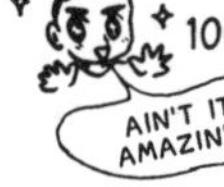
AIN'T IT AMAZIN'!?

IDEA: K. OF TOKYO (A MANGA ASSISTANT)

⇦ BY Y.W. (A MANGA ARTIST)

CHAPTER NINE
AWAKENING MEMORIES

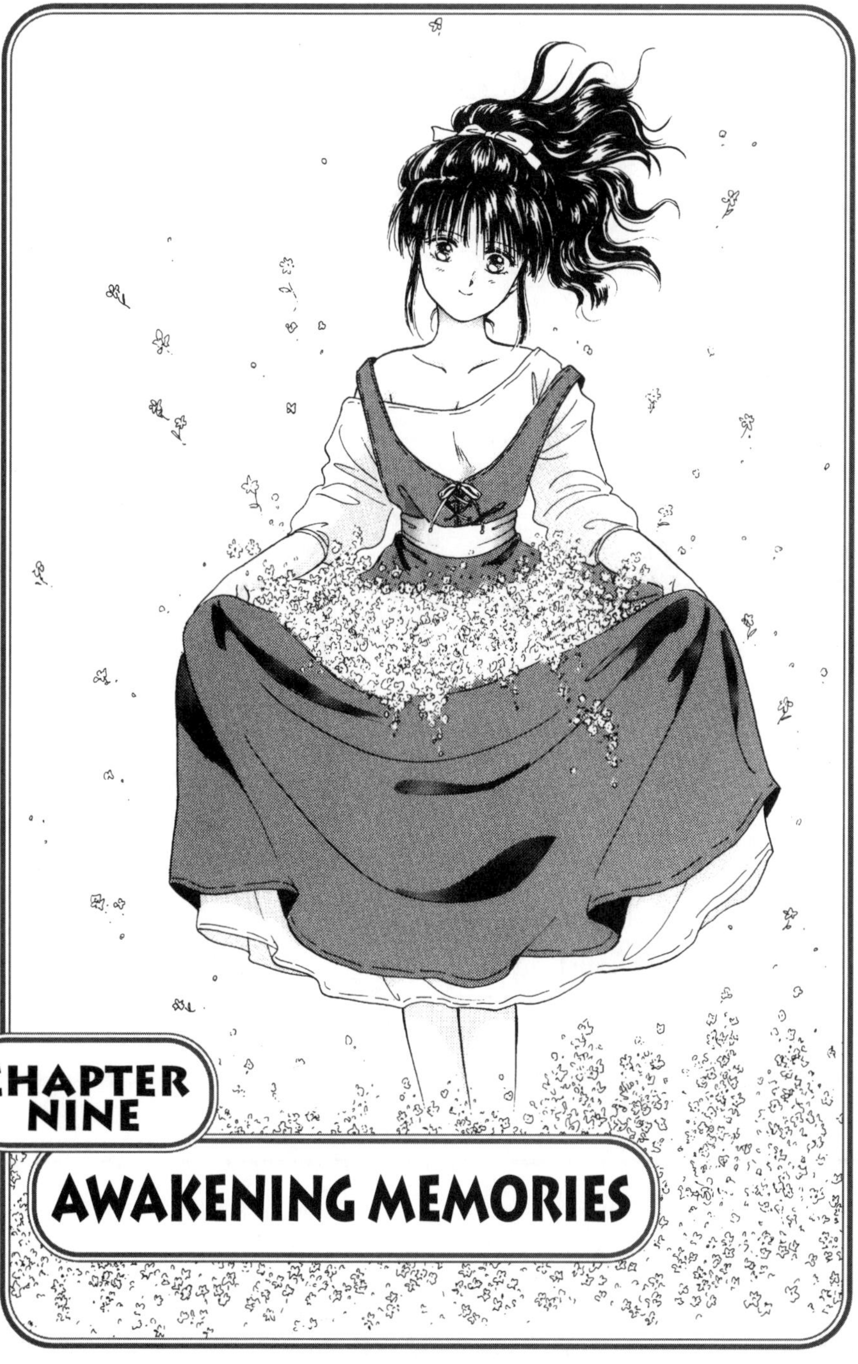

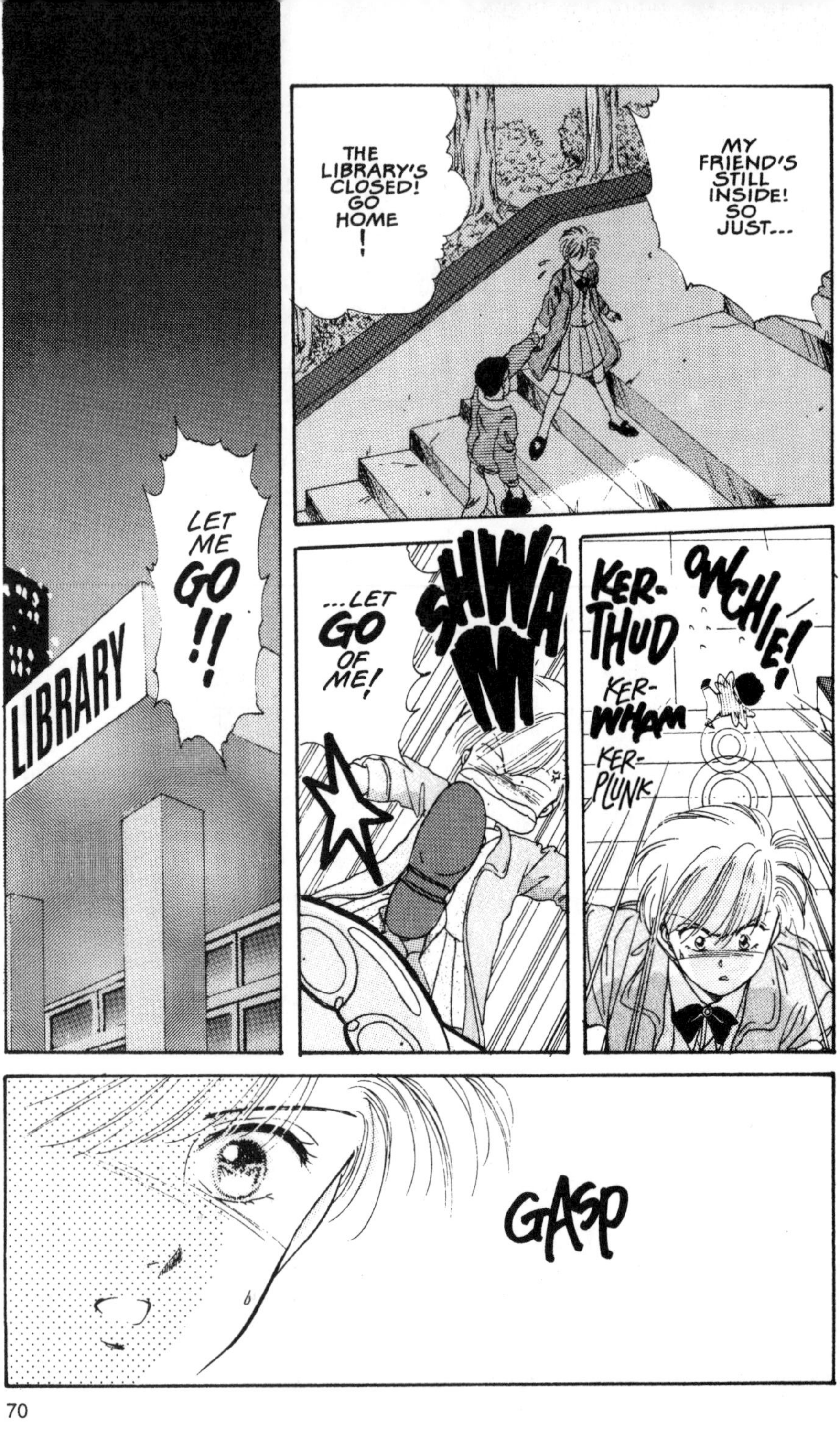
LET ME GO!!
LIBRARY
THE LIBRARY'S CLOSED! GO HOME!
MY FRIEND'S STILL INSIDE! SO JUST...
...LET GO OF ME!
SHWAM
KER-THUD
KER-WHAM
KER-PLUNK
ONCHIE!
GASP

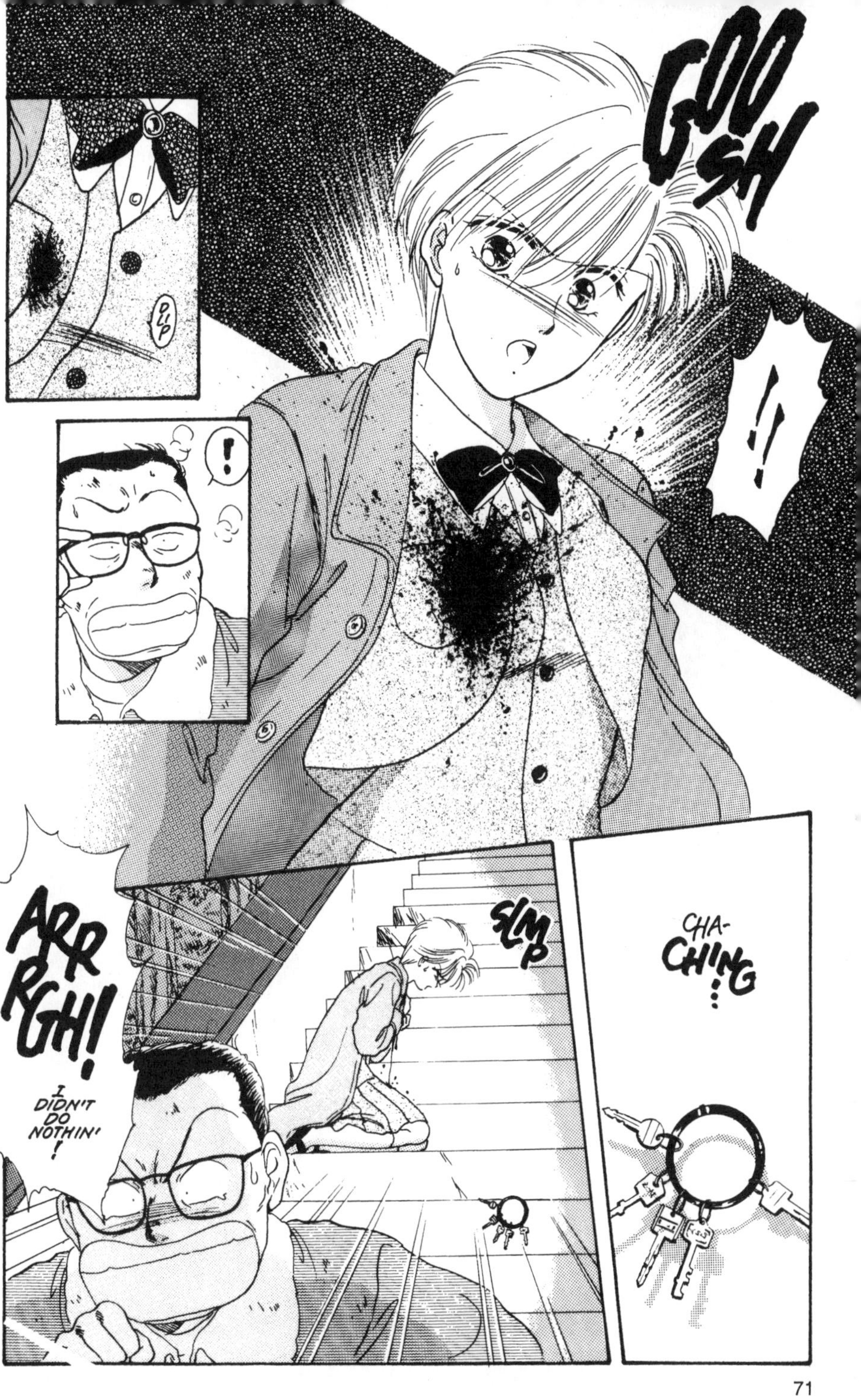
DLIP
!
GOOSH
!!
ARRRGH!
I DIDN'T DO NOTHIN'!
SLMP
CHA-CHING...

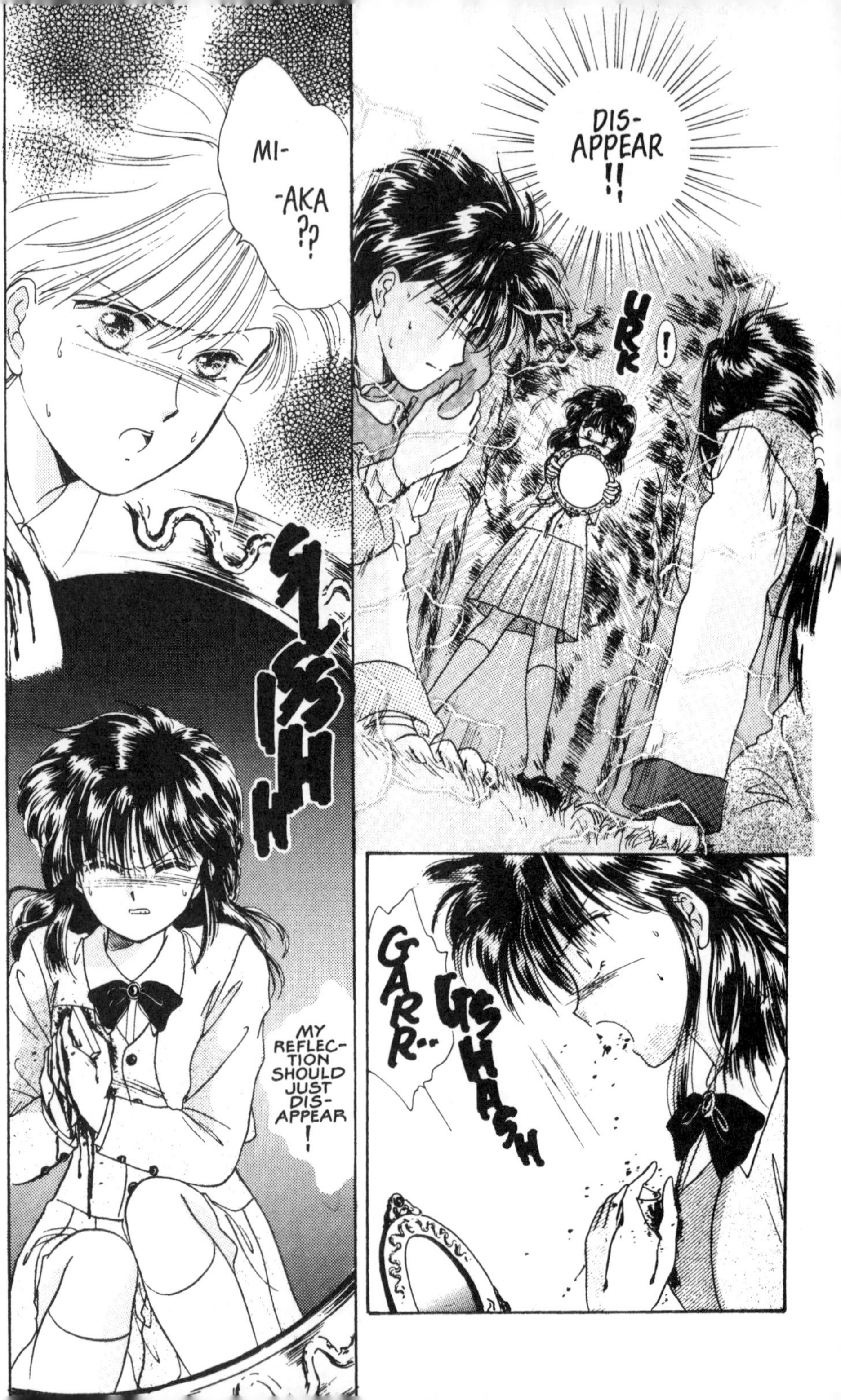
MI- -AKA ??
SLISHH
MY REFLECTION SHOULD JUST DISAPPEAR!
DIS-APPEAR!!
URK
!
GARR..
GUSHASH

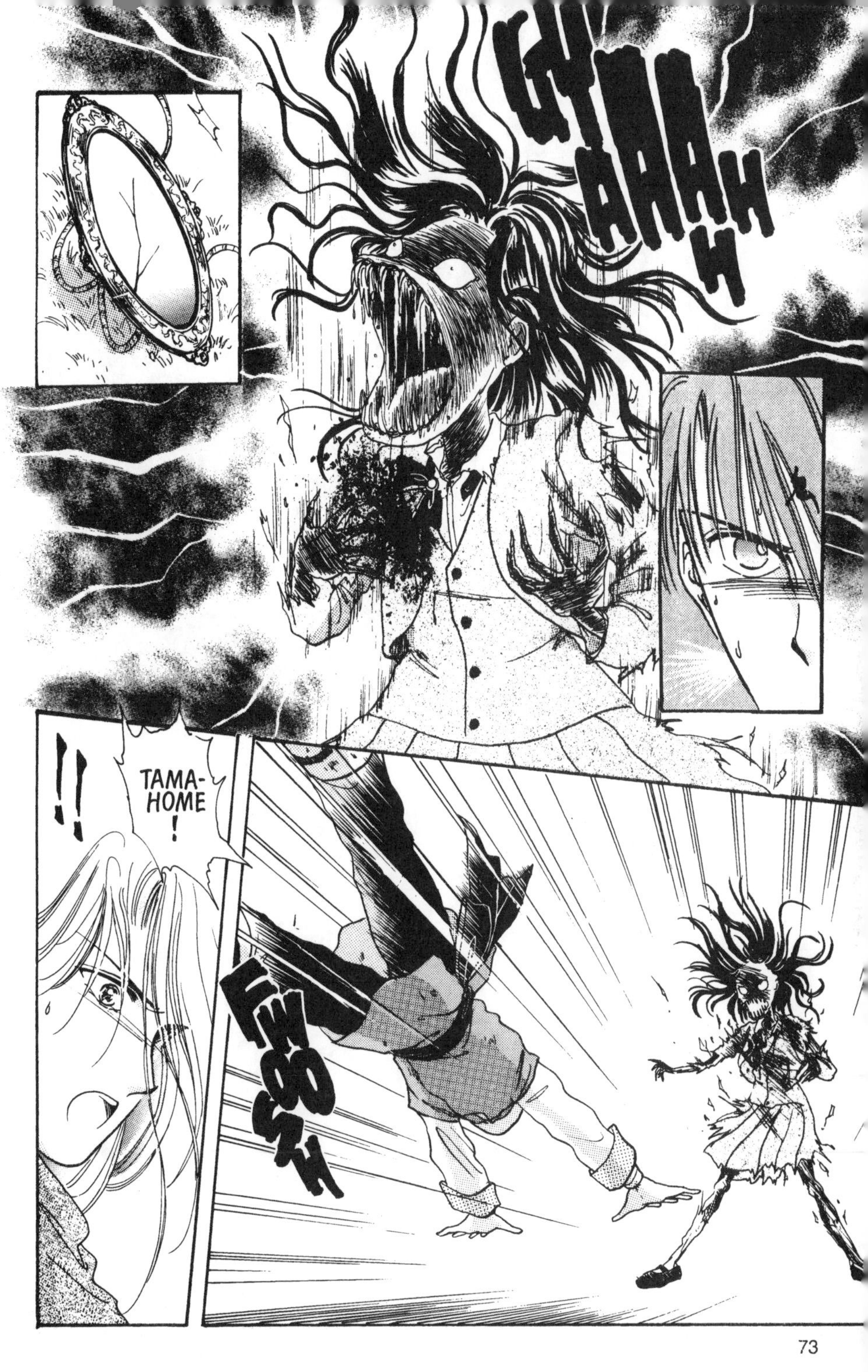
GYAAAAHHHH
!!
TAMA-HOME!
WHOOSH

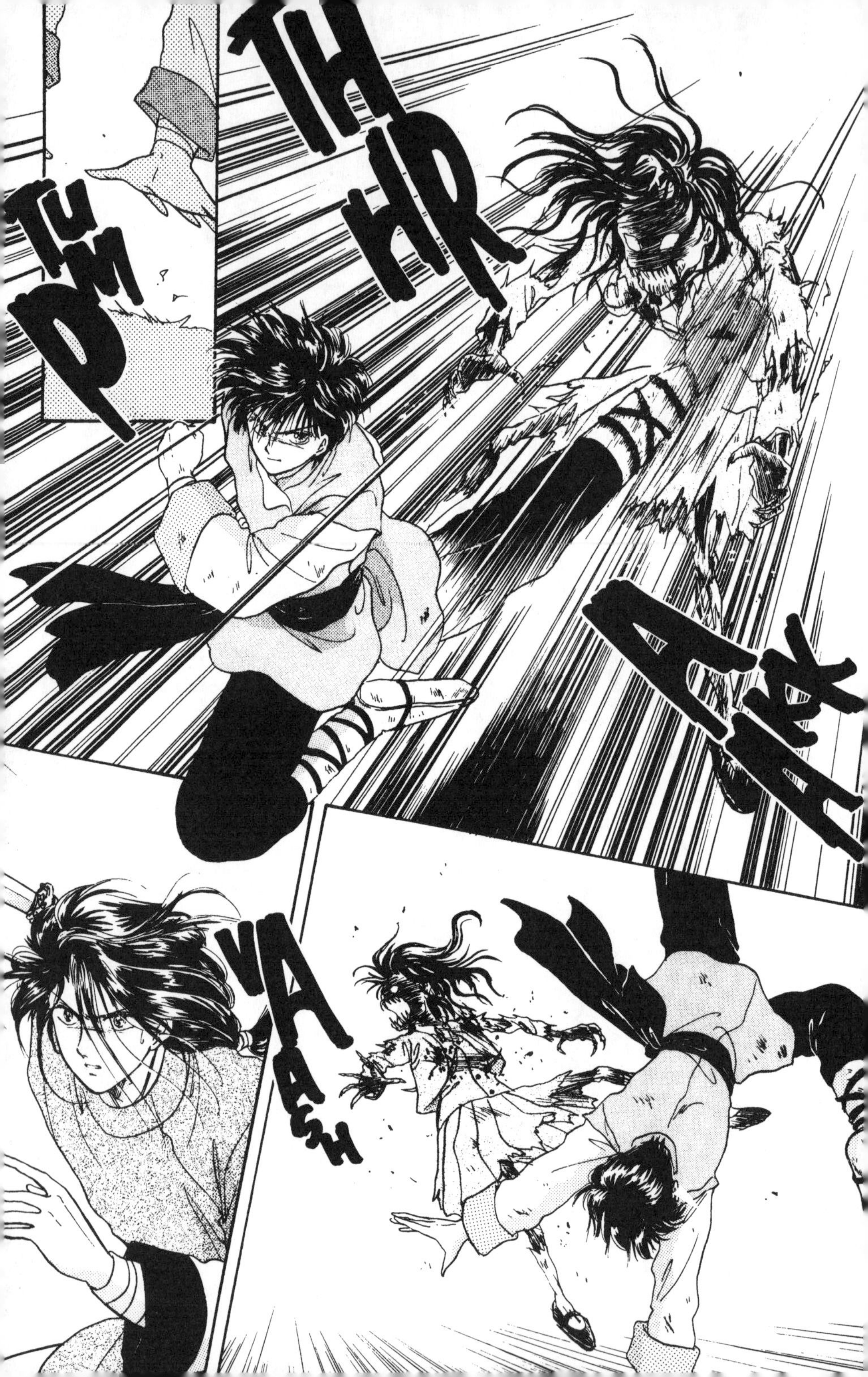
THHR
THUMP
VAASH

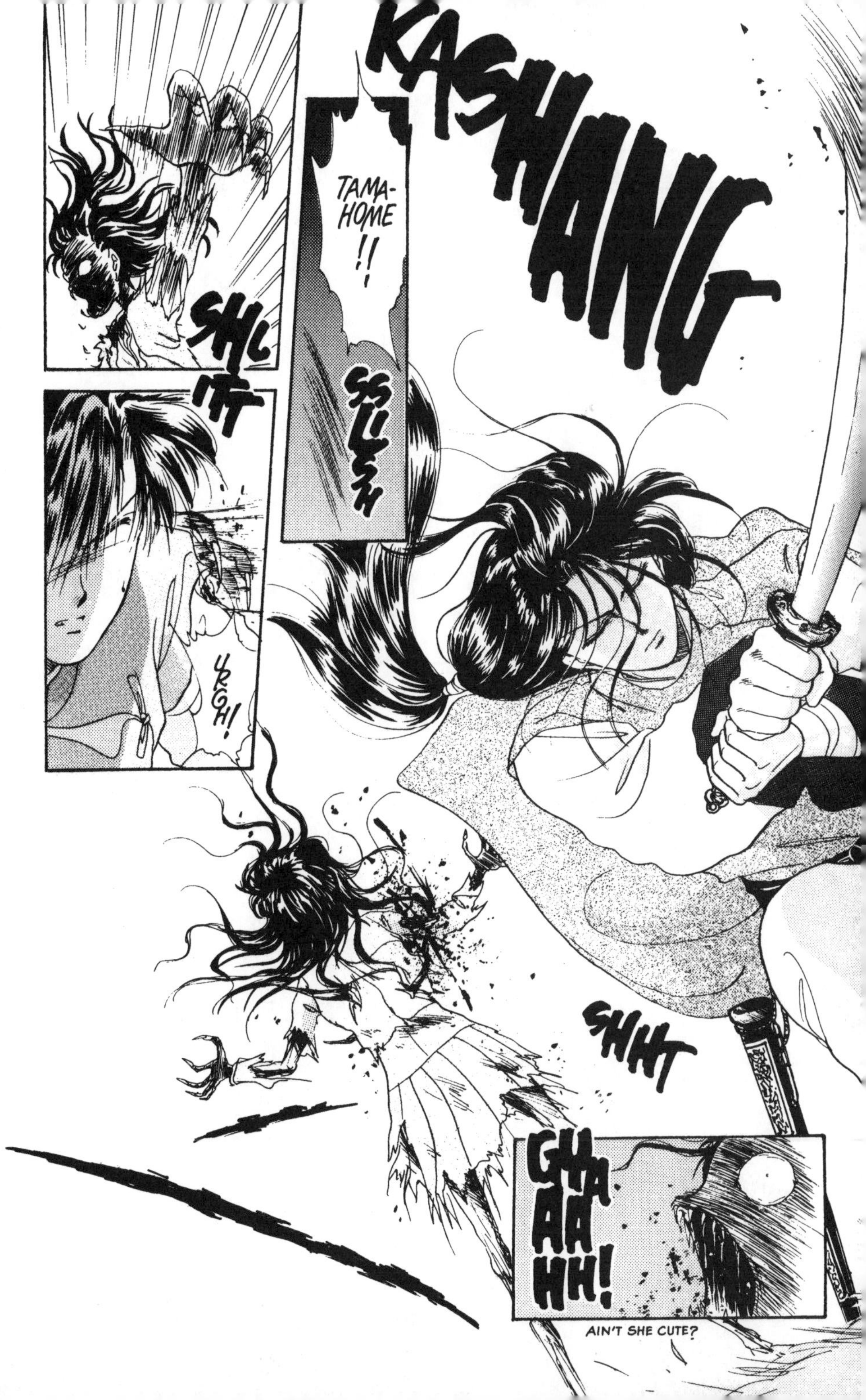
SHUNT
URGH!
TAMA-HOME!!
SSLUSH
KASHANG
SHHT
GHAAAHH!
AIN'T SHE CUTE?

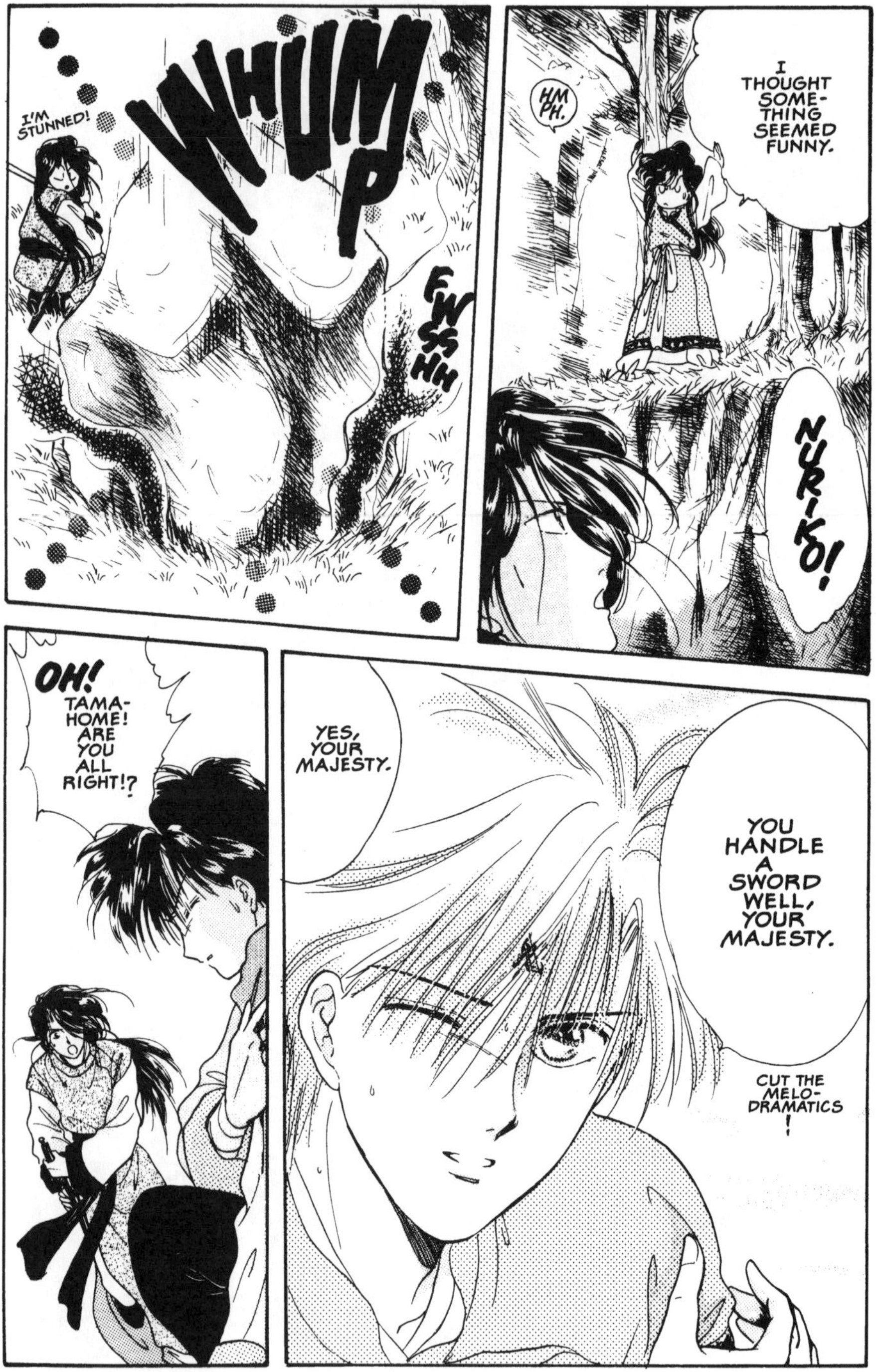
I'M STUNNED!
WHUMP
FWSSHH
HMPH.
I THOUGHT SOMETHING SEEMED FUNNY.
NURIKO!
OH!
TAMAHOME! ARE YOU ALL RIGHT!?
YES, YOUR MAJESTY.
YOU HANDLE A SWORD WELL, YOUR MAJESTY.
CUT THE MELODRAMATICS!

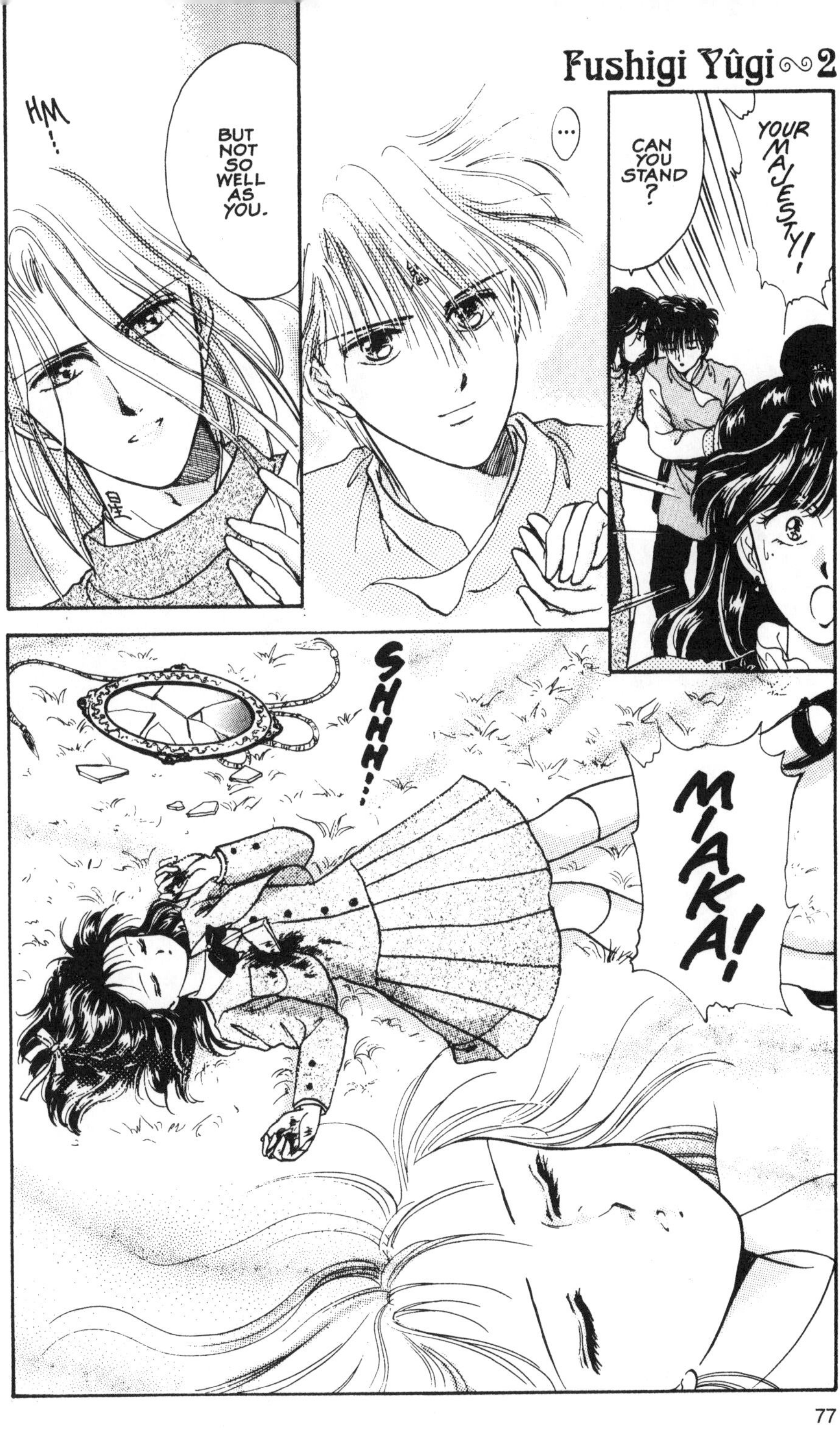
HM...
BUT NOT SO WELL AS YOU.
...
CAN YOU STAND?
YOUR MAJESTY!
SHHH...
MIAKA!

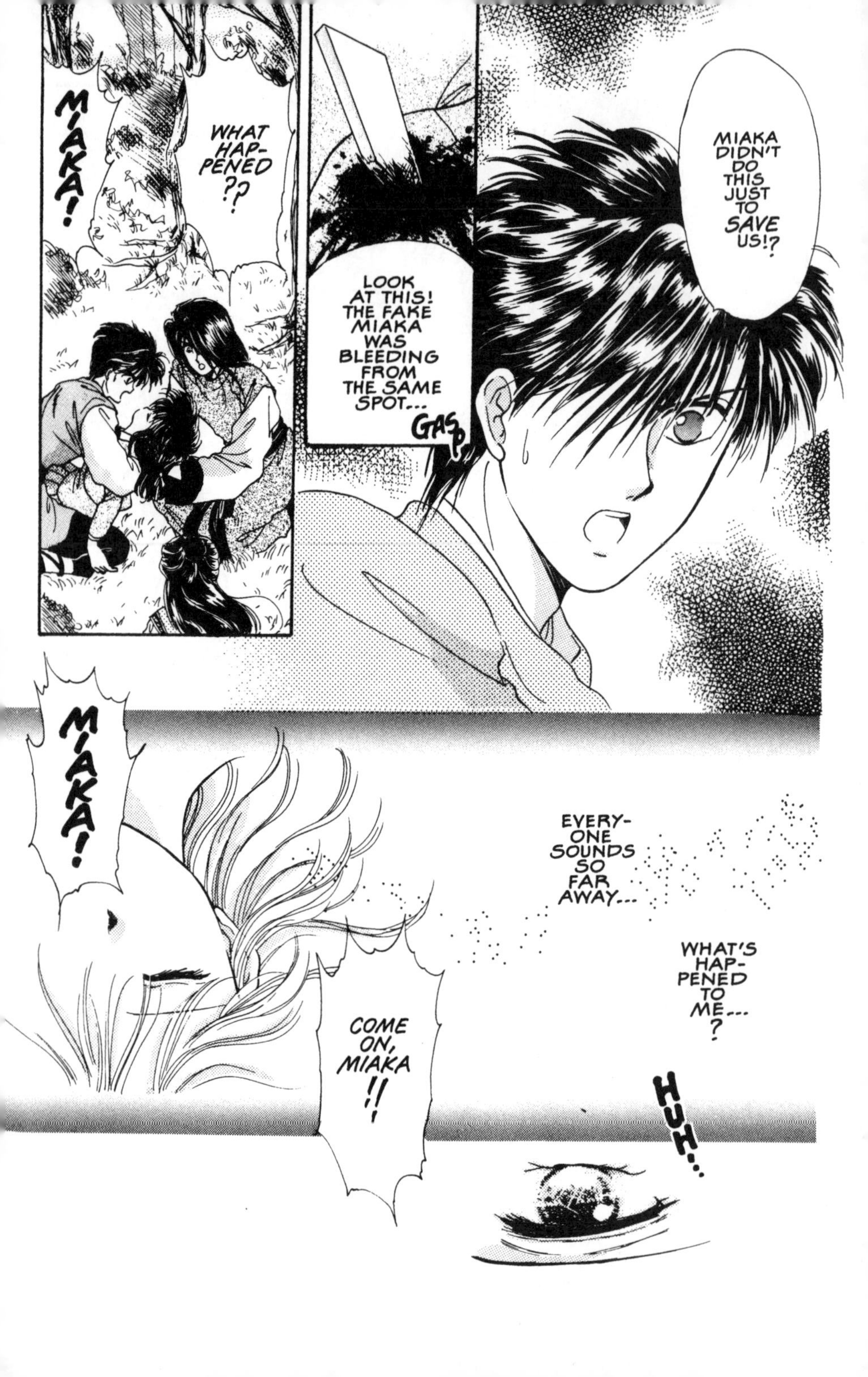
MIAKA!
WHAT HAP-PENED ??
LOOK AT THIS! THE FAKE MIAKA WAS BLEEDING FROM THE SAME SPOT...
GASP
MIAKA DIDN'T DO THIS JUST TO SAVE US!?
MIAKA!
EVERY-ONE SOUNDS SO FAR AWAY...
WHAT'S HAP-PENED TO ME...?
COME ON, MIAKA !!
HUH...

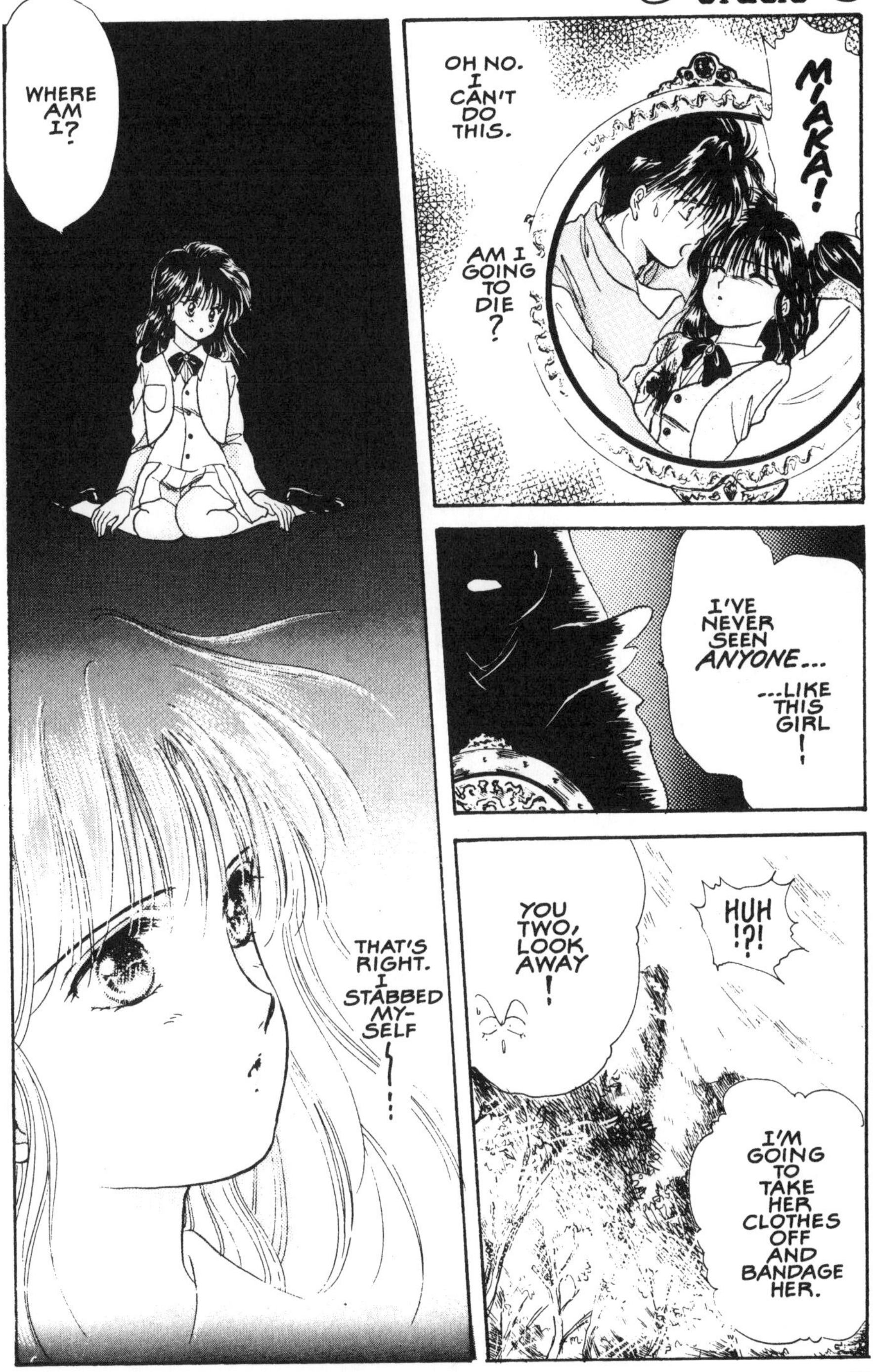
WHERE AM I?
THAT'S RIGHT. I STABBED MY-SELF...!
OH NO. I CAN'T DO THIS.
MIAKA!
AM I GOING TO DIE?
I'VE NEVER SEEN ANYONE...
...LIKE THIS GIRL!
YOU TWO, LOOK AWAY!
HUH!?!
I'M GOING TO TAKE HER CLOTHES OFF AND BANDAGE HER.

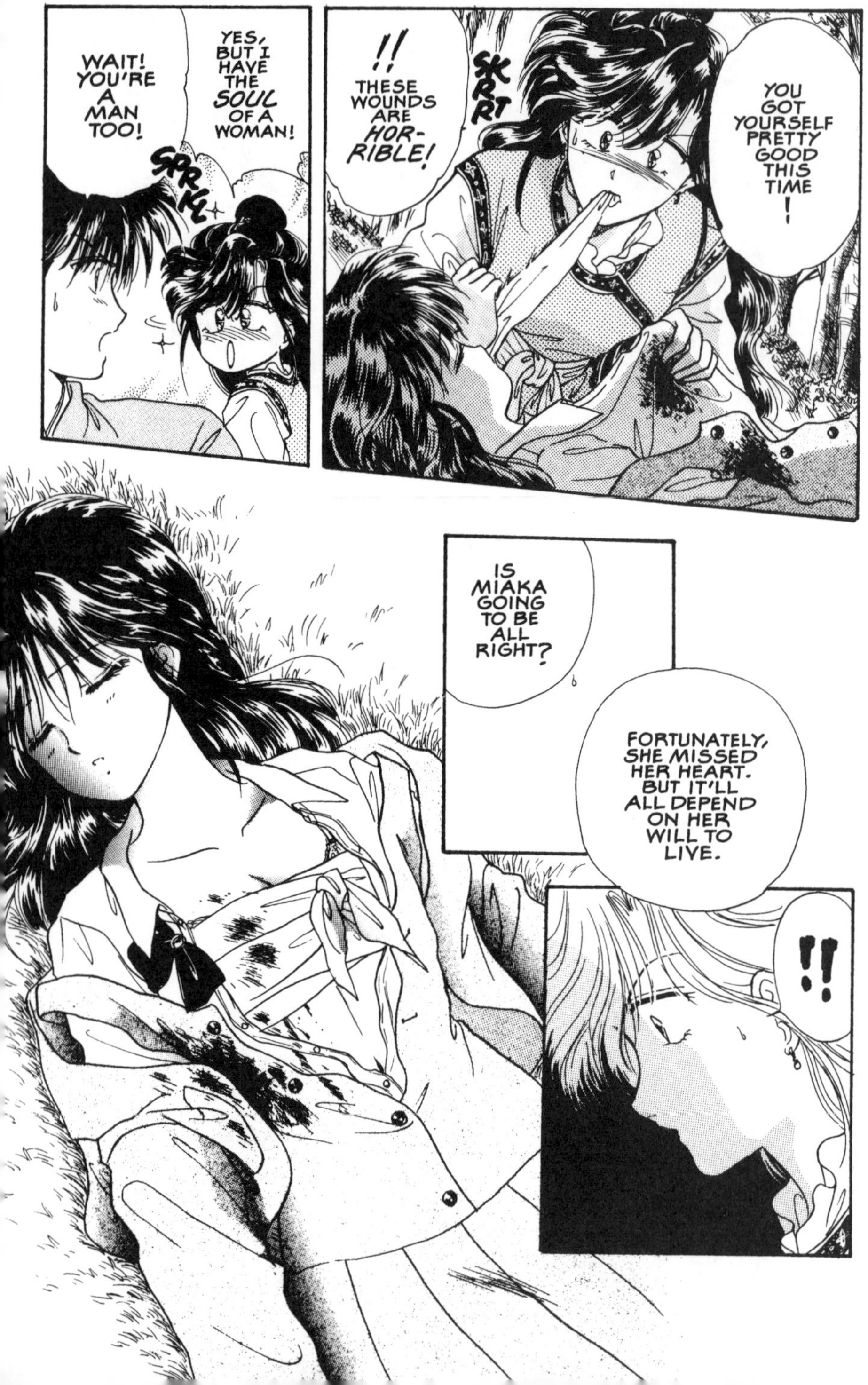
WAIT! YOU'RE A MAN TOO!
YES, BUT I HAVE THE SOUL OF A WOMAN!
SPRKLE
!!
THESE WOUNDS ARE HOR-RIBLE!
SKRRT
YOU GOT YOURSELF PRETTY GOOD THIS TIME!
IS MIAKA GOING TO BE ALL RIGHT?
FORTUNATELY, SHE MISSED HER HEART. BUT IT'LL ALL DEPEND ON HER WILL TO LIVE.
!!

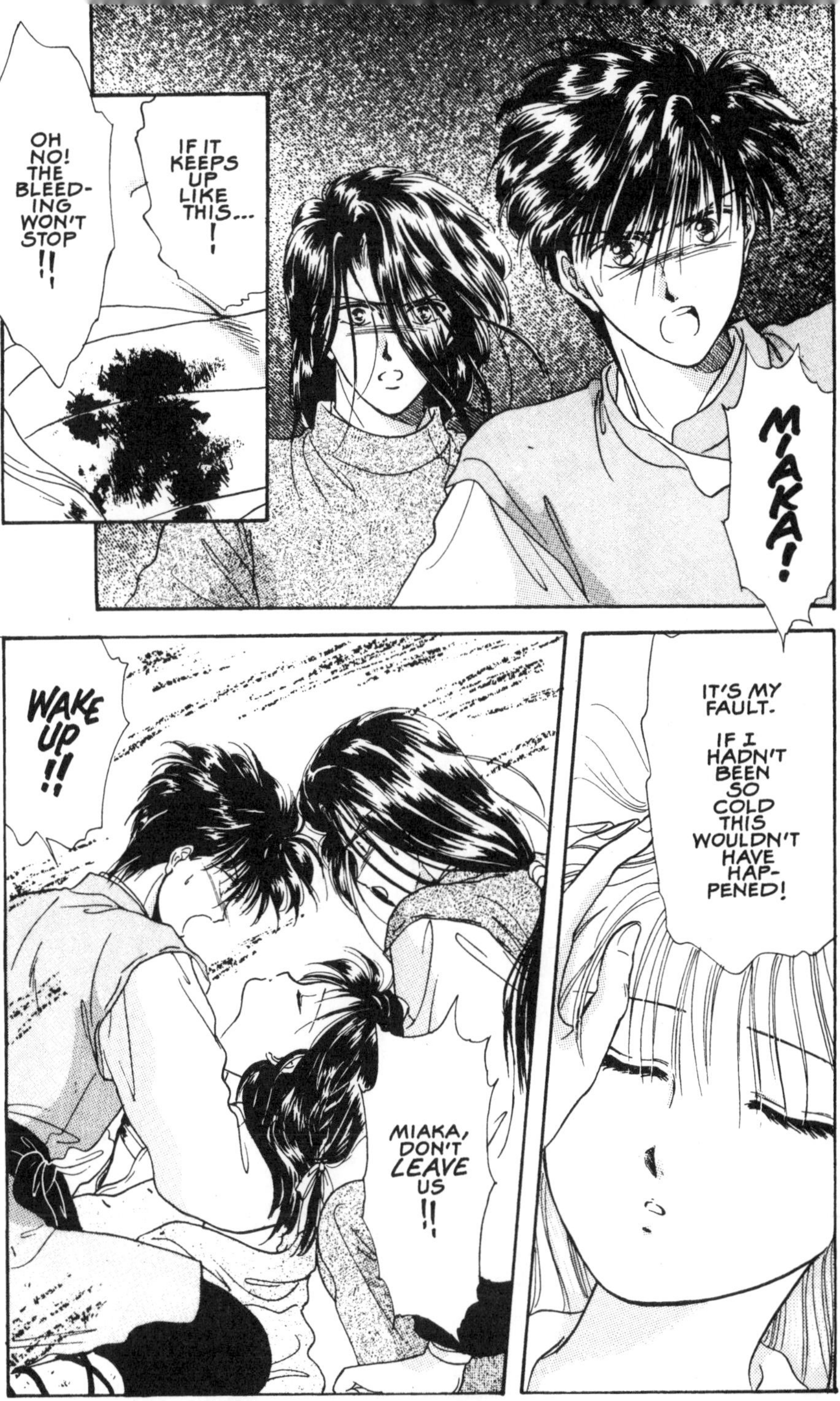
OH NO! THE BLEEDING WON'T STOP!!
IF IT KEEPS UP LIKE THIS...!
MIAKA!
WAKE UP!!
MIAKA, DON'T LEAVE US!!
IT'S MY FAULT.
IF I HADN'T BEEN SO COLD THIS WOULDN'T HAVE HAPPENED!

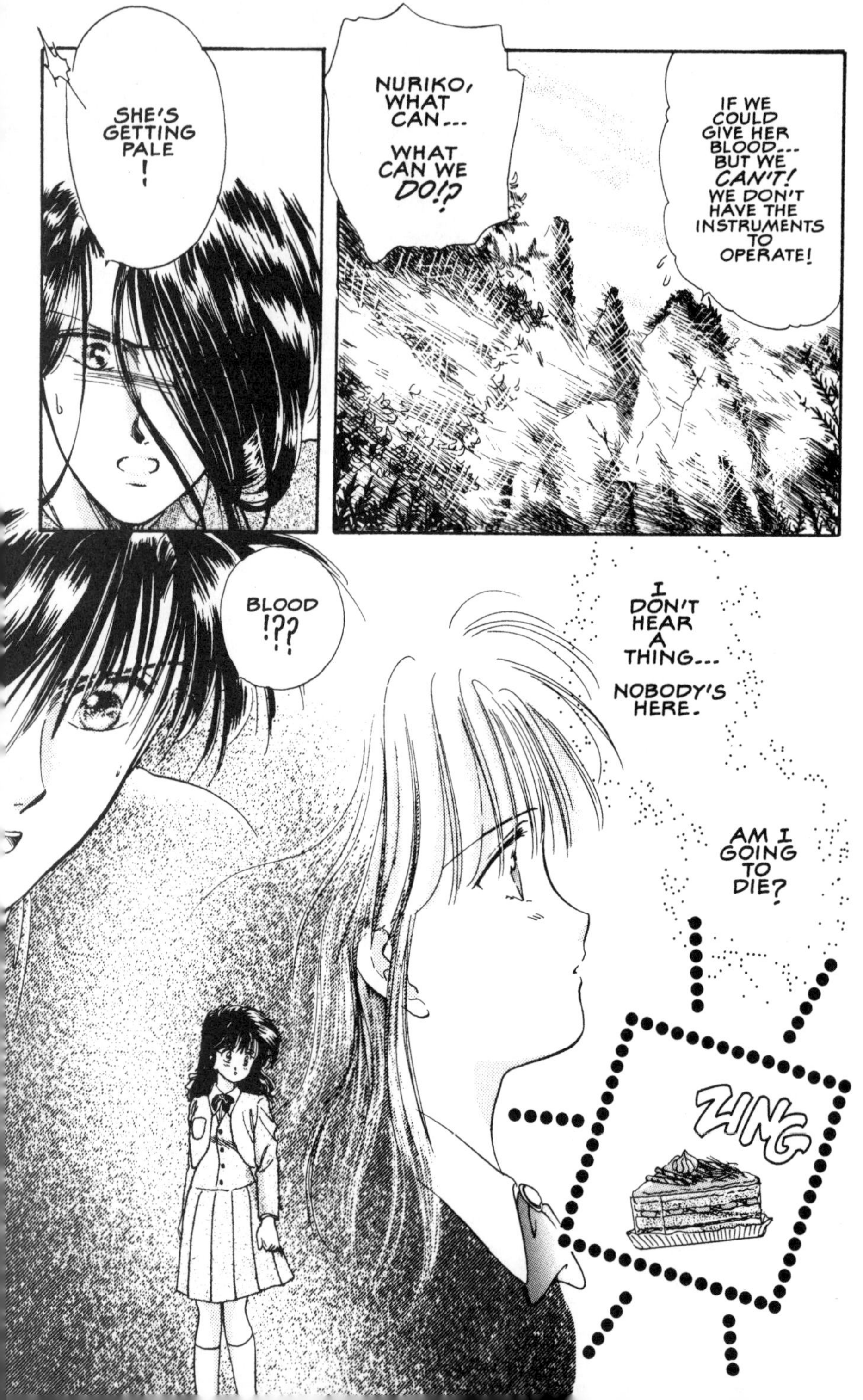
SHE'S GETTING PALE!
NURIKO, WHAT CAN...
WHAT CAN WE DO!?
IF WE COULD GIVE HER BLOOD... BUT WE CAN'T! WE DON'T HAVE THE INSTRUMENTS TO OPERATE!
BLOOD!??
I DON'T HEAR A THING...
NOBODY'S HERE.
AM I GOING TO DIE?
ZING

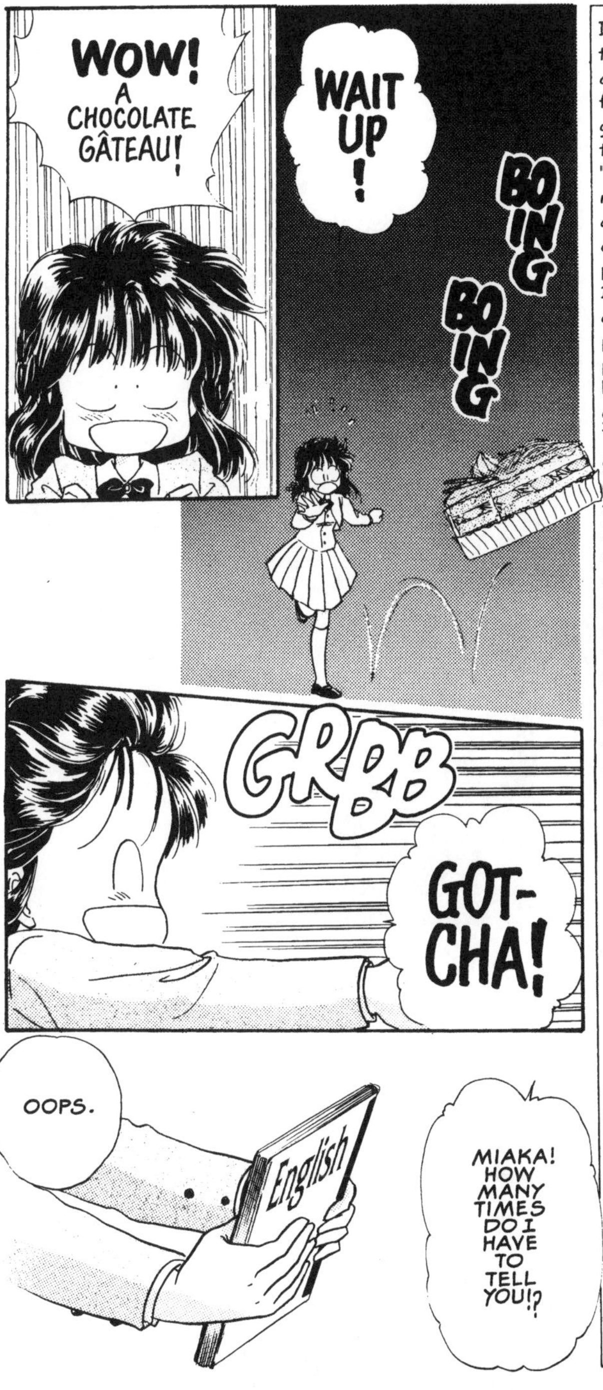
WOW! A CHOCOLATE GÂTEAU!
WAIT UP!
BOING
BOING
GRBB
GOT-CHA!
OOPS.
MIAKA! HOW MANY TIMES DO I HAVE TO TELL YOU!?

I just want you to know, it's not true! I heard there's been some controversy saying "Watase's a sex-fiend!"...*(unbelievable!)* Let's just get this straight! The only comic that comes close to being sexy is "Prepubescence." Quite a few readers told me they had dreams about Asuka and the other characters, so I guess the story left a pretty strong impression. On page 141 of volume 7 of "Prepubescence" I wrote, "I wouldn't want people to think I'm turning into a perv." I didn't mean I was put out by it, I only meant people shouldn't get worked up over the stuff. Teenage girls might get excited and embarrassed and squeal "Oh m'god! She's so dirty," but to girls in their twenties, talking about this kind of stuff is so common, it's nothing special. *So it's not a matter of being a "perv" or not.* So this stuff might shock teenage girls. *You're so young. (Where am I going with this thought?)* If bed scenes are necessary then I have no problem depicting them to the extent that they won't cause any major controversy. But I hate gratuitous sex scenes. Now that the plot is thickening I might have to include a sex scene or two in a serious context. (What? You're happy to hear that?) The characters are developing in volume 1, and in volume 2 they're finally getting to know each other.

But if the sales fall off, I'll have to start drawing autobiographical manga (What the heck would I write about!?). There was quite a bit of...that in the "Prepubescence" side story , but the average age of the readers is pretty high, so I'll be all right. In any case, those scenes represent an expression of love so I don't think they're bad at all. I do think that gratuitous, superficial love scenes might have a bad effect on the reader.

What am I talking about?!?

Watase: Artist for the boys' comic, Shônen Perv.

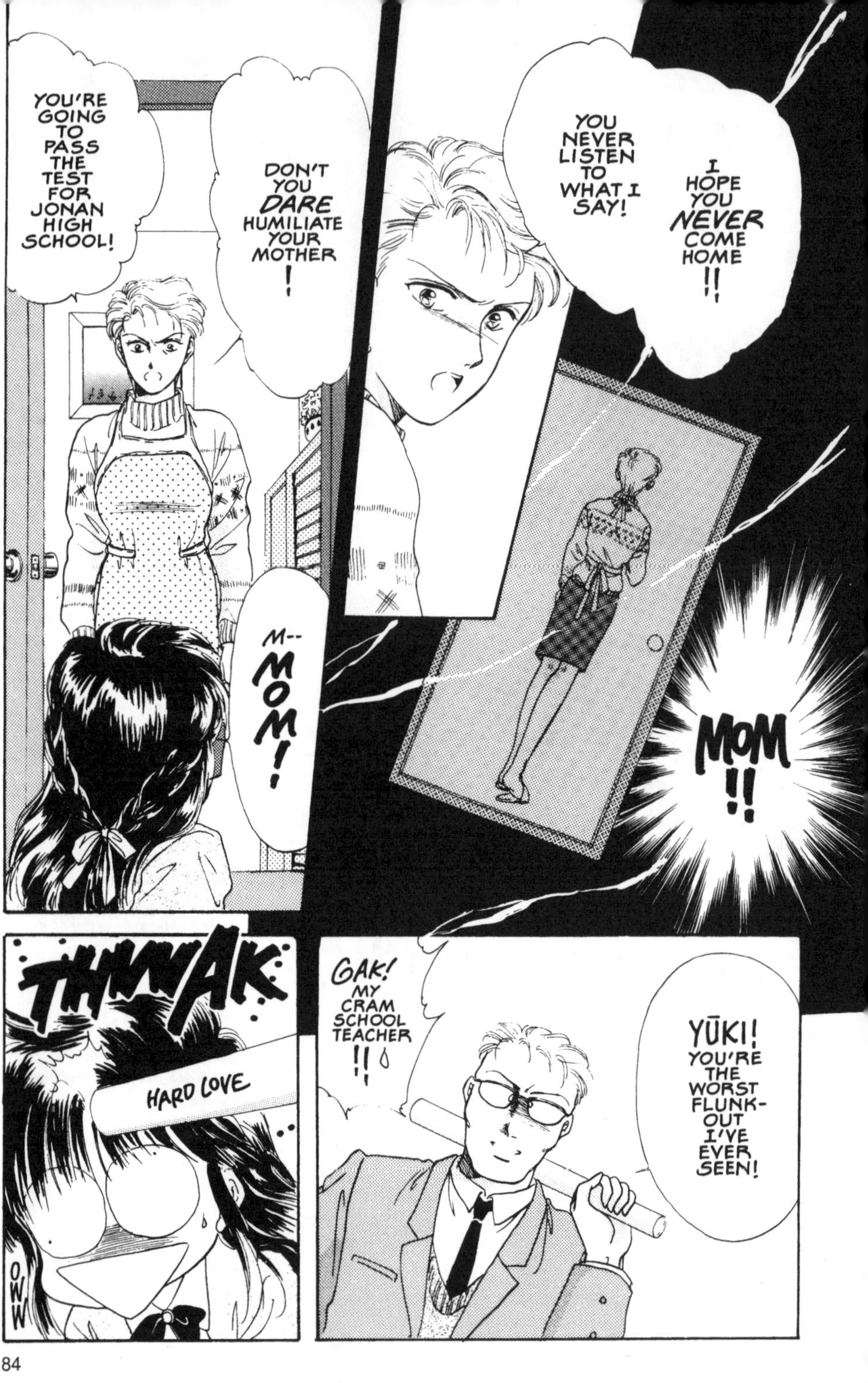

YOU'RE GOING TO PASS THE TEST FOR JONAN HIGH SCHOOL!
DON'T YOU DARE HUMILIATE YOUR MOTHER!
M-- MOM!!
YOU NEVER LISTEN TO WHAT I SAY!
I HOPE YOU NEVER COME HOME!!
MOM!!
THWAK
HARD LOVE
OWW
GAK! MY CRAM SCHOOL TEACHER!!
YŪKI! YOU'RE THE WORST FLUNK-OUT I'VE EVER SEEN!

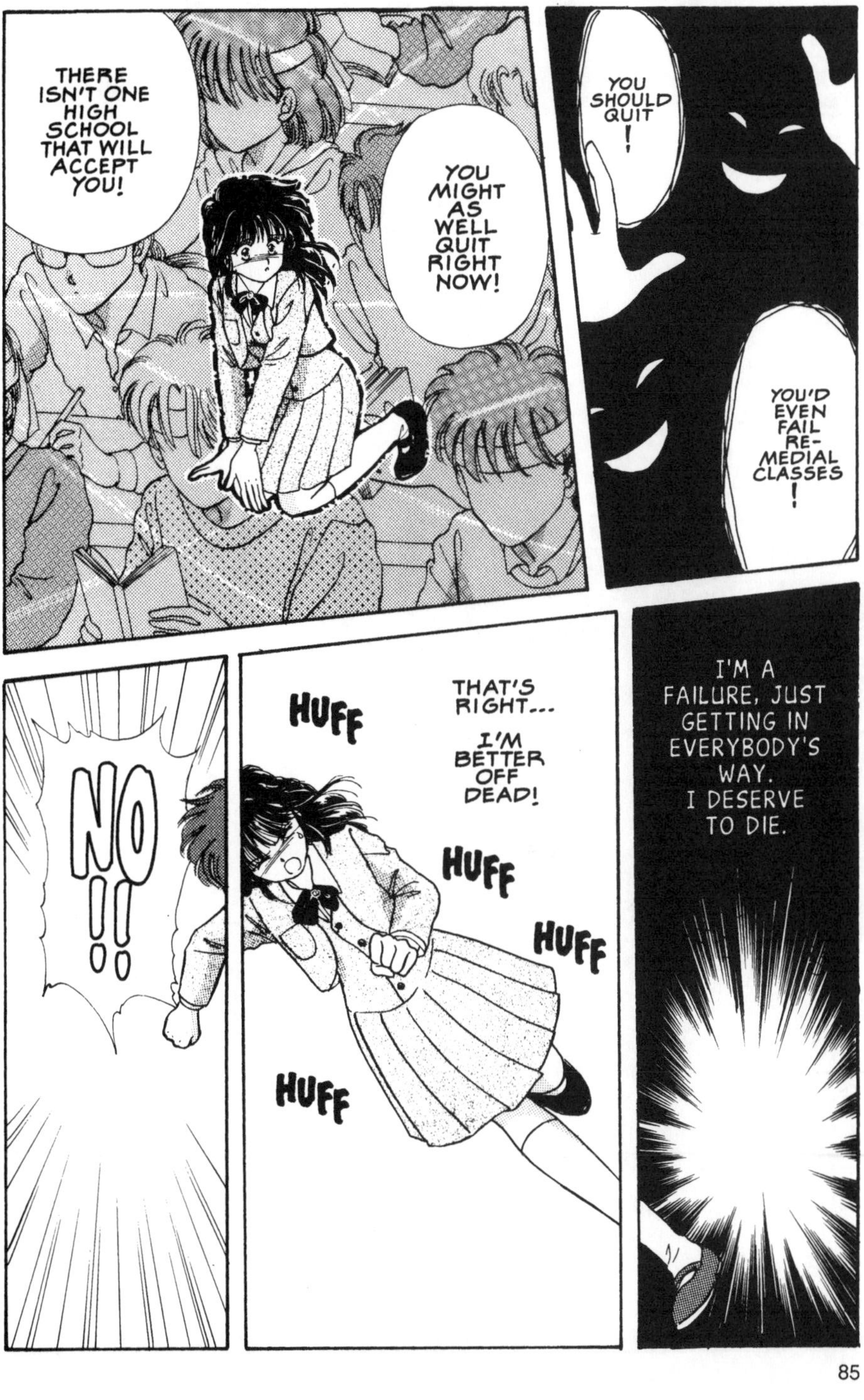
THERE ISN'T ONE HIGH SCHOOL THAT WILL ACCEPT YOU!
YOU MIGHT AS WELL QUIT RIGHT NOW!
YOU SHOULD QUIT!
YOU'D EVEN FAIL RE-MEDIAL CLASSES!
NO!!!!
HUFF
THAT'S RIGHT...
I'M BETTER OFF DEAD!
HUFF
HUFF
HUFF
I'M A FAILURE, JUST GETTING IN EVERYBODY'S WAY. I DESERVE TO DIE.

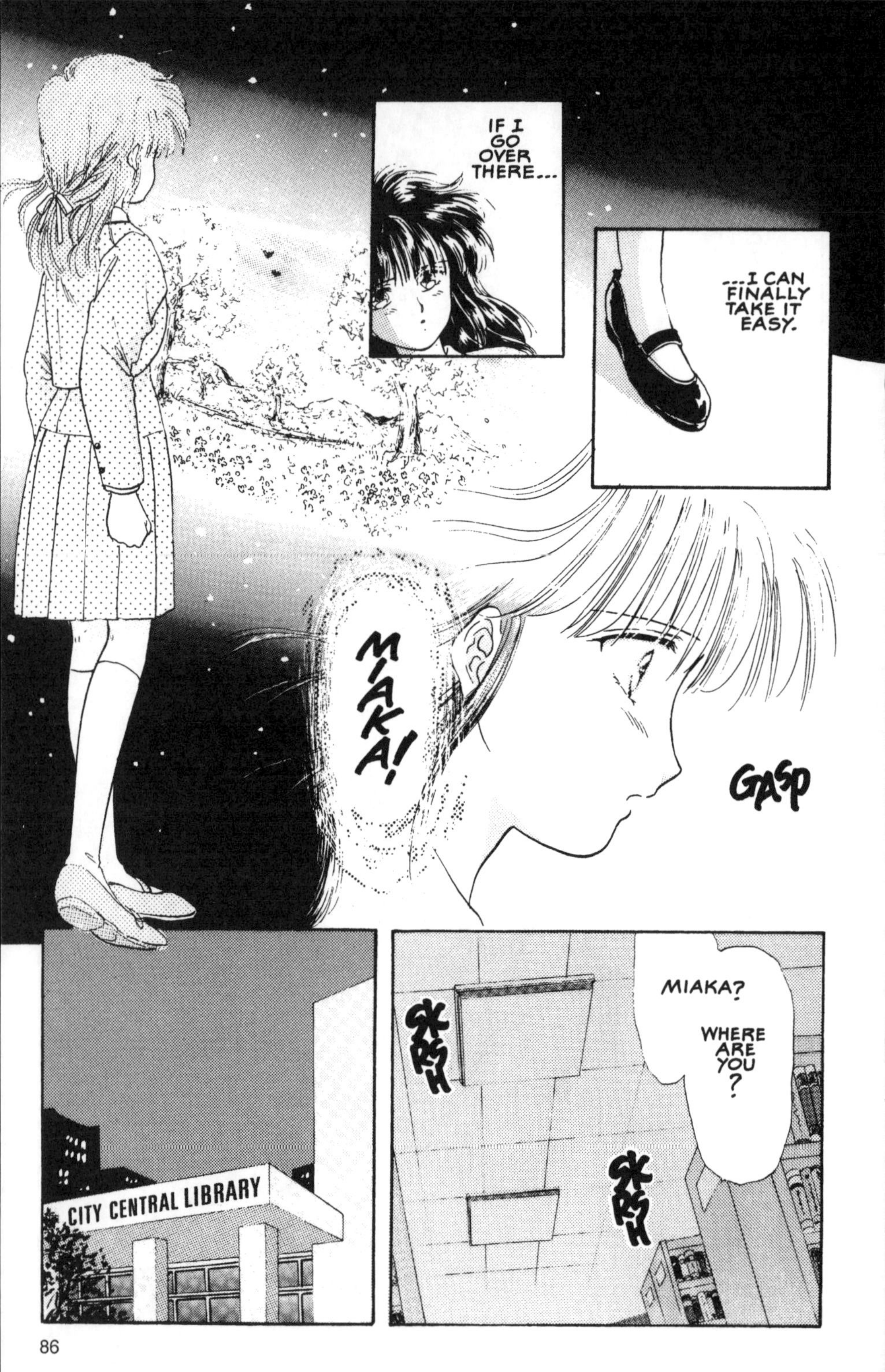
IF I GO OVER THERE...
...I CAN FINALLY TAKE IT EASY.
MIAKA!
GASP
CITY CENTRAL LIBRARY
SKRSH
MIAKA?
WHERE ARE YOU?
SKRSH

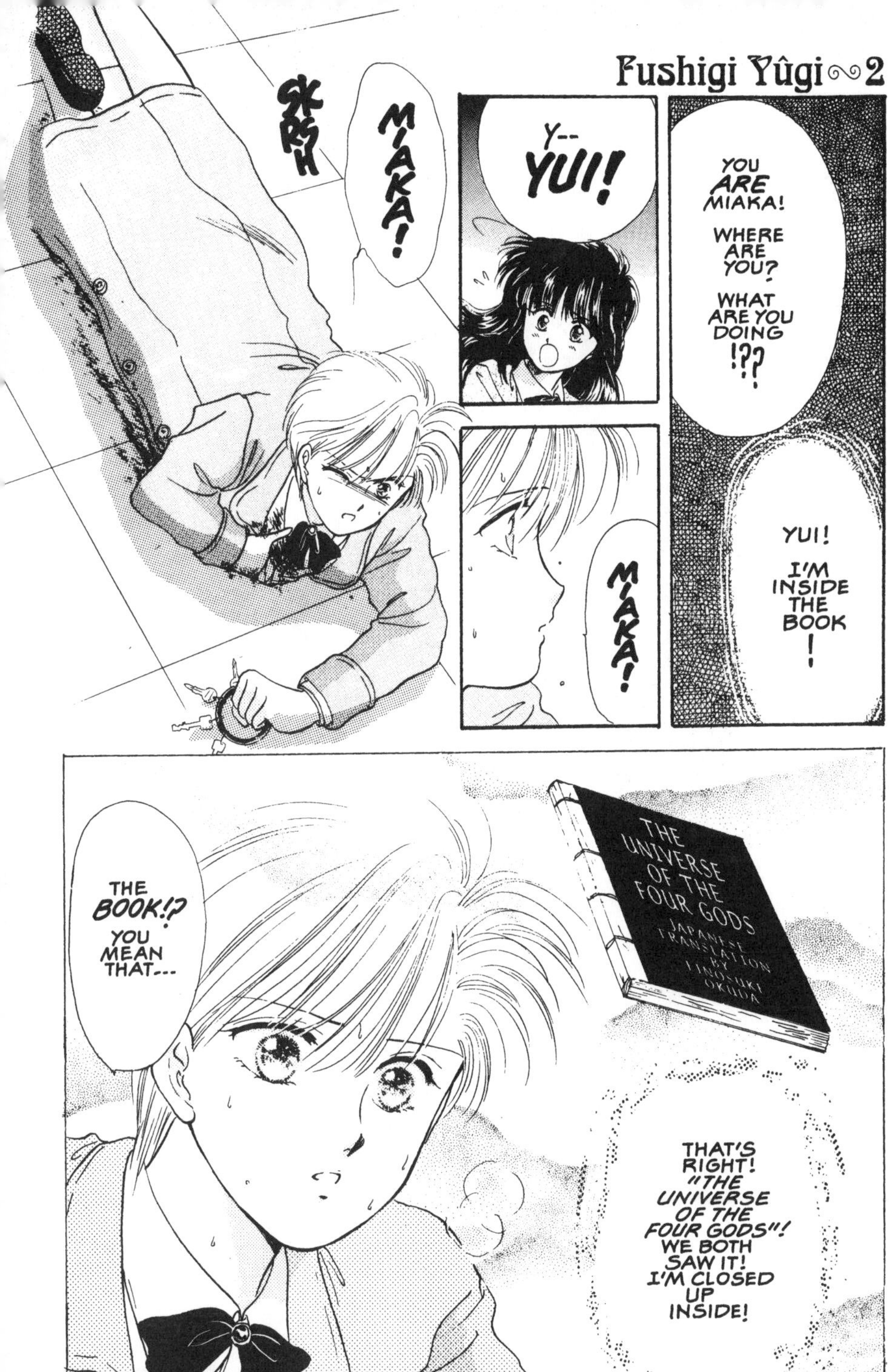
GKRSH
MIAKA!
Y-- YUI!
MIAKA!
YOU ARE MIAKA! WHERE ARE YOU? WHAT ARE YOU DOING !??
YUI! I'M INSIDE THE BOOK !
THE BOOK!? YOU MEAN THAT---
THE UNIVERSE OF THE FOUR GODS
JAPANESE TRANSLATION BY EINOSUKI OKUDA
THAT'S RIGHT! "THE UNIVERSE OF THE FOUR GODS"! WE BOTH SAW IT! I'M CLOSED UP INSIDE!

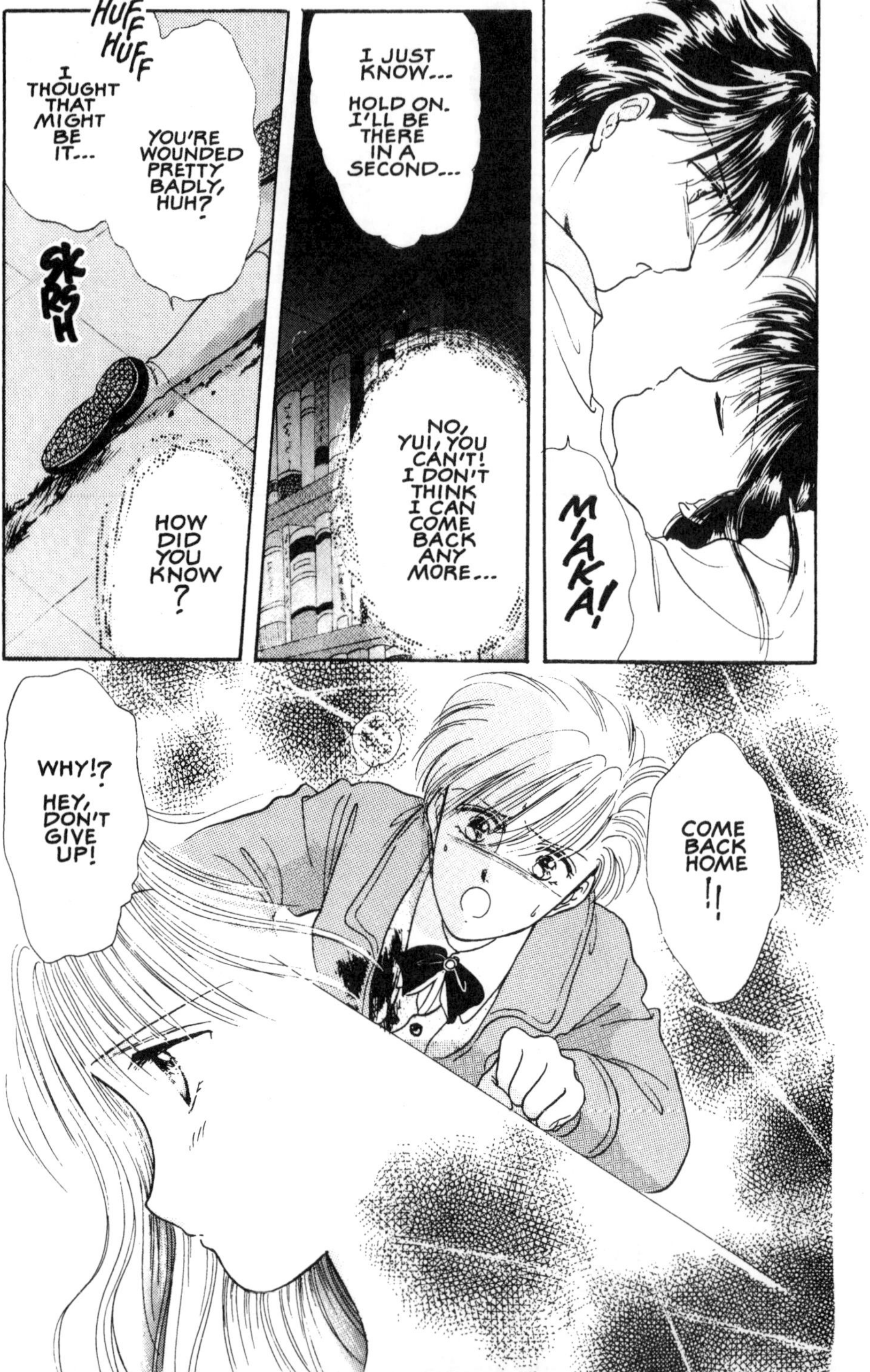
HUFF HUFF
I THOUGHT THAT MIGHT BE IT...
YOU'RE WOUNDED PRETTY BADLY, HUH?
SKRSH
HOW DID YOU KNOW?
I JUST KNOW...
HOLD ON. I'LL BE THERE IN A SECOND...
NO, YUI, YOU CAN'T! I DON'T THINK I CAN COME BACK ANY MORE...
MIAKA!
WHY!? HEY, DON'T GIVE UP!
COME BACK HOME!!

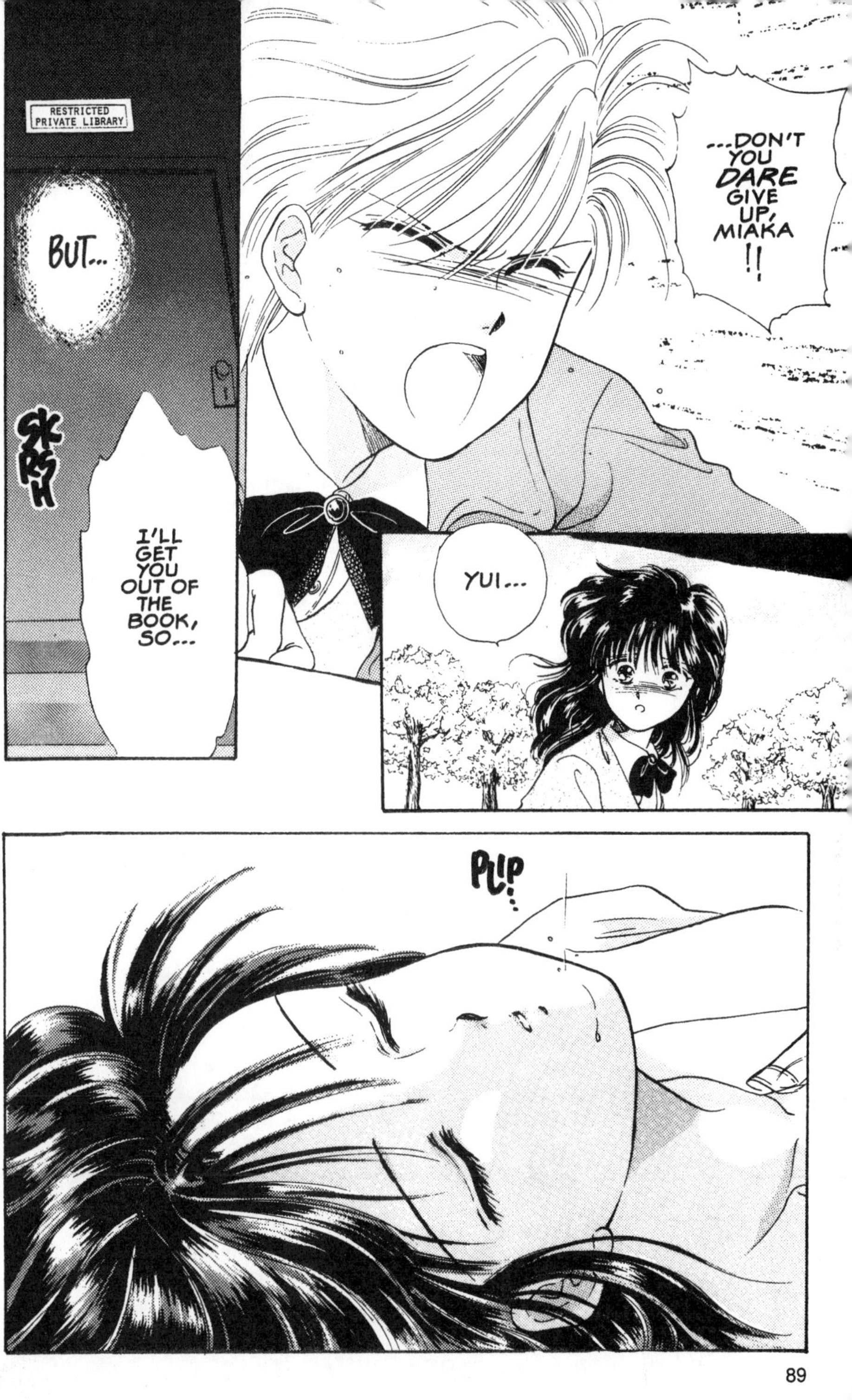
RESTRICTED PRIVATE LIBRARY
BUT...
SKRSH
I'LL GET YOU OUT OF THE BOOK, SO...
...DON'T YOU DARE GIVE UP, MIAKA!!
YUI...
PLIP...

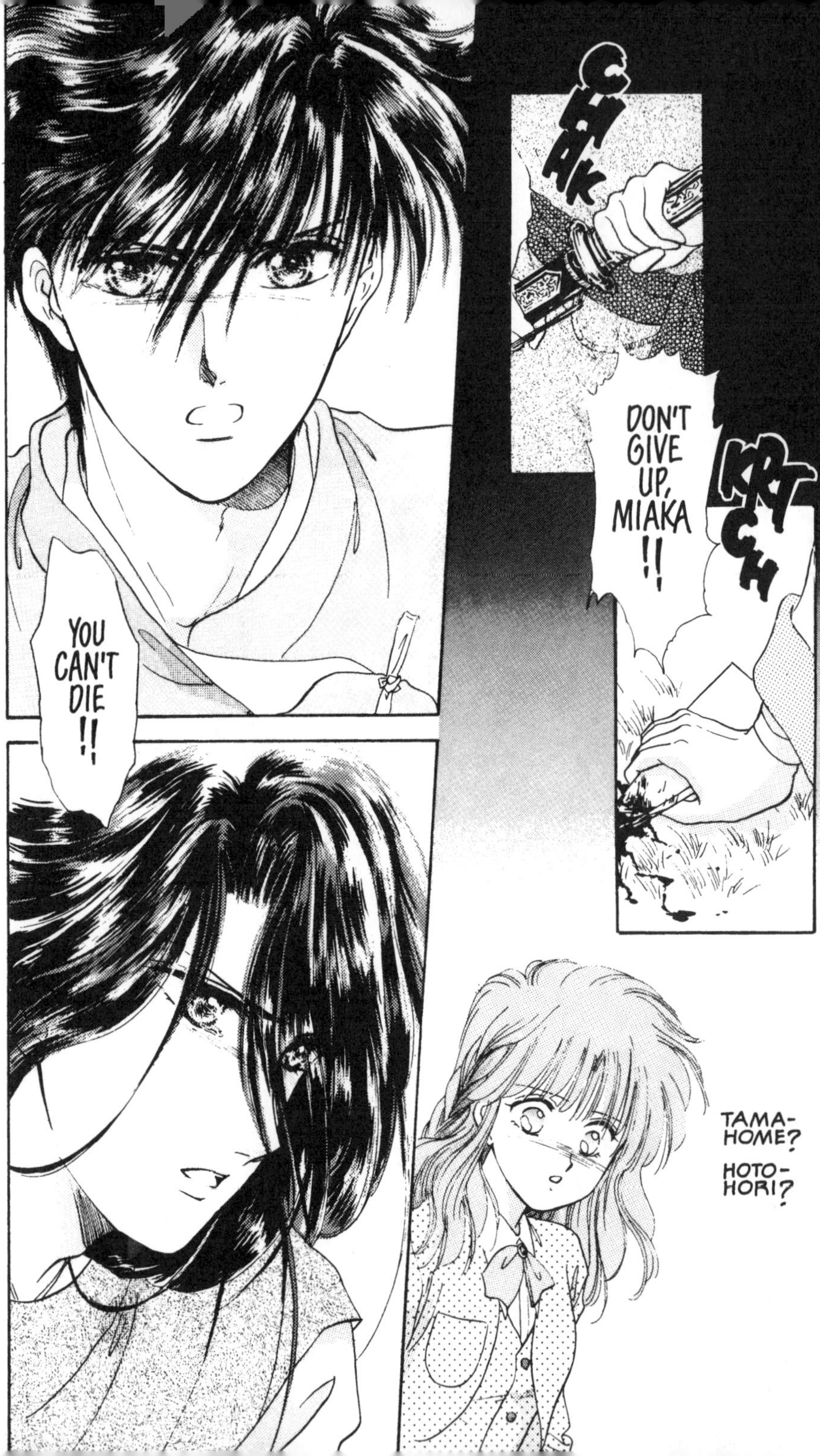
YOU CAN'T DIE!!
CHAK
DON'T GIVE UP, MIAKA!!
KRTCH
TAMA-HOME?
HOTO-HORI?

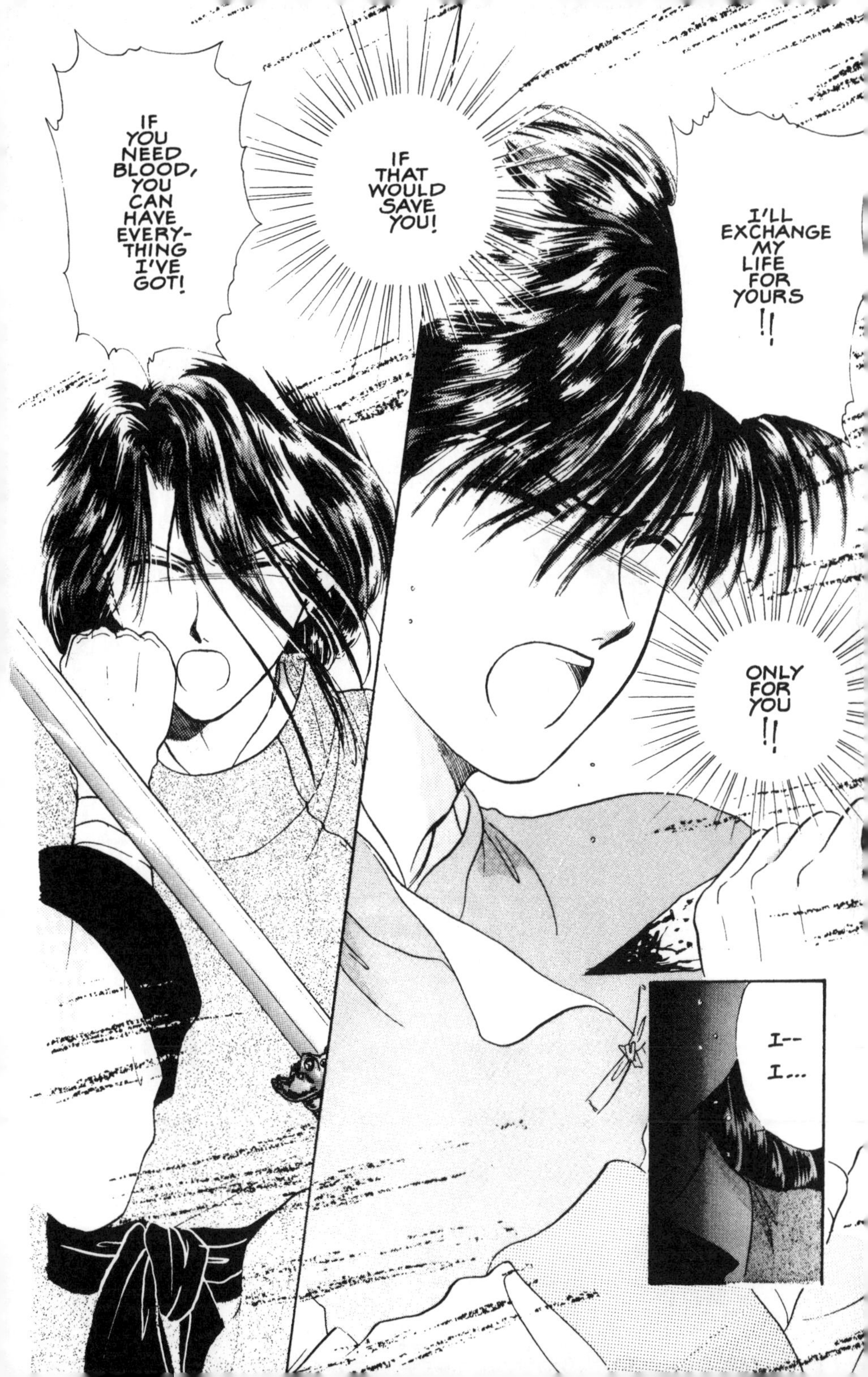
IF YOU NEED BLOOD, YOU CAN HAVE EVERYTHING I'VE GOT!
IF THAT WOULD SAVE YOU!
I'LL EXCHANGE MY LIFE FOR YOURS!!
ONLY FOR YOU!!
I-- I...

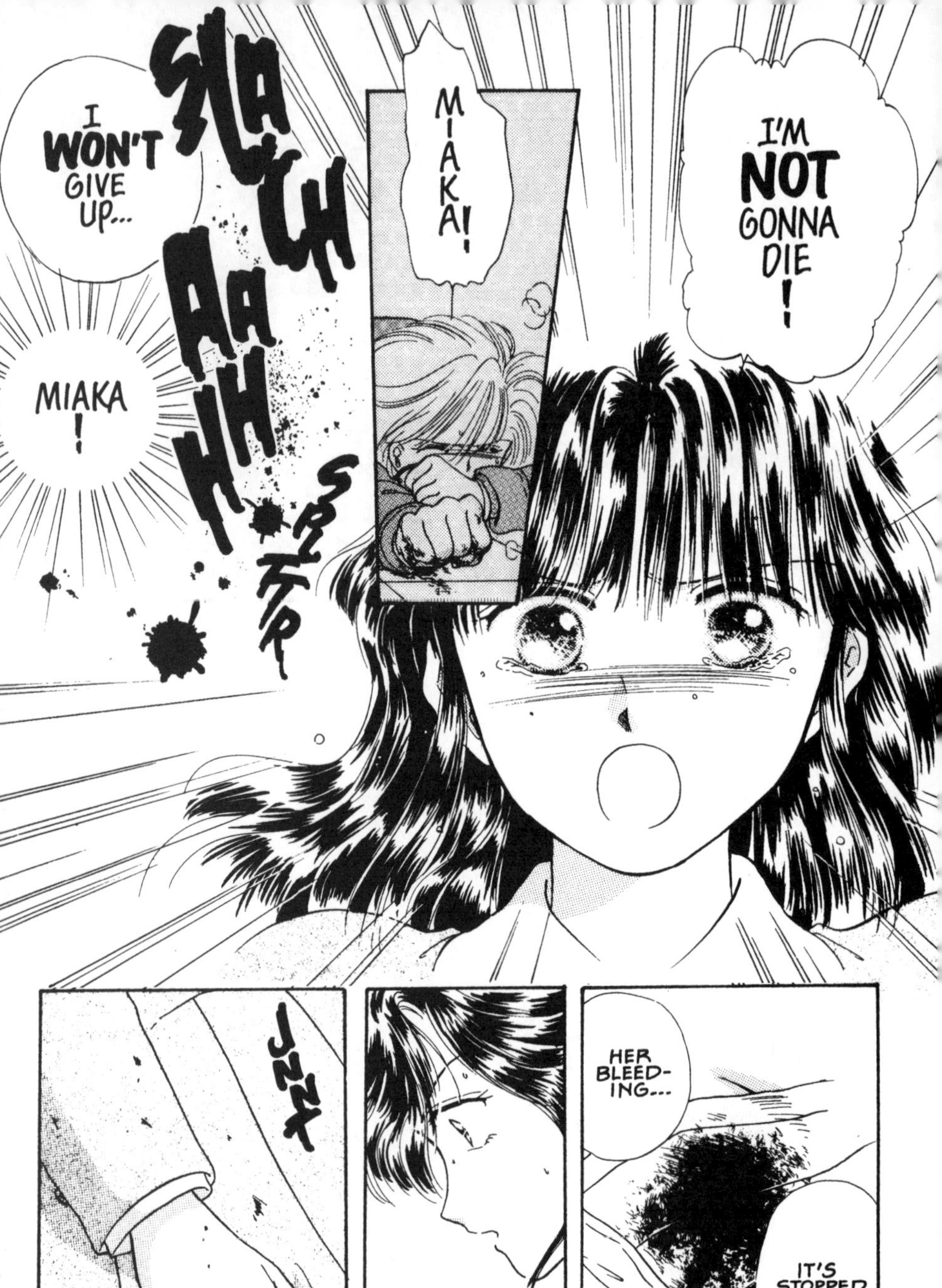
I WON'T GIVE UP...
MIAKA!
I'M NOT GONNA DIE!
MIAKA!
HER BLEED-ING...
IT'S STOPPED!!

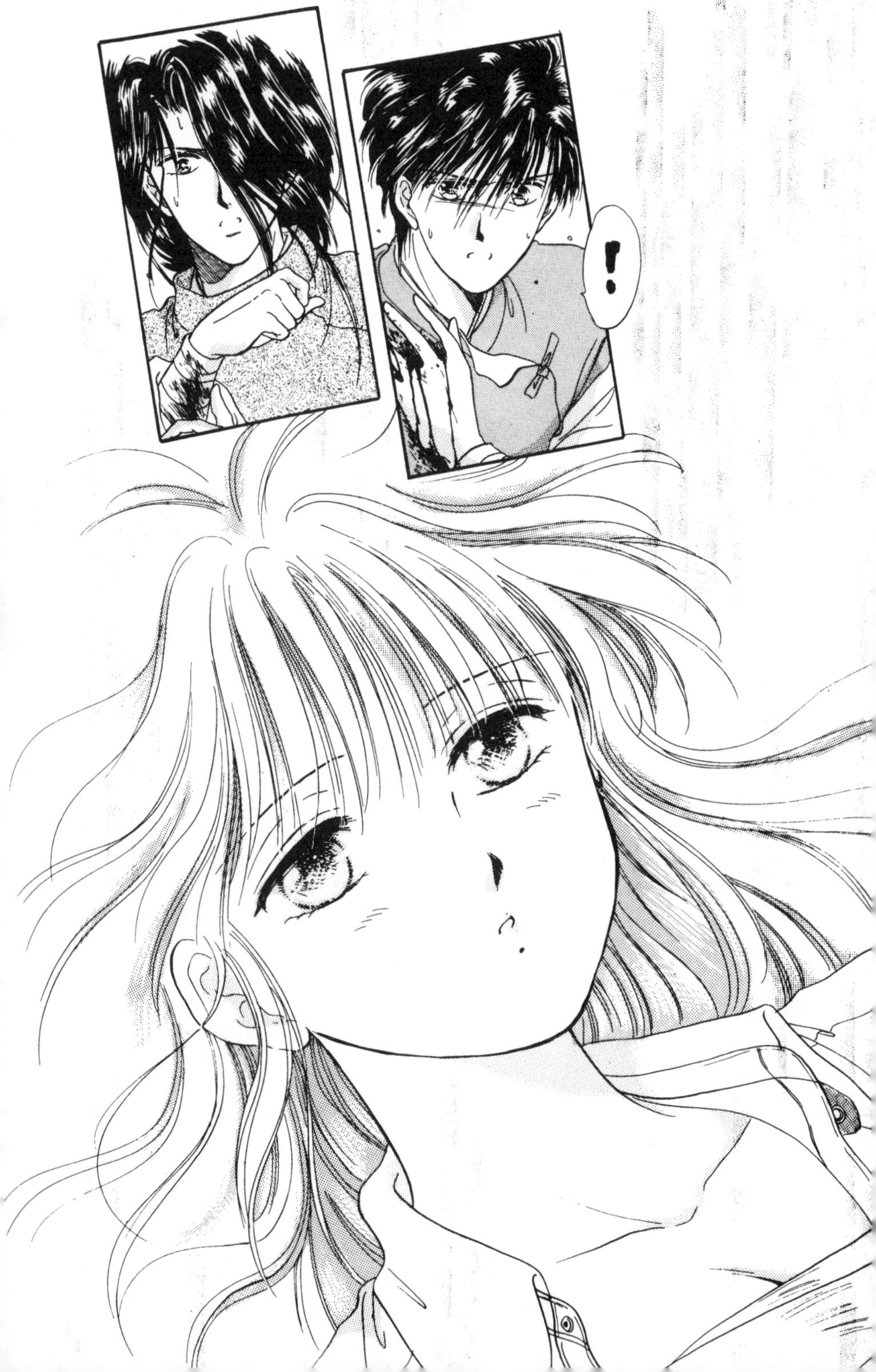
!

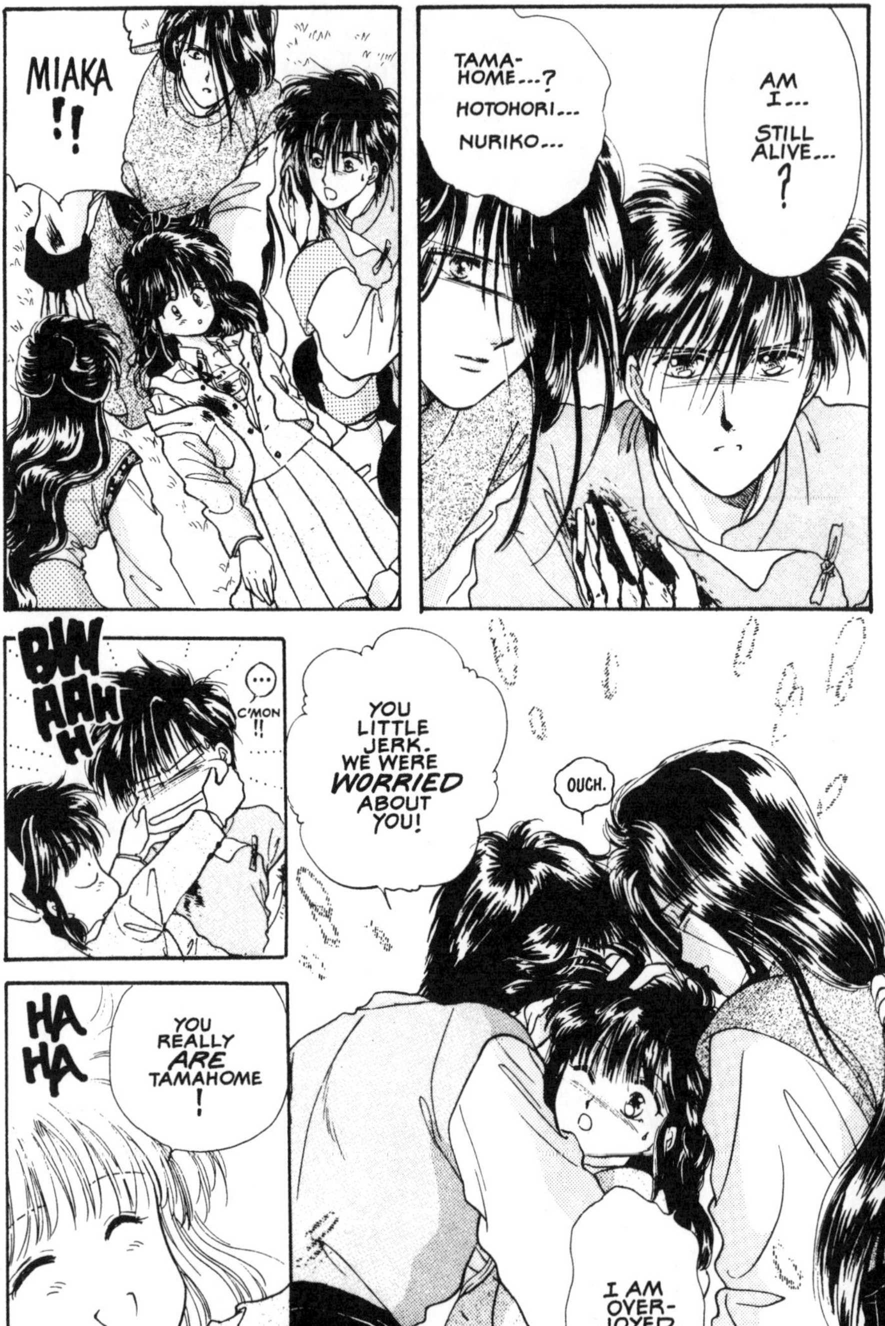
MIAKA!!
TAMA-HOME...? HOTOHORI... NURIKO...
AM I... STILL ALIVE...?
BWAAHH
...
C'MON!!
HA HA
YOU REALLY ARE TAMAHOME!
YOU LITTLE JERK. WE WERE WORRIED ABOUT YOU!
OUCH.
I AM OVER-JOYED.

I NEVER THOUGHT FOR A SECOND THAT A STUPID, OVERLY OPTIMISTIC FOODMONGER LIKE YOU WOULD DIE!

OH, SHRIVEL AND DIE, NURIKO.

IT WAS REALLY DARK. THEN I FOUND THIS BEAUTIFUL PLACE.

BUT EVERYONE WAS CALLING FOR ME.

SO I DIDN'T GO.

THANK YOU.

WHA?

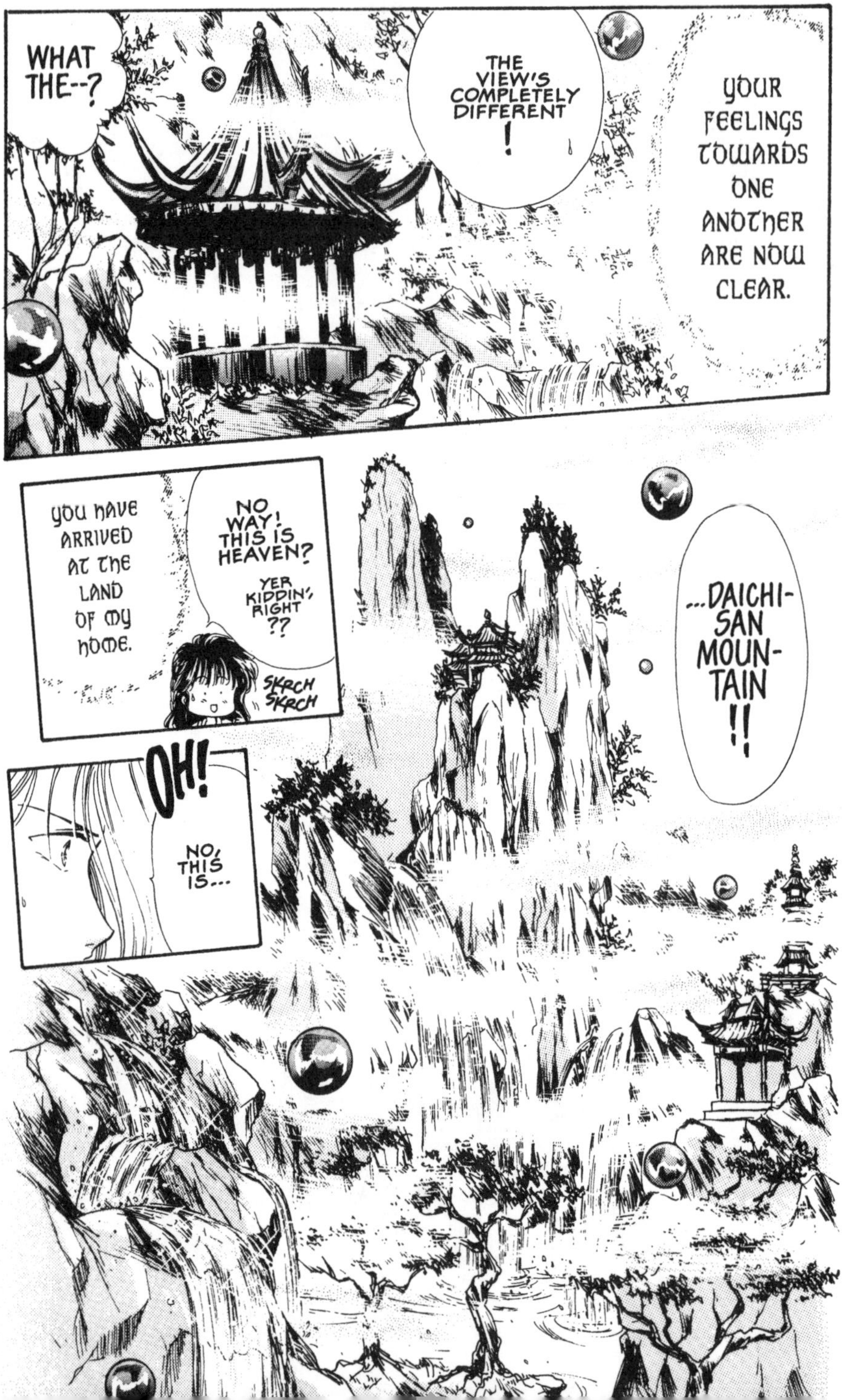
WHAT THE--?
THE VIEW'S COMPLETELY DIFFERENT!
YOUR FEELINGS TOWARDS ONE ANOTHER ARE NOW CLEAR.
YOU HAVE ARRIVED AT THE LAND OF MY HOME.
NO WAY! THIS IS HEAVEN?
YER KIDDIN', RIGHT??
SKRCH SKRCH
OH!
NO, THIS IS...
...DAICHI-SAN MOUNTAIN!!

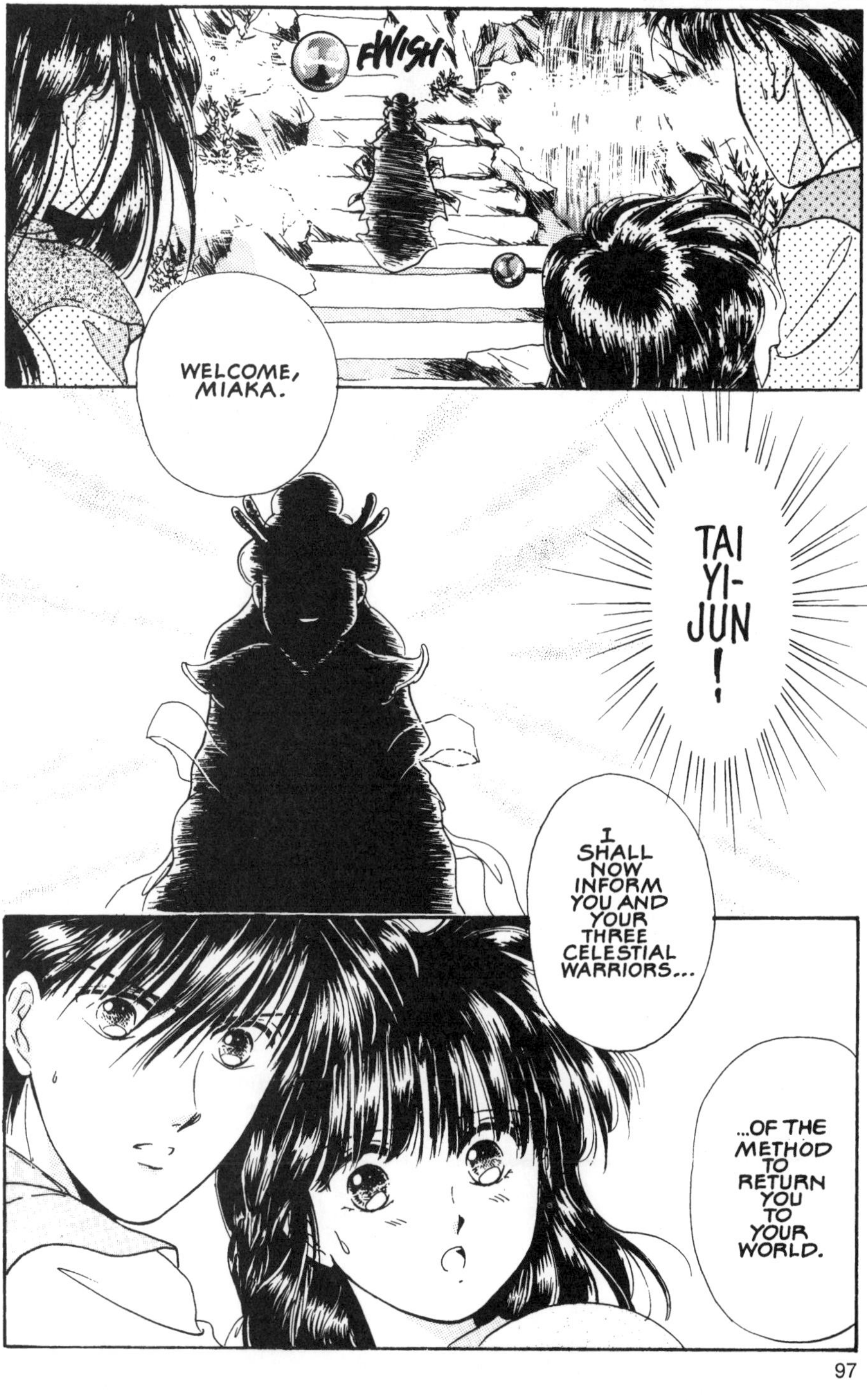
FWISH
WELCOME, MIAKA.
TAI YI-JUN!
I SHALL NOW INFORM YOU AND YOUR THREE CELESTIAL WARRIORS...
...OF THE METHOD TO RETURN YOU TO YOUR WORLD.

WHAT'LL I DO IF EVERYONE LIKES *THIS* BETTER THAN THE ORIGINAL?

PARDON THE PARODY

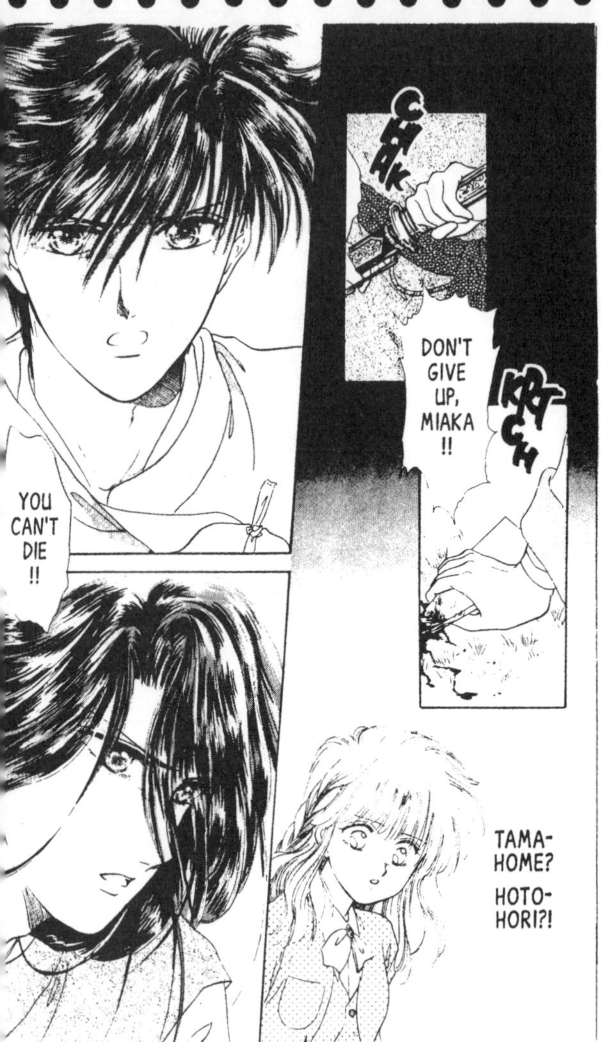
YOU CAN'T DIE!!
CHAK
DON'T GIVE UP, MIAKA!!
KRATCH
TAMA-HOME? HOTO-HORI?!

IDEA - Y.M. ↓

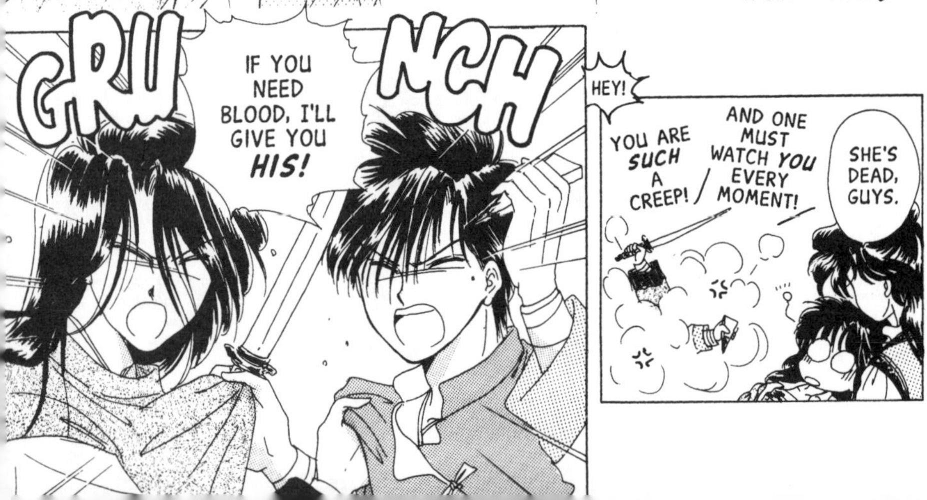
GRU
IF YOU NEED BLOOD, I'LL GIVE YOU *HIS!*
NCH
HEY!
YOU ARE *SUCH* A CREEP!
AND ONE MUST WATCH *YOU* EVERY MOMENT!
SHE'S DEAD, GUYS.

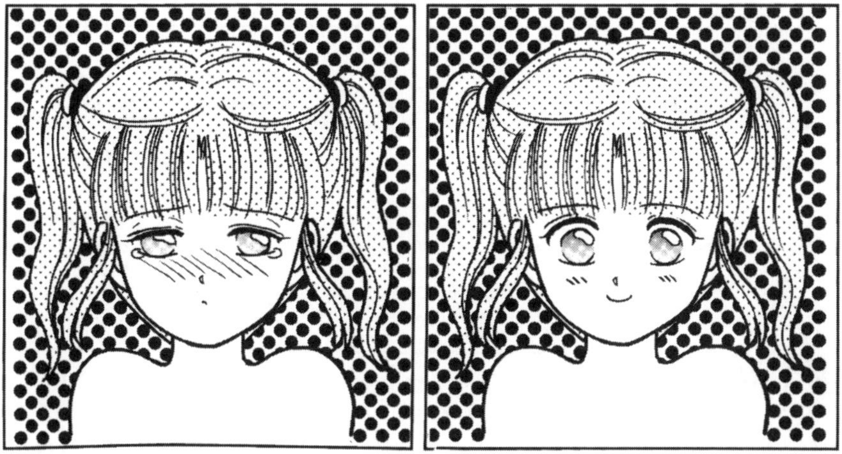

CHAPTER TEN

COME BACK HOME

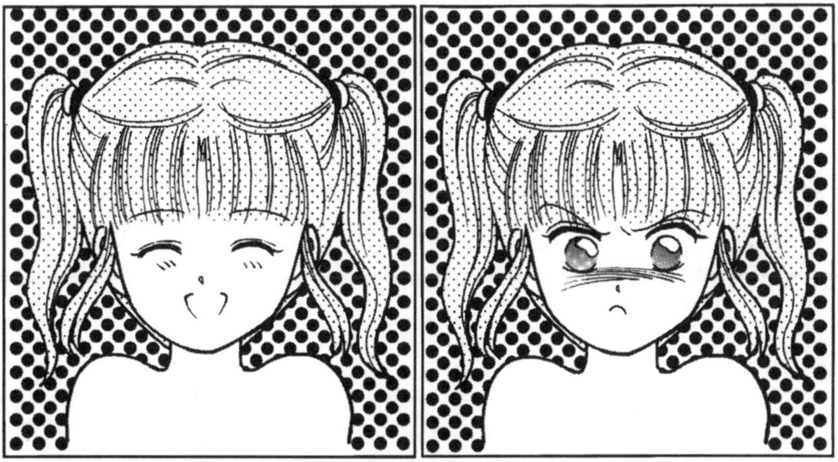

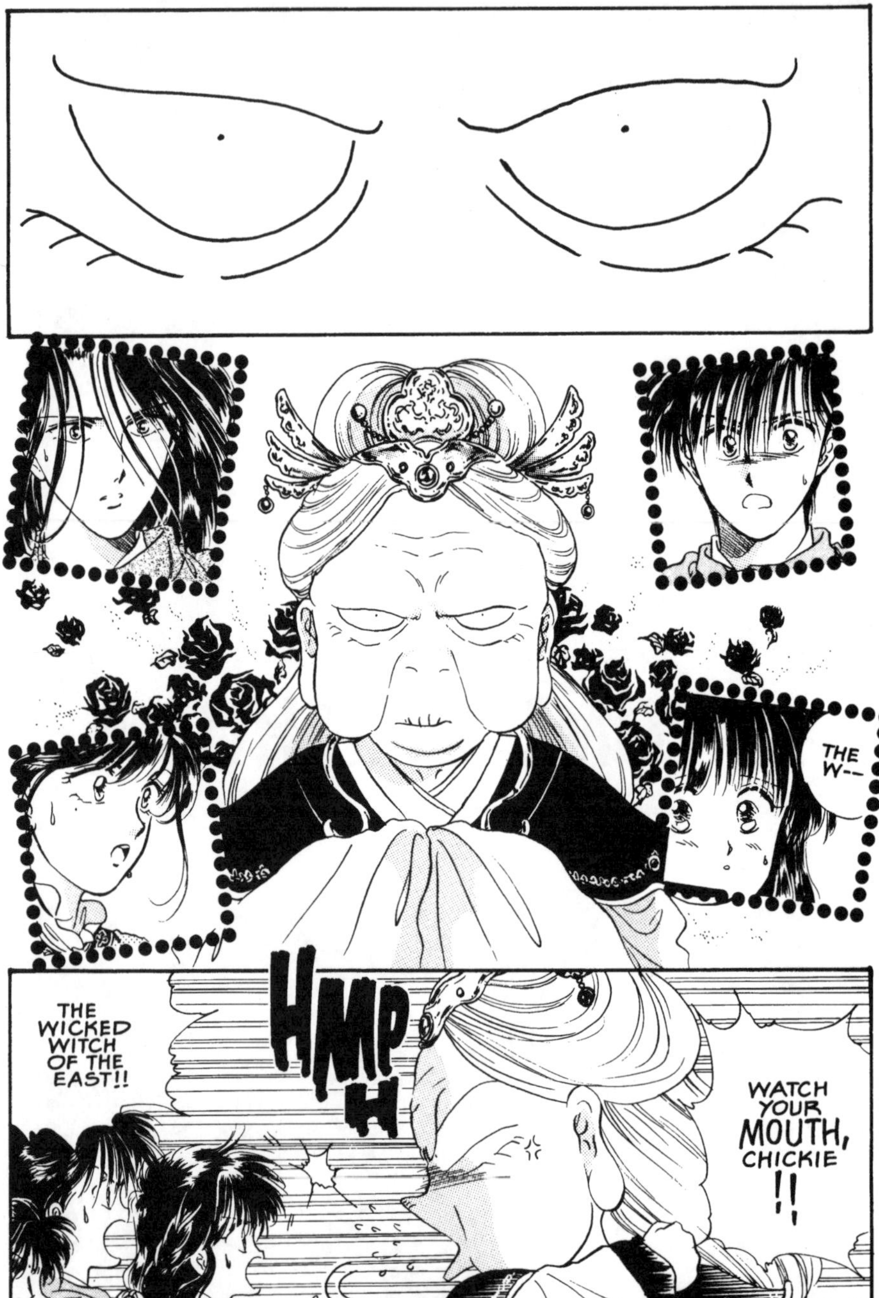
THE W--
THE WICKED WITCH OF THE EAST!!
HMPH
WATCH YOUR MOUTH, CHICKIE !!

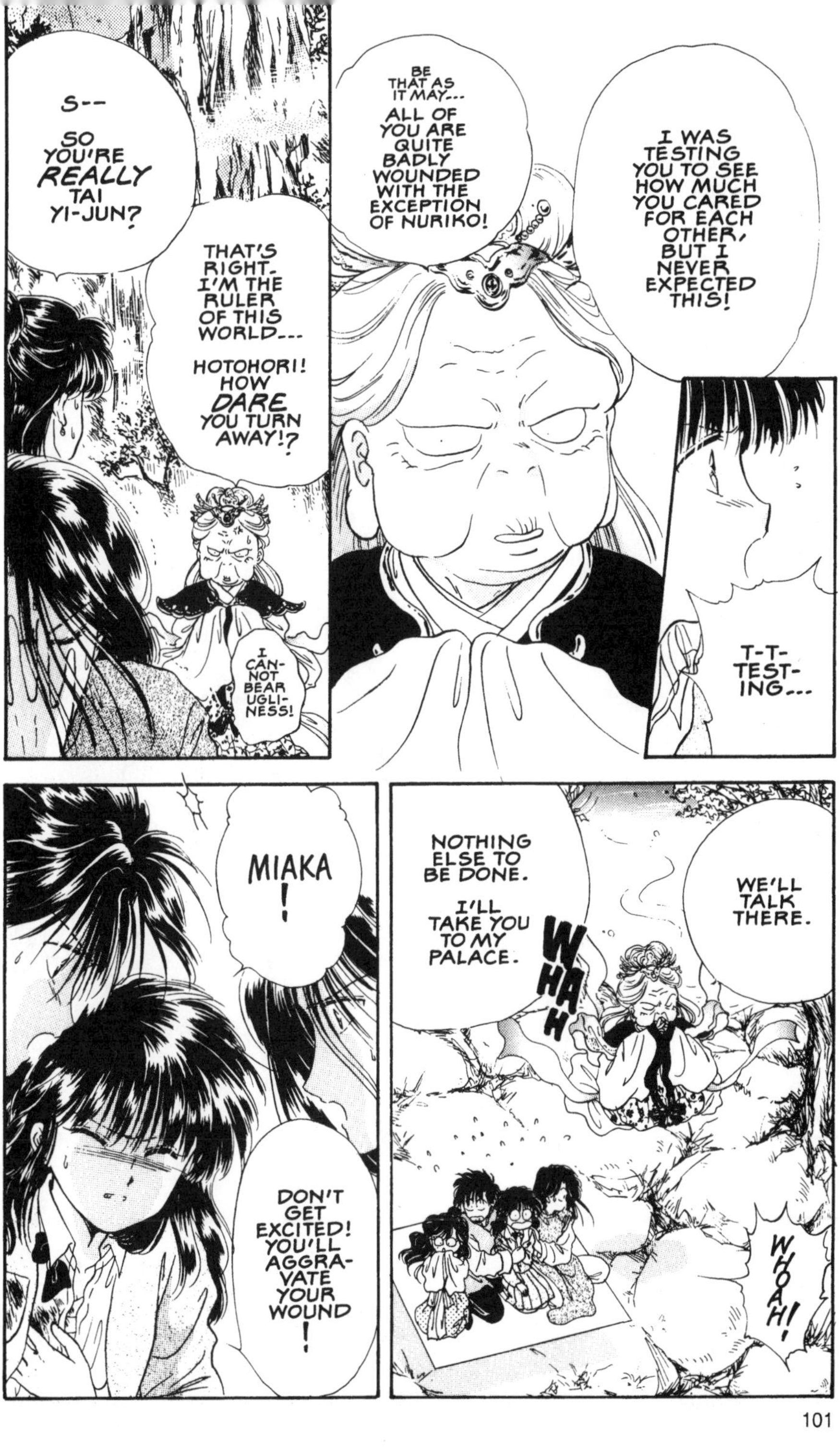
S--
SO YOU'RE REALLY TAI YI-JUN?
THAT'S RIGHT. I'M THE RULER OF THIS WORLD... HOTOHORI! HOW DARE YOU TURN AWAY!?
I CANNOT BEAR UGLINESS!
BE THAT AS IT MAY... ALL OF YOU ARE QUITE BADLY WOUNDED WITH THE EXCEPTION OF NURIKO!
I WAS TESTING YOU TO SEE HOW MUCH YOU CARED FOR EACH OTHER, BUT I NEVER EXPECTED THIS!
T-T-TESTING...
MIAKA!
DON'T GET EXCITED! YOU'LL AGGRAVATE YOUR WOUND!
NOTHING ELSE TO BE DONE. I'LL TAKE YOU TO MY PALACE.
WHAAH
WE'LL TALK THERE.
WHOAH!

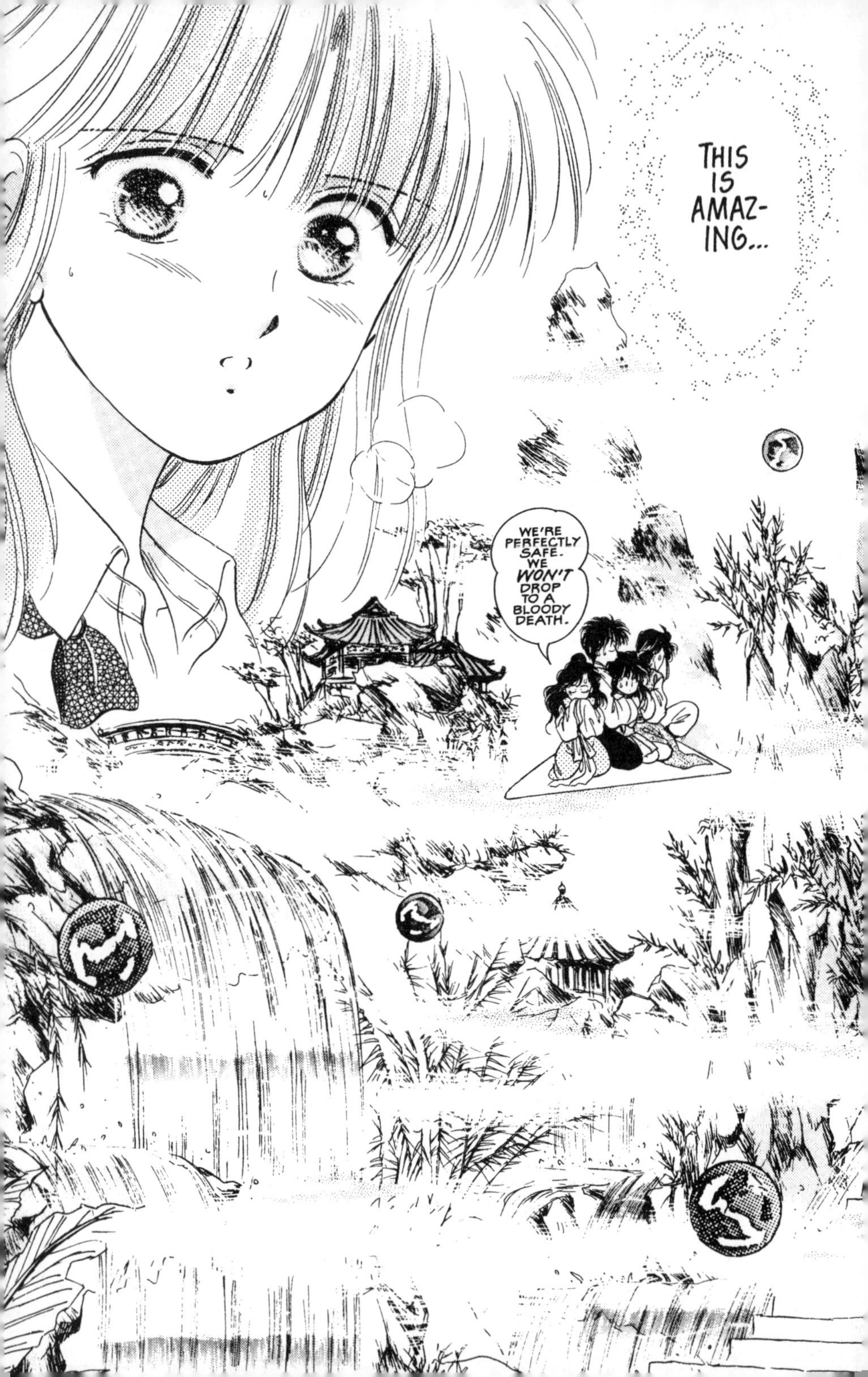
THIS IS AMAZ-ING...
WE'RE PERFECTLY SAFE. WE WON'T DROP TO A BLOODY DEATH.

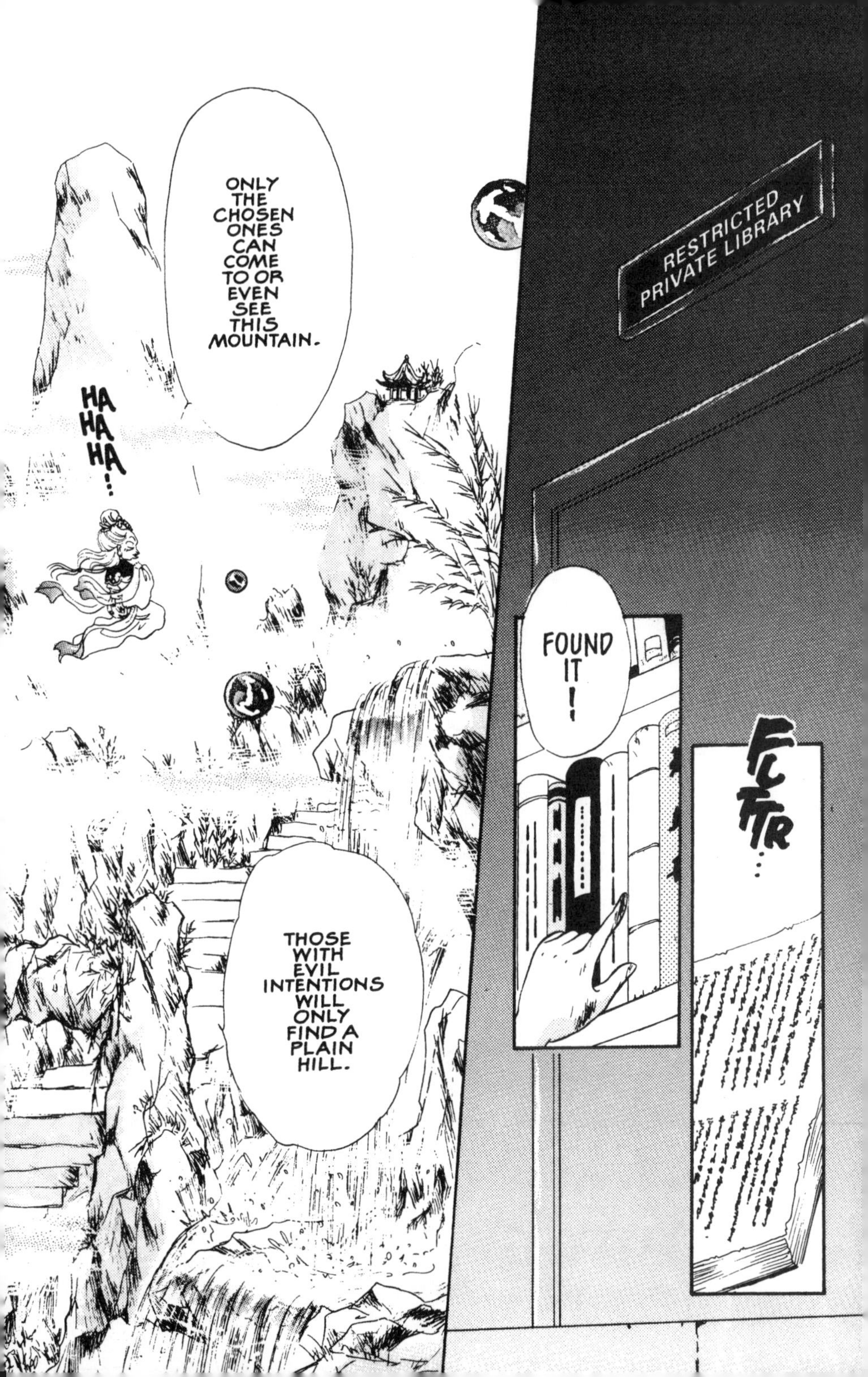
ONLY THE CHOSEN ONES CAN COME TO OR EVEN SEE THIS MOUNTAIN.
HA HA HA...
THOSE WITH EVIL INTENTIONS WILL ONLY FIND A PLAIN HILL.
RESTRICTED PRIVATE LIBRARY
FOUND IT!!
FLTTR...

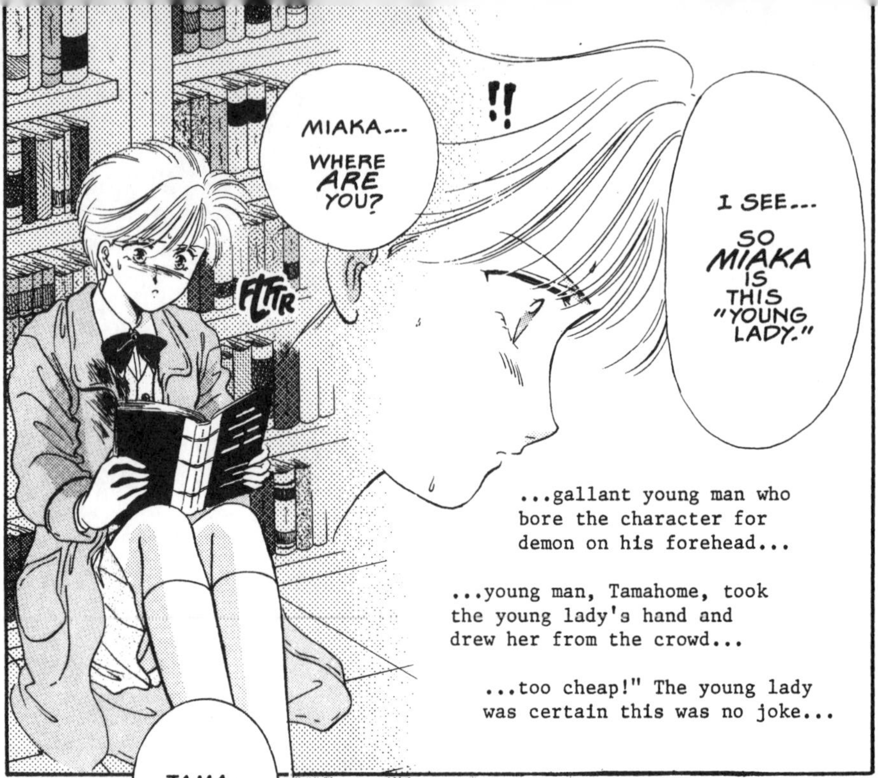
MIAKA... WHERE ARE YOU?
FLTTR
!!
I SEE... SO MIAKA IS THIS "YOUNG LADY."
...gallant young man who bore the character for demon on his forehead...
...young man, Tamahome, took the young lady's hand and drew her from the crowd...
...too cheap!" The young lady was certain this was no joke...

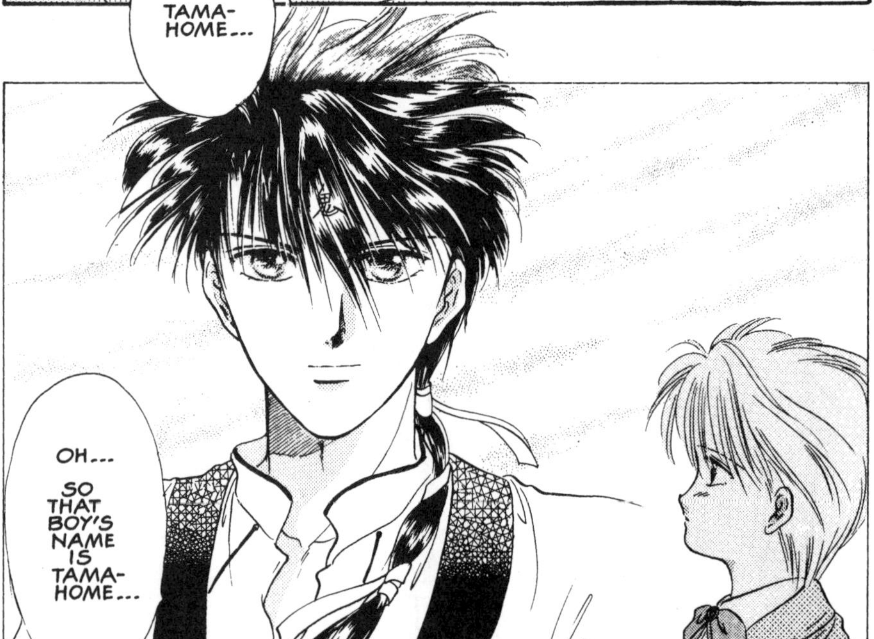
TAMA-HOME...
OH... SO THAT BOY'S NAME IS TAMA-HOME...

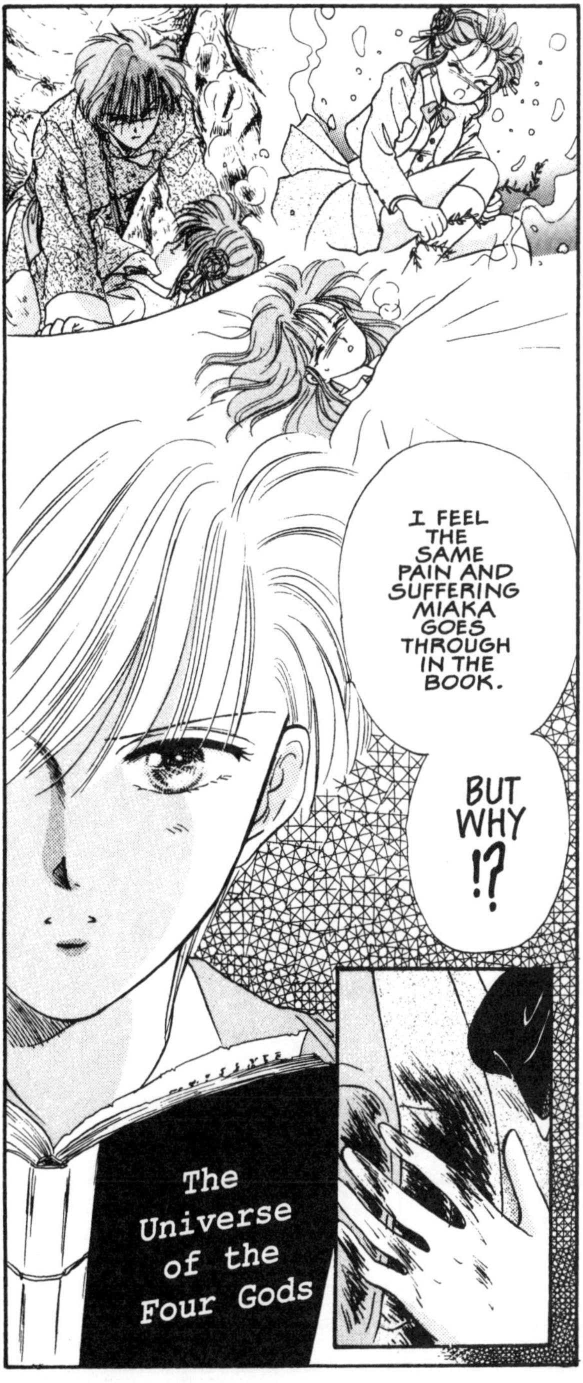
I FEEL THE SAME PAIN AND SUFFERING MIAKA GOES THROUGH IN THE BOOK.
BUT WHY !?
The Universe of the Four Gods

By the way, my profile in "The Watase Newsletter" includes something about my leg size, but that's really my shoe size. I can wear a size 25. 25.5 is a loose fit, but 25 is a little too tight. My shoe size is about average for my height. When I mentioned my age in an earlier chat section, someone said, "So you're 26!" Wrongo! "Prepubescence" began in December of '90, and I started this serial less than a year later. How could I be 26!? I graduated high school only 4 years ago. *sobb sobb*

Oh yeah! Someone from my old high school wrote me! *I've had several letters from students there.* She's in the Manga Research Club! When I entered high school I really wished that this club existed! I had no other choice but to join the art club and cinema club. But all they had me doing was ink and paint on Vifam and Minky Momo cels. I quit both clubs within 6 months. It seems like ages ago. I still remember it clearly though. According to this letter, a teacher I had during my senior year keeps a copy of my manga in his desk! Unbelievable!! I hope he's doing well! I'd never do the chores he assigned, I'd barely pass his math classes. I was a rotten student, but it was a good school. I heard that the name's been changed to "Sakai Girl's High School." I guess all the badges have different designs now. The one thing I didn't like at school was the winter uniform!! I wanted a ribbon or a tie!! (I've graduated so I can criticize them all I want!) Are the uniforms still ugly? Miaka's uniform is a fan favorite because it's cute. I mean, you have to wear your uniform every day. So cute is good.

When I was in school I was so envious of another Sakai school. They were co-ed. *What am I trying to say?* My teachers were very committed. (It was a private school, so the rules were strict.) Thanks for all your help! I loved my time in junior high and high school. I'd like to go back--wear my uniform, carry my bag and joke around with my friends.

I'm sure some of you who are still in school say you hate it, but your school days become a great memory.

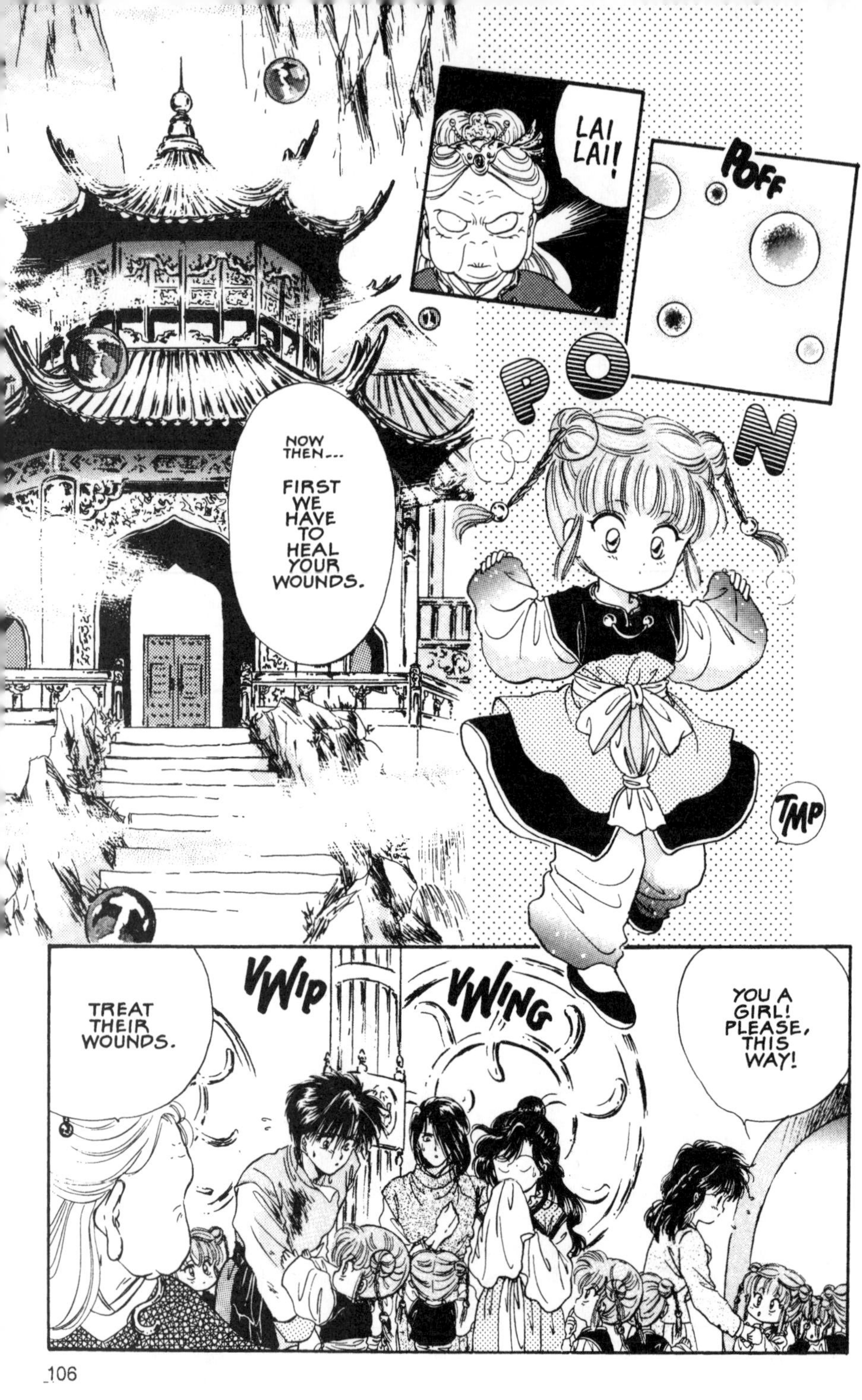
NOW THEN...
FIRST WE HAVE TO HEAL YOUR WOUNDS.
LAI LAI!
POFF
PON
TMP
TREAT THEIR WOUNDS.
VWIP
VWING
YOU A GIRL! PLEASE, THIS WAY!

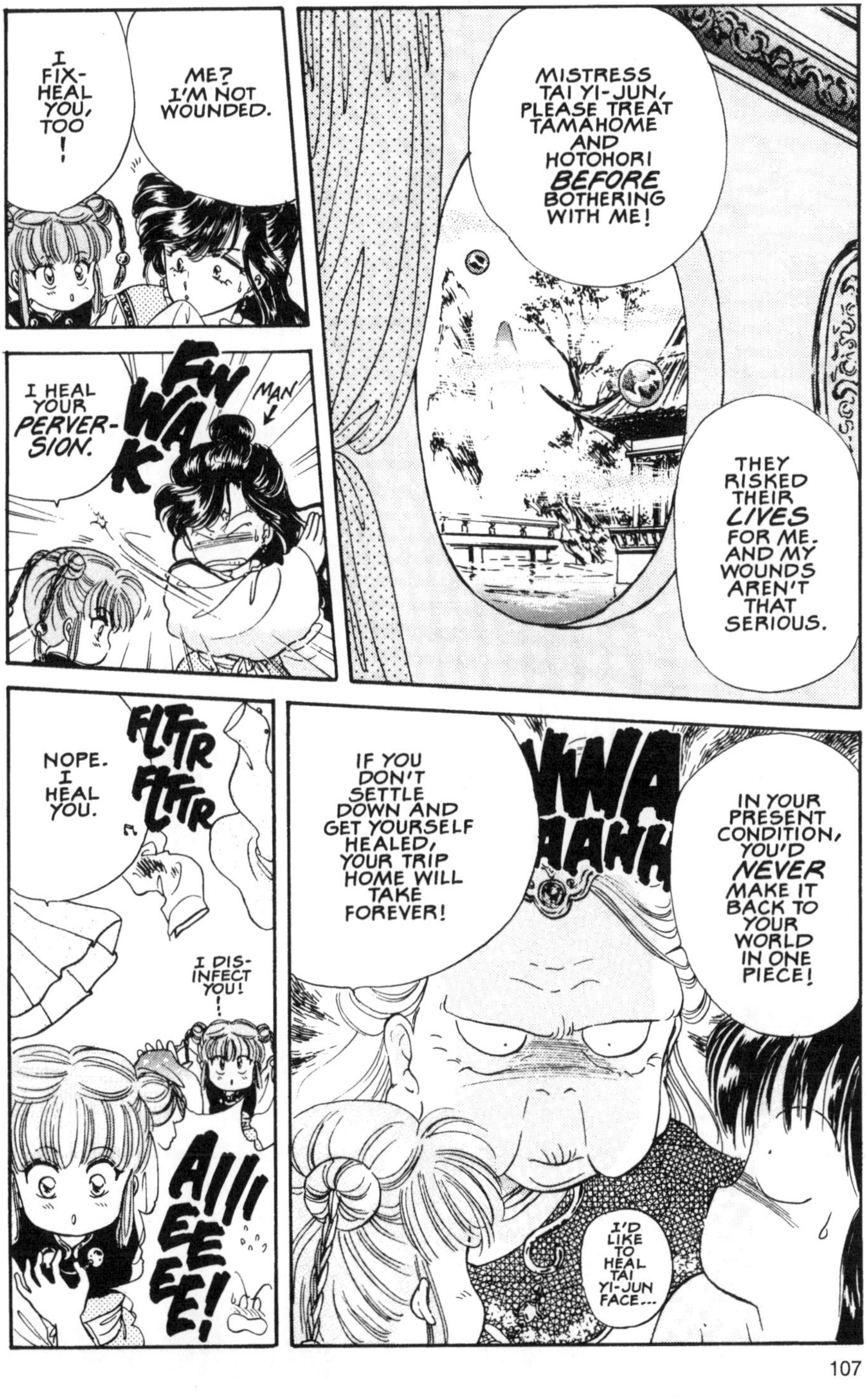
I FIX-HEAL YOU, TOO!
ME? I'M NOT WOUNDED.
I HEAL YOUR *PERVERSION*.
FWWAK
MAN
MISTRESS TAI YI-JUN, PLEASE TREAT TAMAHOME AND HOTOHORI ***BEFORE*** BOTHERING WITH ME!
THEY RISKED THEIR *LIVES* FOR ME. AND MY WOUNDS AREN'T THAT SERIOUS.
NOPE. I HEAL YOU.
FLTTR FLTTTR
I DIS-INFECT YOU!
AIIIEEEEE!
WWAAANH
IF YOU DON'T SETTLE DOWN AND GET YOURSELF HEALED, YOUR TRIP HOME WILL TAKE FOREVER!
IN YOUR PRESENT CONDITION, YOU'D *NEVER* MAKE IT BACK TO YOUR WORLD IN ONE PIECE!
I'D LIKE TO HEAL TAI YI-JUN FACE...

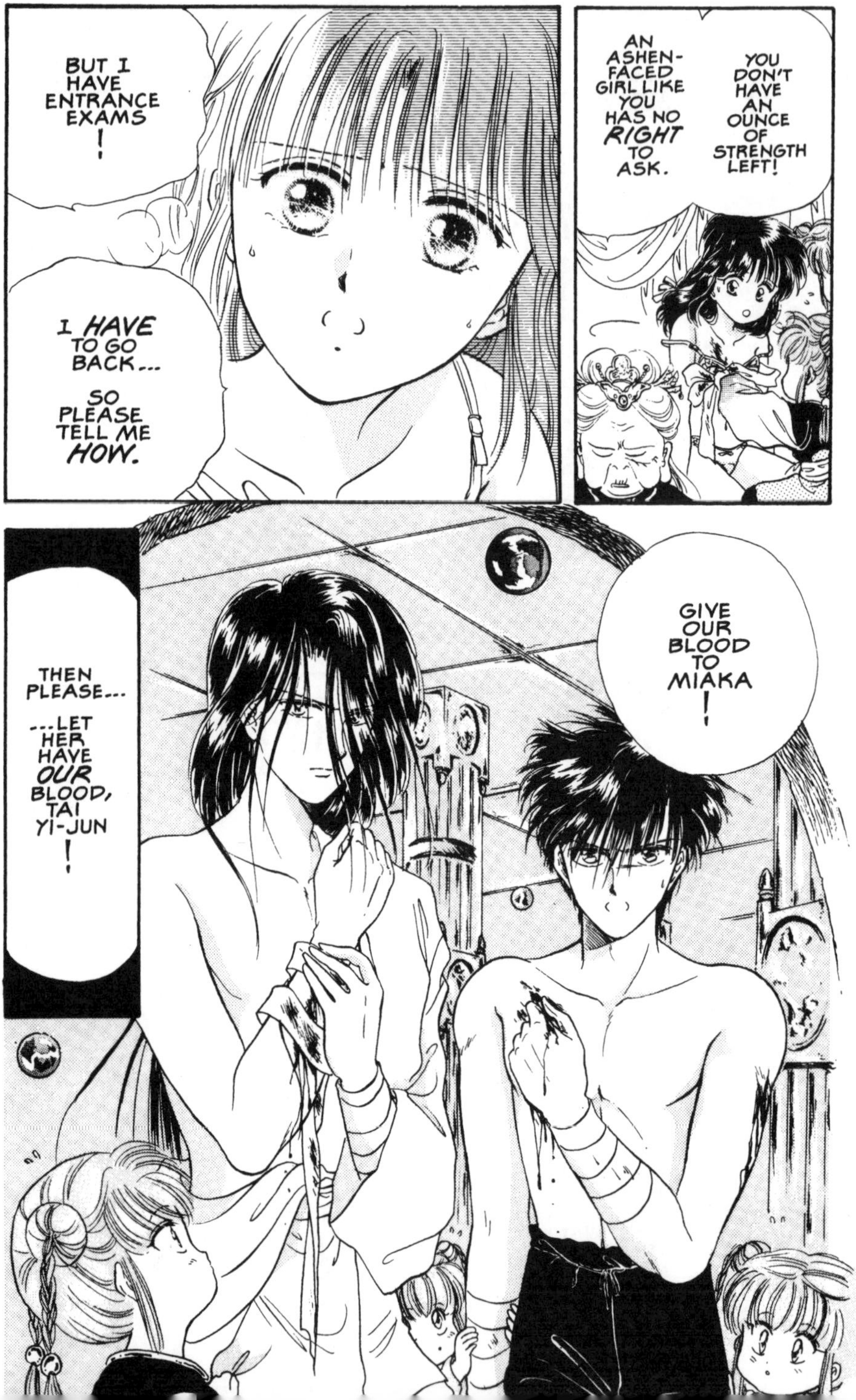
BUT I HAVE ENTRANCE EXAMS!
I HAVE TO GO BACK... SO PLEASE TELL ME HOW.
AN ASHEN-FACED GIRL LIKE YOU HAS NO RIGHT TO ASK.
YOU DON'T HAVE AN OUNCE OF STRENGTH LEFT!
THEN PLEASE... ...LET HER HAVE OUR BLOOD, TAI YI-JUN!
GIVE OUR BLOOD TO MIAKA!

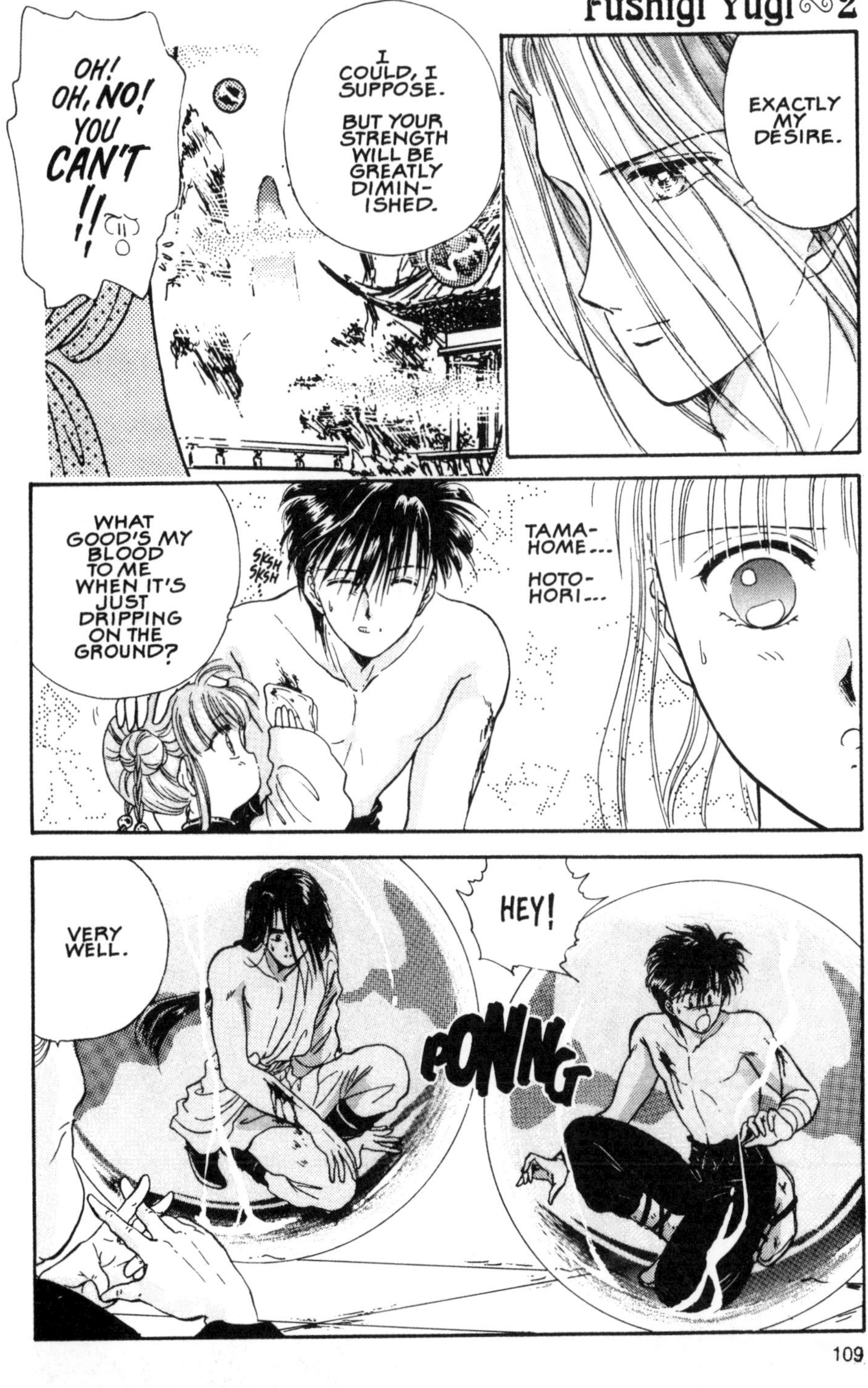
OH! OH, NO! YOU CAN'T!!
I COULD, I SUPPOSE.
BUT YOUR STRENGTH WILL BE GREATLY DIMIN-ISHED.
EXACTLY MY DESIRE.
WHAT GOOD'S MY BLOOD TO ME WHEN IT'S JUST DRIPPING ON THE GROUND?
SKSH SKSH
TAMA-HOME...
HOTO-HORI...
VERY WELL.
HEY!
PONNG

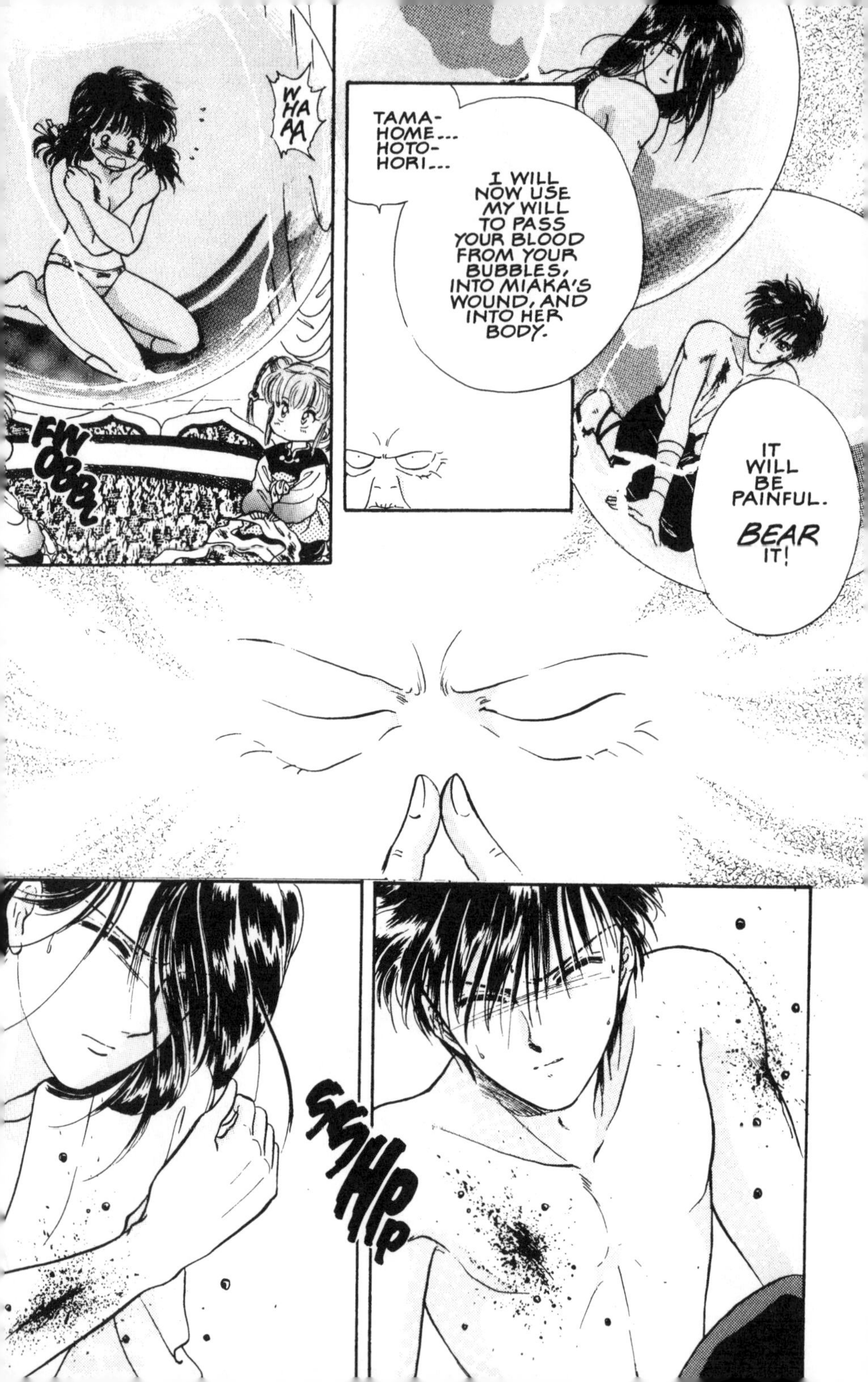

WHAAA
FWOBBB
TAMA-HOME... HOTO-HORI...
I WILL NOW USE MY WILL TO PASS YOUR BLOOD FROM YOUR BUBBLES, INTO MIAKA'S WOUND, AND INTO HER BODY.
IT WILL BE PAINFUL. BEAR IT!
SHHP

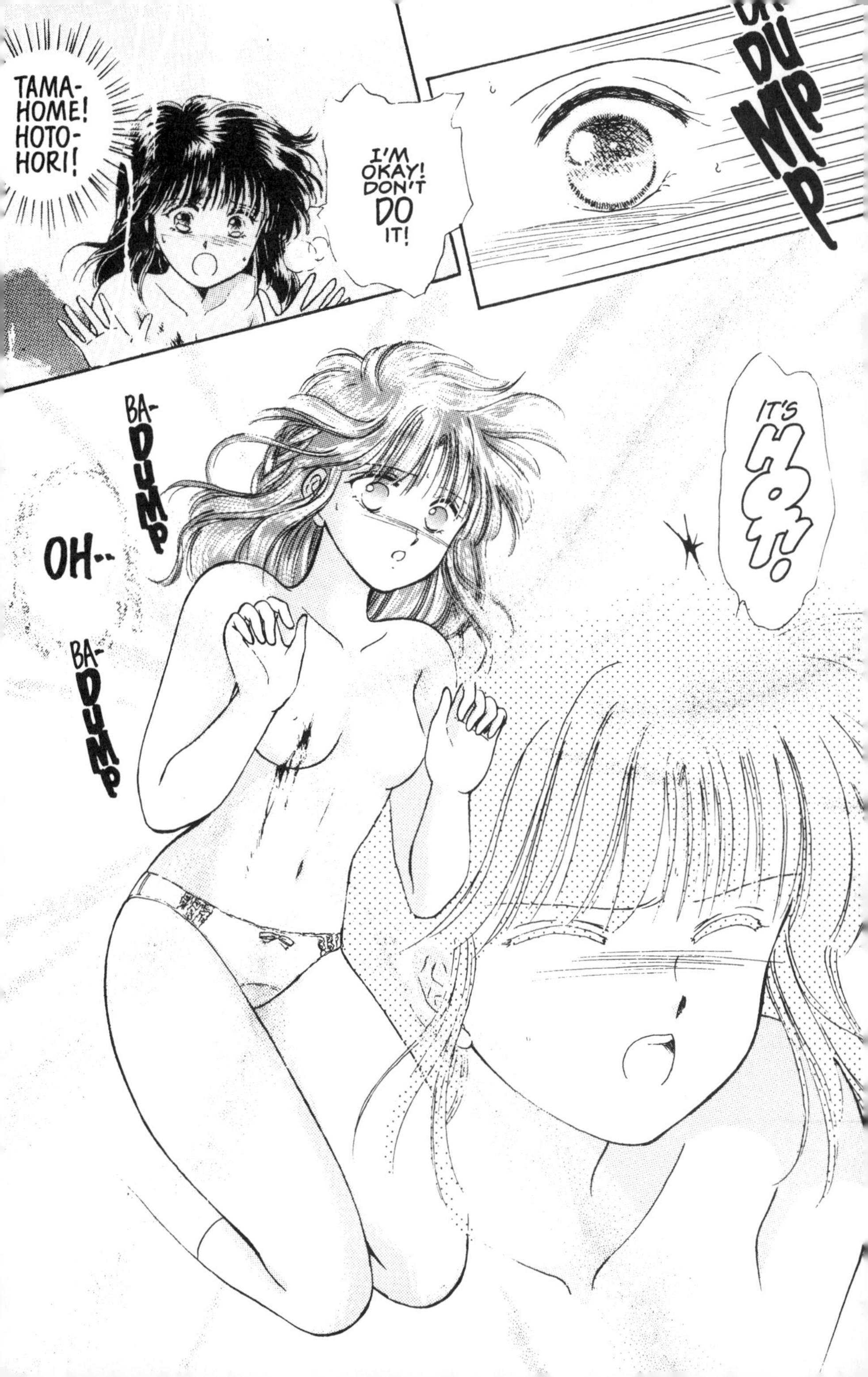
TAMA-HOME! HOTO-HORI!
I'M OKAY! DON'T DO IT!
DUMP
BA-DUMP
OH..
BA-DUMP
IT'S HOT!

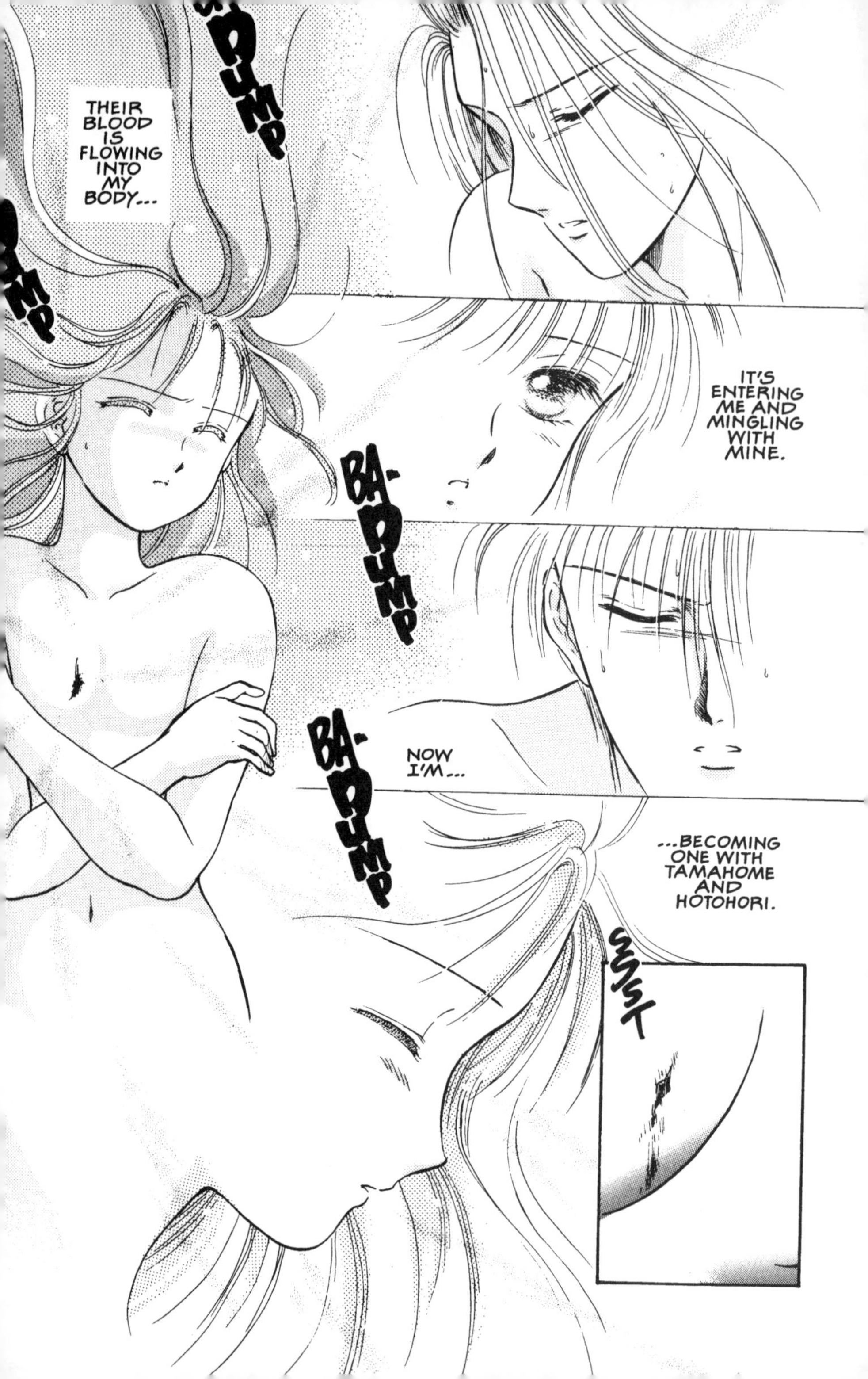
DUMP
THEIR BLOOD IS FLOWING INTO MY BODY...
BA-DUMP
BA-DUMP
IT'S ENTERING ME AND MINGLING WITH MINE.
NOW I'M...
...BECOMING ONE WITH TAMAHOME AND HOTOHORI.
SSST

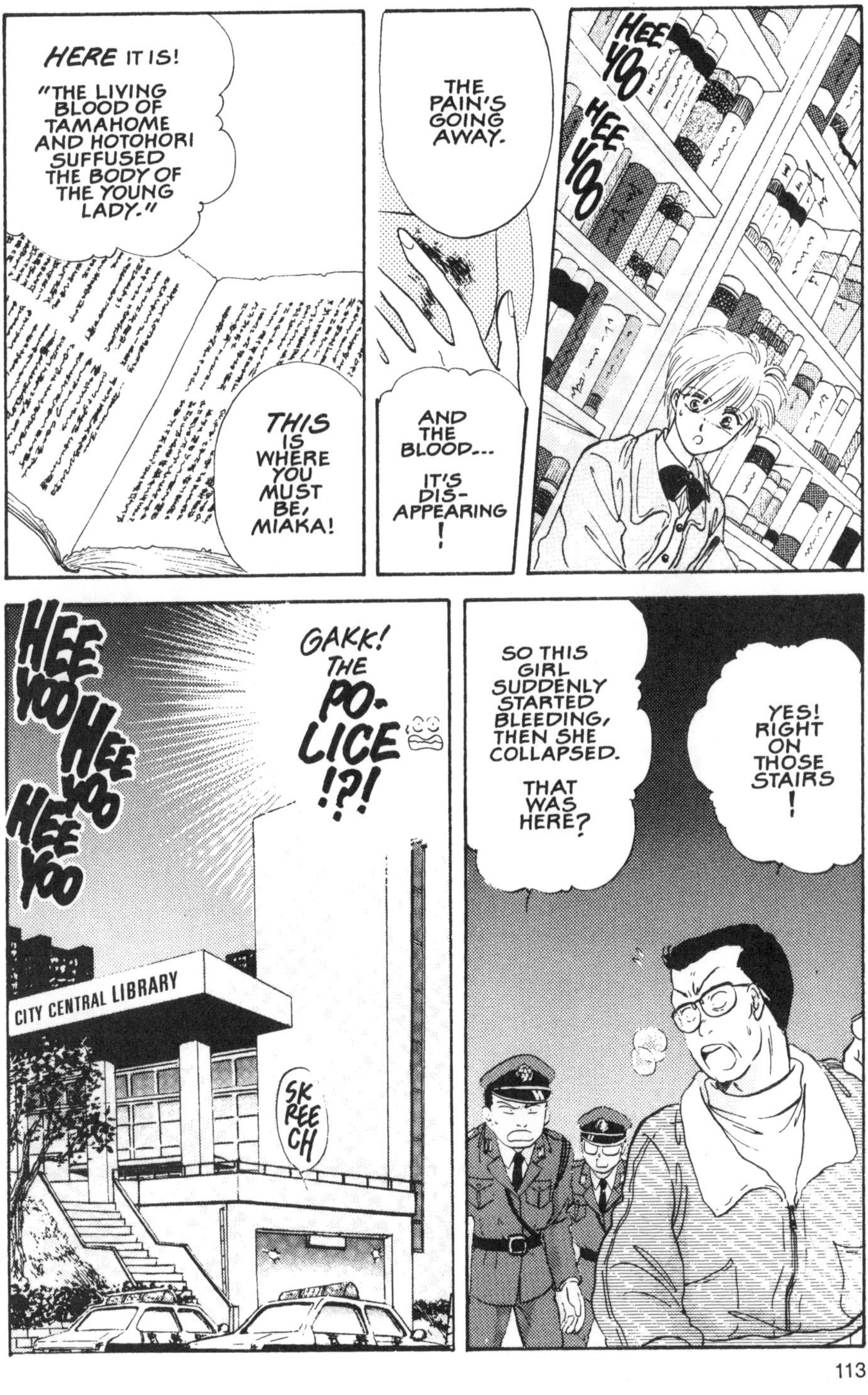
HERE IT IS!
"THE LIVING BLOOD OF TAMAHOME AND HOTOHORI SUFFUSED THE BODY OF THE YOUNG LADY."
THIS IS WHERE YOU MUST BE, MIAKA!
THE PAIN'S GOING AWAY.
AND THE BLOOD... IT'S DIS-APPEARING!
HEE YOO
HEE YOO
HEE YOO HEE YOO HEE YOO
GAKK! THE PO-LICE!?!
CITY CENTRAL LIBRARY
SKREECH
SO THIS GIRL SUDDENLY STARTED BLEEDING, THEN SHE COLLAPSED.
THAT WAS HERE?
YES! RIGHT ON THOSE STAIRS!

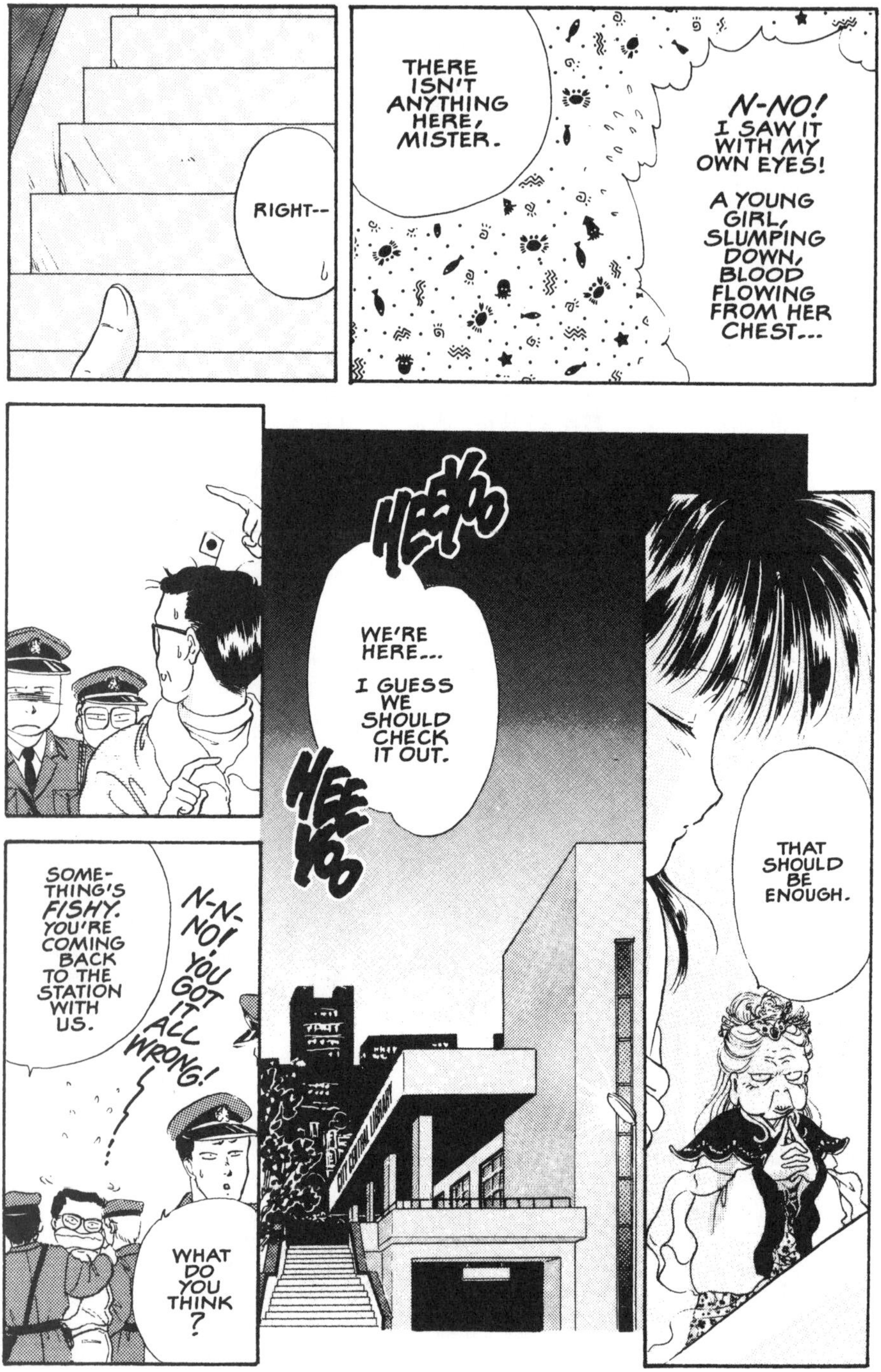
RIGHT--
THERE ISN'T ANYTHING HERE, MISTER.
N-NO! I SAW IT WITH MY OWN EYES!
A YOUNG GIRL, SLUMPING DOWN, BLOOD FLOWING FROM HER CHEST...
SOME-THING'S FISHY. YOU'RE COMING BACK TO THE STATION WITH US.
N-N-NO! YOU GOT IT ALL WRONG!
WHAT DO YOU THINK?
HEEYOO
WE'RE HERE... I GUESS WE SHOULD CHECK IT OUT.
HEEYOO
CITY CENTRAL LIBRARY
THAT SHOULD BE ENOUGH.

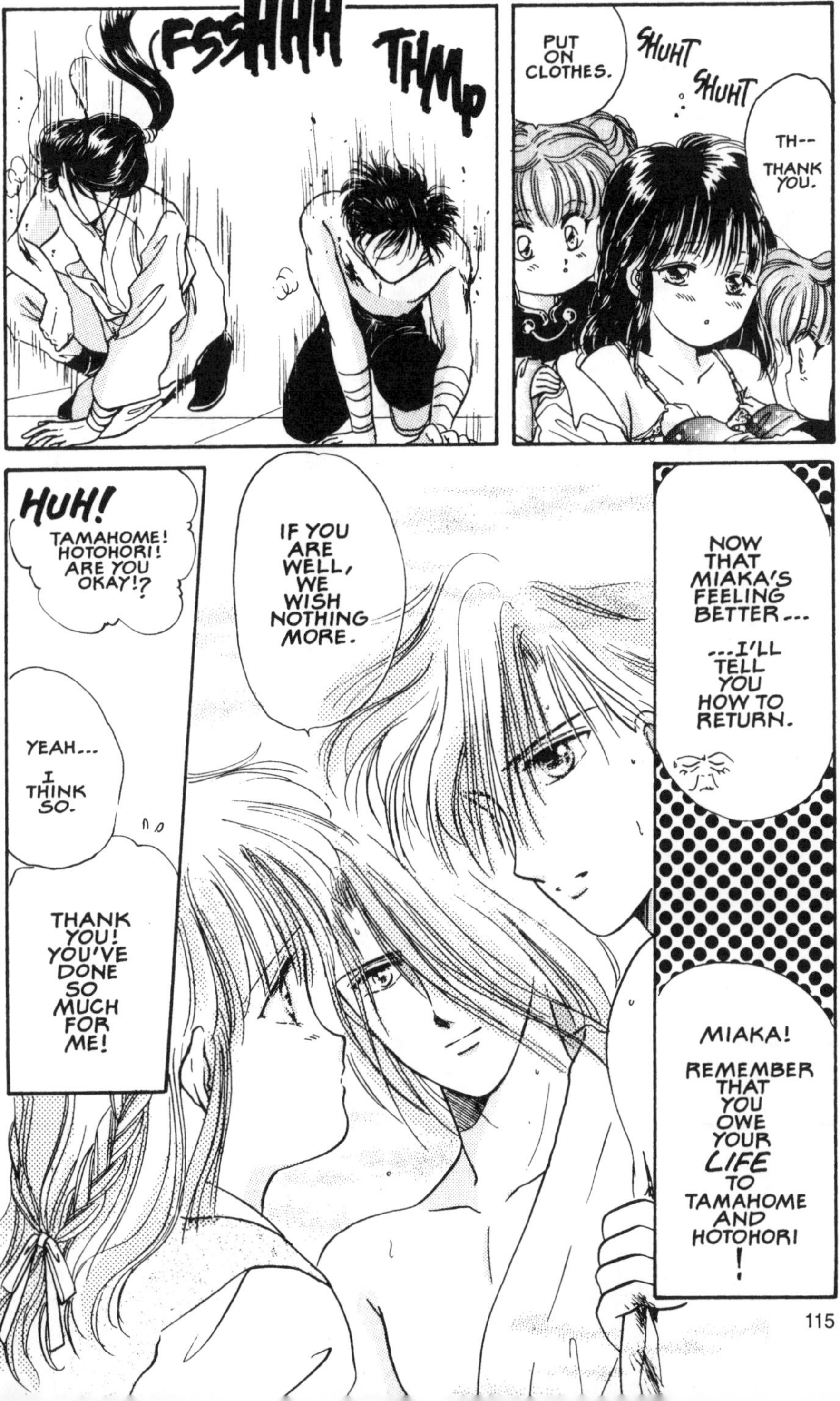
FSSHHH
THMP
PUT ON CLOTHES.
SHUHT
SHUHT
TH-- THANK YOU.
HUH!
TAMAHOME! HOTOHORI! ARE YOU OKAY!?
YEAH... I THINK SO.
THANK YOU! YOU'VE DONE SO MUCH FOR ME!
IF YOU ARE WELL, WE WISH NOTHING MORE.
NOW THAT MIAKA'S FEELING BETTER...
...I'LL TELL YOU HOW TO RETURN.
MIAKA! REMEMBER THAT YOU OWE YOUR LIFE TO TAMAHOME AND HOTOHORI!

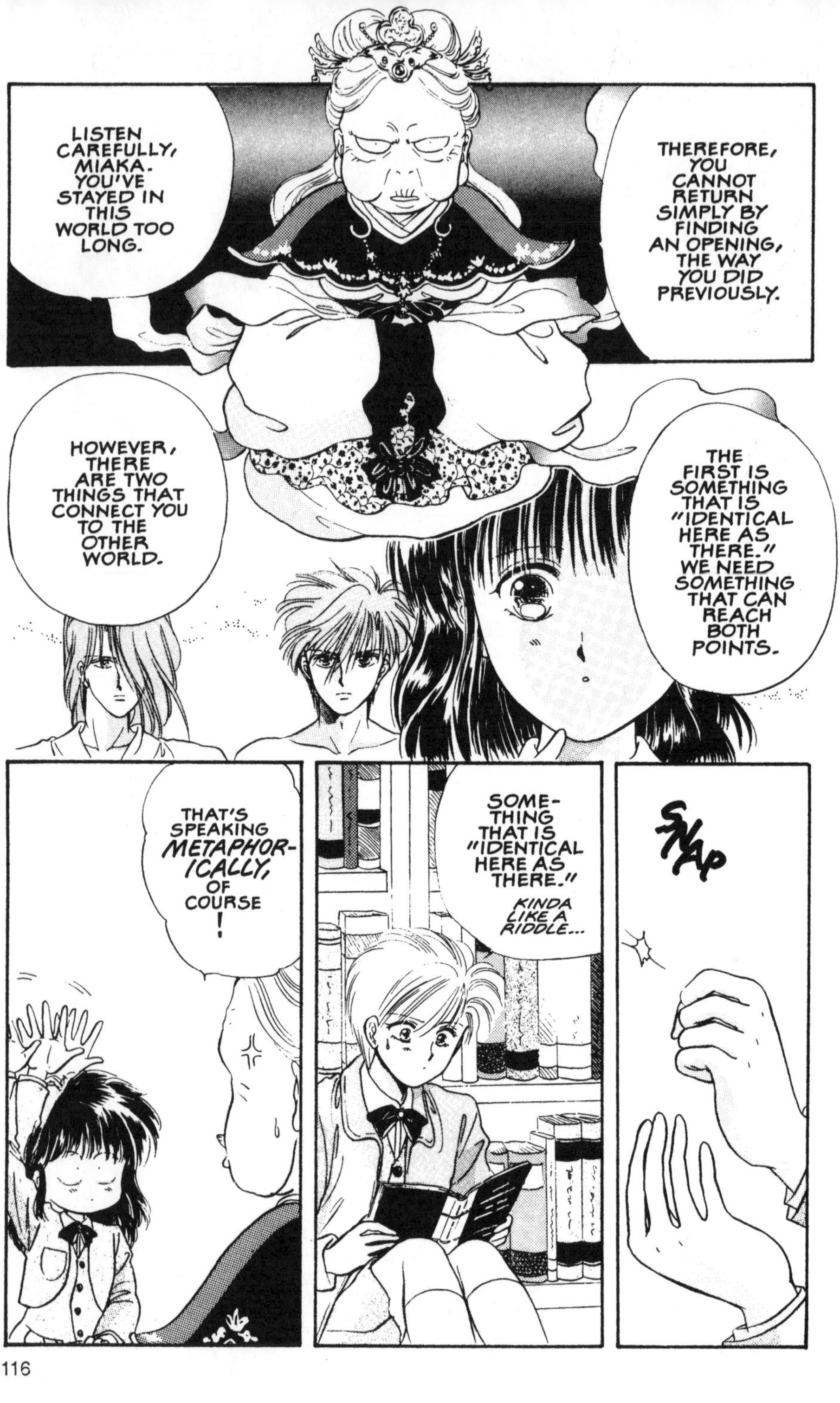
LISTEN CAREFULLY, MIAKA. YOU'VE STAYED IN THIS WORLD TOO LONG.
THEREFORE, YOU CANNOT RETURN SIMPLY BY FINDING AN OPENING, THE WAY YOU DID PREVIOUSLY.
HOWEVER, THERE ARE TWO THINGS THAT CONNECT YOU TO THE OTHER WORLD.
THE FIRST IS SOMETHING THAT IS "IDENTICAL HERE AS THERE." WE NEED SOMETHING THAT CAN REACH BOTH POINTS.
THAT'S SPEAKING METAPHORICALLY, OF COURSE!
SOMETHING THAT IS "IDENTICAL HERE AS THERE."
KINDA LIKE A RIDDLE...
SNAP

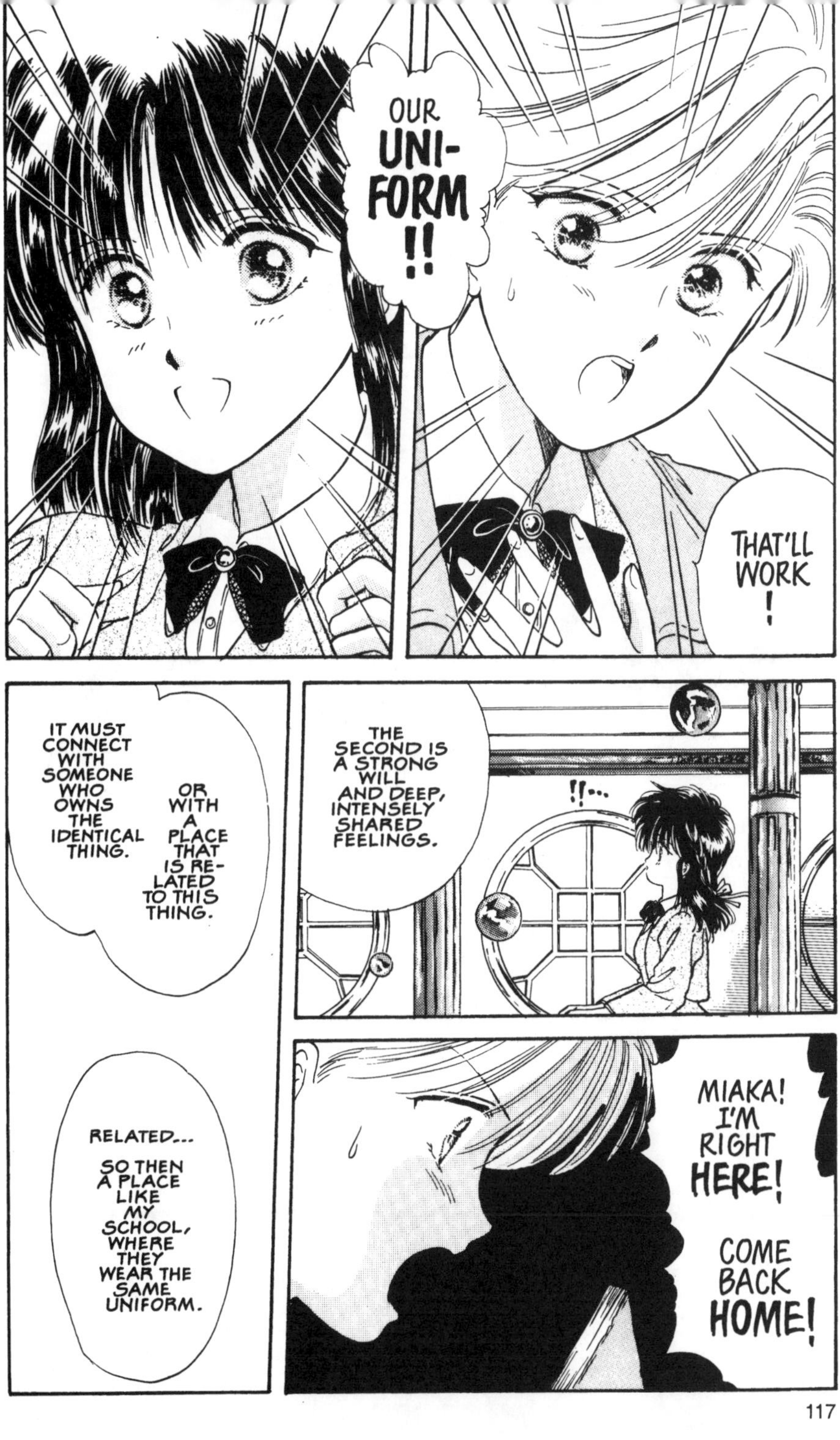
OUR UNI-FORM!!
THAT'LL WORK!
IT MUST CONNECT WITH SOMEONE WHO OWNS THE IDENTICAL THING.
OR WITH A PLACE THAT IS RE-LATED TO THIS THING.
RELATED...
SO THEN A PLACE LIKE MY SCHOOL, WHERE THEY WEAR THE SAME UNIFORM.
THE SECOND IS A STRONG WILL AND DEEP, INTENSELY SHARED FEELINGS.
!!...
MIAKA! I'M RIGHT HERE!
COME BACK HOME!

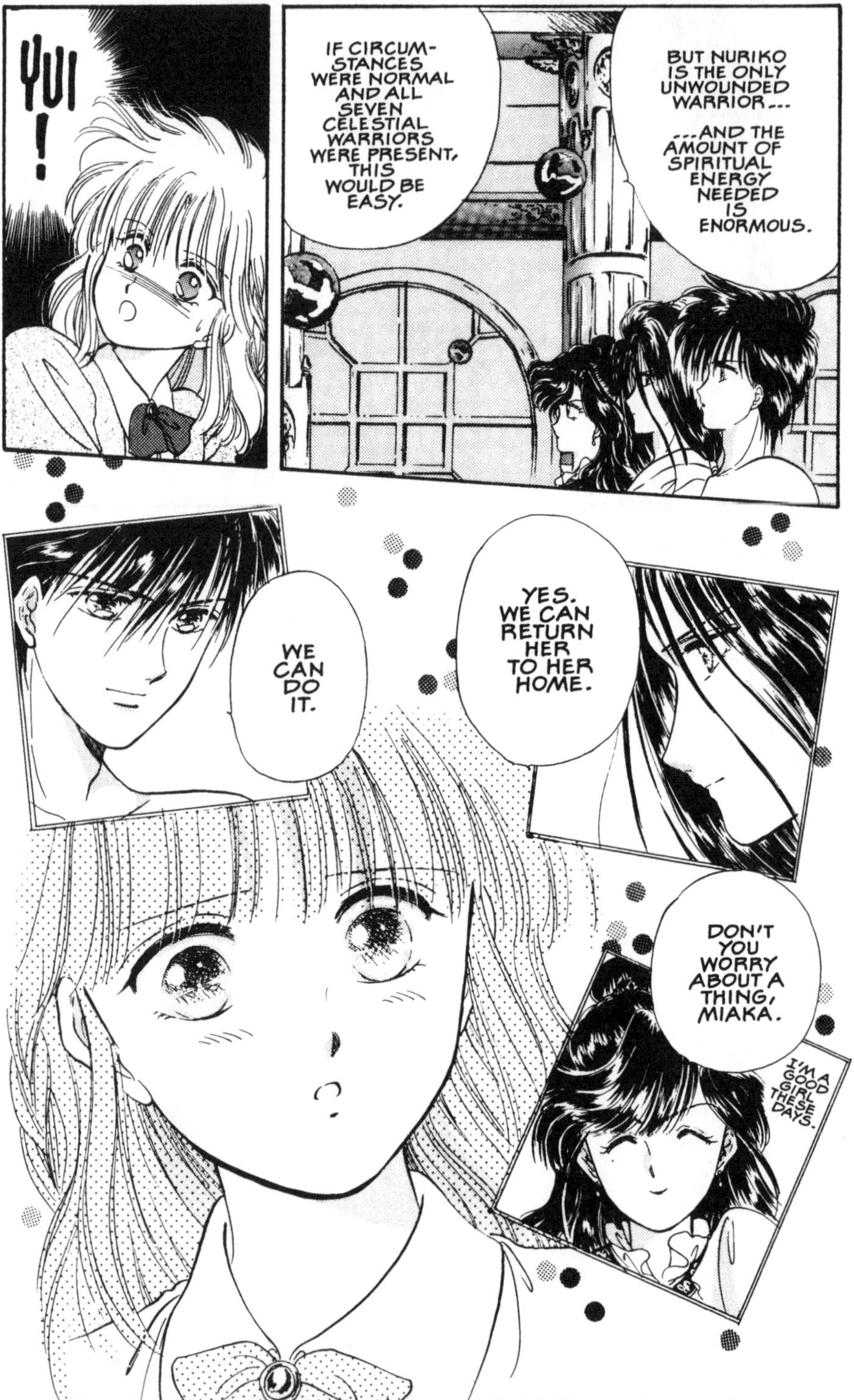
YUI!
IF CIRCUMSTANCES WERE NORMAL AND ALL SEVEN CELESTIAL WARRIORS WERE PRESENT, THIS WOULD BE EASY.
BUT NURIKO IS THE ONLY UNWOUNDED WARRIOR...
...AND THE AMOUNT OF SPIRITUAL ENERGY NEEDED IS ENORMOUS.
WE CAN DO IT.
YES. WE CAN RETURN HER TO HER HOME.
DON'T YOU WORRY ABOUT A THING, MIAKA.
I'M A GOOD GIRL THESE DAYS.

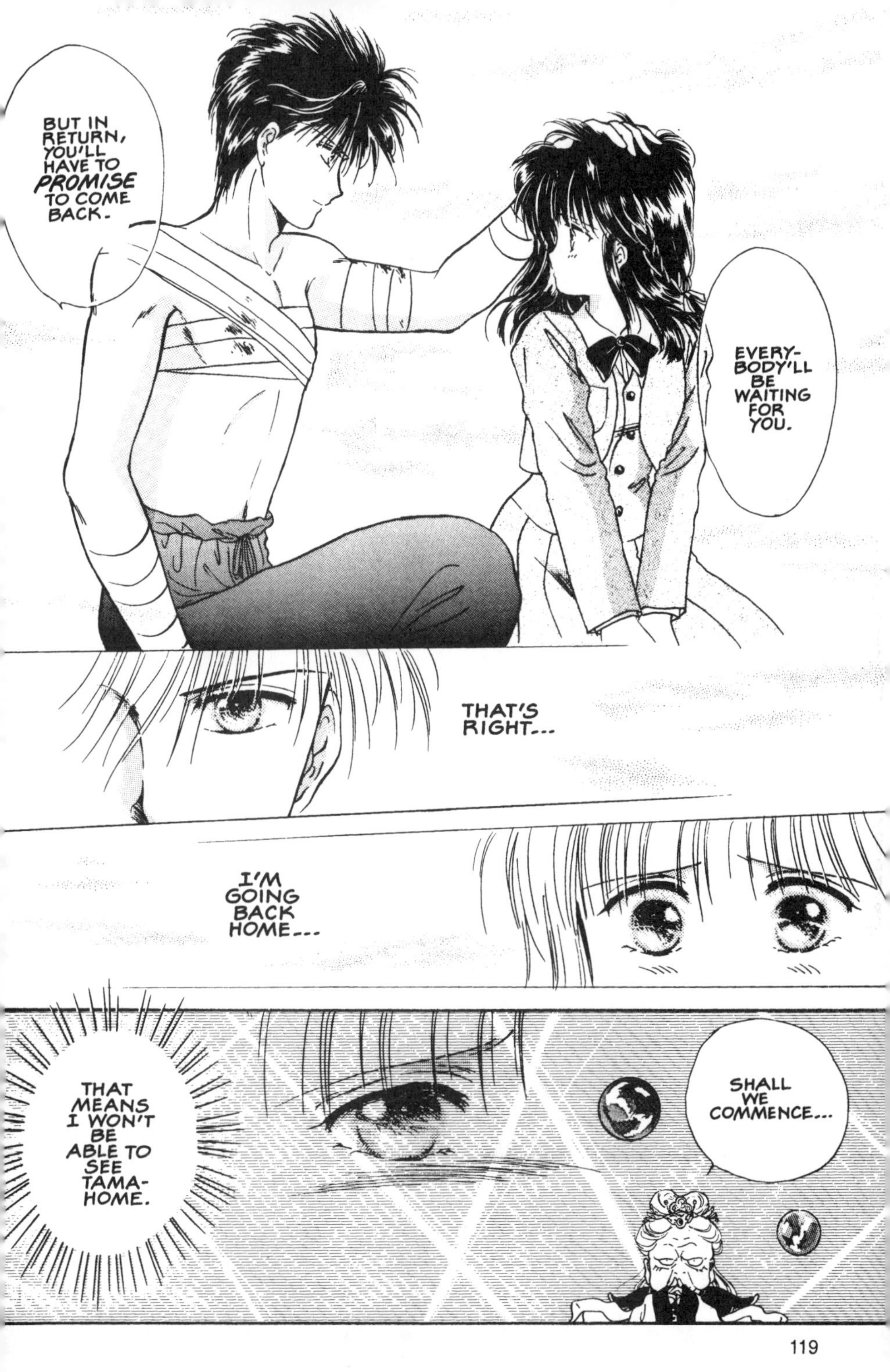

BUT IN RETURN, YOU'LL HAVE TO *PROMISE* TO COME BACK.
EVERYBODY'LL BE WAITING FOR YOU.
THAT'S RIGHT...
I'M GOING BACK HOME...
THAT MEANS I WON'T BE ABLE TO SEE TAMAHOME.
SHALL WE COMMENCE...

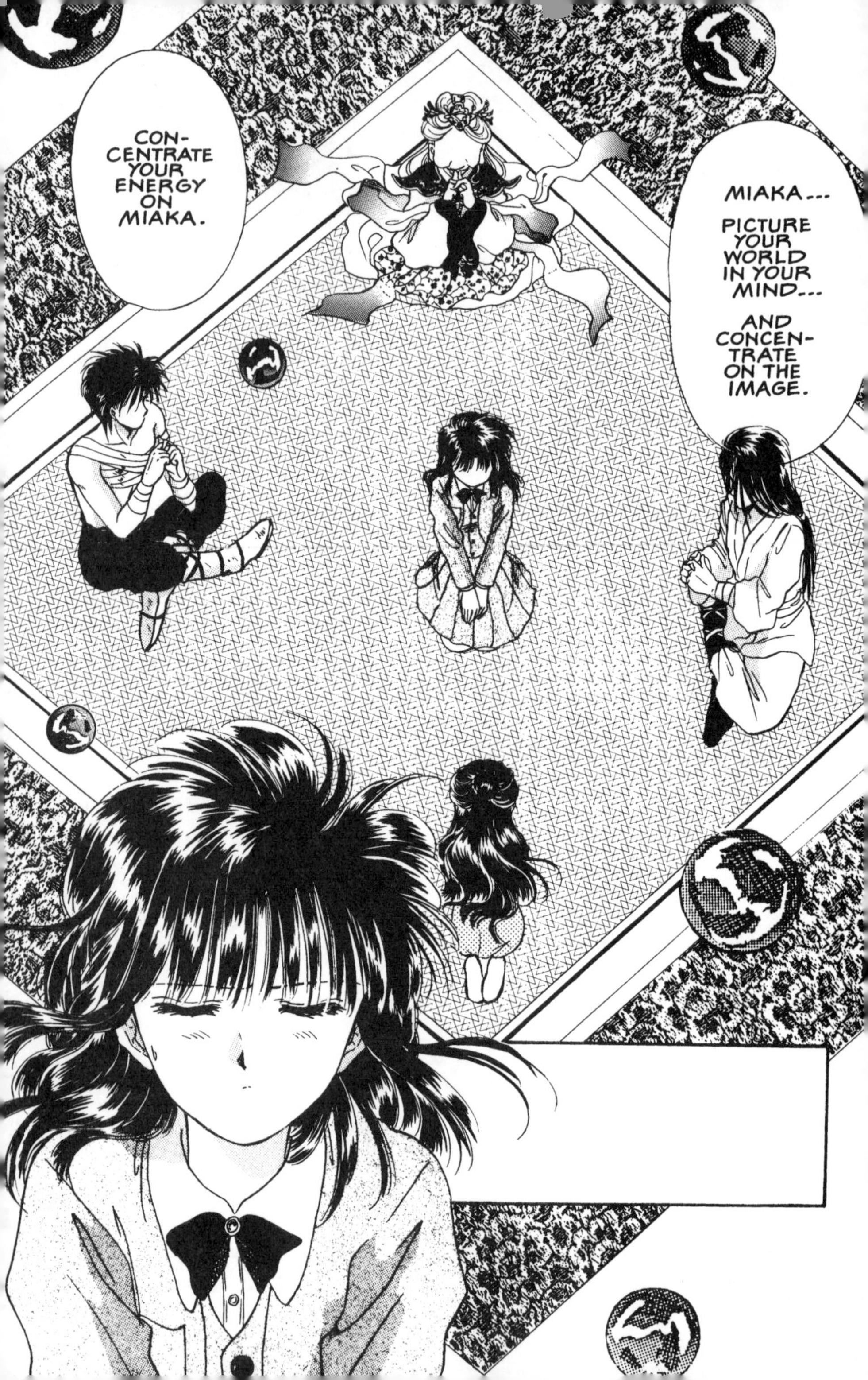
CON-CENTRATE YOUR ENERGY ON MIAKA.
MIAKA...
PICTURE YOUR WORLD IN YOUR MIND...
AND CONCEN-TRATE ON THE IMAGE.

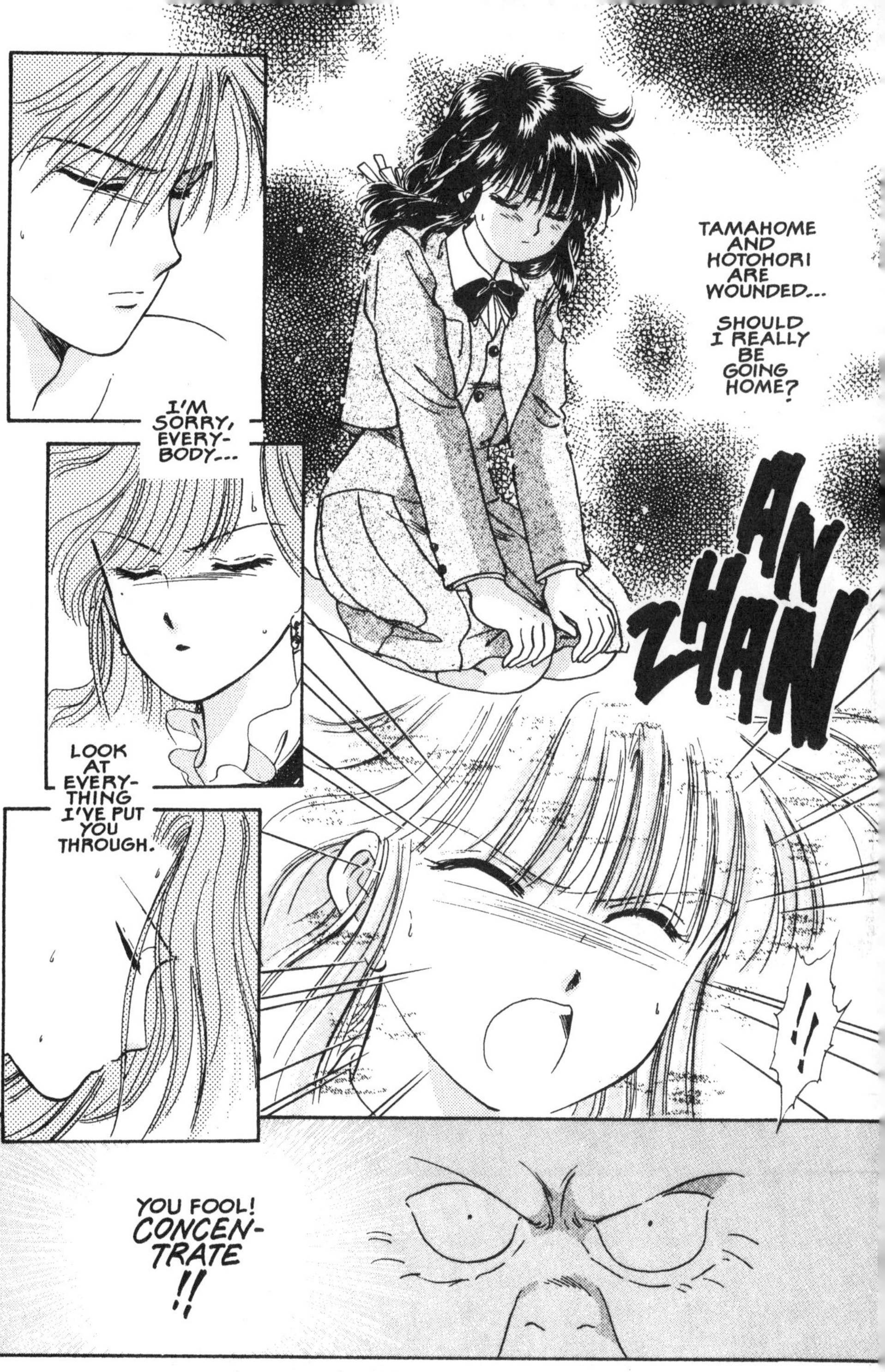
I'M SORRY, EVERYBODY...
LOOK AT EVERYTHING I'VE PUT YOU THROUGH.
TAMAHOME AND HOTOHORI ARE WOUNDED...
SHOULD I REALLY BE GOING HOME?
AN ZHAN
!!
YOU FOOL! CONCENTRATE !!

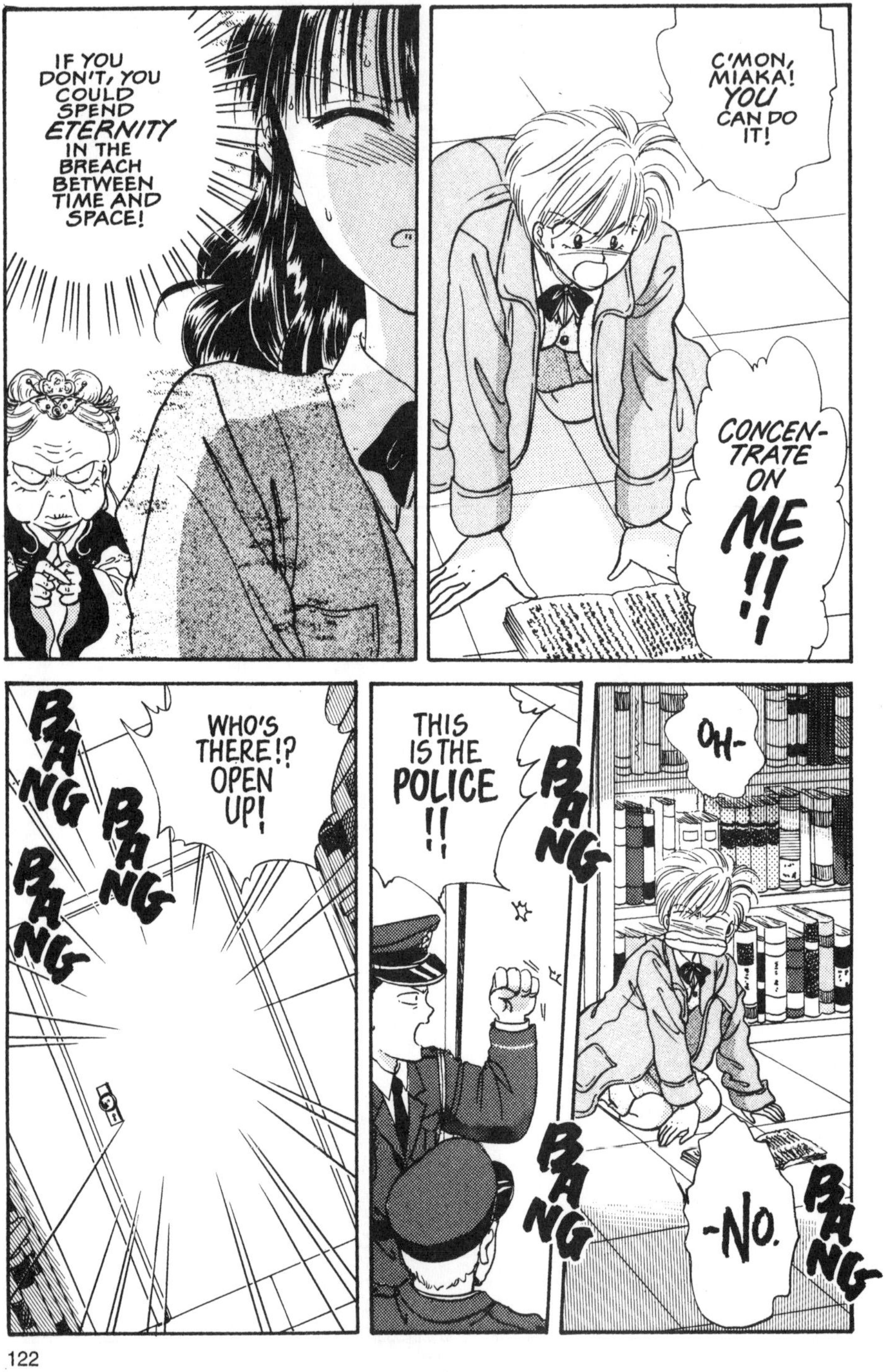
IF YOU DON'T, YOU COULD SPEND ETERNITY IN THE BREACH BETWEEN TIME AND SPACE!
C'MON, MIAKA! YOU CAN DO IT!
CONCENTRATE ON ME!!
BANG BANG BANG
WHO'S THERE!? OPEN UP!
THIS IS THE POLICE!!
BANG
OH-
BANG
-NO.
BANG

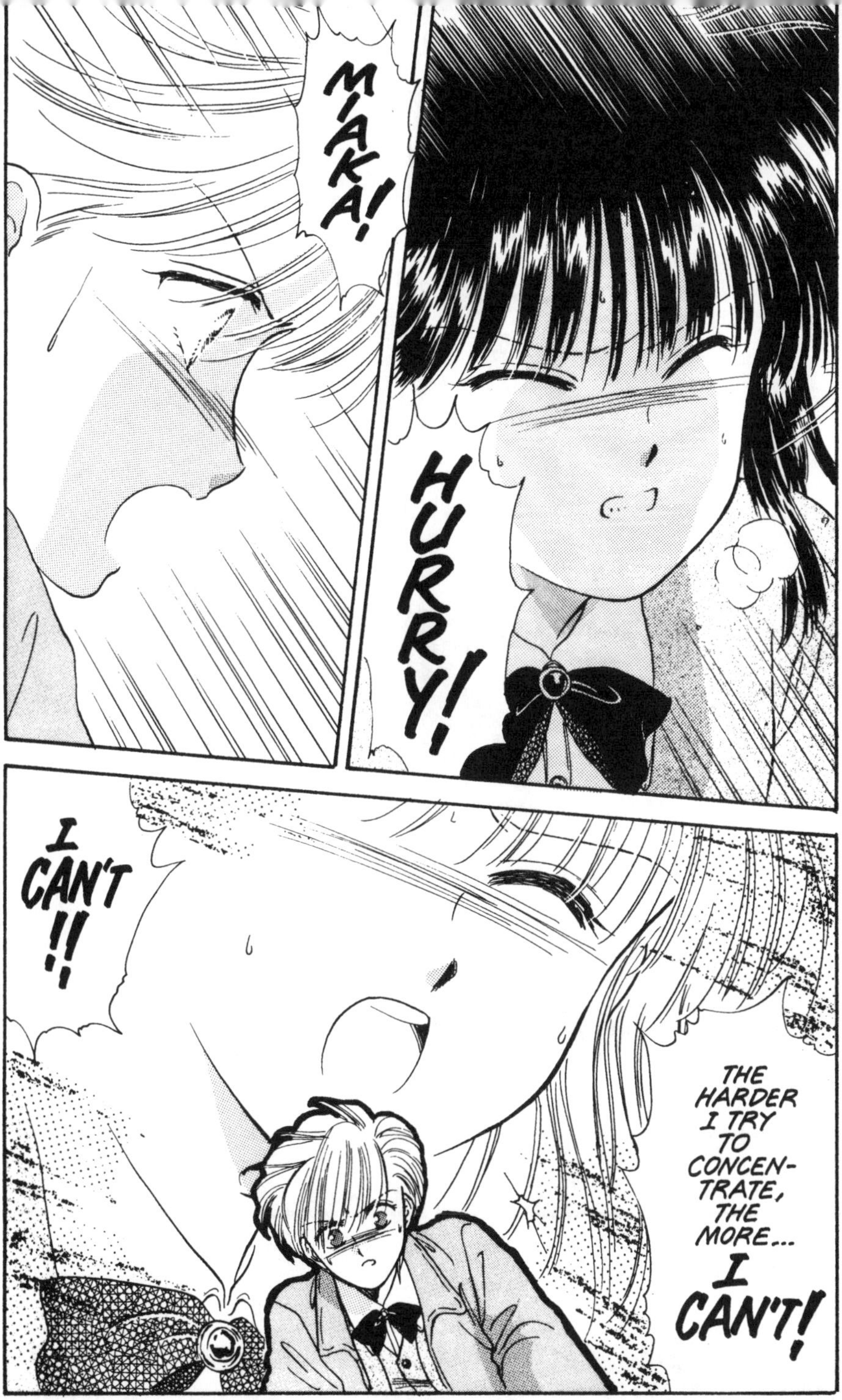
MIAKA!
HURRY!
I CAN'T !!
THE HARDER I TRY TO CONCENTRATE, THE MORE...
I CAN'T!

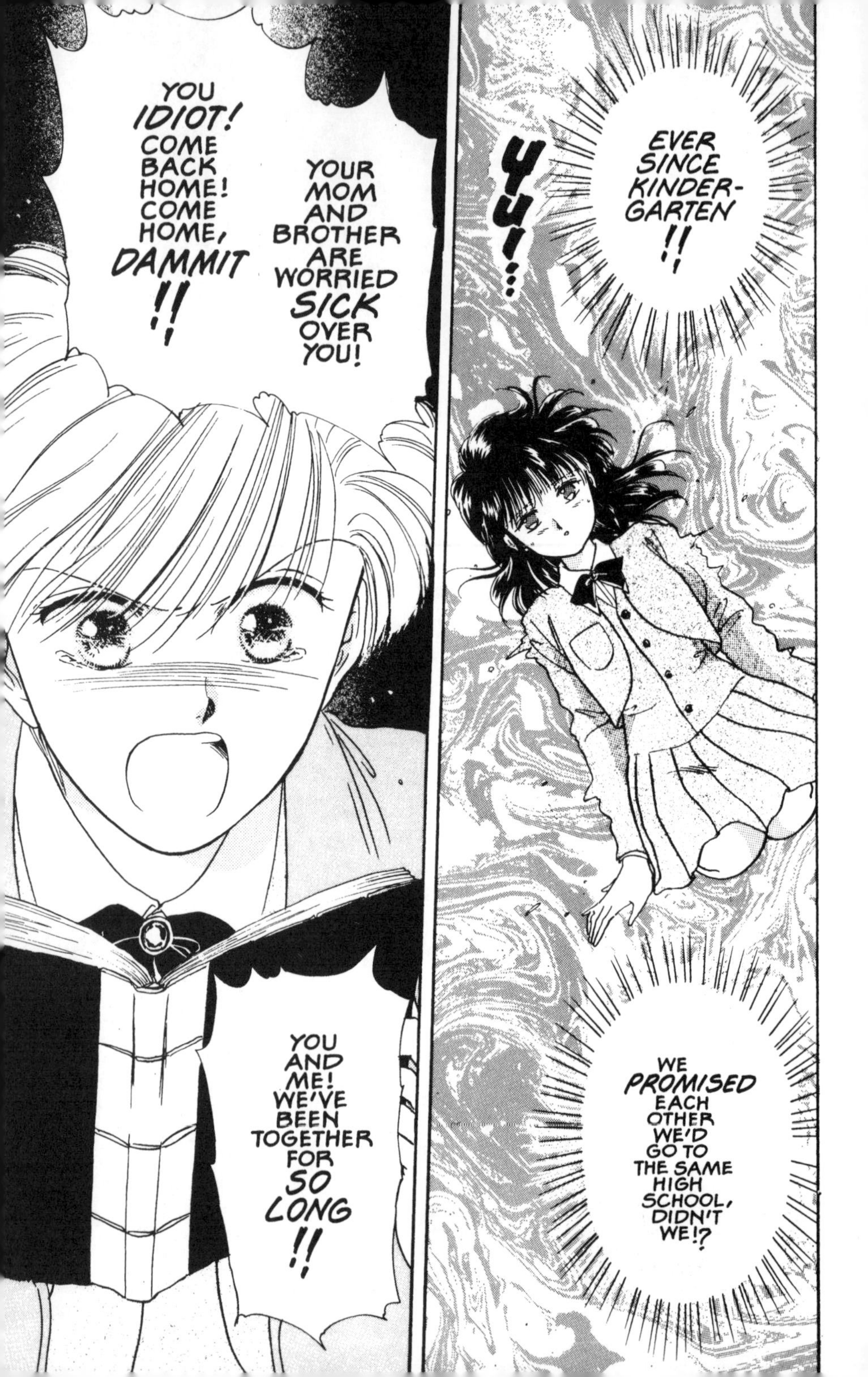
YOU IDIOT! COME BACK HOME! COME HOME, DAMMIT!!
YOUR MOM AND BROTHER ARE WORRIED SICK OVER YOU!
YOU AND ME! WE'VE BEEN TOGETHER FOR SO LONG!!
YUI!..
EVER SINCE KINDER-GARTEN!!
WE PROMISED EACH OTHER WE'D GO TO THE SAME HIGH SCHOOL, DIDN'T WE!?

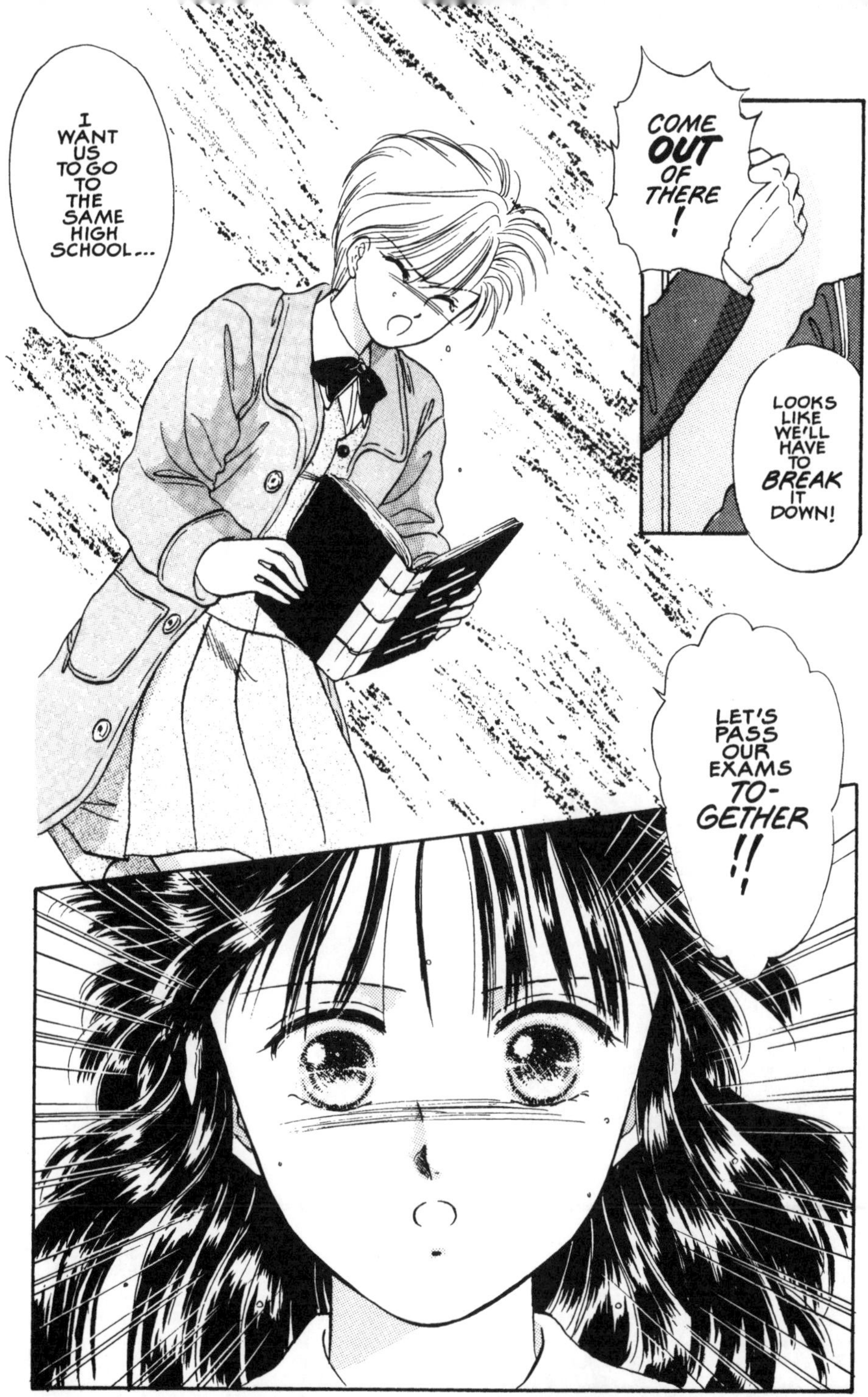
I WANT US TO GO TO THE SAME HIGH SCHOOL...
COME OUT OF THERE!
LOOKS LIKE WE'LL HAVE TO BREAK IT DOWN!
LET'S PASS OUR EXAMS TO-GETHER!!

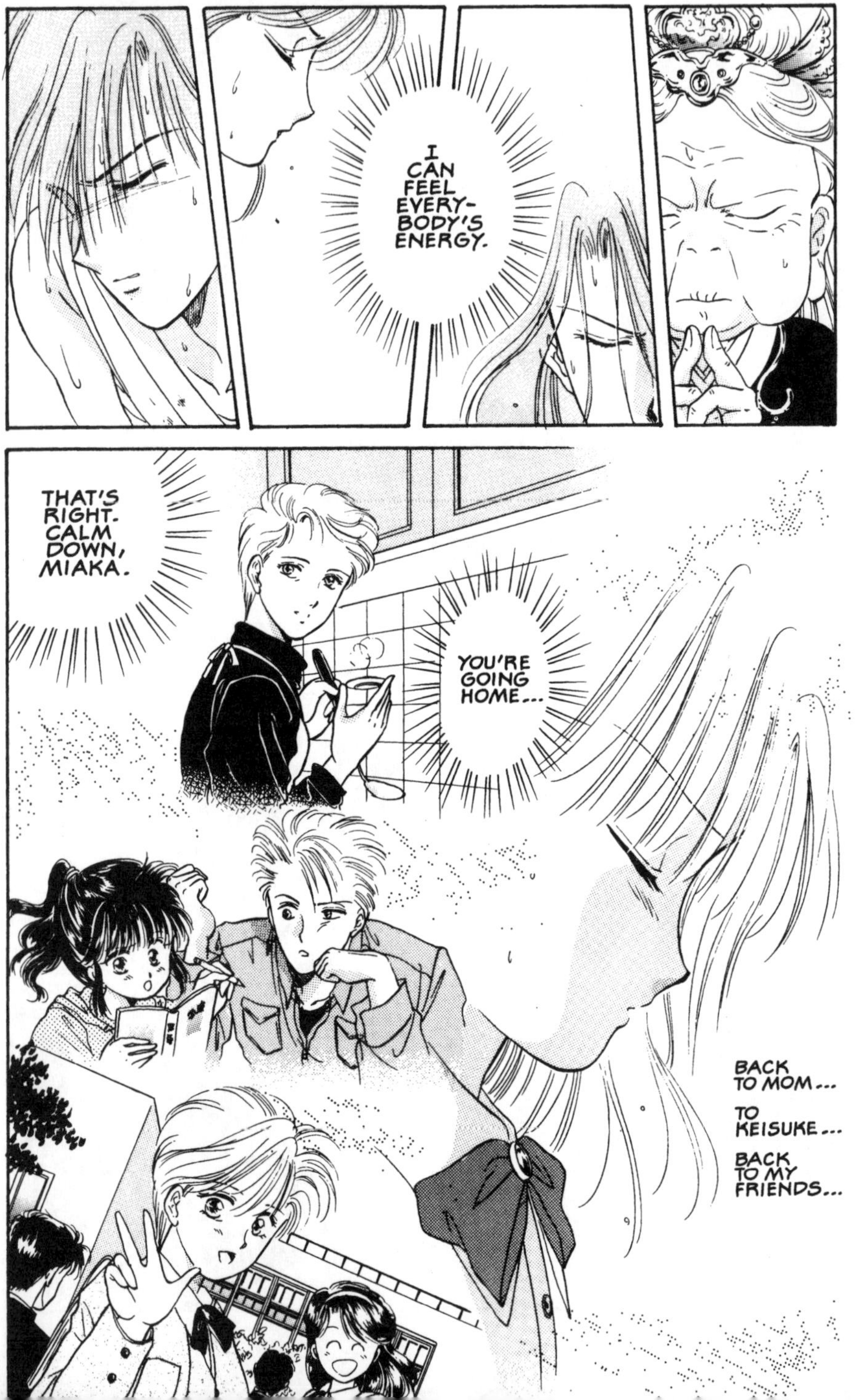
I CAN FEEL EVERY-BODY'S ENERGY.
THAT'S RIGHT. CALM DOWN, MIAKA.
YOU'RE GOING HOME...
BACK TO MOM...
TO KEISUKE...
BACK TO MY FRIENDS...

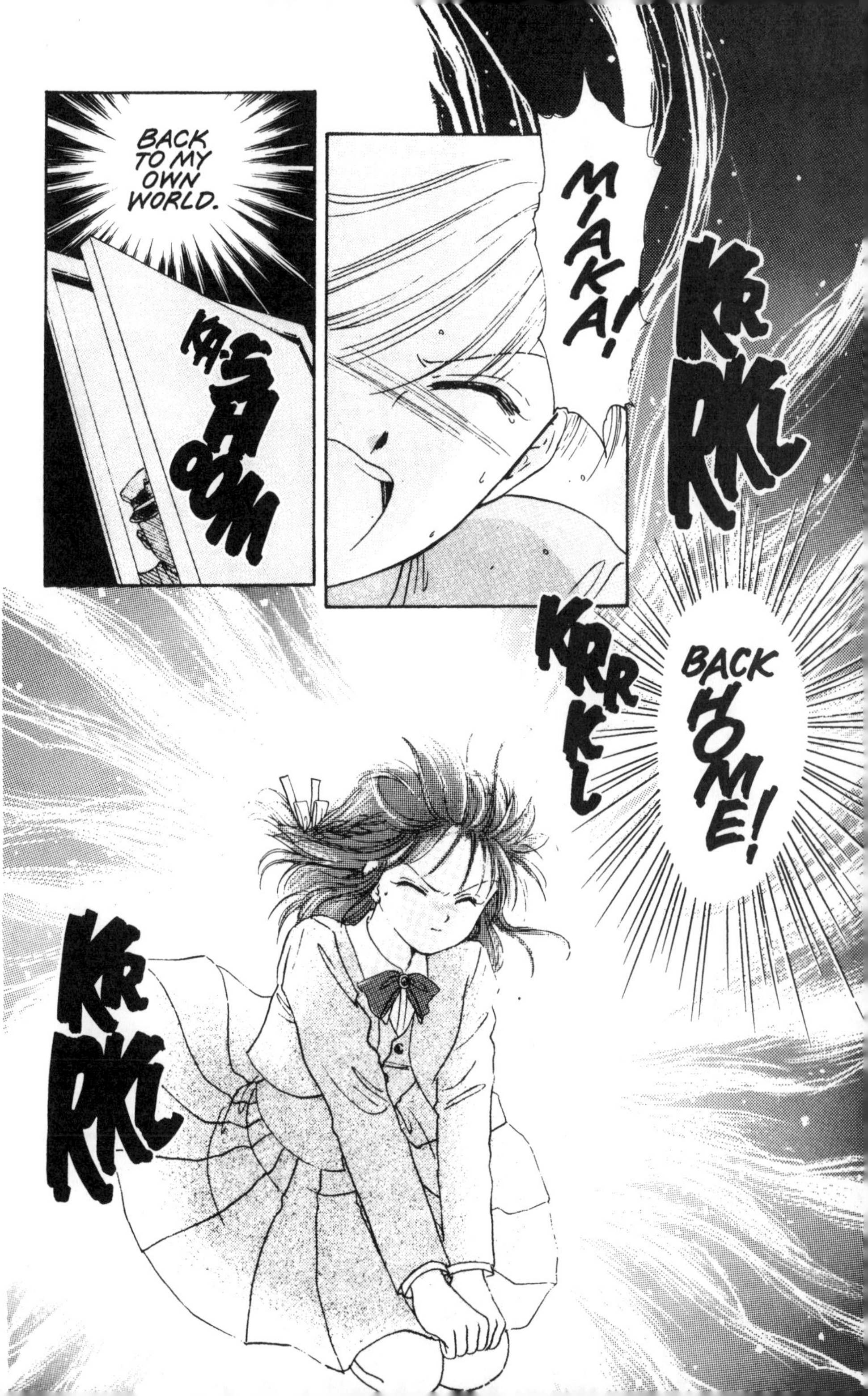
BACK TO MY OWN WORLD.
KA-SHOOM
MIAKA!
KRRKL
KRRKL
KRRKL
BACK HOME!

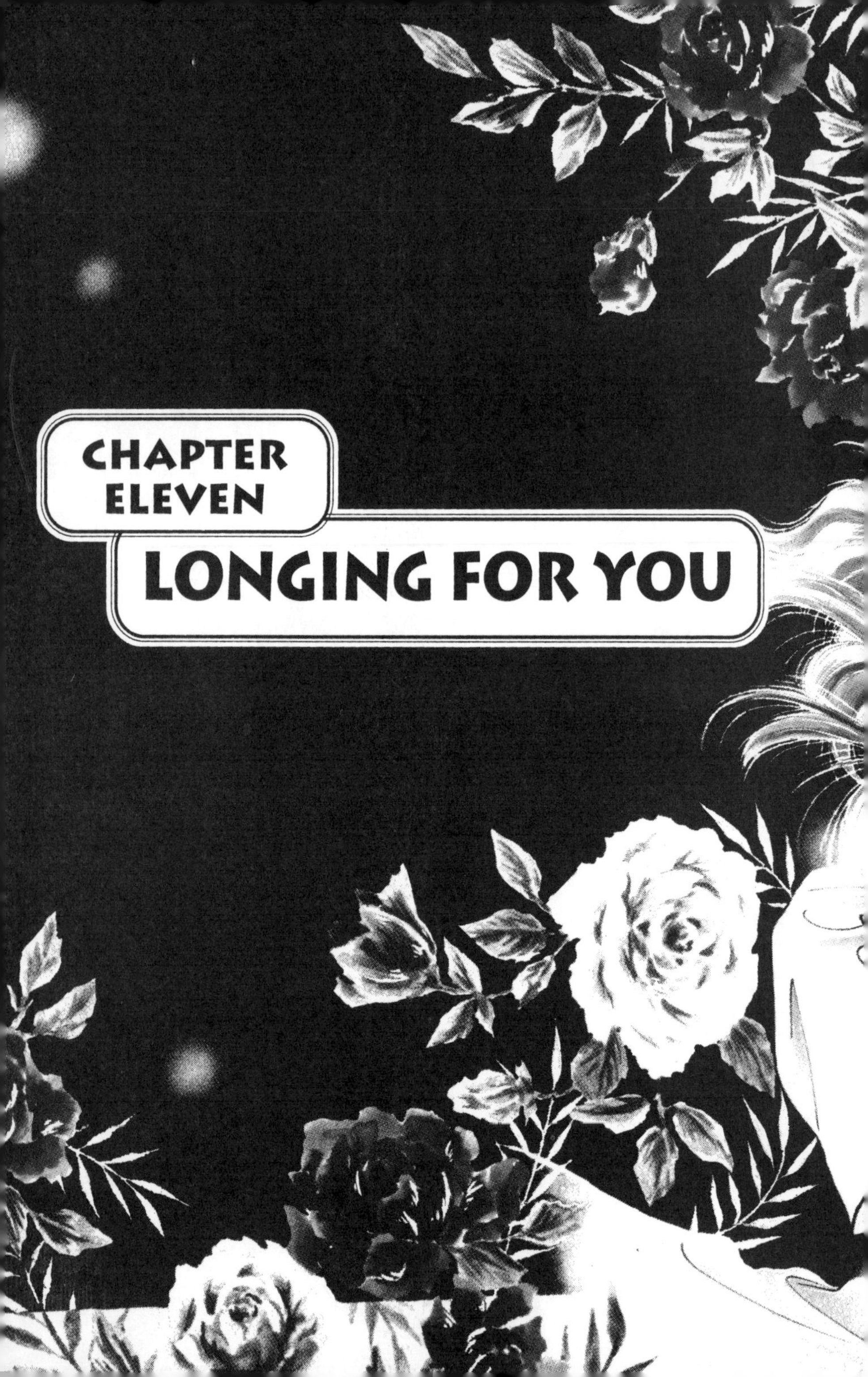
CHAPTER ELEVEN
LONGING FOR YOU

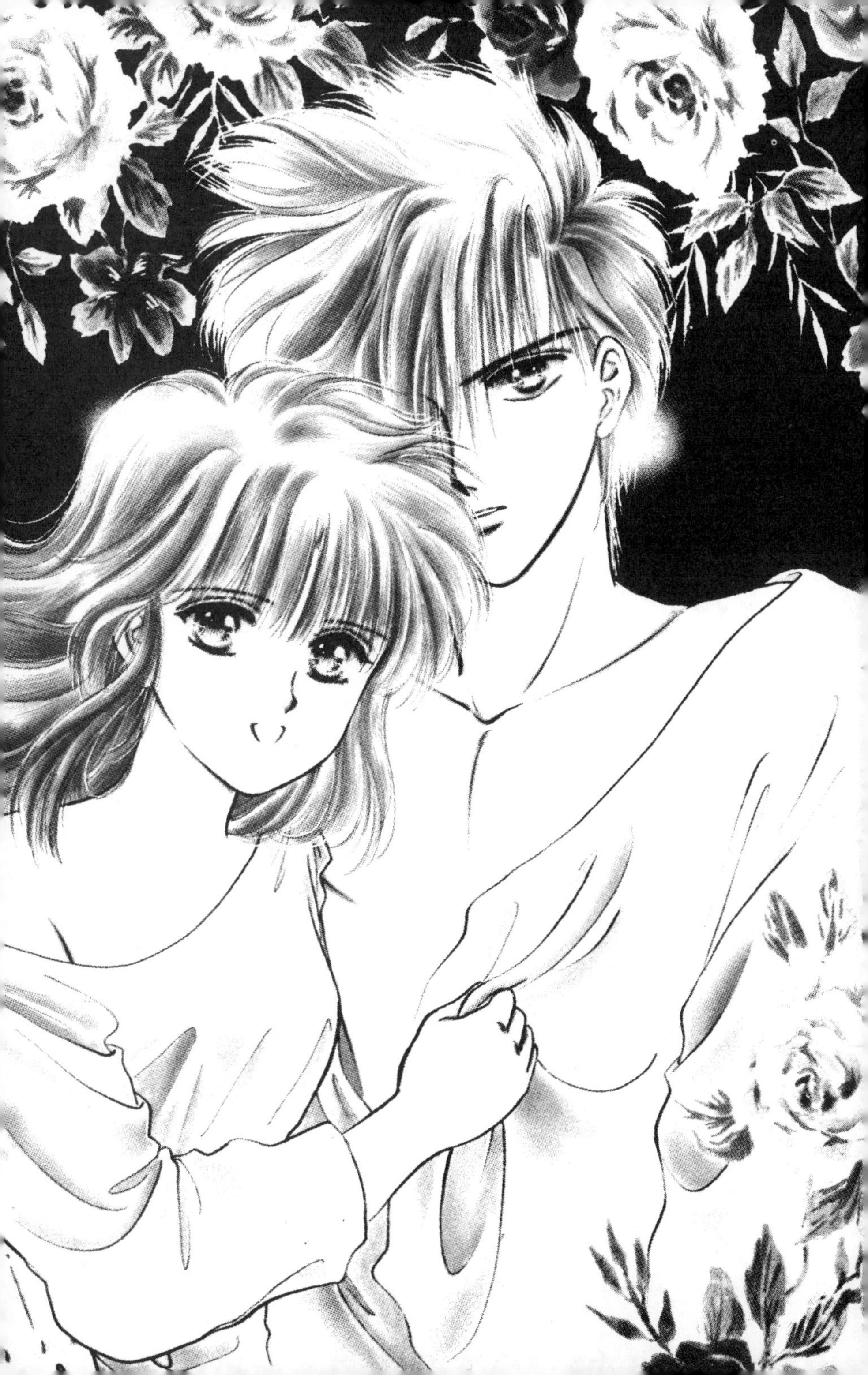

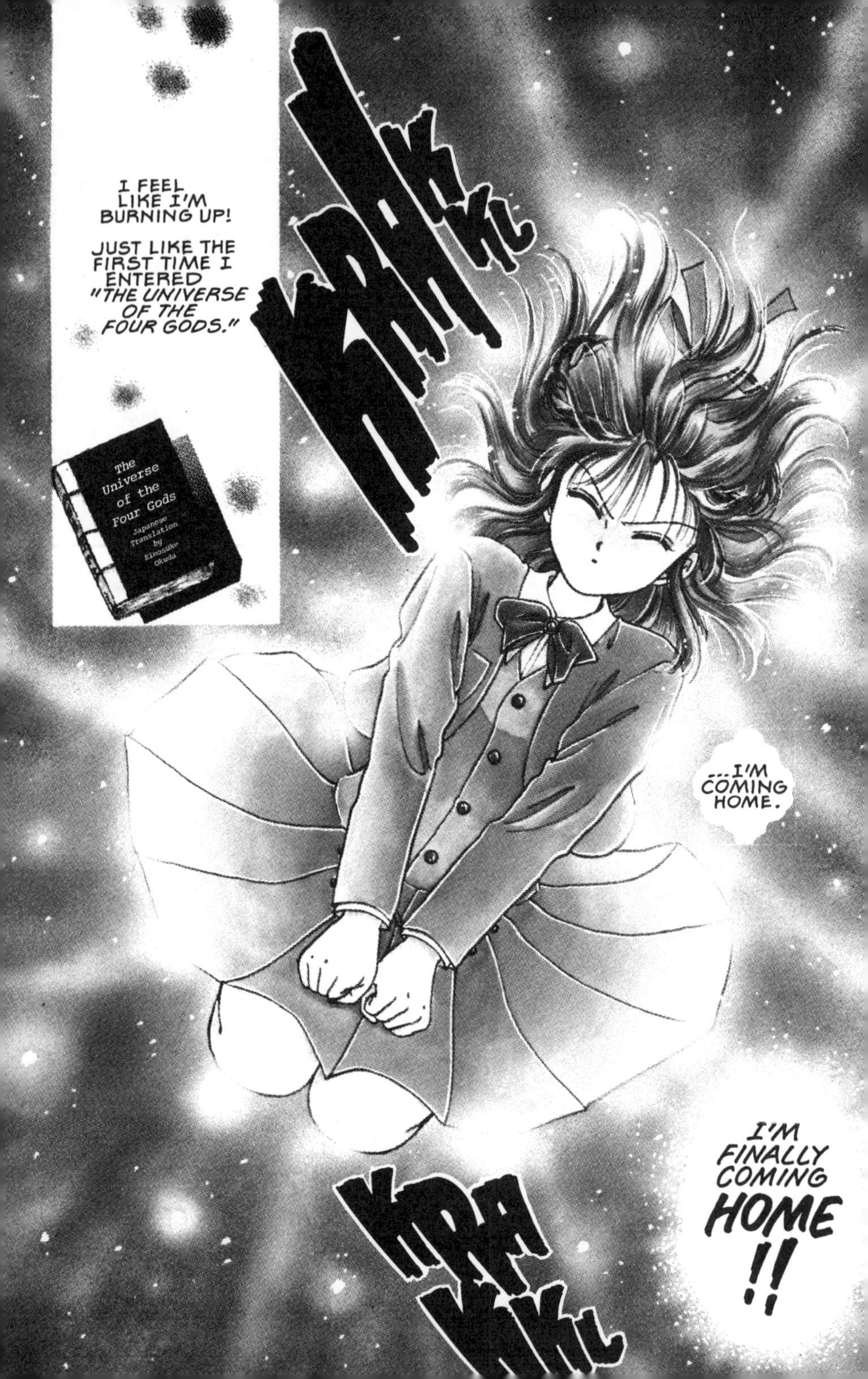

I FEEL LIKE I'M BURNING UP!
JUST LIKE THE FIRST TIME I ENTERED "THE UNIVERSE OF THE FOUR GODS."
The Universe of the Four Gods
Japanese Translation by Einosuke Okuda
...I'M COMING HOME.
I'M FINALLY COMING HOME !!

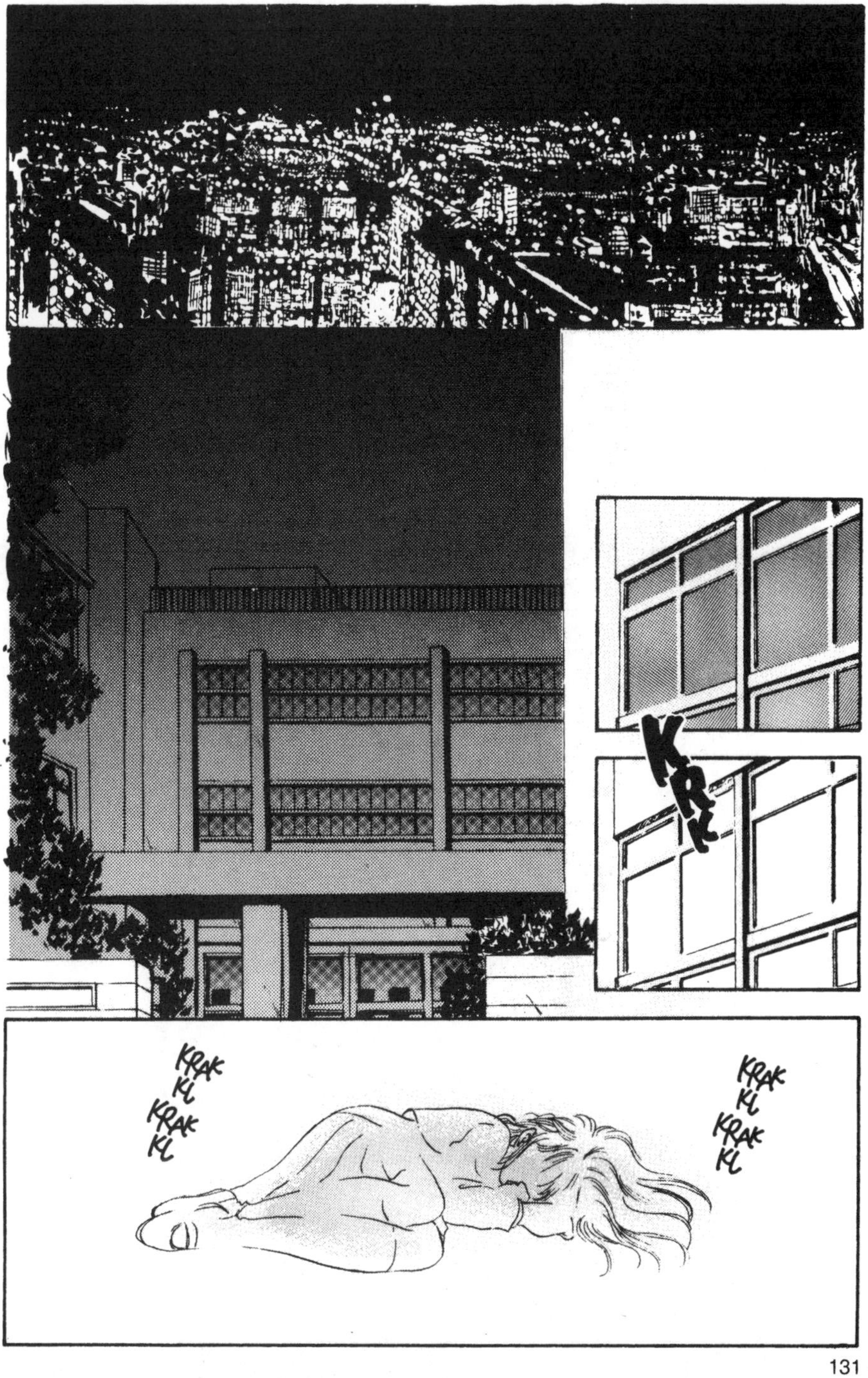
KRK
KRAK
KL
KRAK
KL
KRAK
KL
KRAK
KL

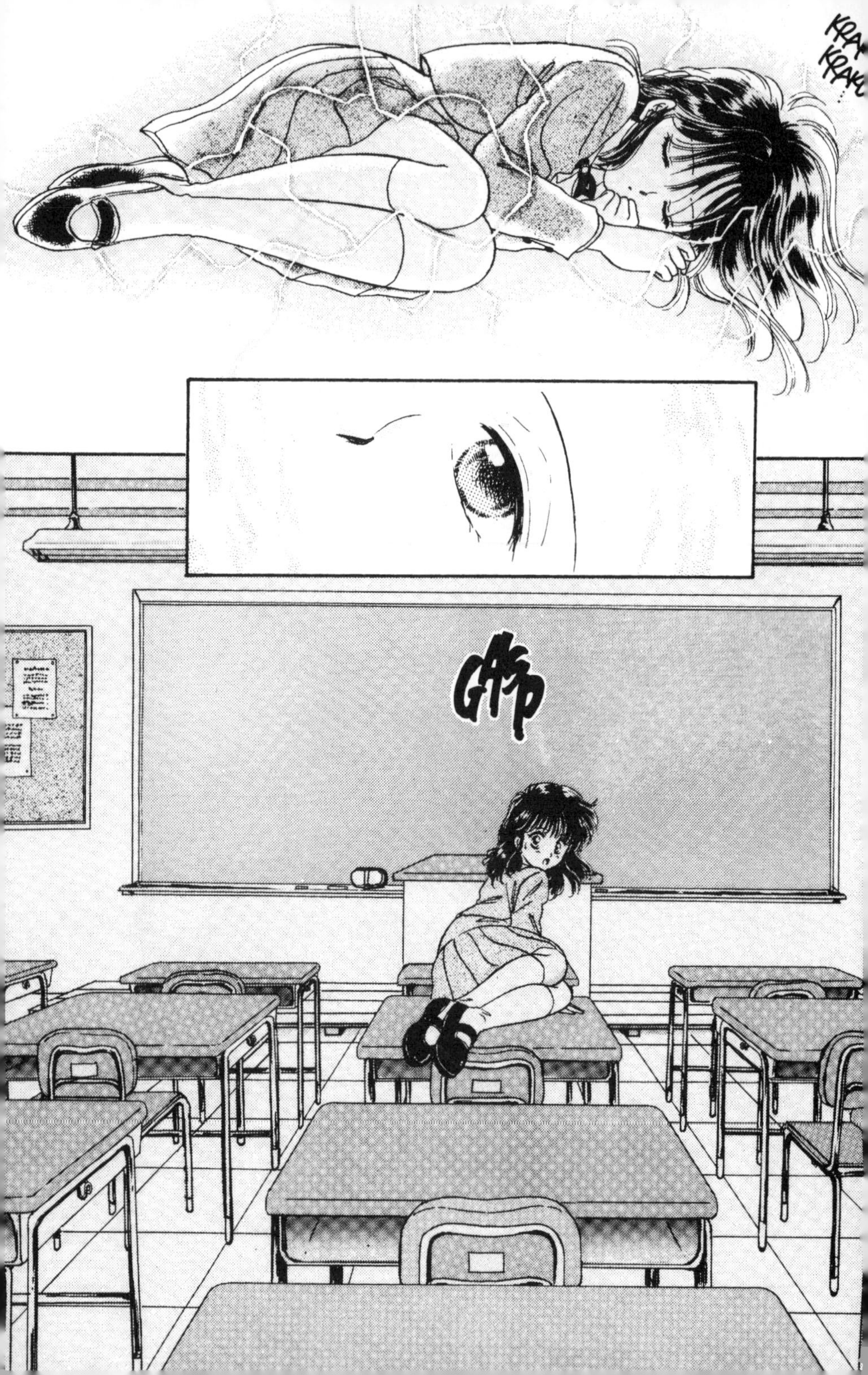
KRAK KRAK...
GASP

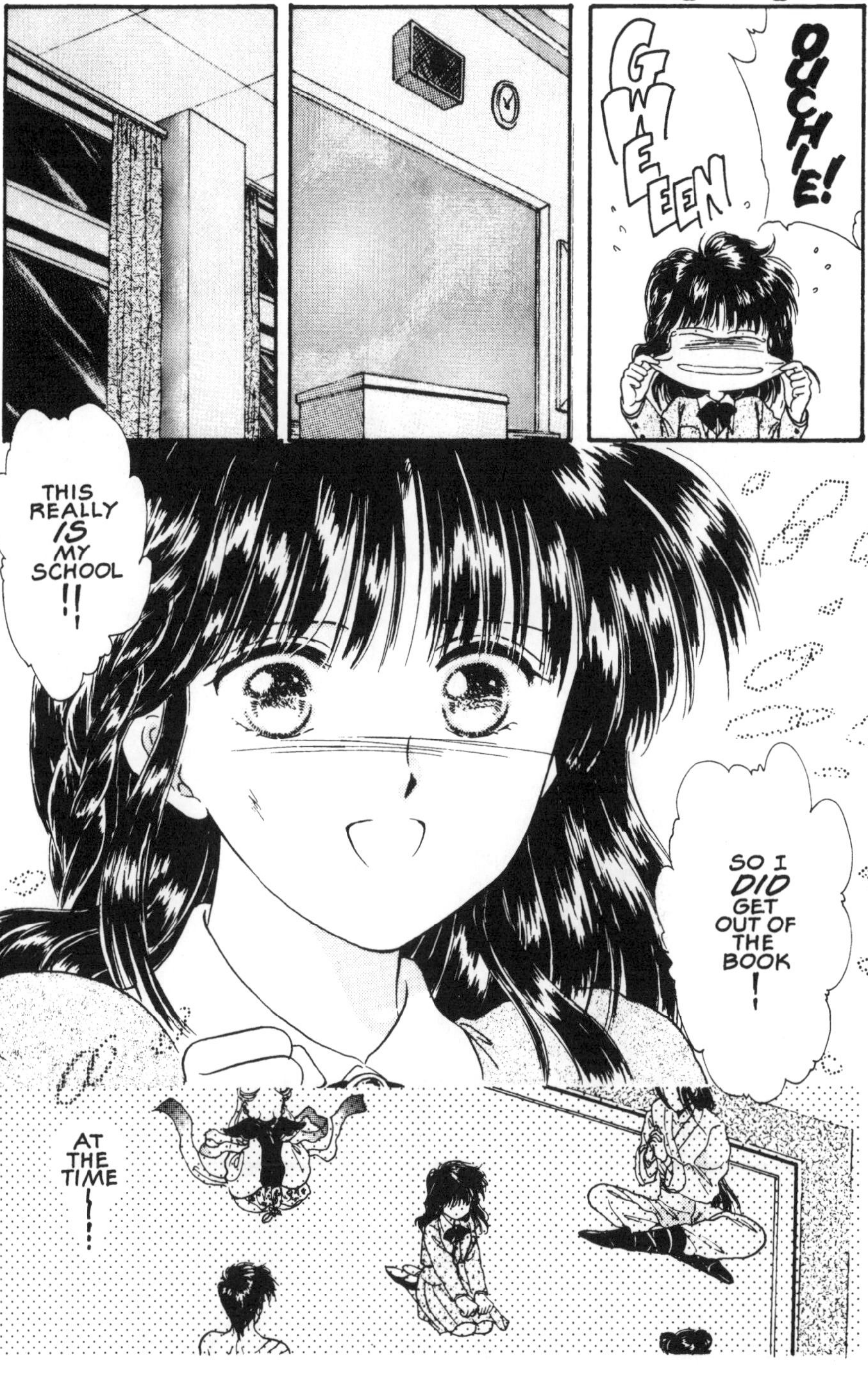
GWEEEEN
OUCHIE!
THIS REALLY *IS* MY SCHOOL !!
SO I *DID* GET OUT OF THE BOOK !
AT THE TIME ---!!

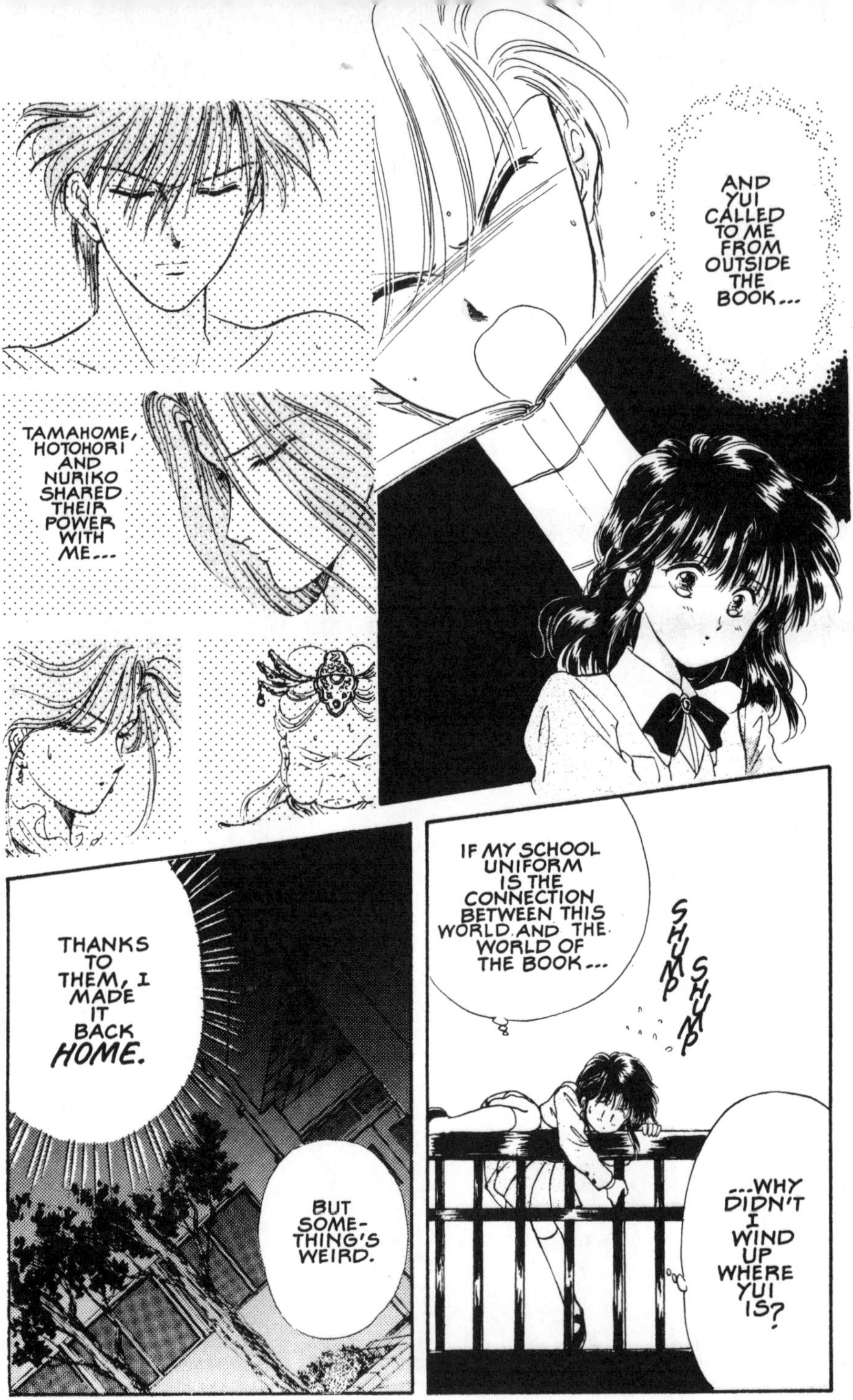
TAMAHOME, HOTOHORI AND NURIKO SHARED THEIR POWER WITH ME...
AND YUI CALLED TO ME FROM OUTSIDE THE BOOK...
THANKS TO THEM, I MADE IT BACK HOME.
BUT SOMETHING'S WEIRD.
IF MY SCHOOL UNIFORM IS THE CONNECTION BETWEEN THIS WORLD AND THE WORLD OF THE BOOK...
SHUMP SHUMP
...WHY DIDN'T I WIND UP WHERE YUI IS?

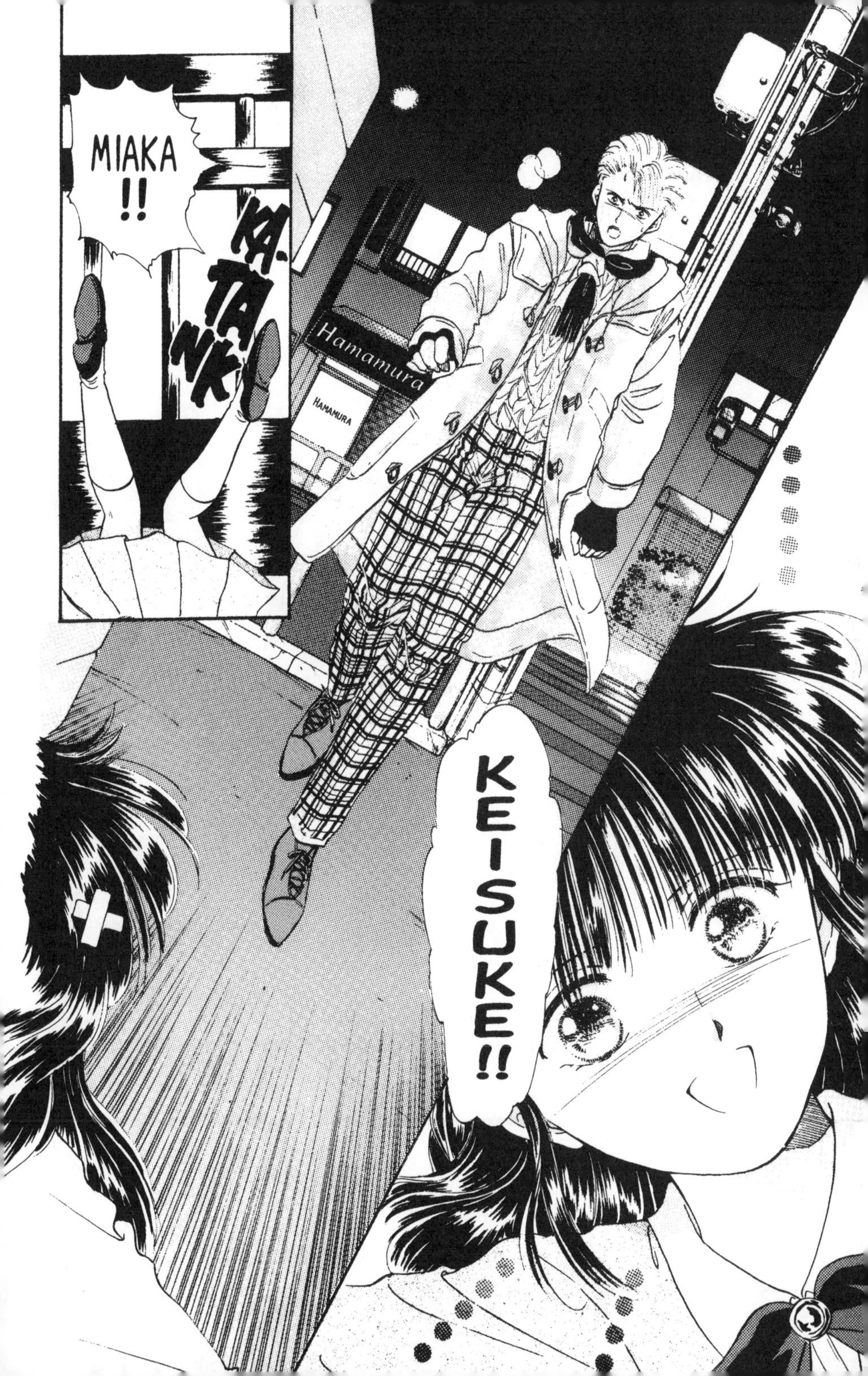
MIAKA!!
KA-TANK
Hamamura
HAMAMURA
KEISUKE!!

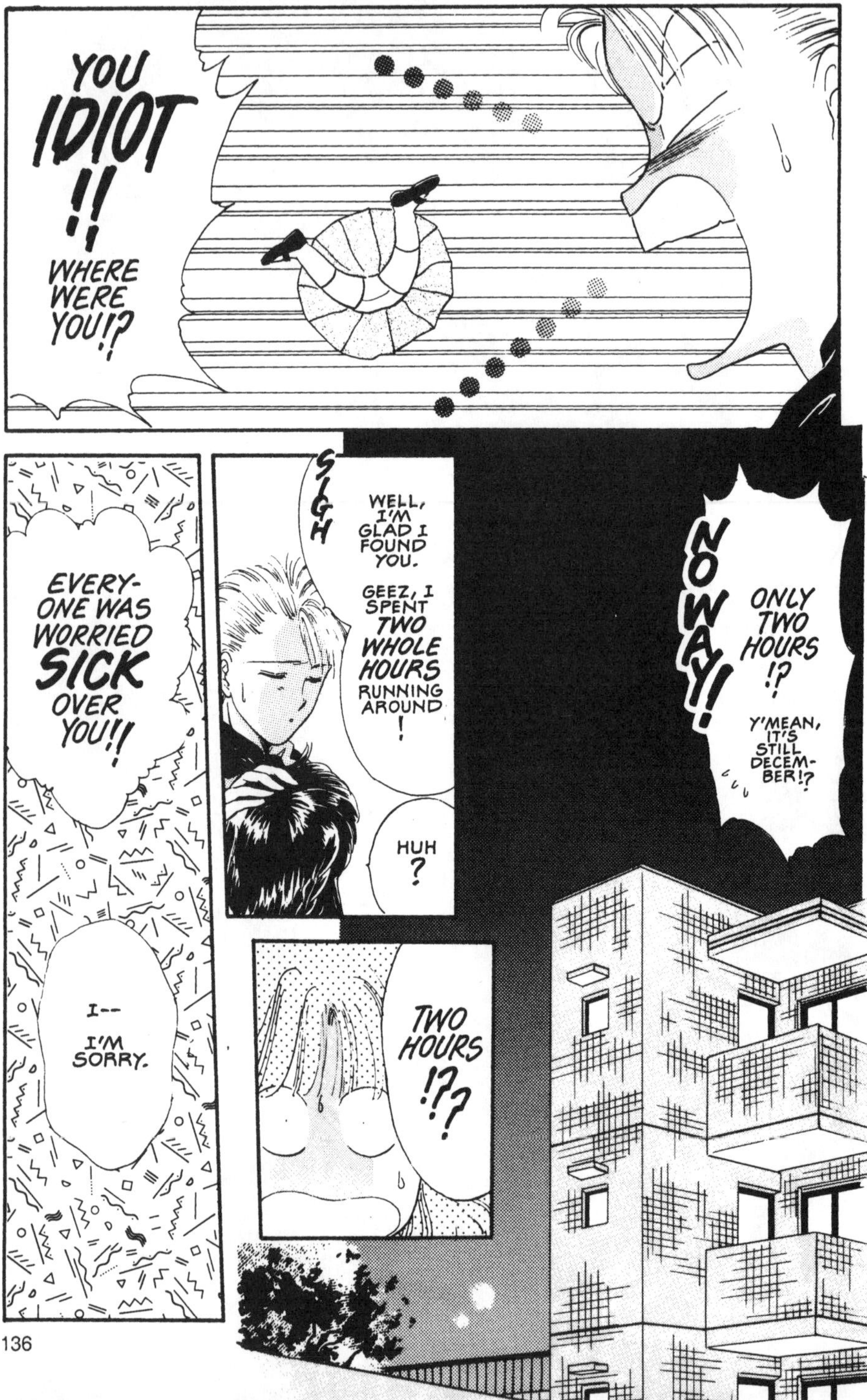

YOU IDIOT!!
WHERE WERE YOU!?
EVERY-ONE WAS WORRIED SICK OVER YOU!!
I-- I'M SORRY.
SIGH
WELL, I'M GLAD I FOUND YOU.
GEEZ, I SPENT TWO WHOLE HOURS RUNNING AROUND!
HUH?
TWO HOURS!??
NO WAY!!
ONLY TWO HOURS!?
Y'MEAN, IT'S STILL DECEM-BER!?

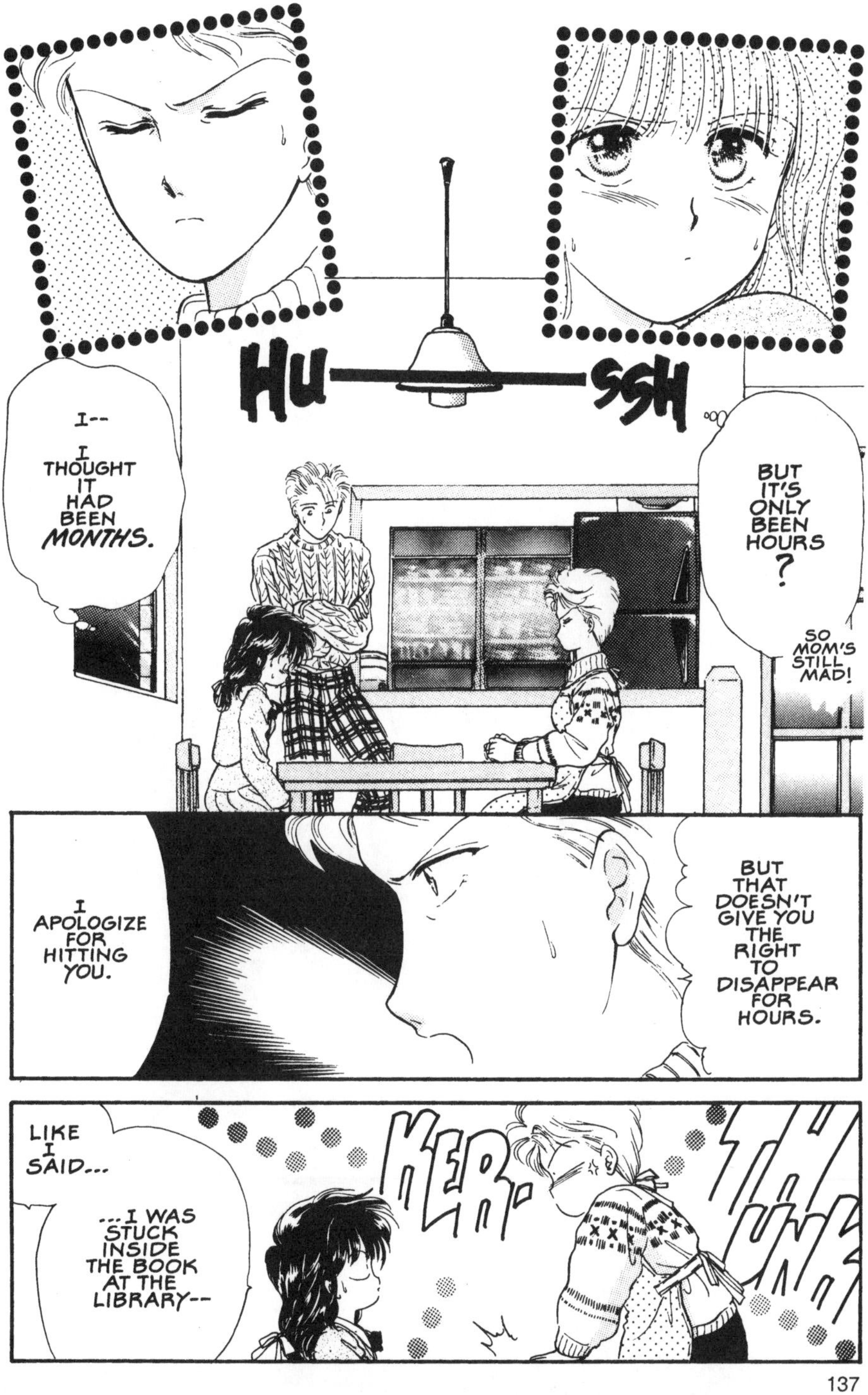
HU—SSH
I-- I THOUGHT IT HAD BEEN MONTHS.
BUT IT'S ONLY BEEN HOURS?
SO MOM'S STILL MAD!
I APOLOGIZE FOR HITTING YOU.
BUT THAT DOESN'T GIVE YOU THE RIGHT TO DISAPPEAR FOR HOURS.
LIKE I SAID...
...I WAS STUCK INSIDE THE BOOK AT THE LIBRARY--
KER-
THUNK

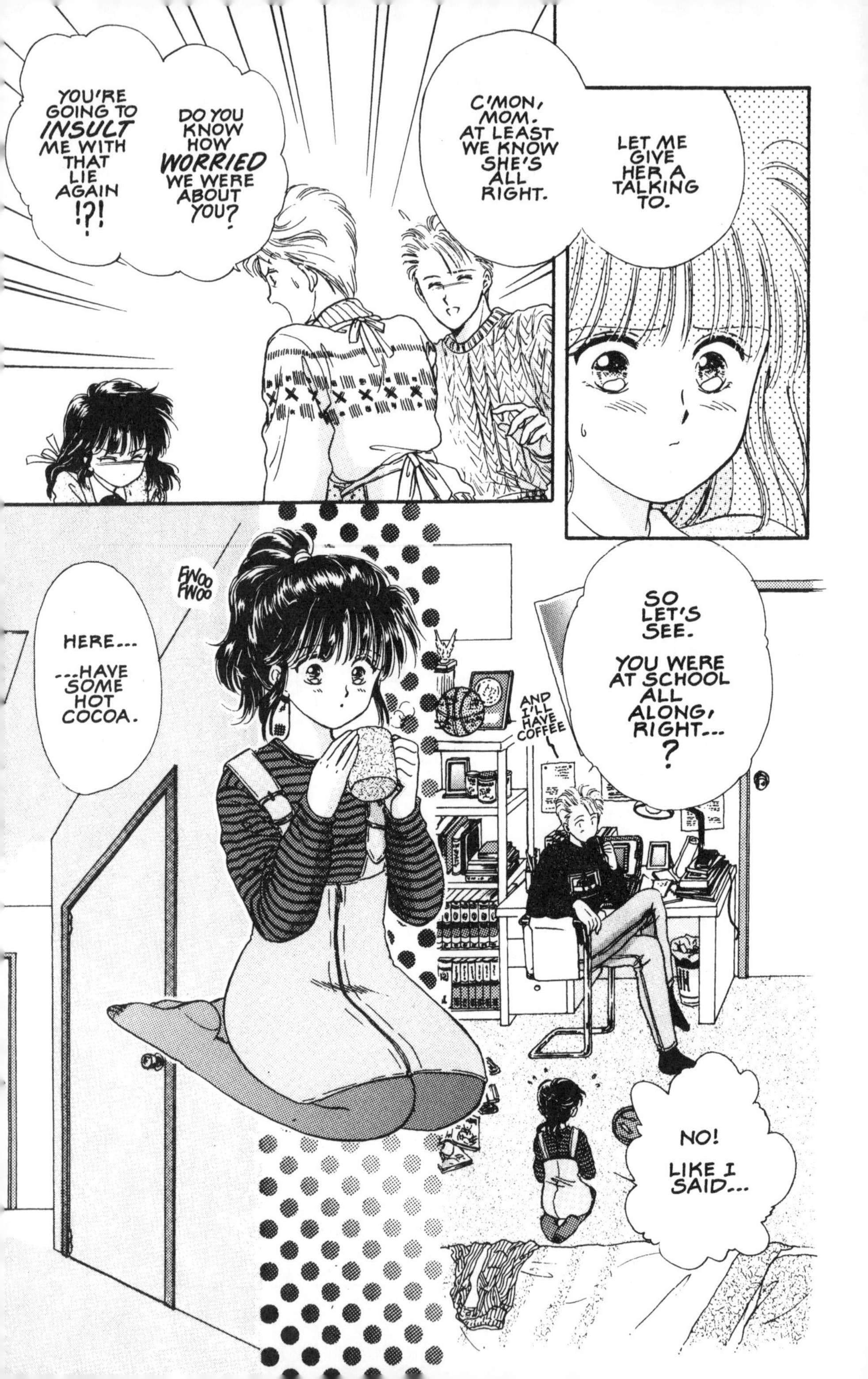

YOU'RE GOING TO INSULT ME WITH THAT LIE AGAIN !?!
DO YOU KNOW HOW WORRIED WE WERE ABOUT YOU?
C'MON, MOM. AT LEAST WE KNOW SHE'S ALL RIGHT.
LET ME GIVE HER A TALKING TO.
FWOO FWOO
HERE...
...HAVE SOME HOT COCOA.
AND I'LL HAVE COFFEE
SO LET'S SEE.
YOU WERE AT SCHOOL ALL ALONG, RIGHT... ?
NO!
LIKE I SAID...

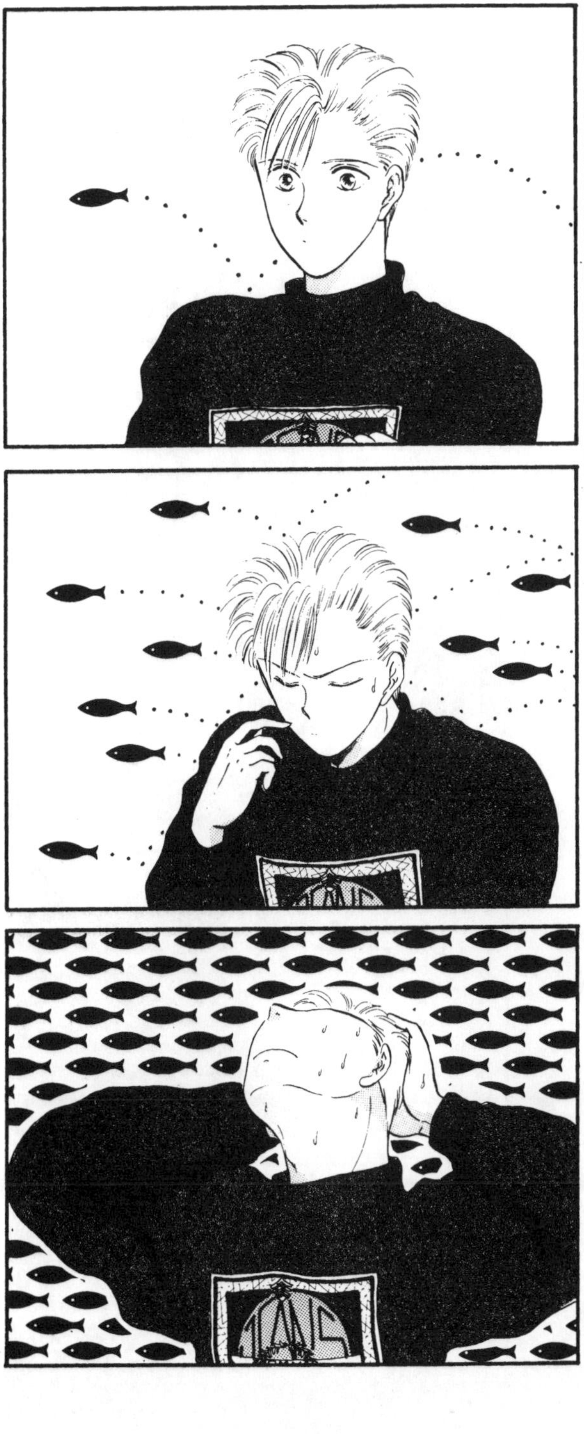

Here's a little confession. I really like Miaka's older brother, Keisuke. If he existed I might really fall for him. His younger classmates would fall for him--he's so nice. He probably would have been the captain of whatever team he was on. If both he and his friend had a crush on the same girl, he would pair the girl up with his friend. He's really fond of his sister (not like she's his pet or anything). My assistant, S., on the other hand is part of the "Tamahome" faction. I gotta say... Yeah, I like Tamahome too, as a manga character. I guess Tamahome's the most popular amongst you readers. I heard that one of the reasons for his popularity is that he resembles Manato in "Prepubescence." S. was totally mortified by this comment, insisting that they had totally different personalities. I suppose Tamahome wouldn't exactly be thrilled to find he was popular because he looked like someone else. Asuka and Miaka are both my main characters and so have the same look, but their personalities are totally different. (But do they look so much alike? Well maybe they do, but should every manga artist have to draw a different face for every new protagonist?) I think that Tamahome is more mature than Manato. Manato's an ordinary urban high-school boy. He DOES have his lighter side, though. Tamahome, on the other hand, had to work hard and mature, so he's more in control of his feelings. He might seem a little insensitive (e.g. when Nuriko says something outrageous), but that's not his true self at all. In fact, he might be more sensitive than Hotohori. He has some powerful emotions kept inside. I've never written a character like him before. Tamahome is really strong, but he might have some profound weaknesses. He seems really upbeat when in fact he has a dark side. He can be emotional and yet be cool. He has a child-like face yet he can be so mature. So S. and I think that he is full of contradictory traits...

So that's what he's like!

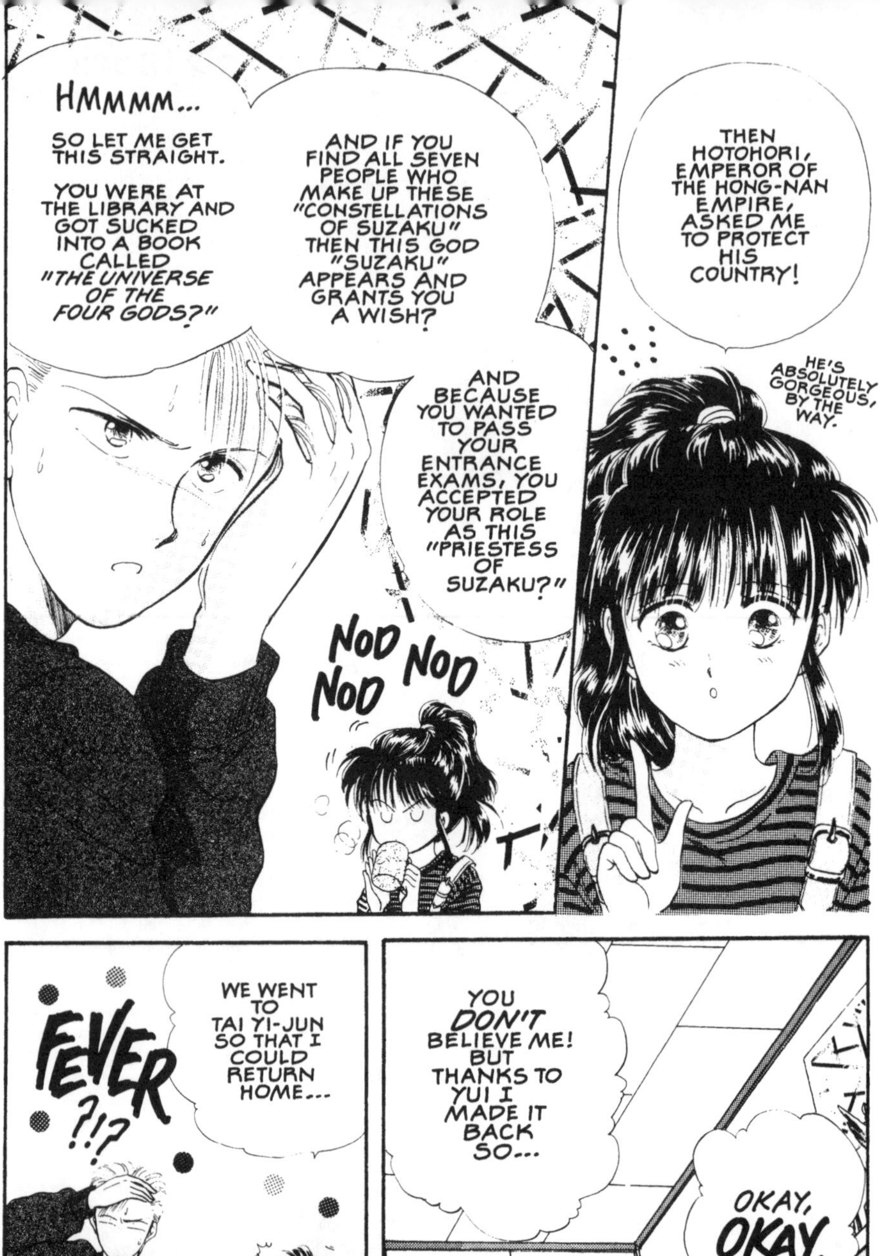
HMMMM...
SO LET ME GET THIS STRAIGHT.
YOU WERE AT THE LIBRARY AND GOT SUCKED INTO A BOOK CALLED "THE UNIVERSE OF THE FOUR GODS?"
AND IF YOU FIND ALL SEVEN PEOPLE WHO MAKE UP THESE "CONSTELLATIONS OF SUZAKU" THEN THIS GOD "SUZAKU" APPEARS AND GRANTS YOU A WISH?
AND BECAUSE YOU WANTED TO PASS YOUR ENTRANCE EXAMS, YOU ACCEPTED YOUR ROLE AS THIS "PRIESTESS OF SUZAKU?"
NOD NOD NOD
THEN HOTOHORI, EMPEROR OF THE HONG-NAN EMPIRE, ASKED ME TO PROTECT HIS COUNTRY!
HE'S ABSOLUTELY GORGEOUS, BY THE WAY.
WE WENT TO TAI YI-JUN SO THAT I COULD RETURN HOME...
FEVER ?!?
YOU DON'T BELIEVE ME! BUT THANKS TO YUI I MADE IT BACK SO...
OKAY, OKAY.

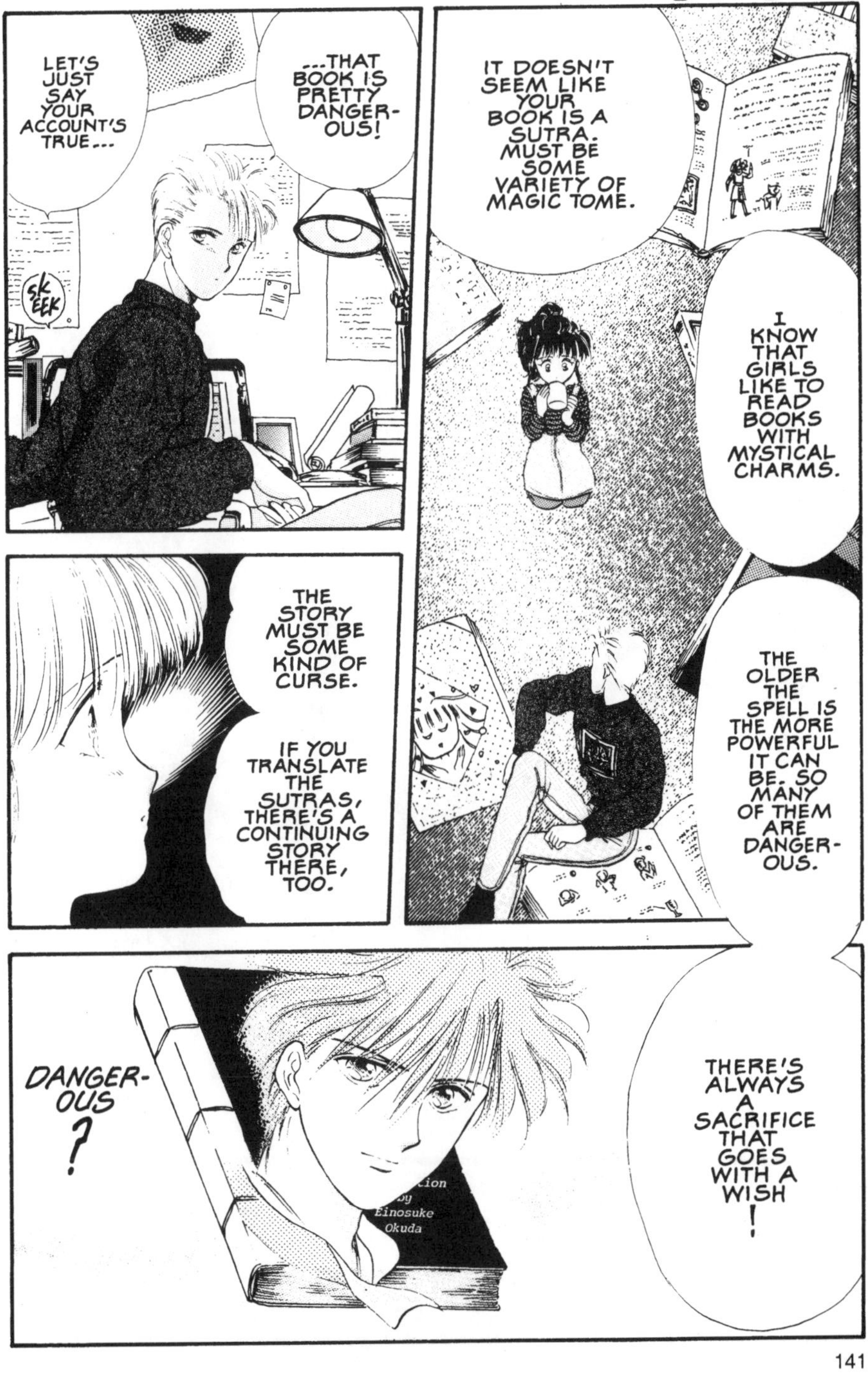
LET'S JUST SAY YOUR ACCOUNT'S TRUE...
...THAT BOOK IS PRETTY DANGER-OUS!
SK EEK
THE STORY MUST BE SOME KIND OF CURSE.
IF YOU TRANSLATE THE SUTRAS, THERE'S A CONTINUING STORY THERE, TOO.
IT DOESN'T SEEM LIKE YOUR BOOK IS A SUTRA. MUST BE SOME VARIETY OF MAGIC TOME.
I KNOW THAT GIRLS LIKE TO READ BOOKS WITH MYSTICAL CHARMS.
THE OLDER THE SPELL IS THE MORE POWERFUL IT CAN BE. SO MANY OF THEM ARE DANGER-OUS.
DANGER-OUS?
Einosuke Okuda
THERE'S ALWAYS A SACRIFICE THAT GOES WITH A WISH!

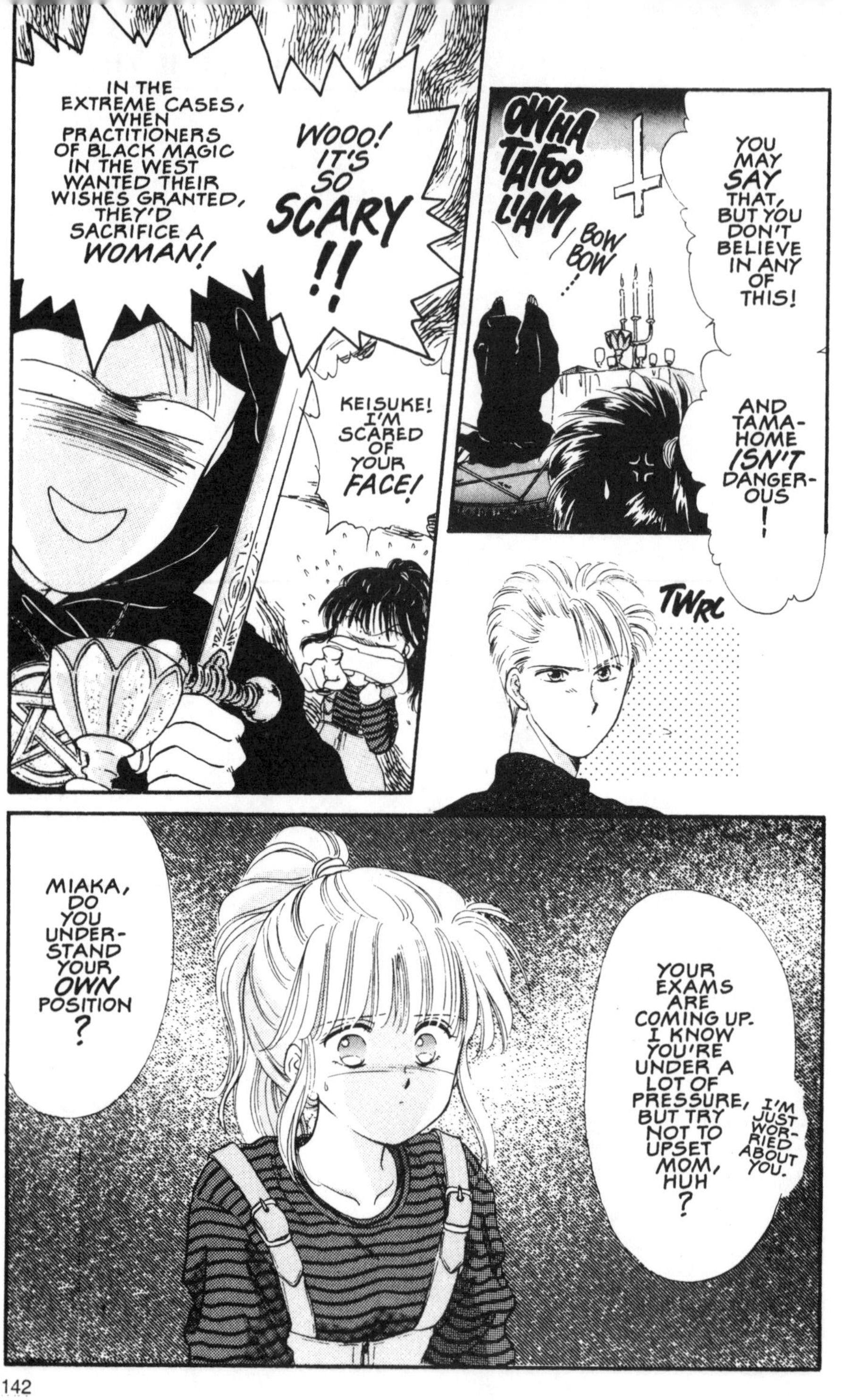
IN THE EXTREME CASES, WHEN PRACTITIONERS OF BLACK MAGIC IN THE WEST WANTED THEIR WISHES GRANTED, THEY'D SACRIFICE A WOMAN!
WOOO! IT'S SO SCARY!!
KEISUKE! I'M SCARED OF YOUR FACE!
OWHA TAFOO LIAM
BOW BOW...
YOU MAY SAY THAT, BUT YOU DON'T BELIEVE IN ANY OF THIS!
AND TAMAHOME ISN'T DANGEROUS!
TWRL
MIAKA, DO YOU UNDERSTAND YOUR OWN POSITION?
YOUR EXAMS ARE COMING UP. I KNOW YOU'RE UNDER A LOT OF PRESSURE, BUT TRY NOT TO UPSET MOM, HUH?
I'M JUST WORRIED ABOUT YOU.

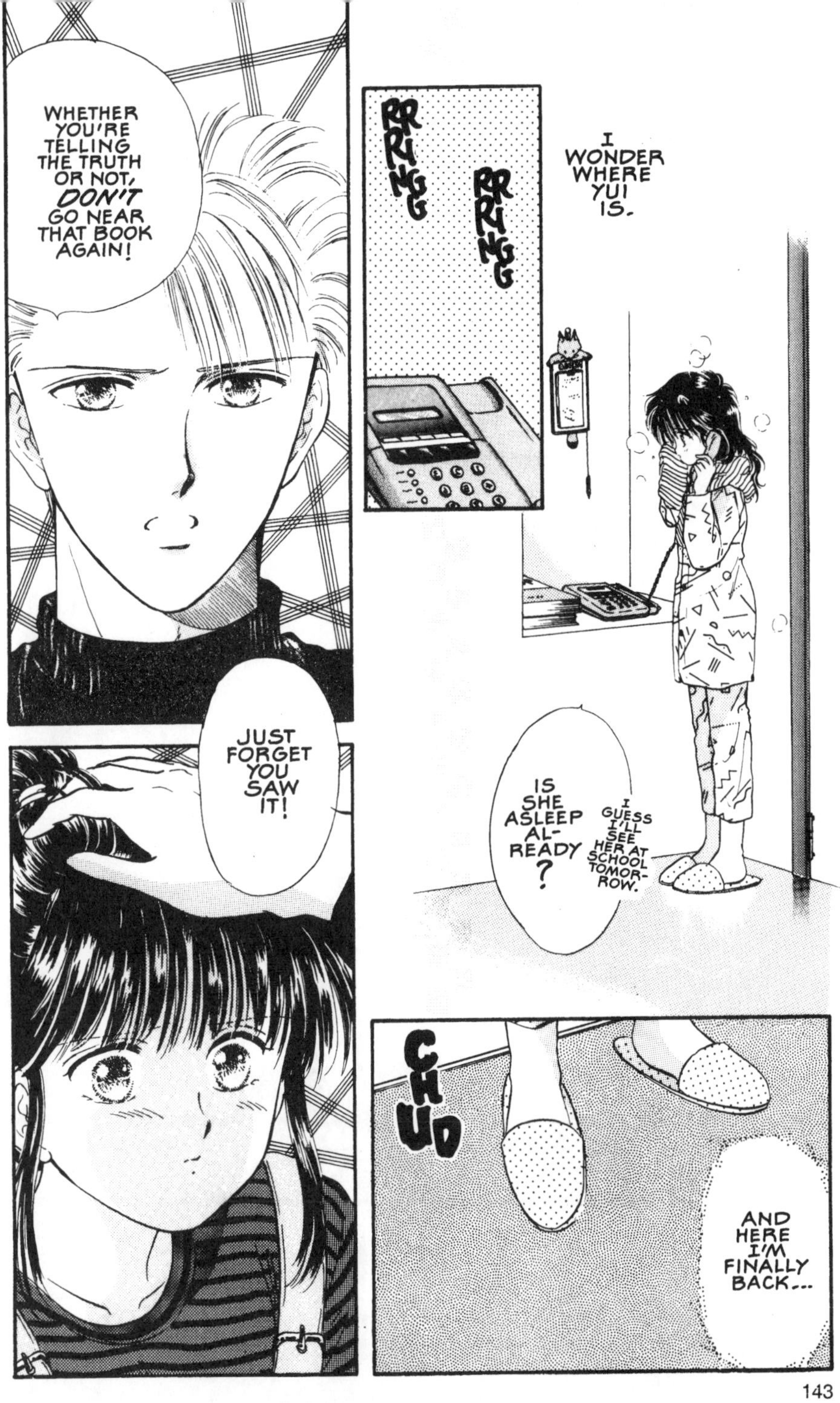
WHETHER YOU'RE TELLING THE TRUTH OR NOT, DON'T GO NEAR THAT BOOK AGAIN!
JUST FORGET YOU SAW IT!
RRRING RRRING
I WONDER WHERE YUI IS.
IS SHE ASLEEP AL-READY?
I GUESS I'LL SEE HER AT SCHOOL TOMOR-ROW.
CHUD
AND HERE I'M FINALLY BACK...

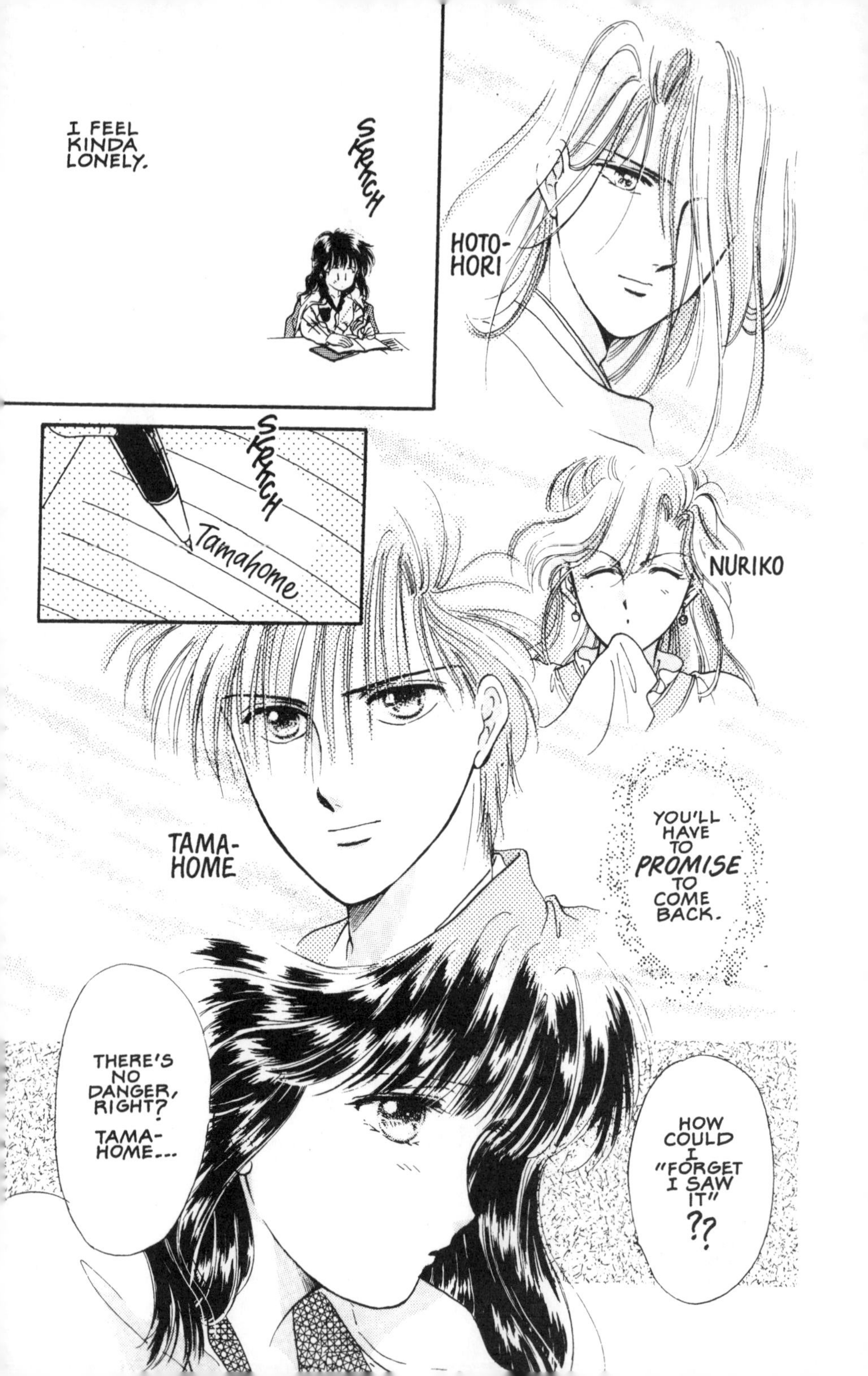

I FEEL KINDA LONELY.
SKRKCH
HOTO-HORI
SKRKCH
Tamahome
NURIKO
TAMA-HOME
YOU'LL HAVE TO PROMISE TO COME BACK.
THERE'S NO DANGER, RIGHT?
TAMA-HOME...
HOW COULD I "FORGET I SAW IT"??

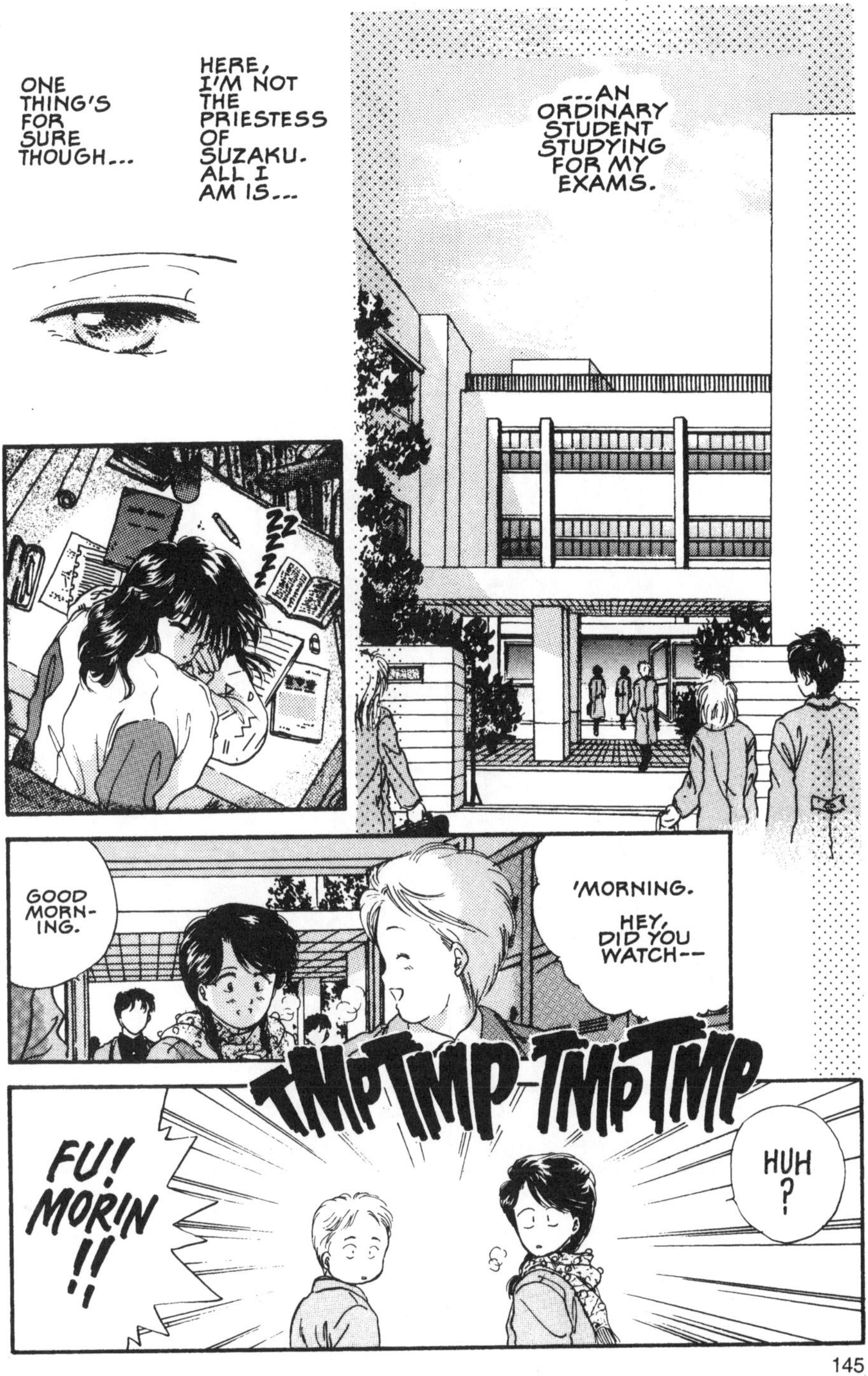
ONE THING'S FOR SURE THOUGH...
HERE, I'M NOT THE PRIESTESS OF SUZAKU. ALL I AM IS...
...AN ORDINARY STUDENT STUDYING FOR MY EXAMS.
ZZZZZ
GOOD MORN-ING.
'MORNING.
HEY, DID YOU WATCH--
TMP TMP TMP TMP
FU! MORIN!!
HUH?

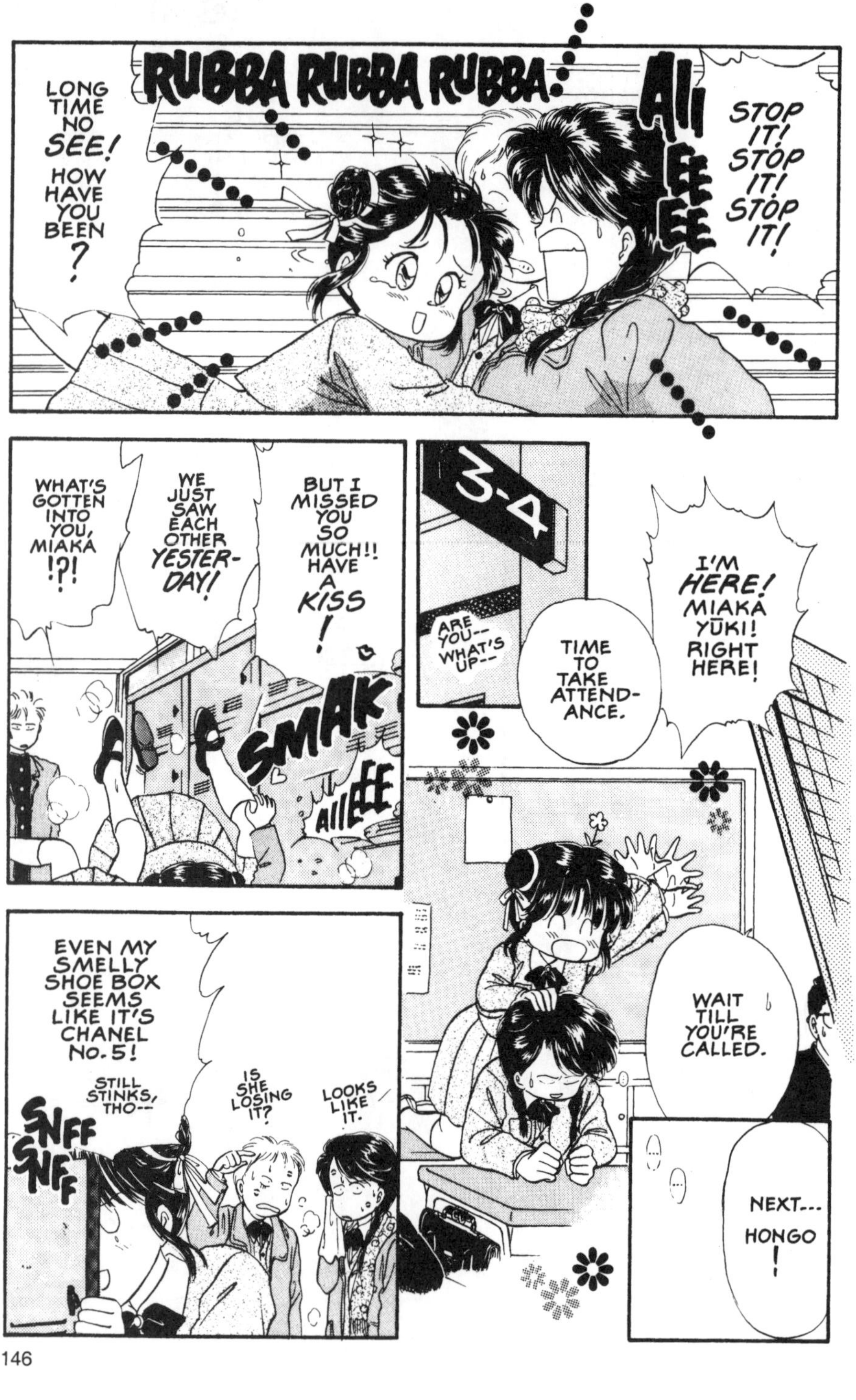
RUBBA RUBBA RUBBA
LONG TIME NO SEE! HOW HAVE YOU BEEN?
AIIEEEEE
STOP IT! STOP IT! STOP IT!
WHAT'S GOTTEN INTO YOU, MIAKA !?!
WE JUST SAW EACH OTHER YESTERDAY!
BUT I MISSED YOU SO MUCH!! HAVE A KISS!
SMAK
AIIEEEE
3-4
ARE YOU-- WHAT'S UP--
TIME TO TAKE ATTENDANCE.
I'M HERE! MIAKA YŪKI! RIGHT HERE!
WAIT TILL YOU'RE CALLED.
EVEN MY SMELLY SHOE BOX SEEMS LIKE IT'S CHANEL No. 5!
SNFF SNFF
STILL STINKS, THO--
IS SHE LOSING IT?
LOOKS LIKE IT.
...
...
NEXT... HONGO!

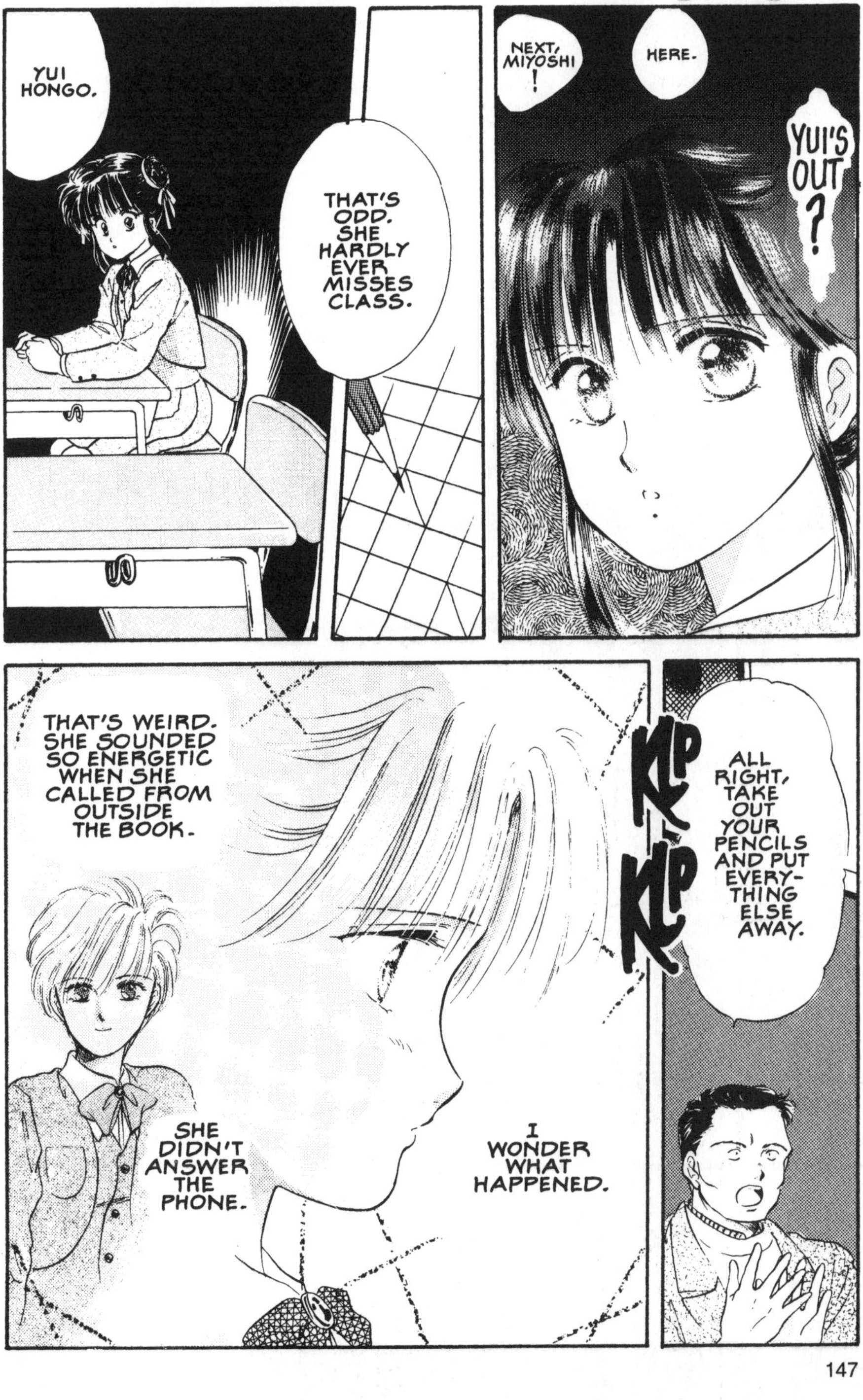
YUI HONGO.
THAT'S ODD. SHE HARDLY EVER MISSES CLASS.
NEXT, MIYOSHI!
HERE.
YUI'S OUT?
THAT'S WEIRD. SHE SOUNDED SO ENERGETIC WHEN SHE CALLED FROM OUTSIDE THE BOOK.
SHE DIDN'T ANSWER THE PHONE.
I WONDER WHAT HAPPENED.
KLP KLP KLP
ALL RIGHT, TAKE OUT YOUR PENCILS AND PUT EVERY-THING ELSE AWAY.

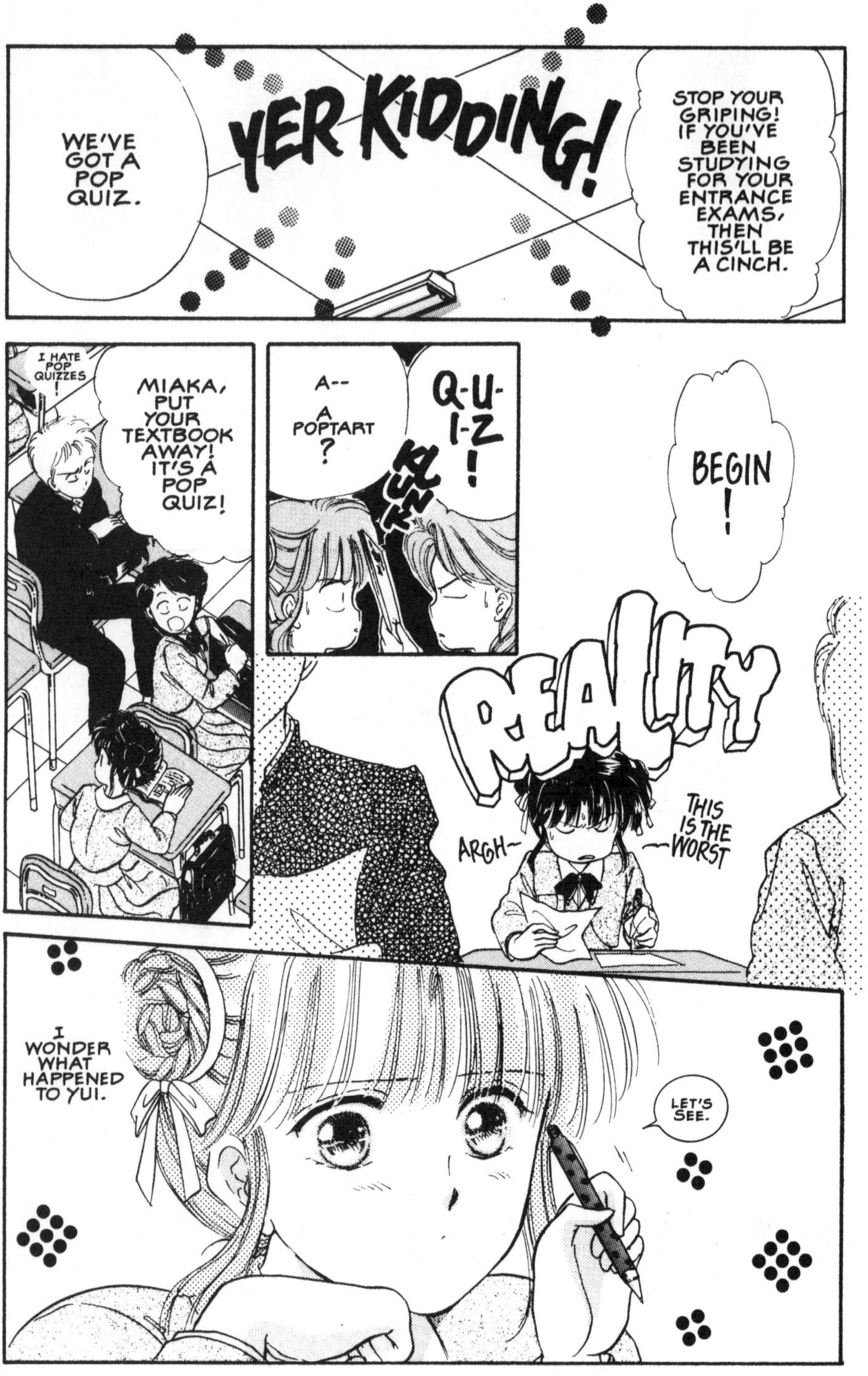
WE'VE GOT A POP QUIZ.
YER KIDDING!
STOP YOUR GRIPING! IF YOU'VE BEEN STUDYING FOR YOUR ENTRANCE EXAMS, THEN THIS'LL BE A CINCH.
I HATE POP QUIZZES!
MIAKA, PUT YOUR TEXTBOOK AWAY! IT'S A POP QUIZ!
A-- A POPTART?
Q-U-I-Z!
KLUNK
BEGIN!
REALITY
ARGH~
THIS IS THE WORST
I WONDER WHAT HAPPENED TO YUI.
LET'S SEE.

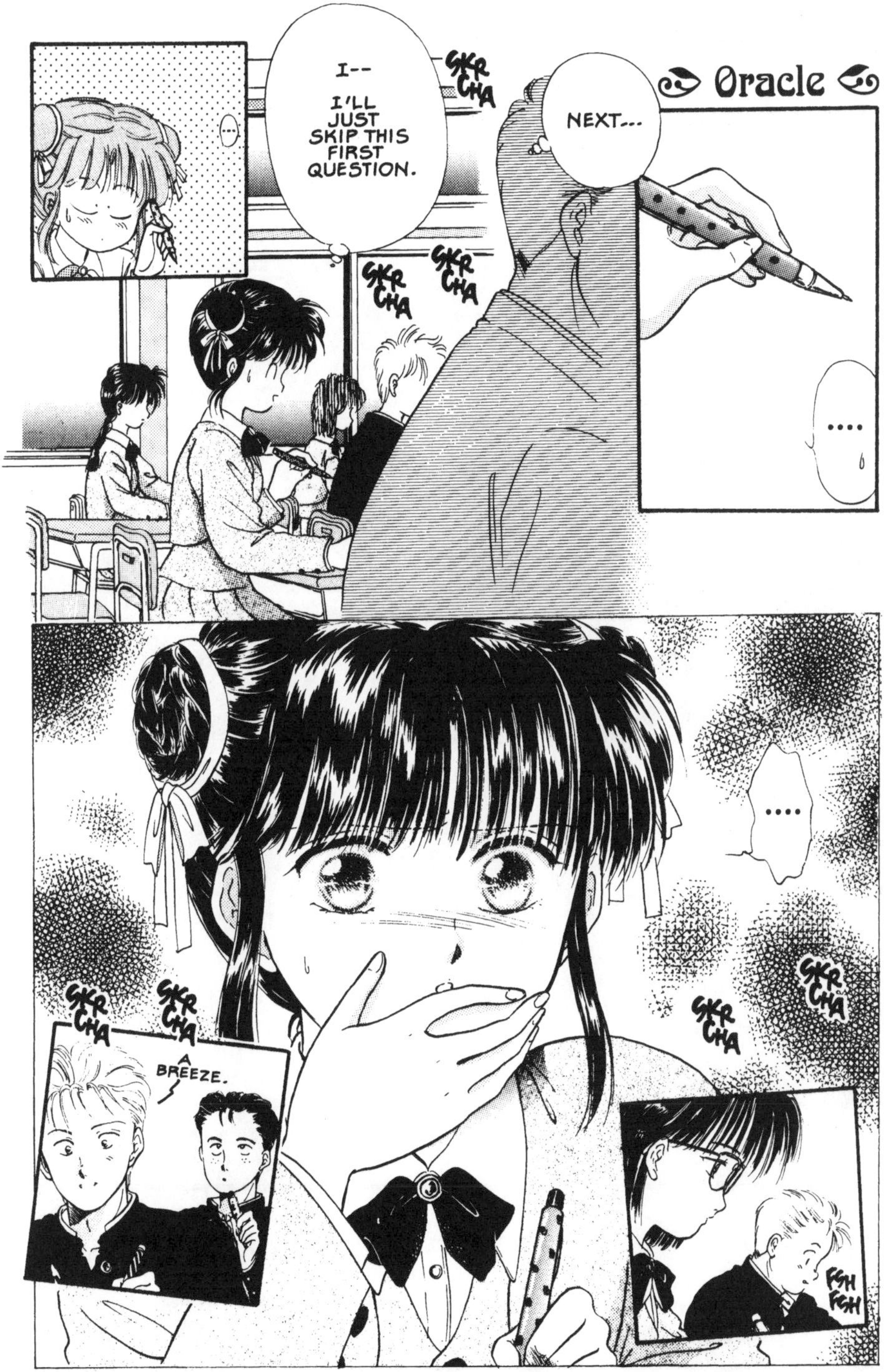
...
I--
I'LL JUST SKIP THIS FIRST QUESTION.
SKR CHA
SKR CHA
SKR CHA
NEXT...
....
....
SKR CHA
SKR CHA
SKR CHA
SKR CHA
A BREEZE.
FSH FSH

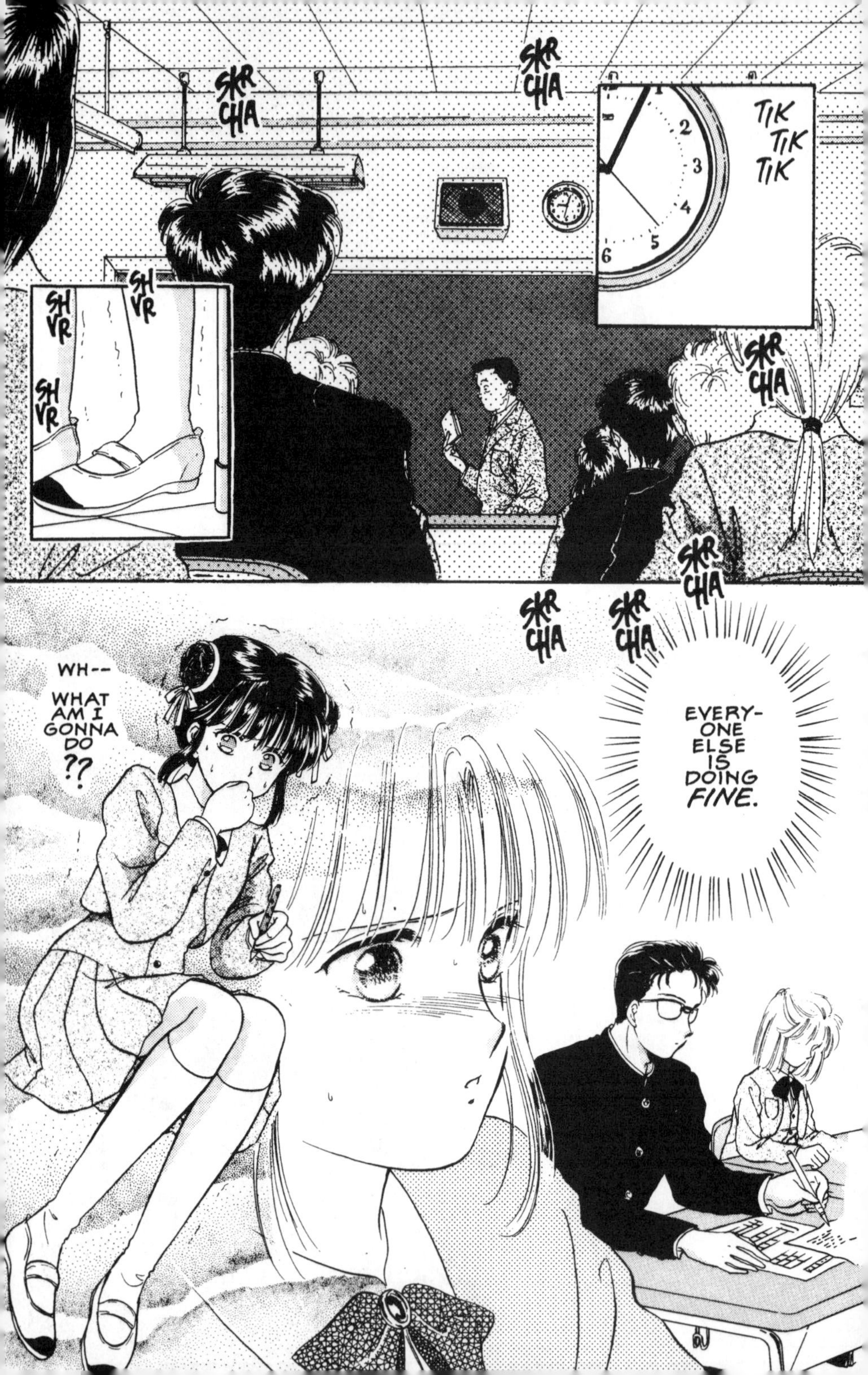
SKR CHA
SKR CHA
TIK TIK TIK
SH VR
SH VR
SH VR
SKR CHA
SKR CHA
SKR CHA
SKR CHA
WH--
WHAT AM I GONNA DO ??
EVERY-ONE ELSE IS DOING *FINE*.

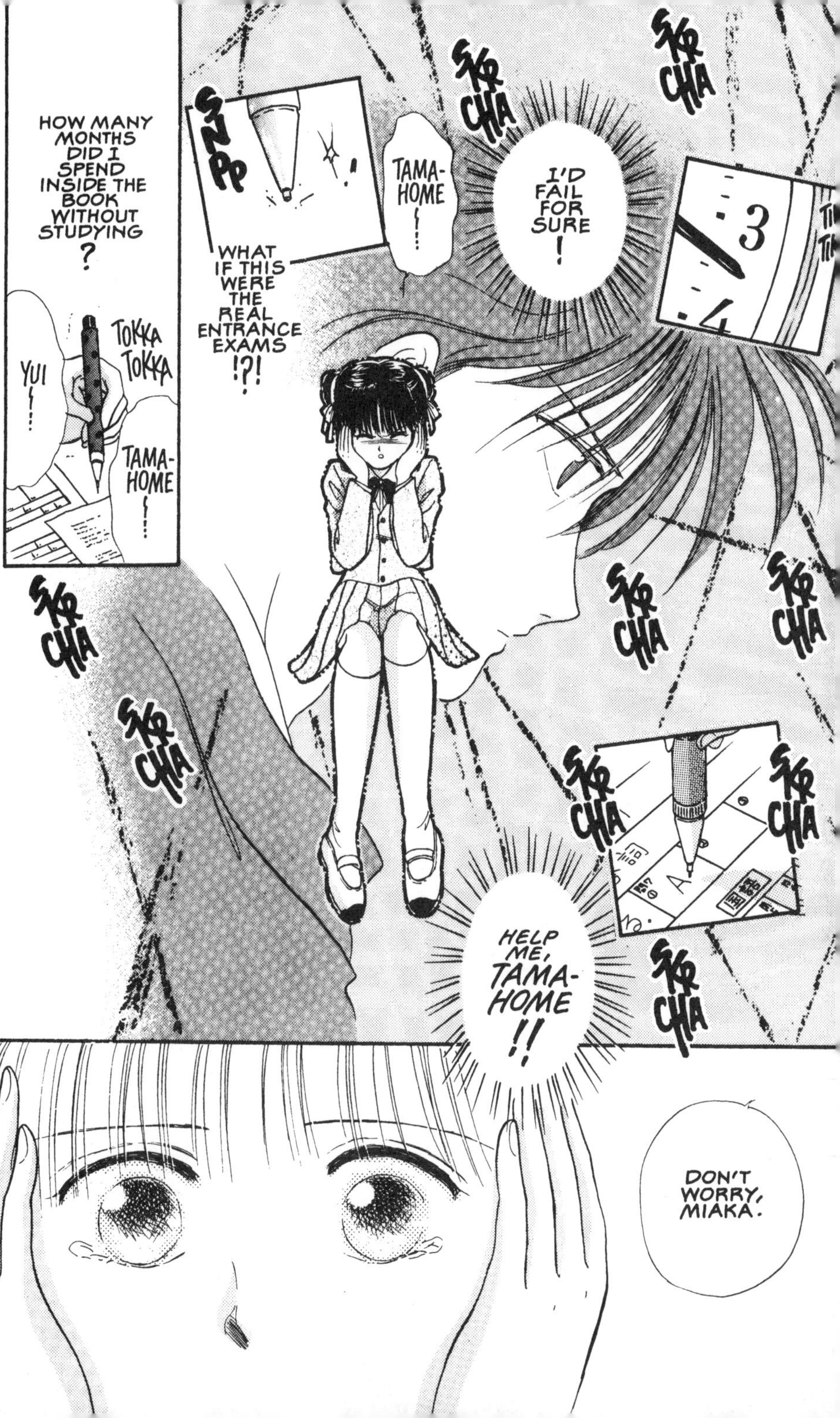
HOW MANY MONTHS DID I SPEND INSIDE THE BOOK WITHOUT STUDYING ?
YUI ...!
TOKKA TOKKA
TAMA-HOME ...!
SNPP
WHAT IF THIS WERE THE REAL ENTRANCE EXAMS !?!
TAMA-HOME ...!
SKRCHA
SKRCHA
I'D FAIL FOR SURE !
SKRCHA
SKRCHA
SKRCHA
SKRCHA
SKRCHA
SKRCHA
SKRCHA
HELP ME, TAMA-HOME !!
SKRCHA
DON'T WORRY, MIAKA.

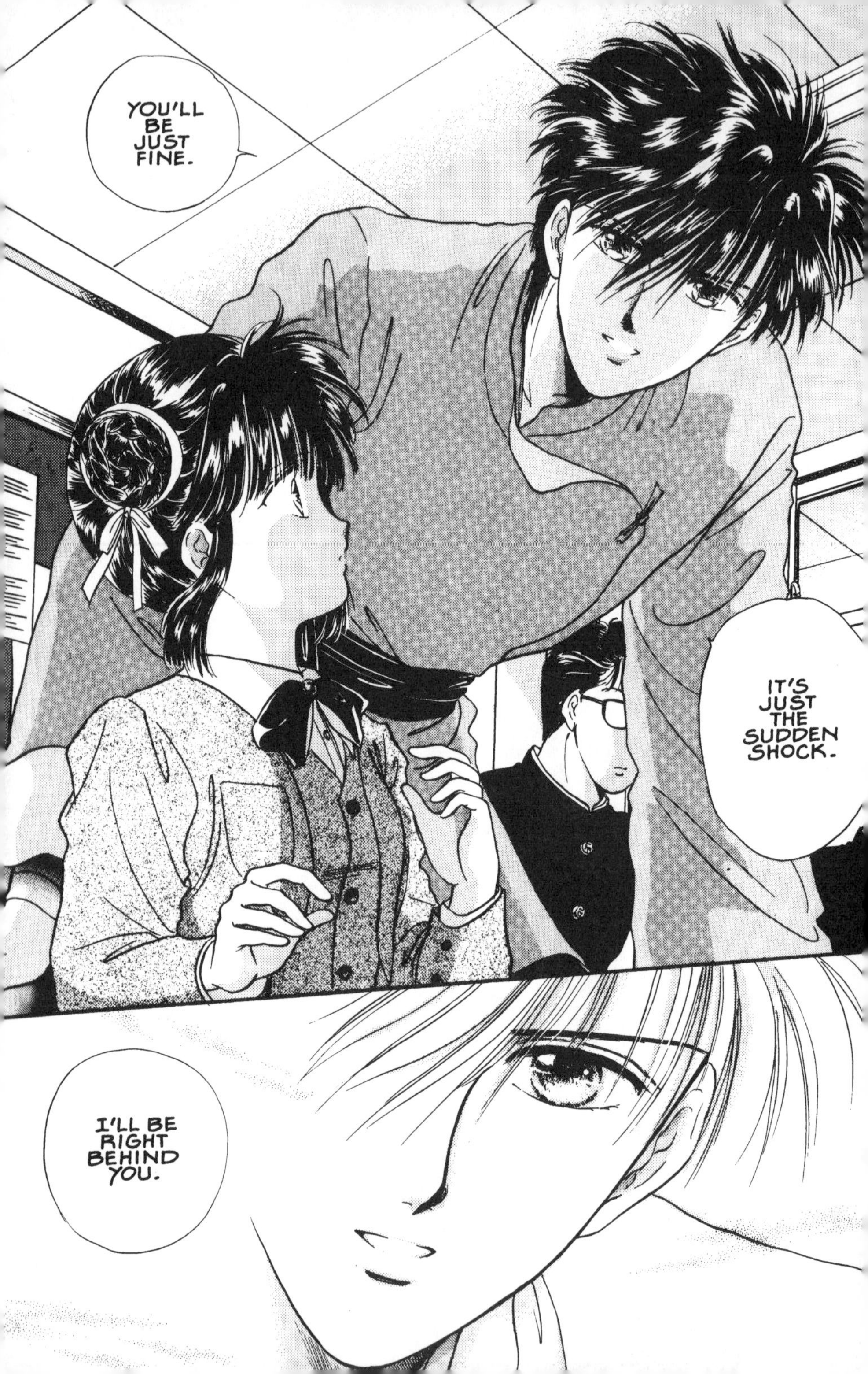
YOU'LL BE JUST FINE.
IT'S JUST THE SUDDEN SHOCK.
I'LL BE RIGHT BEHIND YOU.

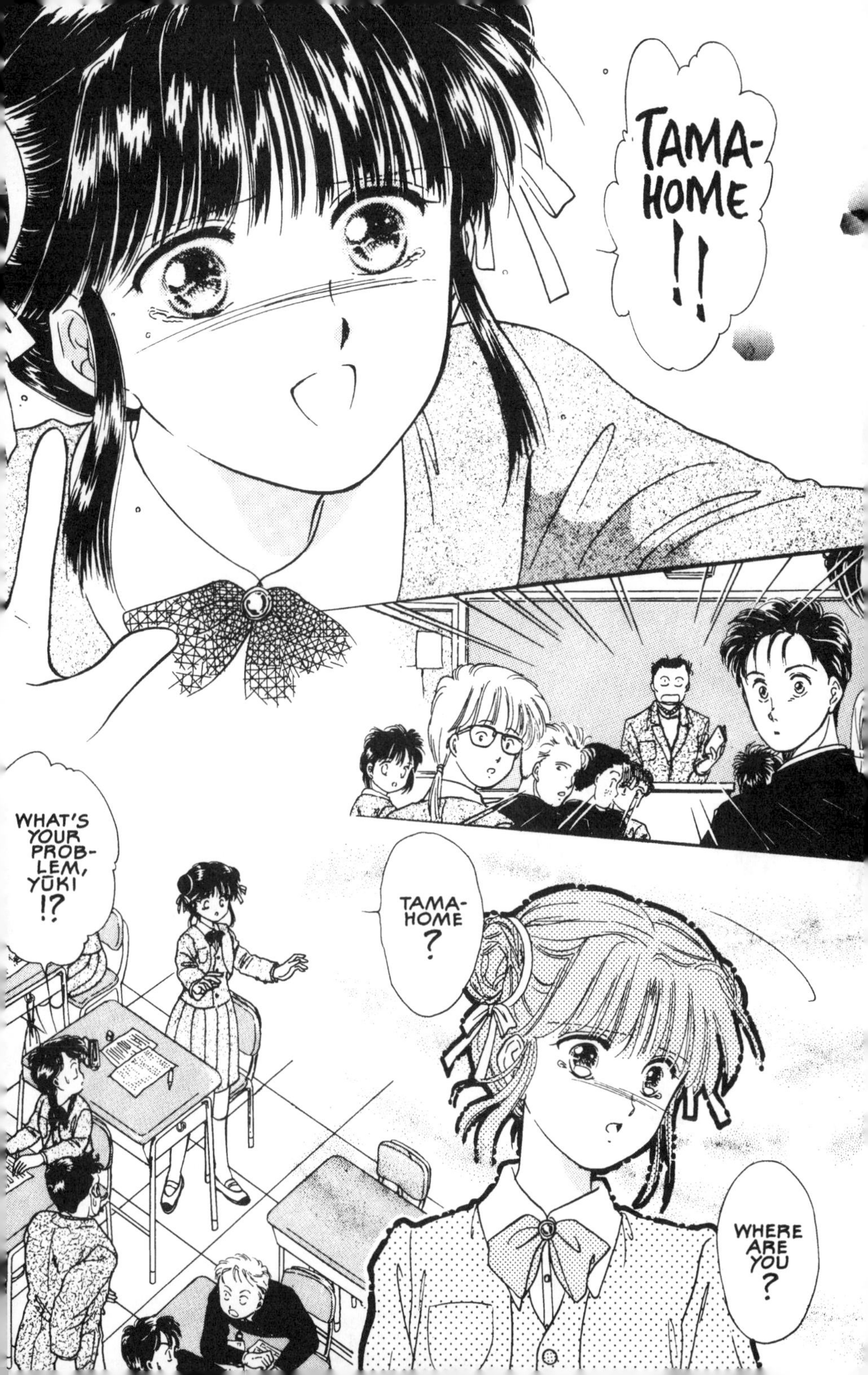
TAMA-HOME !!
WHAT'S YOUR PROB-LEM, YŪKI !?
TAMA-HOME ?
WHERE ARE YOU ?

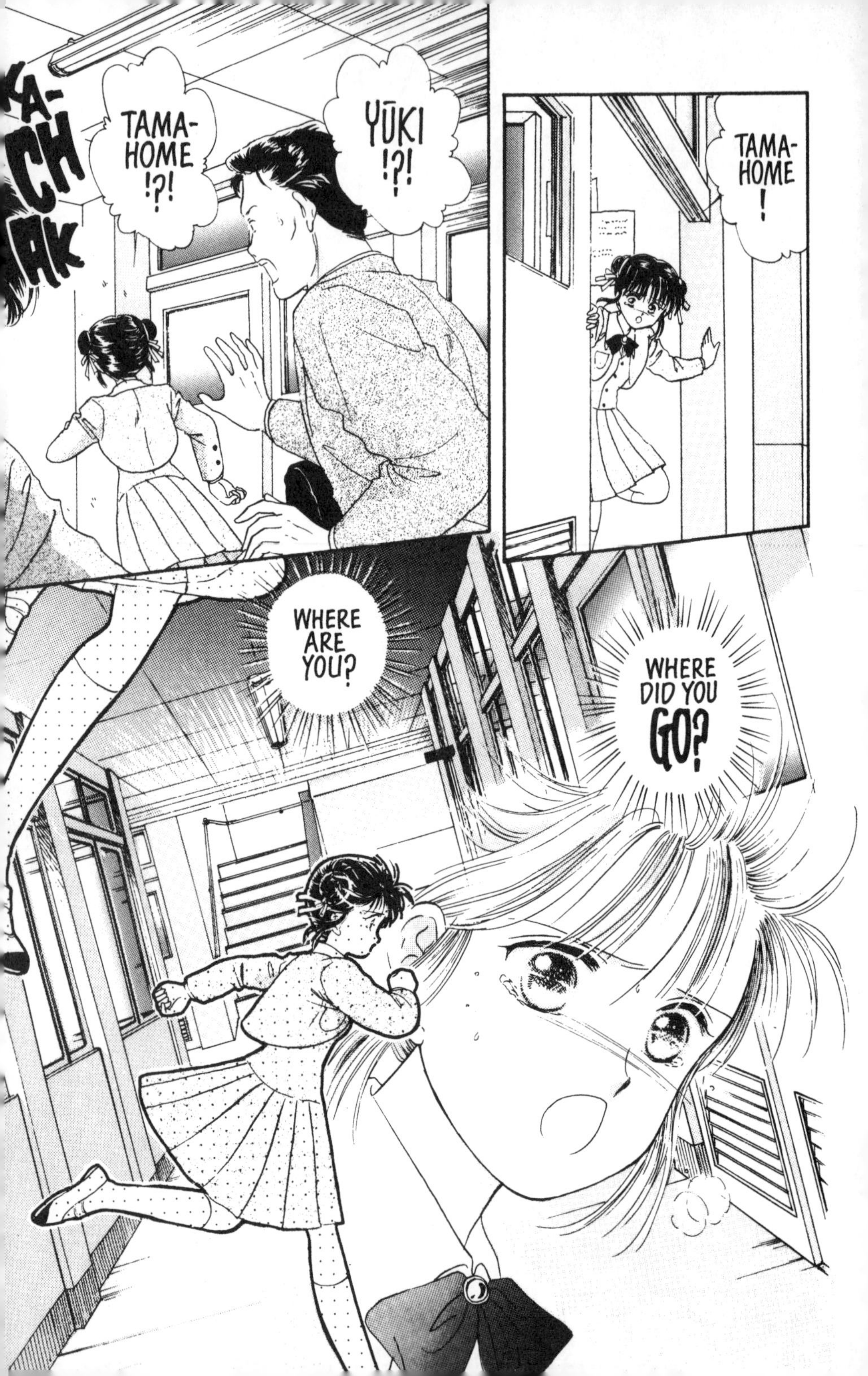
KA-
CH
TAMA-HOME !?!
YŪKI !?!
TAMA-HOME !
WHERE ARE YOU?
WHERE DID YOU GO?

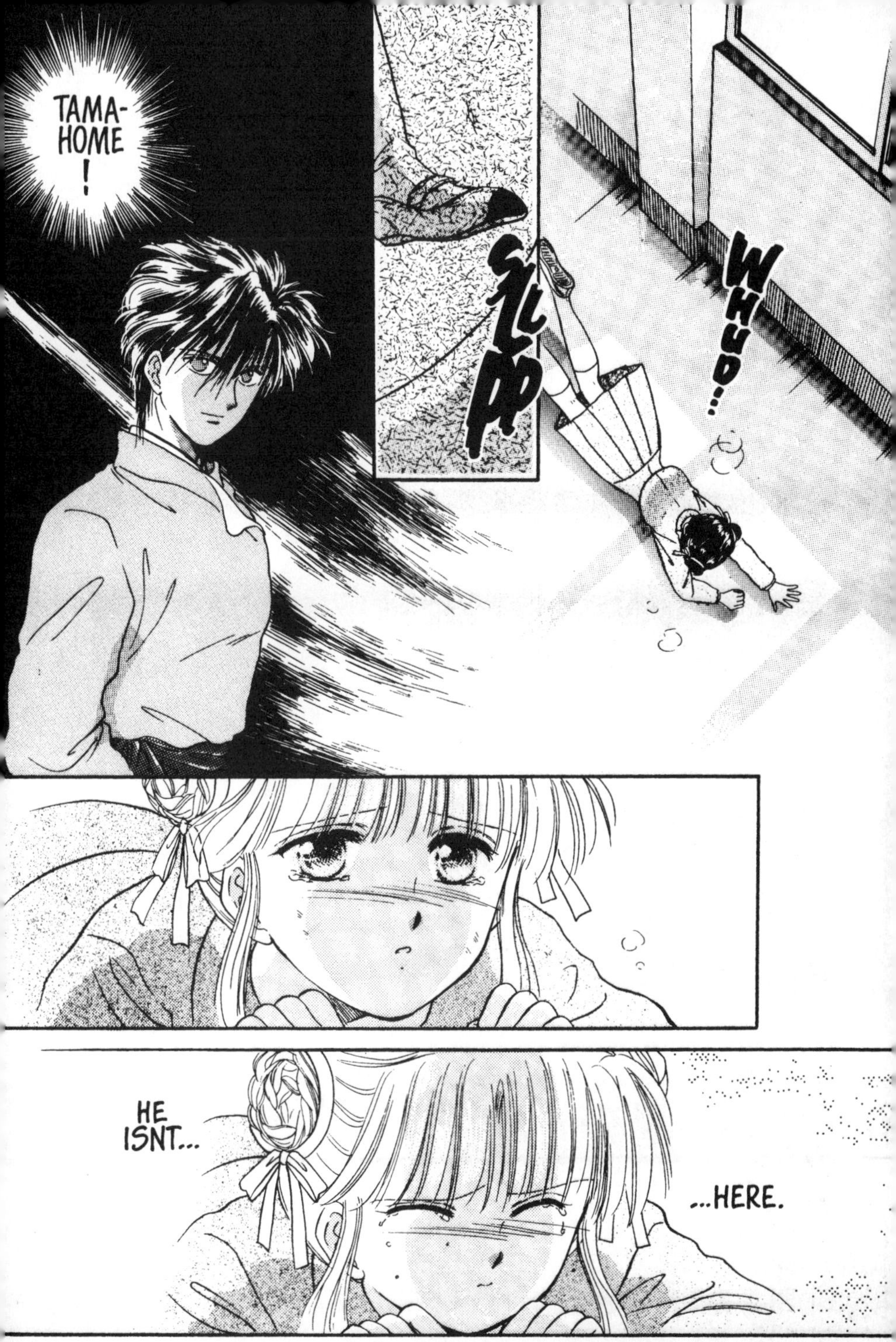
TAMA-HOME!
SLIPP
WHUD...
HE ISNT...
...HERE.

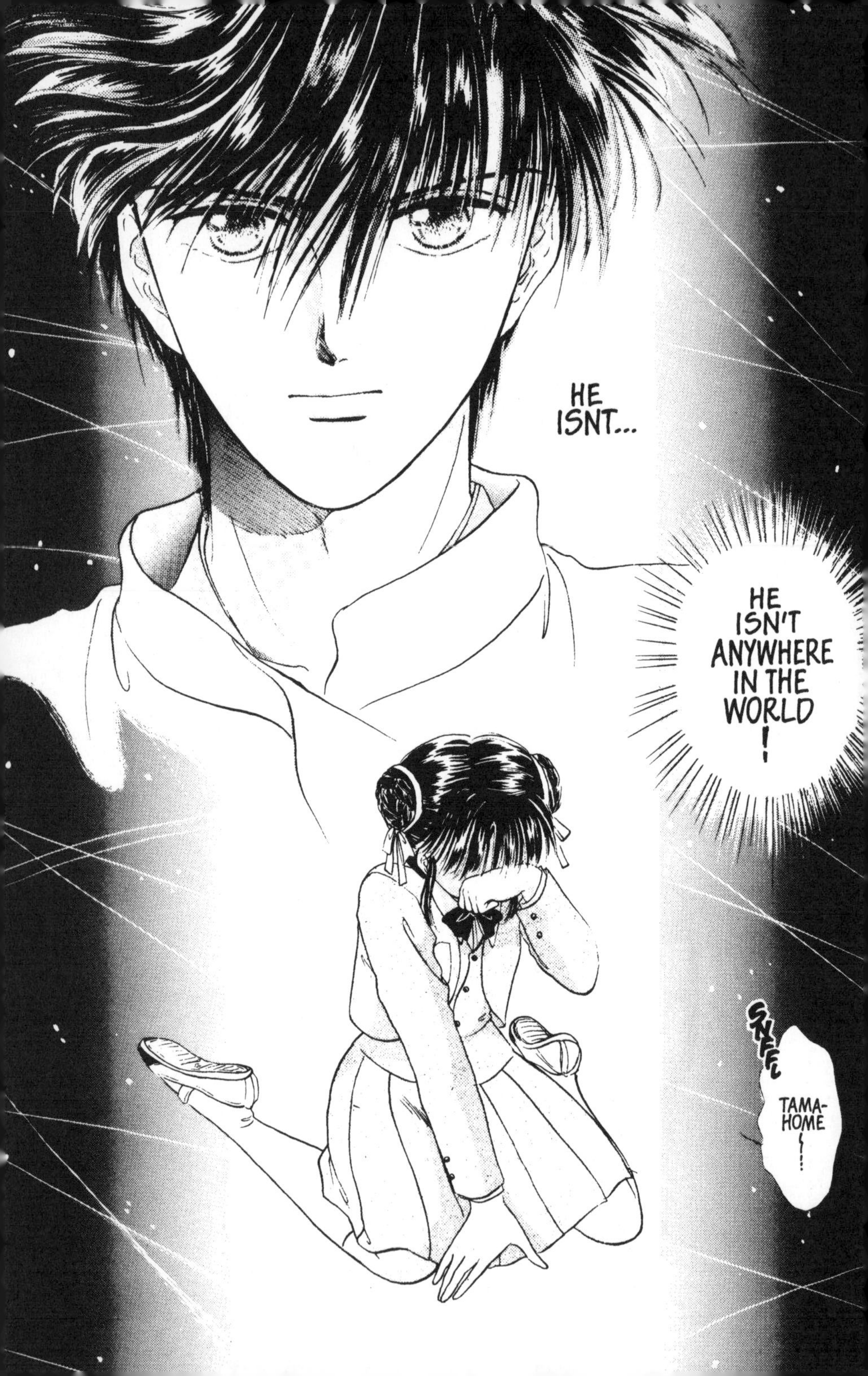
HE ISNT...
HE ISN'T ANYWHERE IN THE WORLD!
SNFFL
TAMA-HOME!!

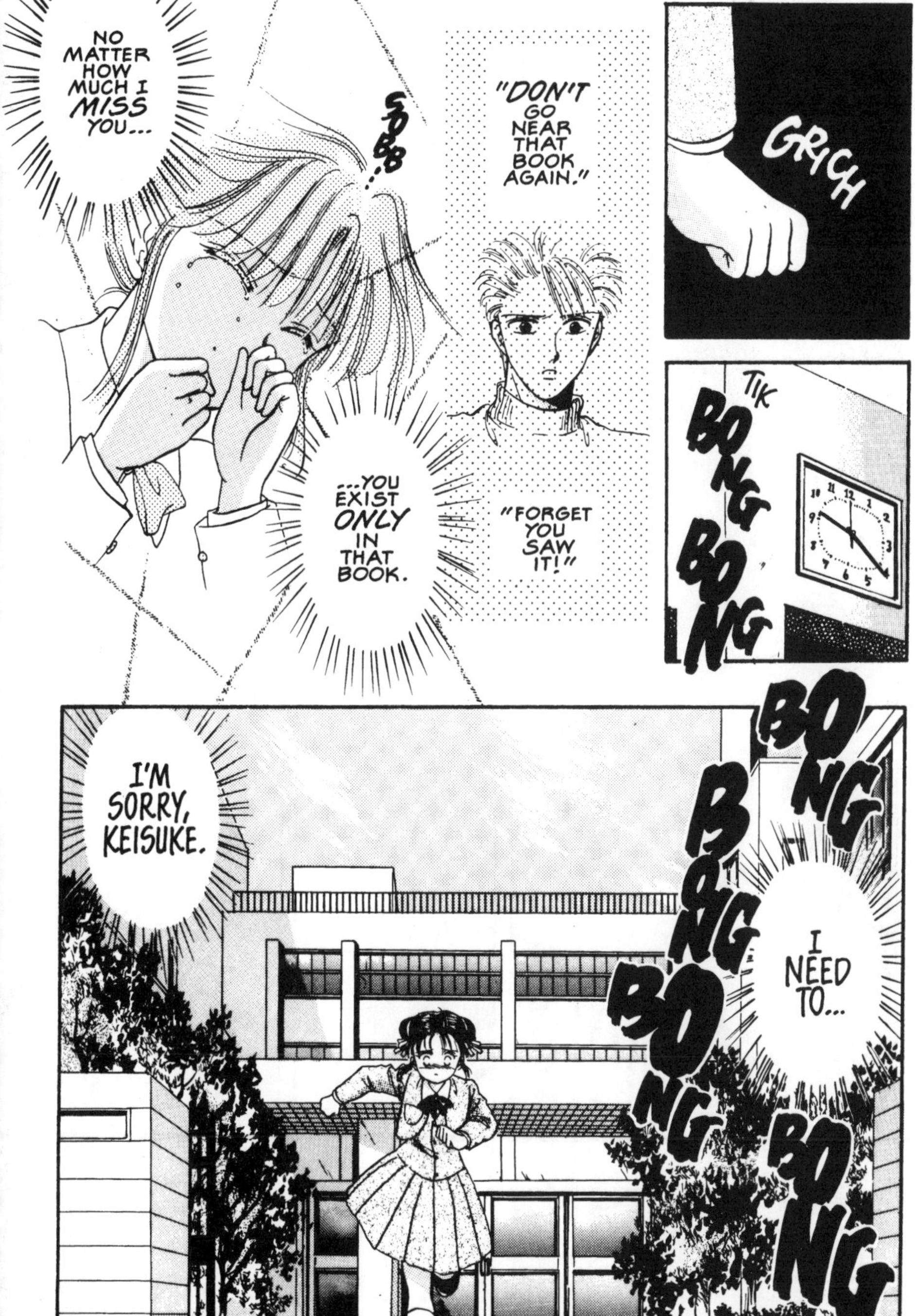
NO MATTER HOW MUCH I MISS YOU...
SOBB...
...YOU EXIST ONLY IN THAT BOOK.
"DON'T GO NEAR THAT BOOK AGAIN."
"FORGET YOU SAW IT!"
GRICH
TIK
BONG BONG
I'M SORRY, KEISUKE.
BONG BONG BONG BONG BONG
I NEED TO...

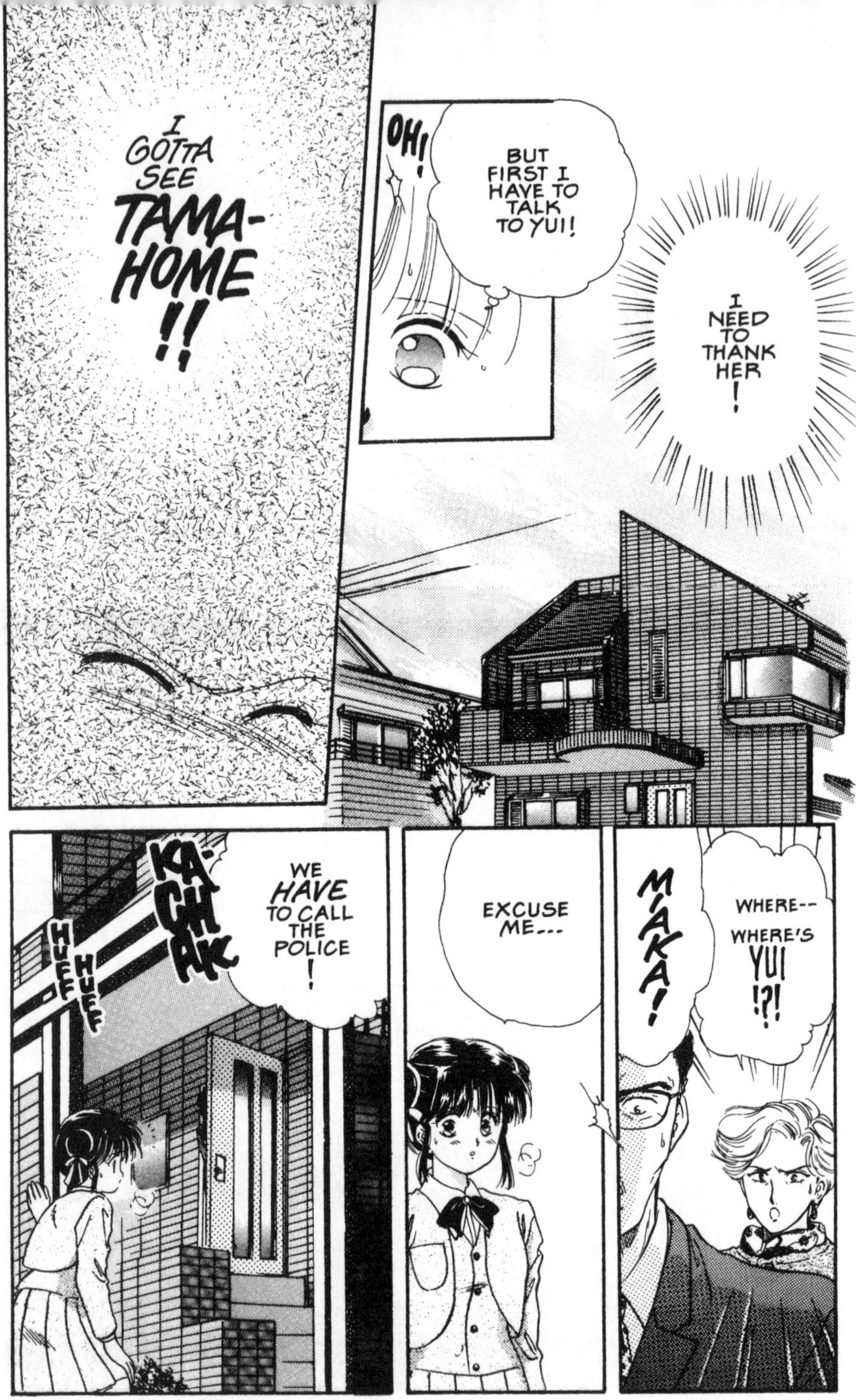
I GOTTA SEE TAMA-HOME!!
OH!
BUT FIRST I HAVE TO TALK TO YUI!
I NEED TO THANK HER!
KA-CHAK
HUFF HUFF
WE HAVE TO CALL THE POLICE!
EXCUSE ME...
MIAKA!
WHERE-- WHERE'S YUI!?!

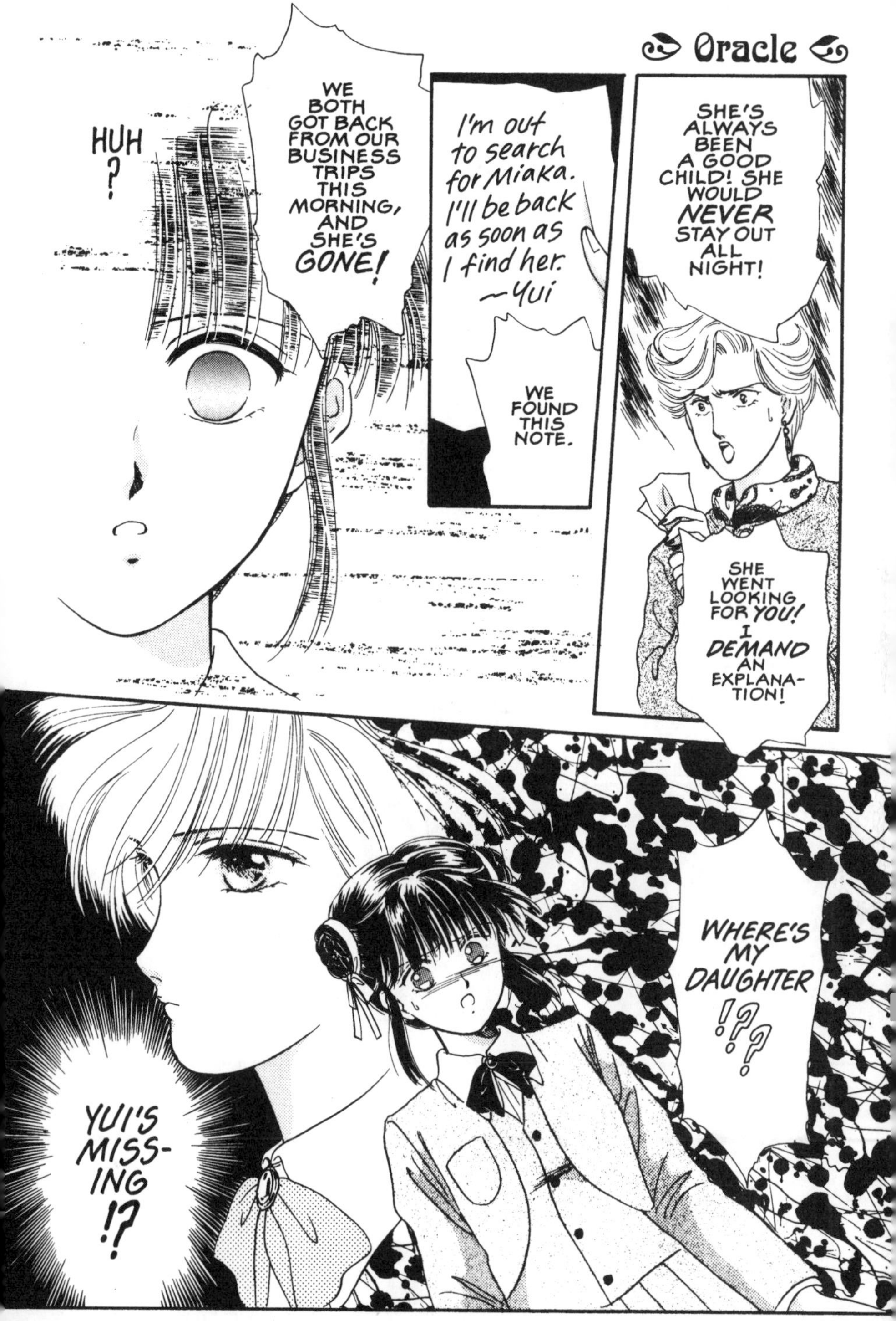
WE BOTH GOT BACK FROM OUR BUSINESS TRIPS THIS MORNING, AND SHE'S GONE!
HUH?
I'm out to search for Miaka. I'll be back as soon as I find her. ~Yui
WE FOUND THIS NOTE.
SHE'S ALWAYS BEEN A GOOD CHILD! SHE WOULD NEVER STAY OUT ALL NIGHT!
SHE WENT LOOKING FOR YOU! I DEMAND AN EXPLANATION!
WHERE'S MY DAUGHTER!??
YUI'S MISSING!?

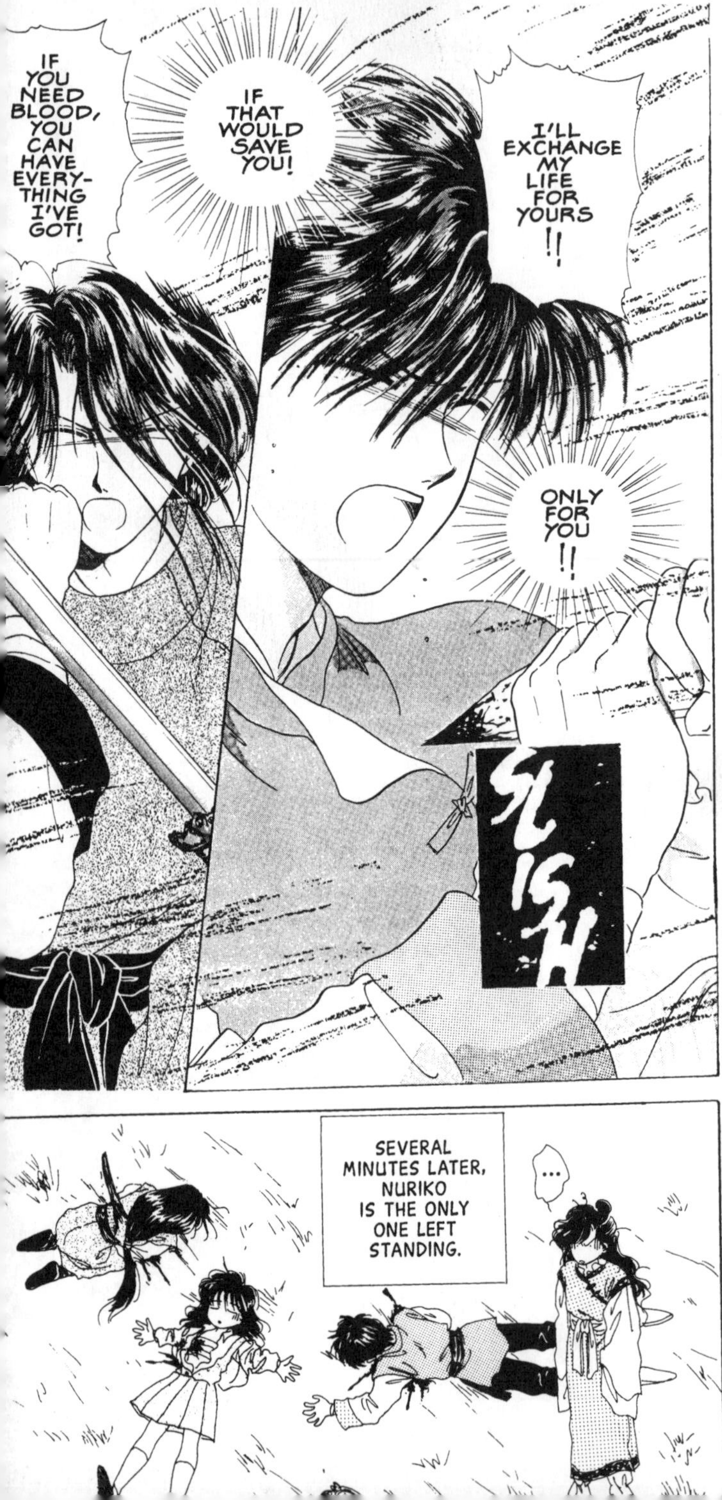
IF YOU NEED BLOOD, YOU CAN HAVE EVERY-THING I'VE GOT!
IF THAT WOULD SAVE YOU!
I'LL EXCHANGE MY LIFE FOR YOURS!!
ONLY FOR YOU!!
SLISH
SEVERAL MINUTES LATER, NURIKO IS THE ONLY ONE LEFT STANDING.
...

PARDON THE PARODY

WHY IS IT ALWAYS OUT OF CHAPTER 9?

⇦ BY Y.W. (MANGA ARTIST)

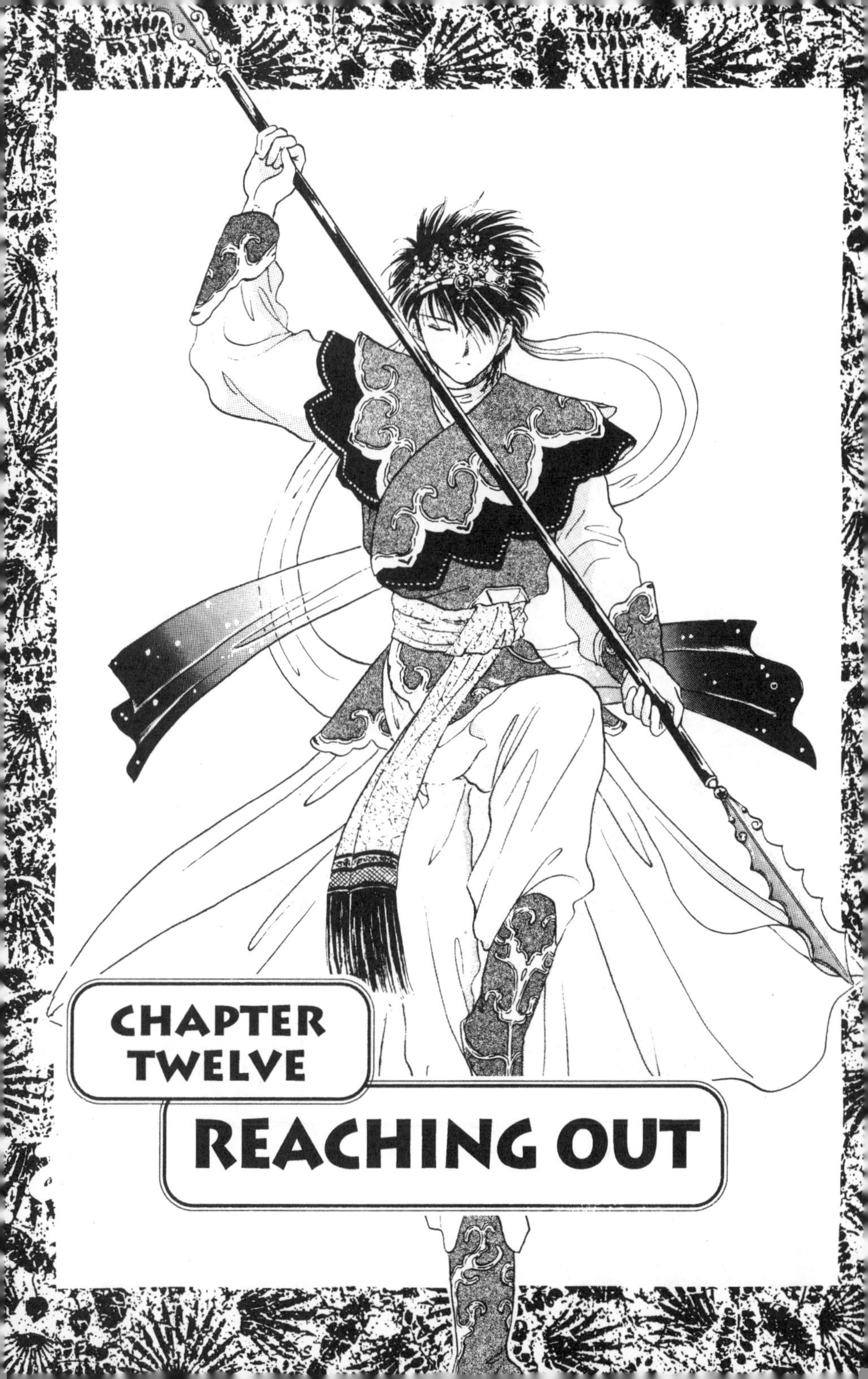
CHAPTER TWELVE
REACHING OUT

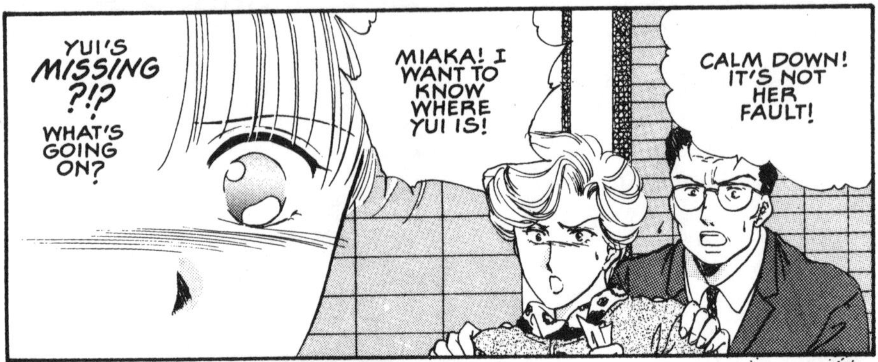
YUI'S *MISSING* ?!? WHAT'S GOING ON?
MIAKA! I WANT TO KNOW WHERE YUI IS!
CALM DOWN! IT'S NOT HER FAULT!

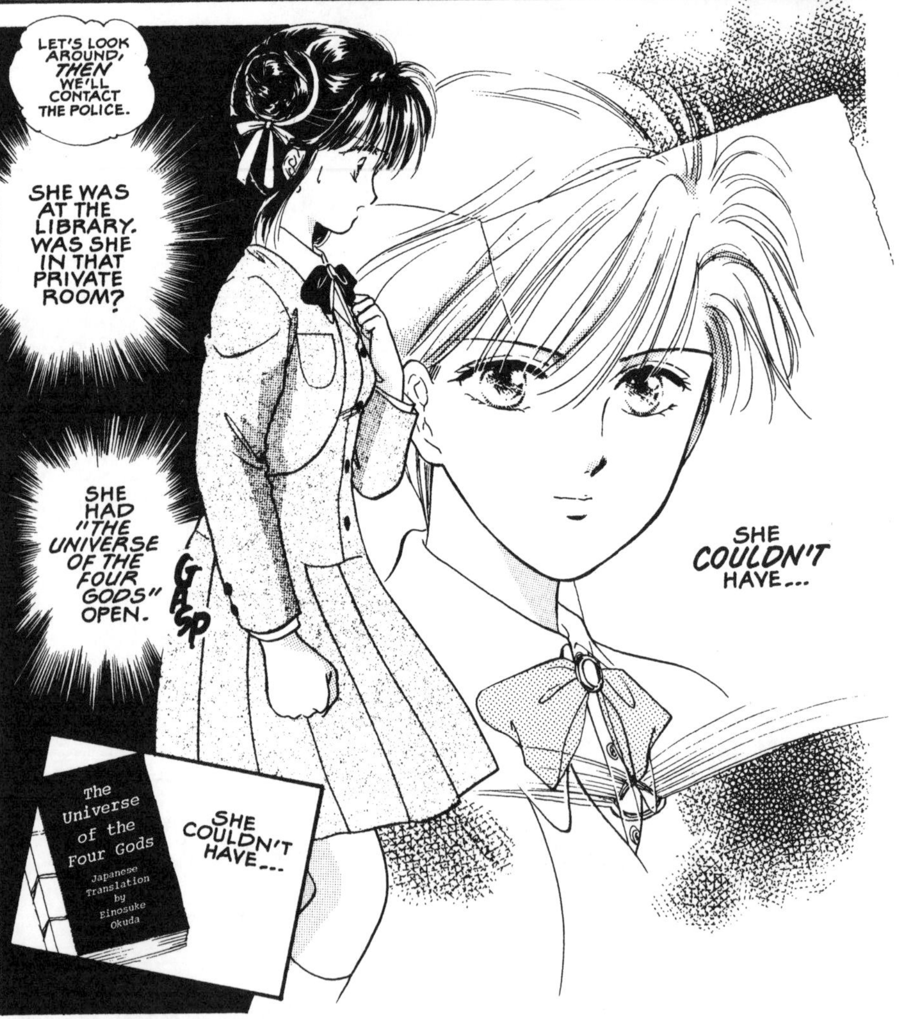
LET'S LOOK AROUND, *THEN* WE'LL CONTACT THE POLICE.
SHE WAS AT THE LIBRARY. WAS SHE IN THAT PRIVATE ROOM?
SHE HAD *"THE UNIVERSE OF THE FOUR GODS"* OPEN.
GASP
SHE *COULDN'T* HAVE...
The Universe of the Four Gods
Japanese Translation by Einosuke Okuda
SHE COULDN'T HAVE...

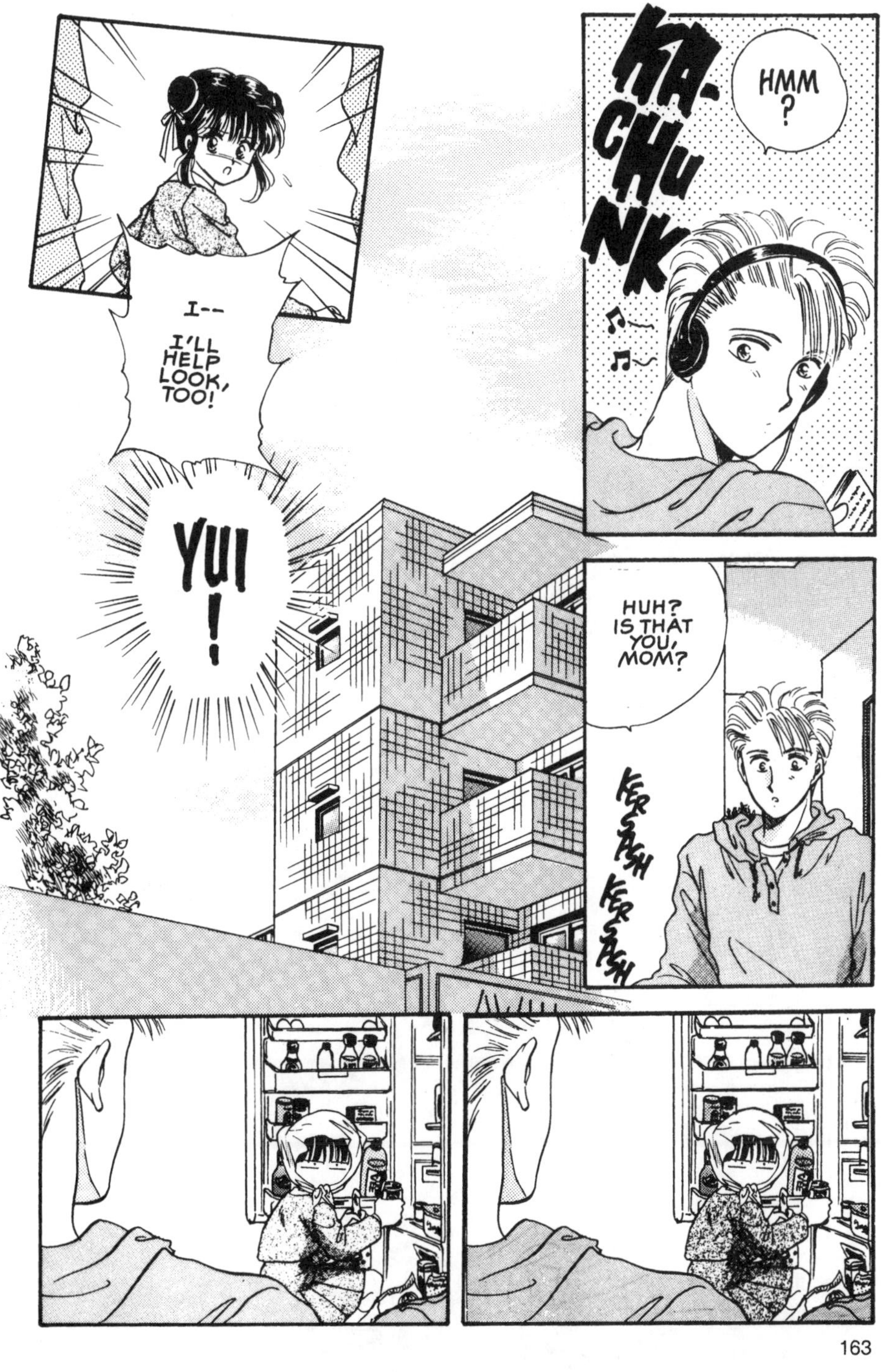
I--
I'LL HELP LOOK, TOO!
YUI !
KA-CHUNK
HMM ?
HUH? IS THAT YOU, MOM?
KERSPASH KERSPASH

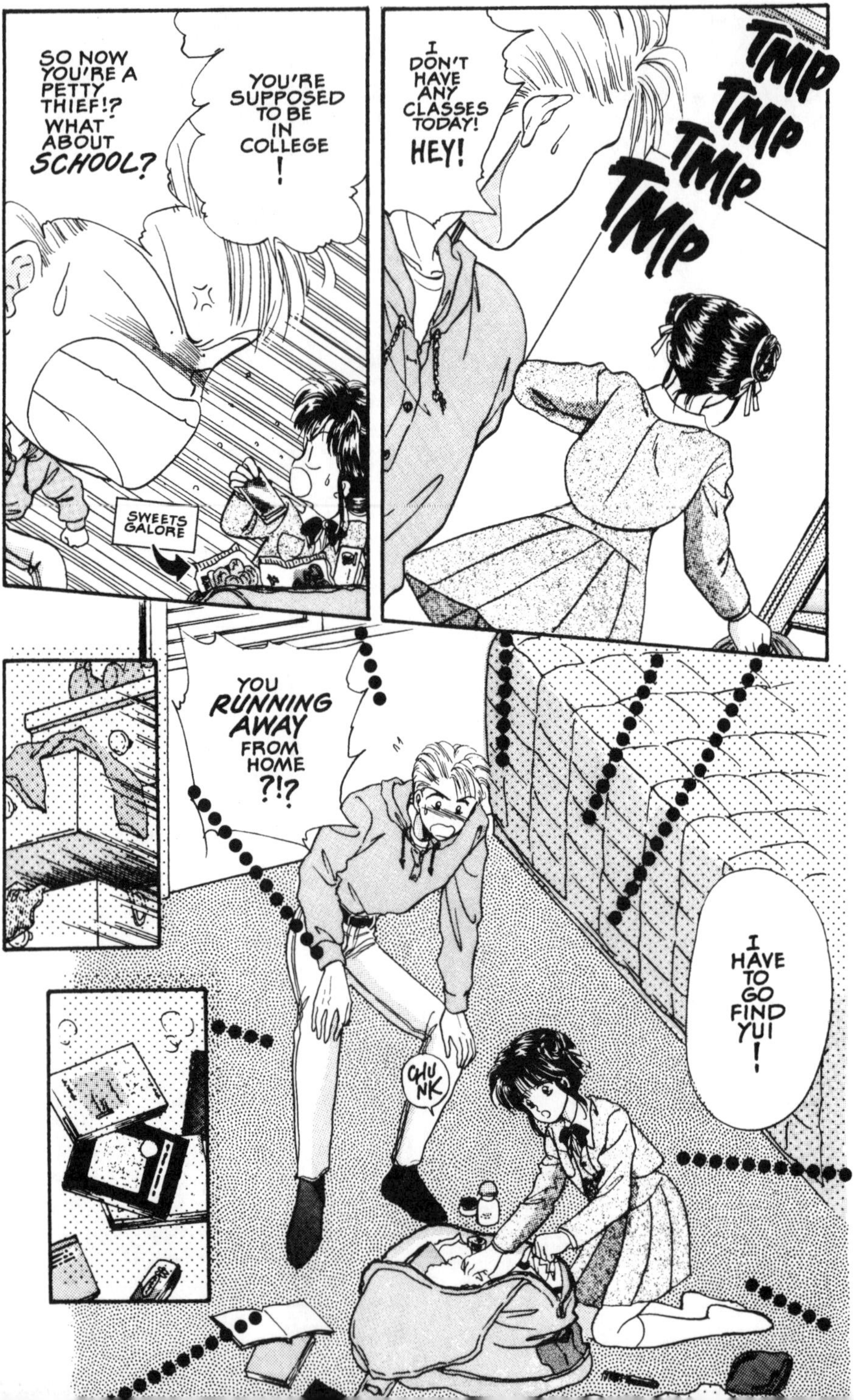
SO NOW YOU'RE A PETTY THIEF!? WHAT ABOUT SCHOOL?
YOU'RE SUPPOSED TO BE IN COLLEGE!
SWEETS GALORE
I DON'T HAVE ANY CLASSES TODAY! HEY!
TMP TMP TMP TMP
YOU RUNNING AWAY FROM HOME?!?
CHUNK
I HAVE TO GO FIND YUI!

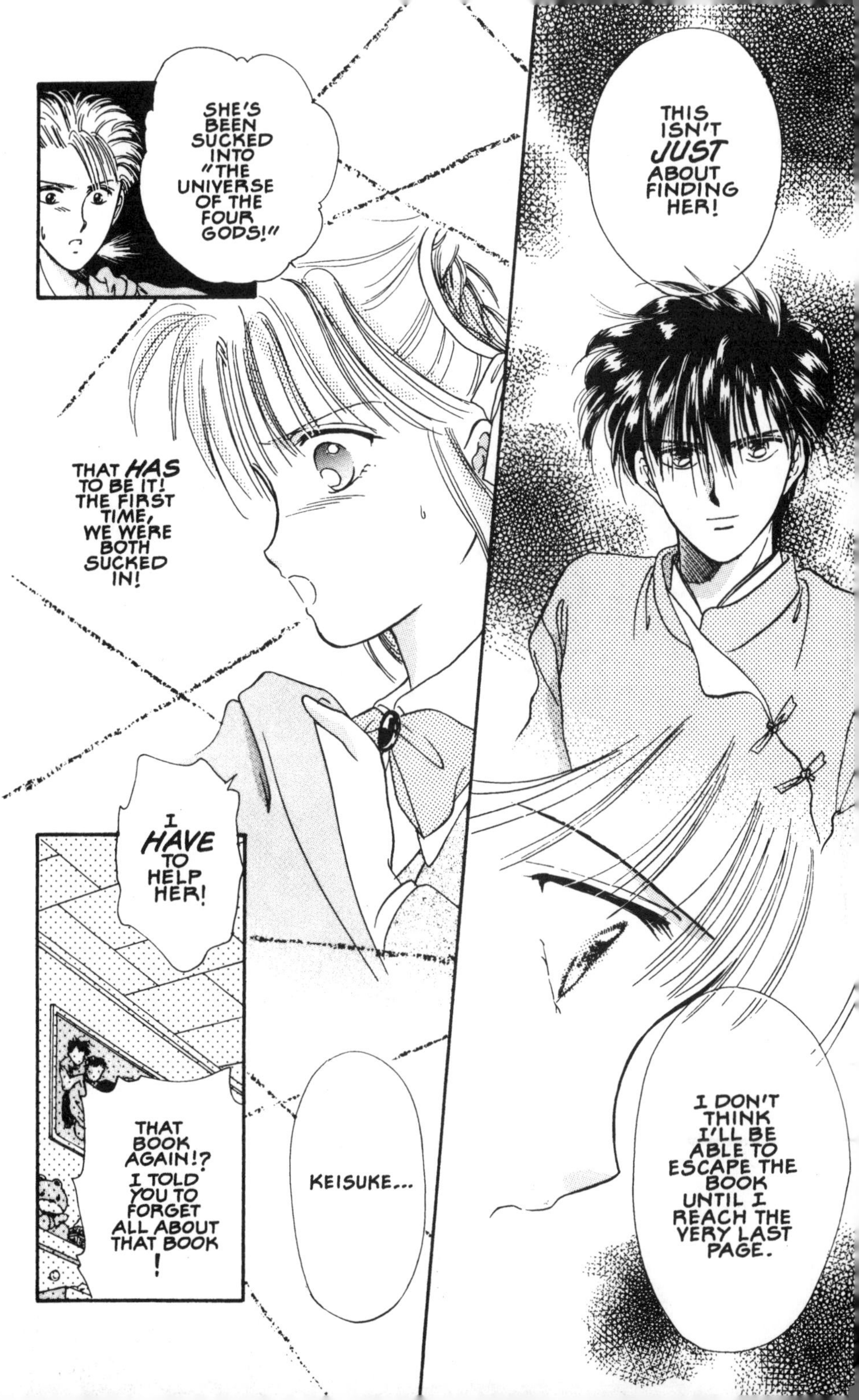
SHE'S BEEN SUCKED INTO "THE UNIVERSE OF THE FOUR GODS!"
THAT HAS TO BE IT! THE FIRST TIME, WE WERE BOTH SUCKED IN!
I HAVE TO HELP HER!
THAT BOOK AGAIN!? I TOLD YOU TO FORGET ALL ABOUT THAT BOOK!
KEISUKE...
THIS ISN'T JUST ABOUT FINDING HER!
I DON'T THINK I'LL BE ABLE TO ESCAPE THE BOOK UNTIL I REACH THE VERY LAST PAGE.

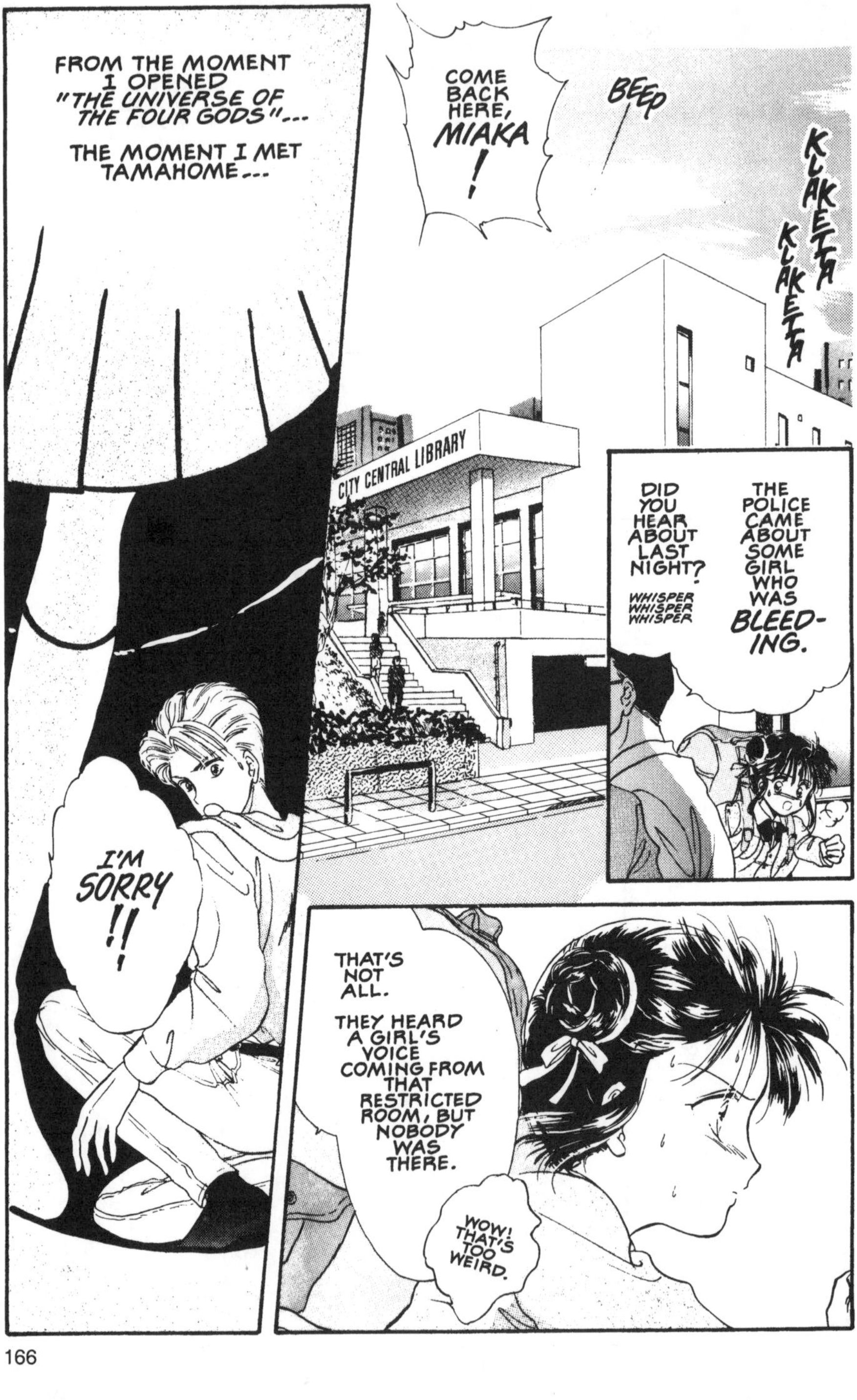

FROM THE MOMENT I OPENED "THE UNIVERSE OF THE FOUR GODS"...
THE MOMENT I MET TAMAHOME...
I'M SORRY!!
COME BACK HERE, MIAKA!
BEEP
KLAKETTA KLAKETTA
CITY CENTRAL LIBRARY
DID YOU HEAR ABOUT LAST NIGHT?
WHISPER WHISPER WHISPER
THE POLICE CAME ABOUT SOME GIRL WHO WAS BLEEDING.
THAT'S NOT ALL.
THEY HEARD A GIRL'S VOICE COMING FROM THAT RESTRICTED ROOM, BUT NOBODY WAS THERE.
WOW! THAT'S TOO WEIRD.

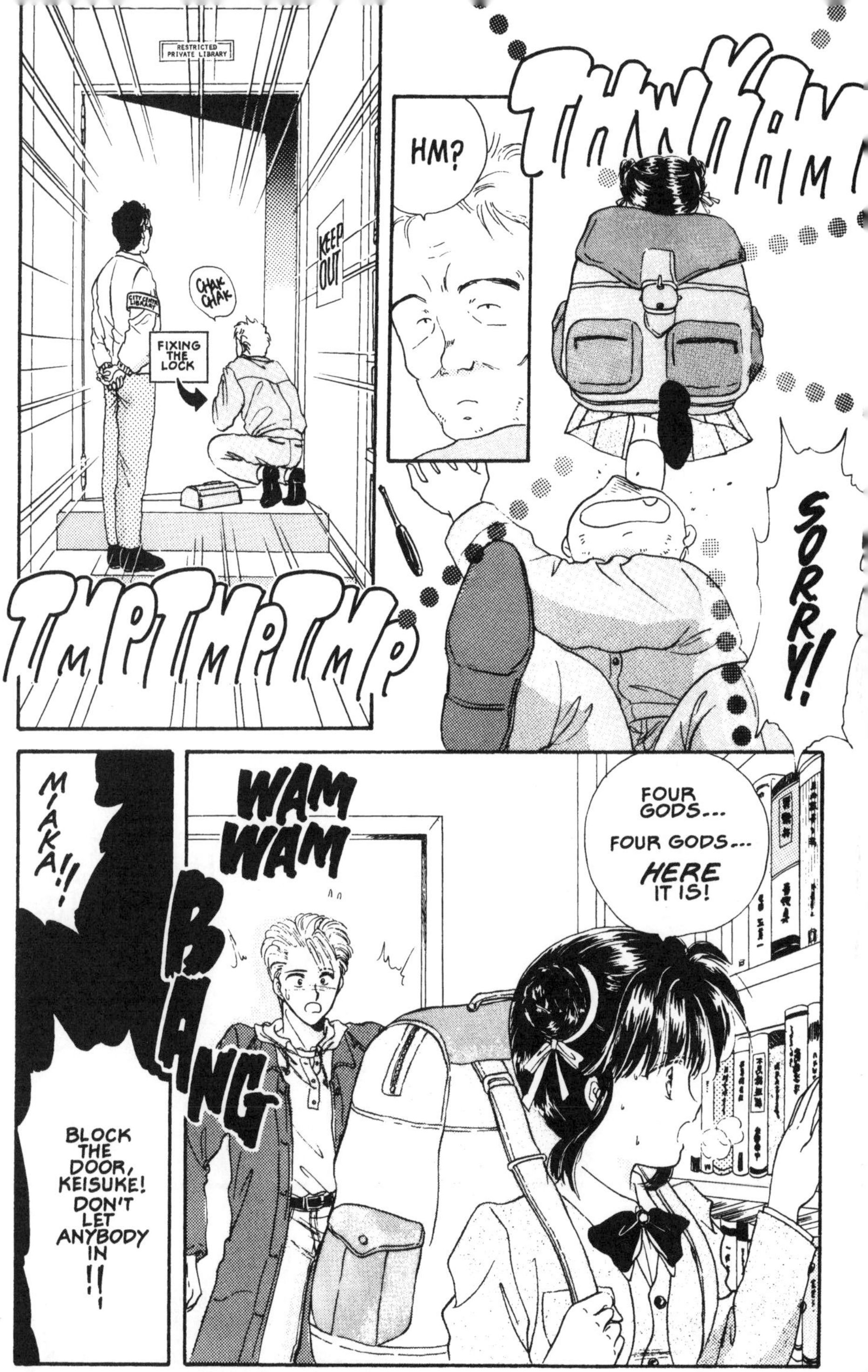
RESTRICTED PRIVATE LIBRARY
KEEP OUT
CITY CENTRAL LIBRARY
CHAK CHAK
FIXING THE LOCK
TMP TMP TMP
HM?
THAM THAM
SORRY!
MIAKA!!
WAM WAM
BANG
FOUR GODS...
FOUR GODS...
HERE IT IS!
BLOCK THE DOOR, KEISUKE! DON'T LET ANYBODY IN!!

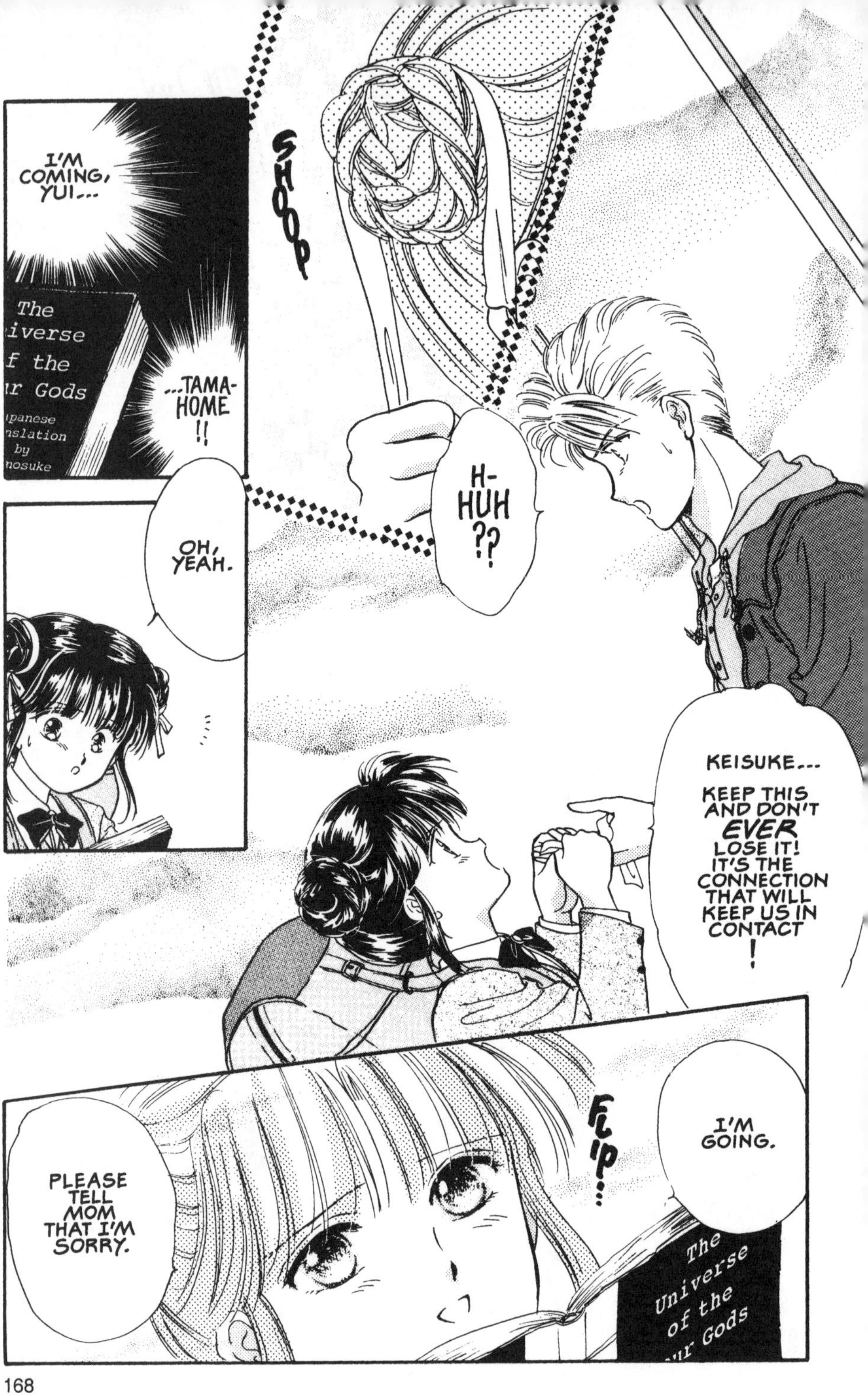
I'M COMING, YUI...
The
iverse
f the
r Gods
panese
nslation
by
nosuke
...TAMA-HOME!!
SHOOP
H-HUH??
OH, YEAH.
KEISUKE... KEEP THIS AND DON'T EVER LOSE IT! IT'S THE CONNECTION THAT WILL KEEP US IN CONTACT!
PLEASE TELL MOM THAT I'M SORRY.
FLIP...
I'M GOING.
The Universe of the
ur Gods

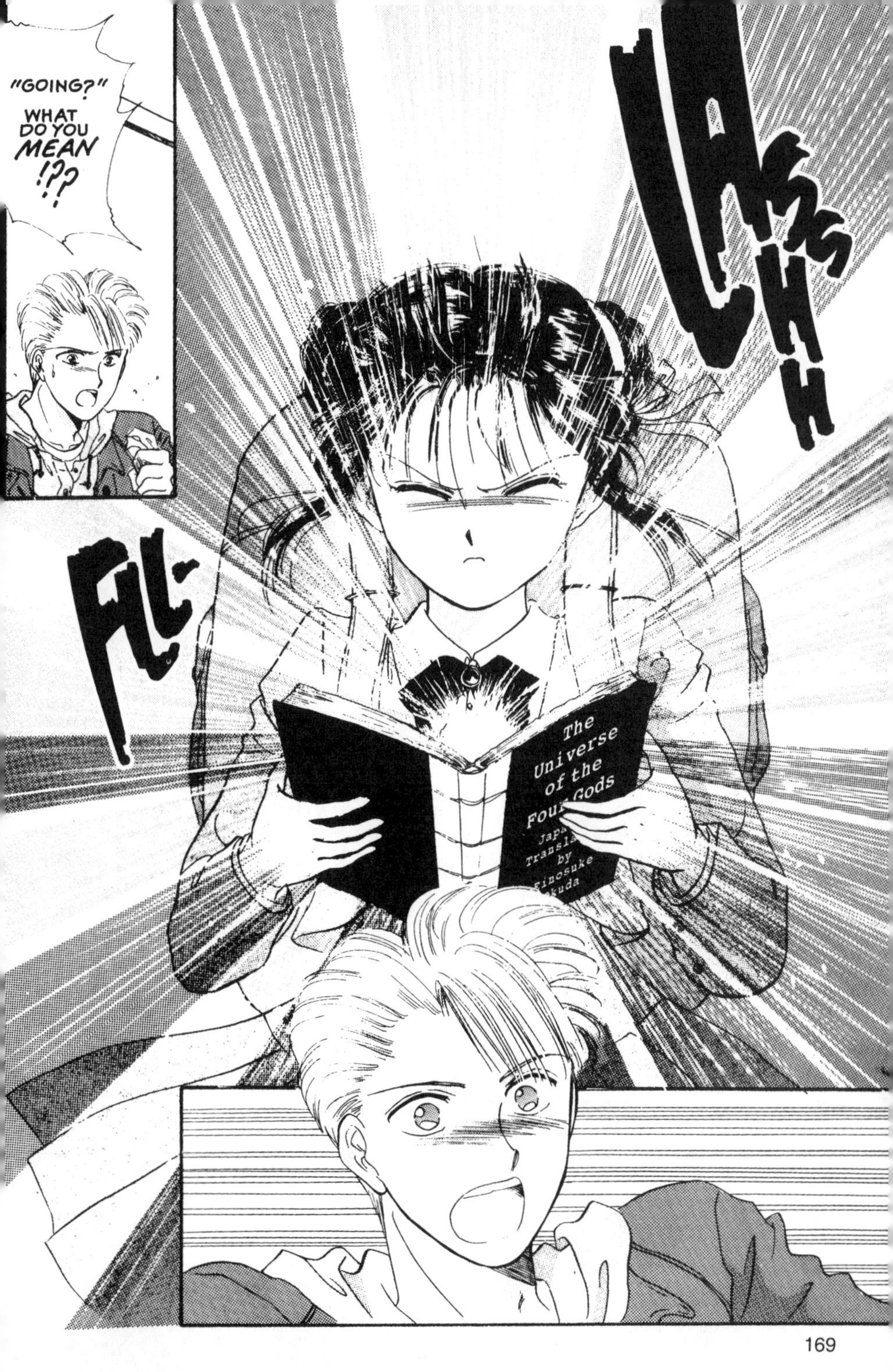
"GOING?" WHAT DO YOU MEAN !??
FL-
ASSHHH
The Universe of the
Gods
by

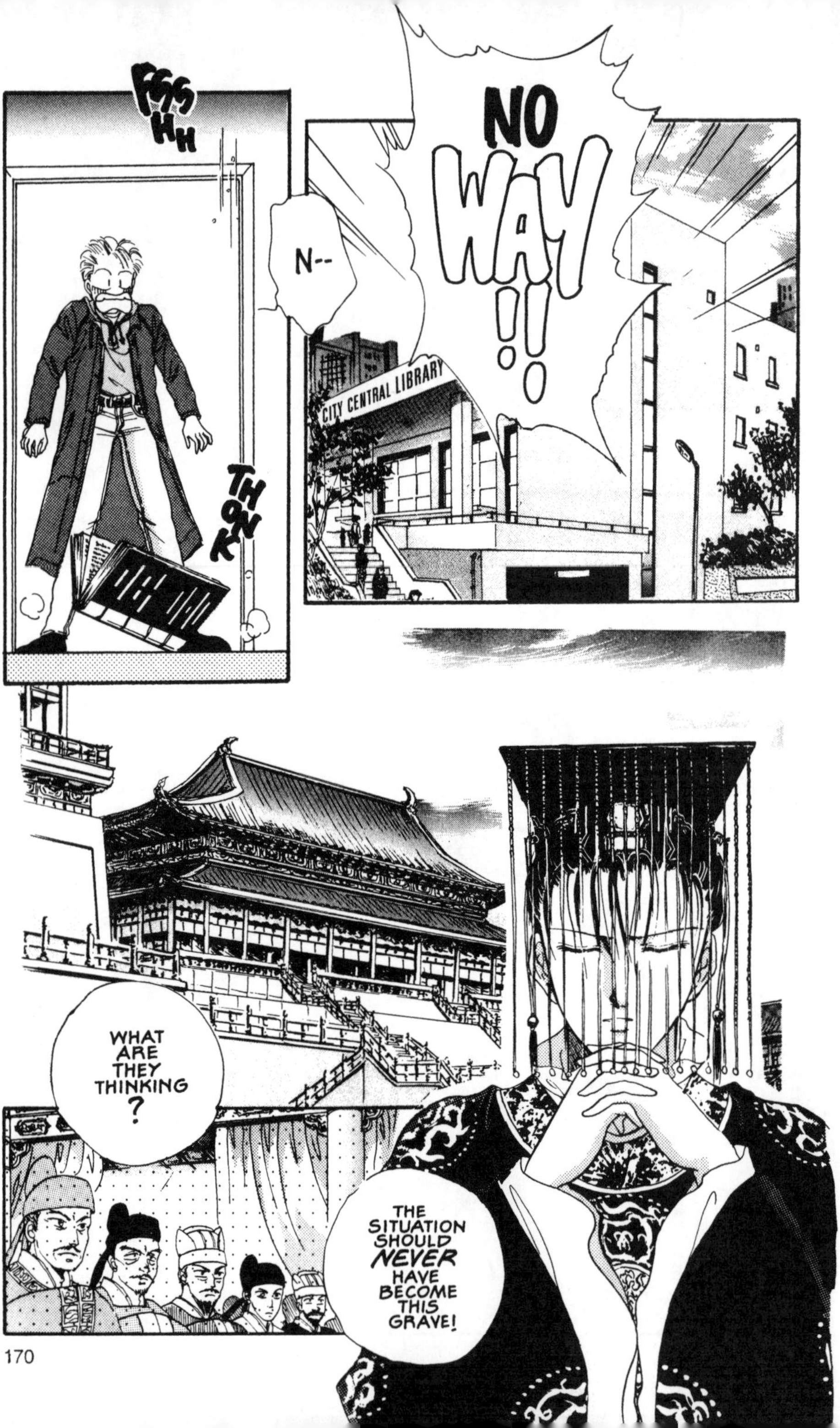
FSSSHH
THONK
N--
NO WAY!!!
CITY CENTRAL LIBRARY
WHAT ARE THEY THINKING?
THE SITUATION SHOULD *NEVER* HAVE BECOME THIS GRAVE!

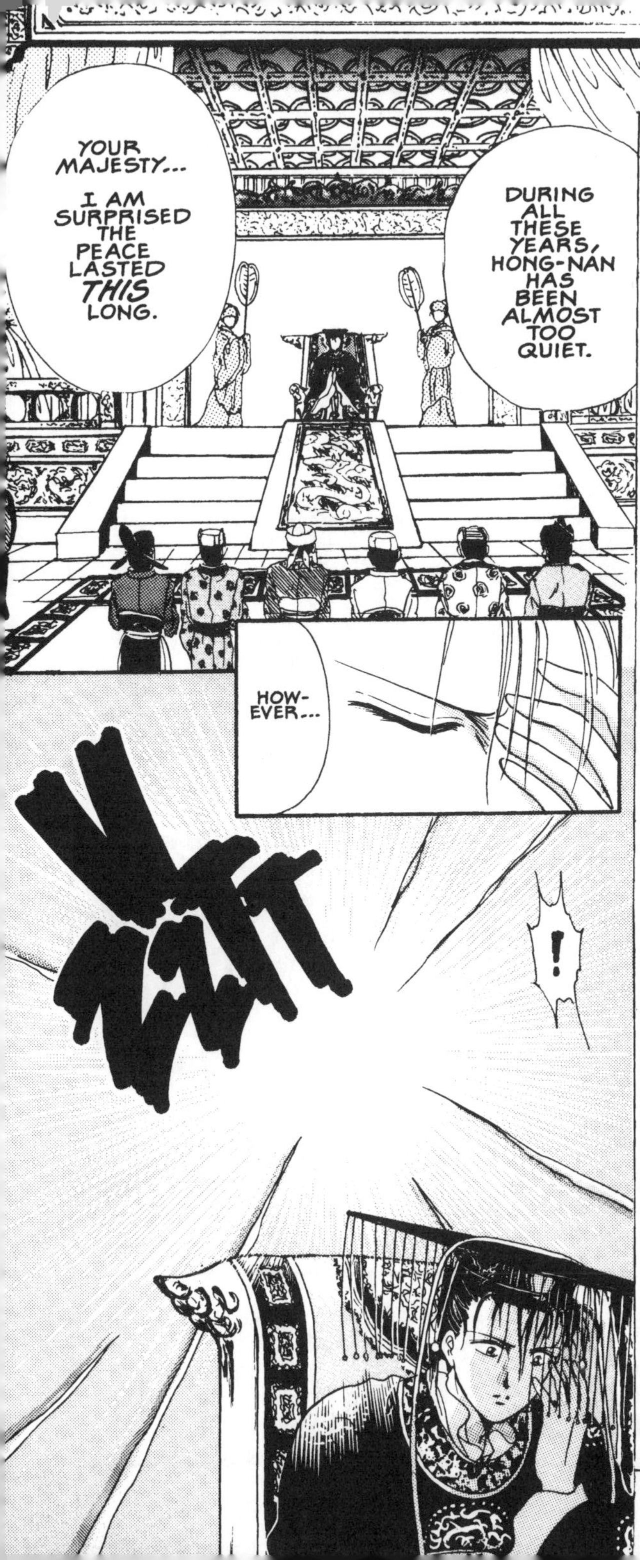
YOUR MAJESTY... I AM SURPRISED THE PEACE LASTED THIS LONG.
DURING ALL THESE YEARS, HONG-NAN HAS BEEN ALMOST TOO QUIET.
HOW-EVER...
!

Fushigi Yûgi ∾ 2

While Asuka has suffered through many hard times, the only hardship for Miaka is studying for the entrance exams (which are pretty hard, to be sure). She has a nice brother; she's carefree and childish. That's why she'll never have the same mature quality Asuka has. I was wondering why this was, only to realize that they had different upbringings, so their personalities would have to differ. I surprised myself. My protagonists are all the same in their energy and outlook. But in terms of her naiveté, Miaka is just an average junior-high-school girl. Unlike Asuka who soon finds happiness, Miaka's life is going to get worse and worse. She might mature like Asuka as the story comes to a close. But the pain makes them grow, and growth is something I enjoy seeing. It's interesting to see how these characters grow up on their own. It isn't one of the things I plan.
By the way, my friends have started to like either Hotohori or Nuriko. Putting Hotohori aside for a moment... They all hated Nuriko when she (he) kissed Tamahome. Later, they started warming up to him, but once they found out he was gay, they disliked him again. Now that's a busy character! Recently, I'm glad to say that I've been hearing from more and more people who like him. I like him a lot! Children who read about cross-dressers don't like them, but readers who've graduated middle school seem to like that type of character a lot. This story is going to be really long so I'll do my best to make it through to the end. Stick with me, okay? The situation has been pretty hard up to this point, but this was the easy part! Miaka and Tamahome are really going to suffer. But however much they suffer, it's going to be twice as hard on me! You see, I'm just too nice and sweet a person. Ten demerits to anyone who just threw this book on the floor and stomped on it.

To be continued in the next issue!!

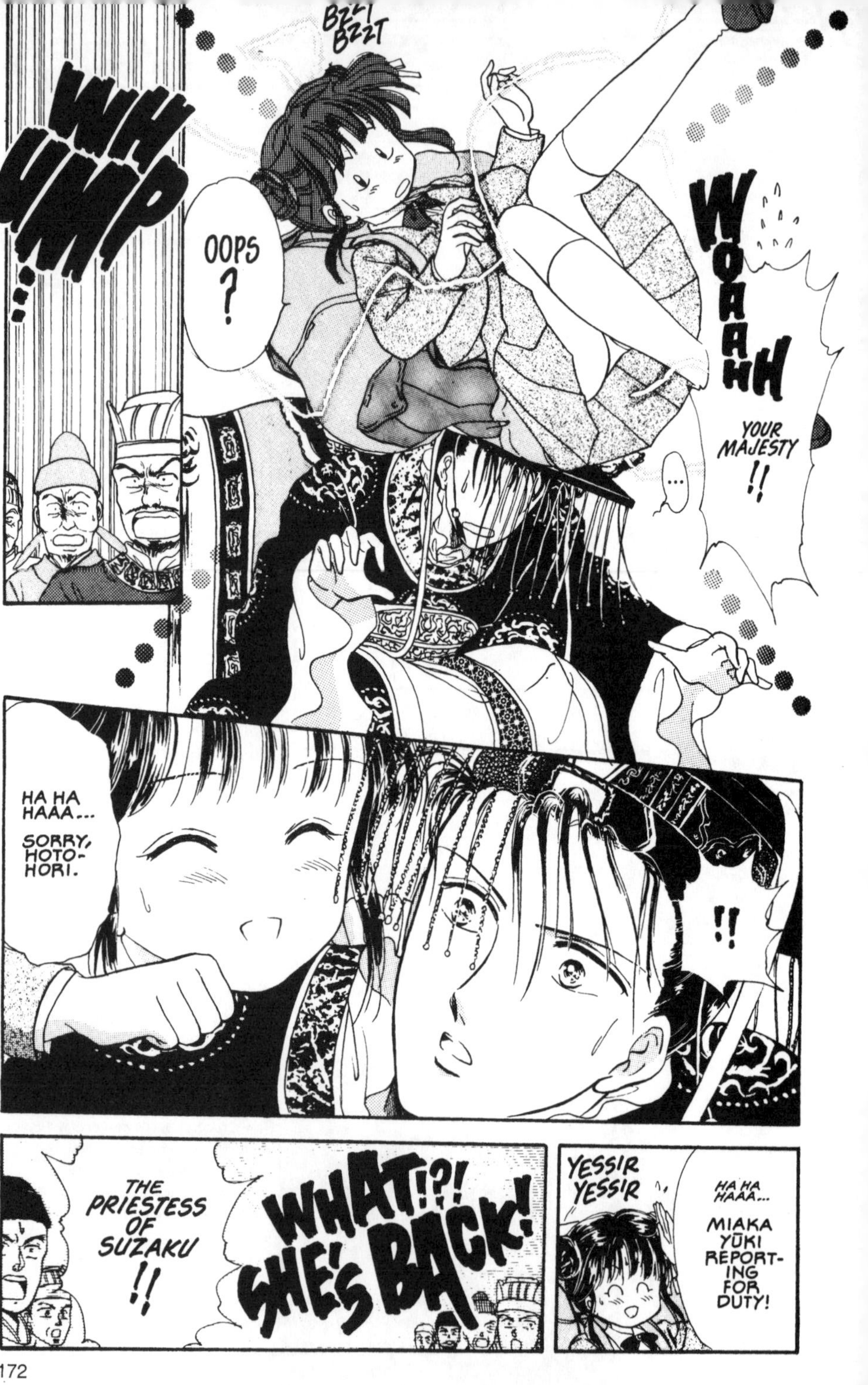
BZZT BZZT
WHUMP!...
OOPS ?
WOAAHH
YOUR MAJESTY !!
...
HA HA HAAA... SORRY, HOTOHORI.
!!
THE PRIESTESS OF SUZAKU !!
WHAT!?! SHE'S BACK!
YESSIR YESSIR
HA HA HAAA... MIAKA YŪKI REPORTING FOR DUTY!

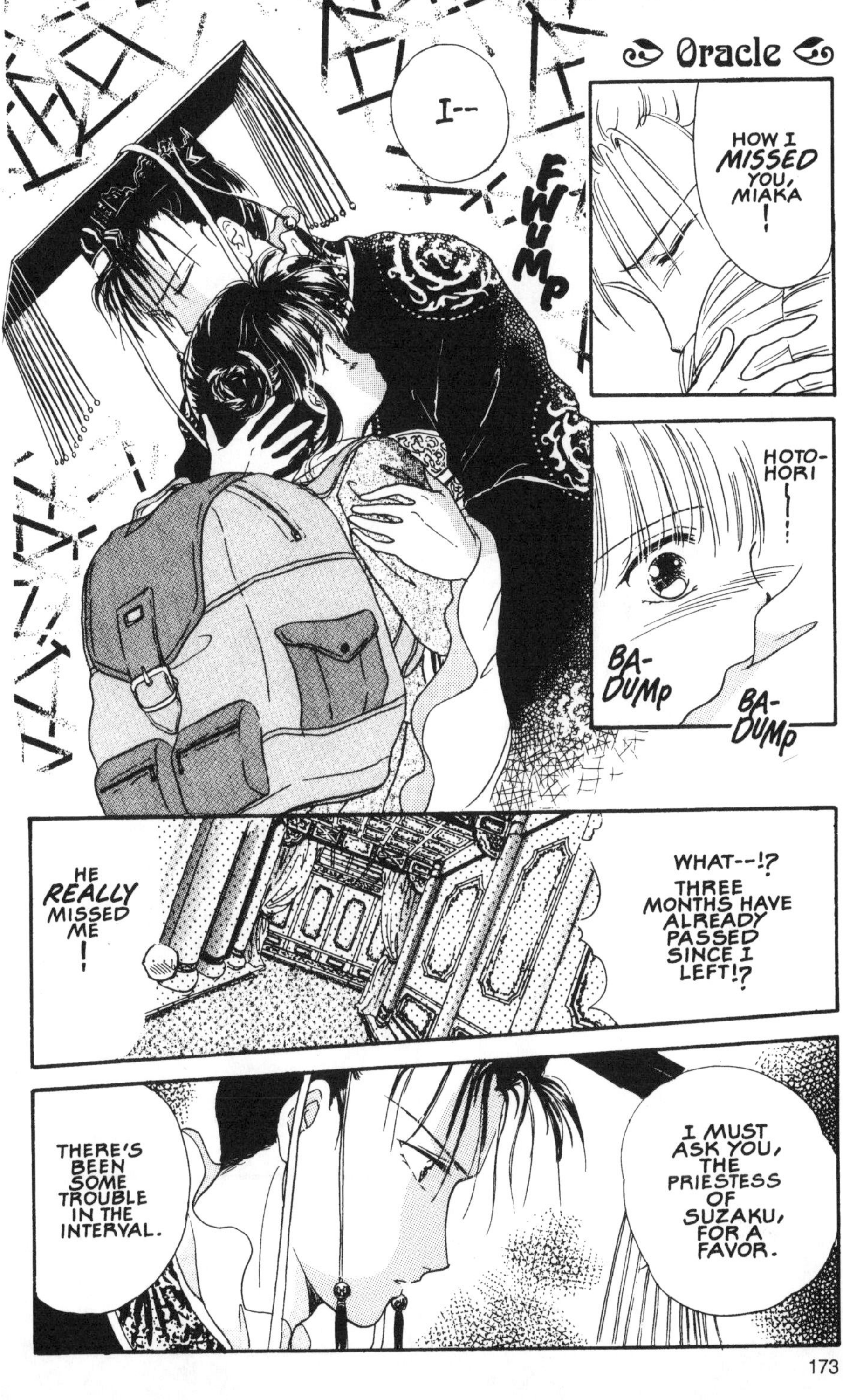
I--
FWUMP
HOW I MISSED YOU, MIAKA!
HOTO-HORI...!
BA-DUMP
BA-DUMP
HE REALLY MISSED ME!
WHAT--!? THREE MONTHS HAVE ALREADY PASSED SINCE I LEFT!?
THERE'S BEEN SOME TROUBLE IN THE INTERVAL.
I MUST ASK YOU, THE PRIESTESS OF SUZAKU, FOR A FAVOR.

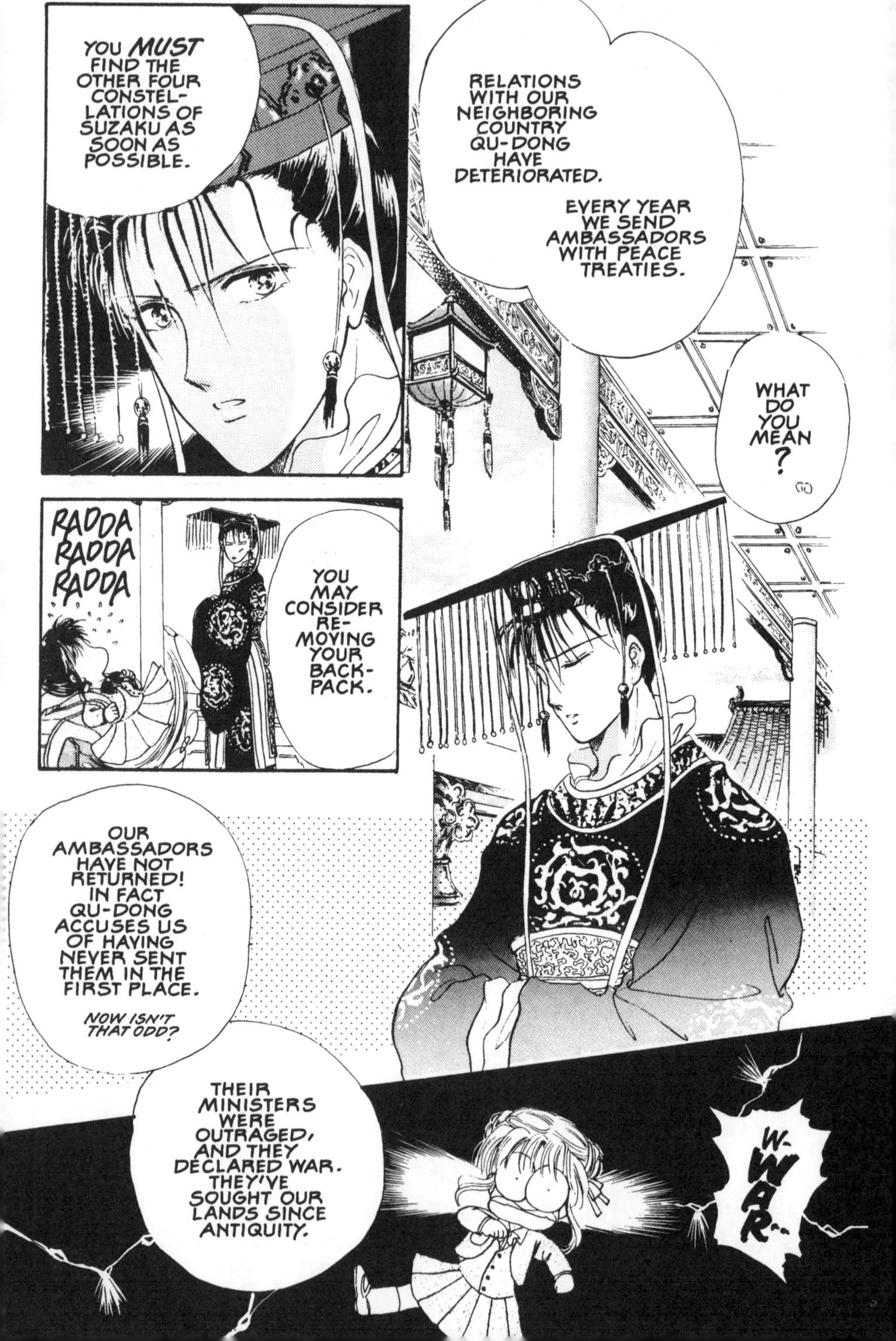
YOU MUST FIND THE OTHER FOUR CONSTEL-LATIONS OF SUZAKU AS SOON AS POSSIBLE.
RADDA RADDA RADDA
YOU MAY CONSIDER RE-MOVING YOUR BACK-PACK.
RELATIONS WITH OUR NEIGHBORING COUNTRY QU-DONG HAVE DETERIORATED.
EVERY YEAR WE SEND AMBASSADORS WITH PEACE TREATIES.
WHAT DO YOU MEAN?
OUR AMBASSADORS HAVE NOT RETURNED! IN FACT QU-DONG ACCUSES US OF HAVING NEVER SENT THEM IN THE FIRST PLACE.
NOW ISN'T THAT ODD?
THEIR MINISTERS WERE OUTRAGED, AND THEY DECLARED WAR. THEY'VE SOUGHT OUR LANDS SINCE ANTIQUITY.
W-WAR--

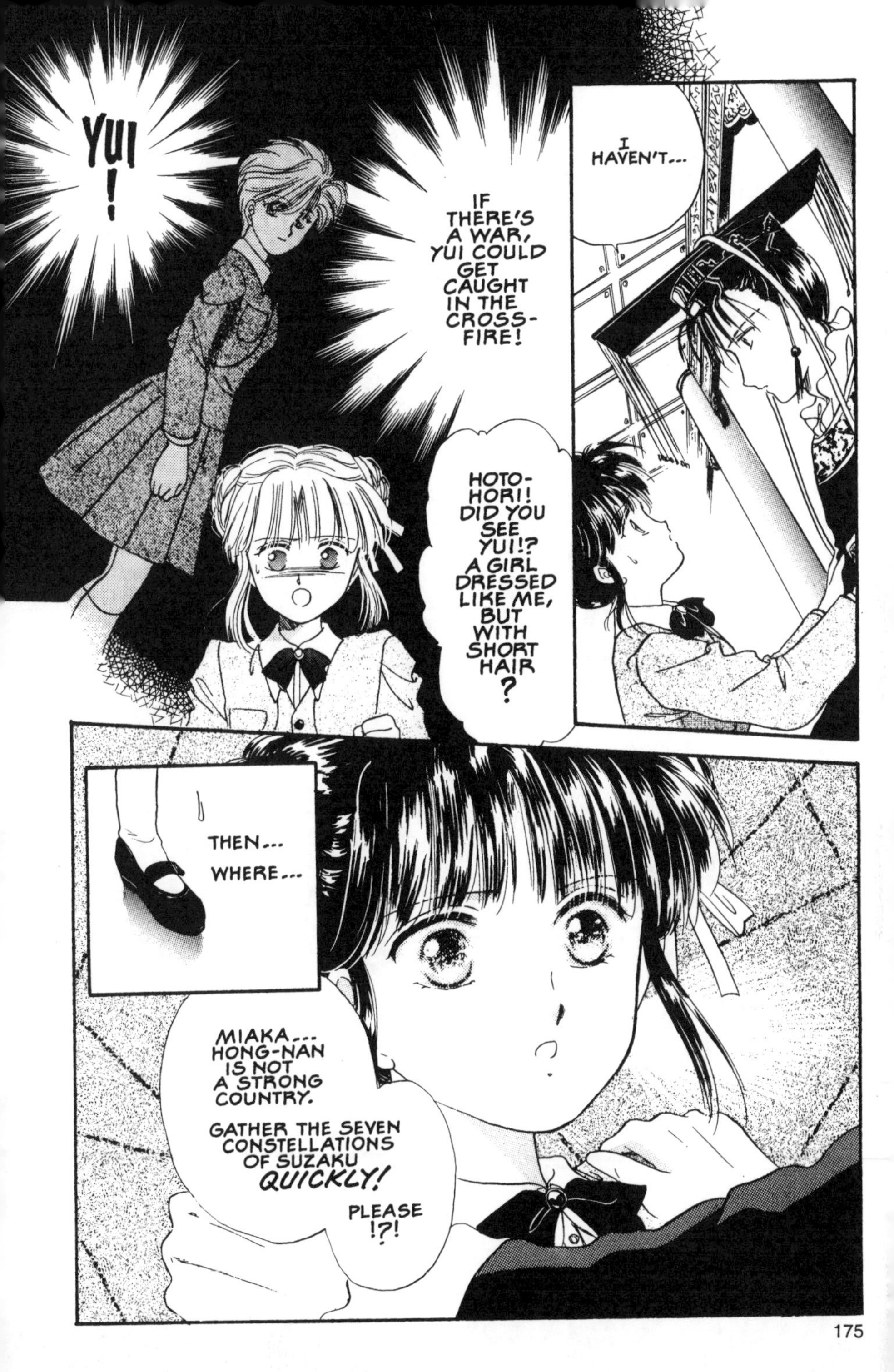
YUI!
IF THERE'S A WAR, YUI COULD GET CAUGHT IN THE CROSS-FIRE!
HOTO-HORI! DID YOU SEE YUI!? A GIRL DRESSED LIKE ME, BUT WITH SHORT HAIR?
I HAVEN'T...
THEN... WHERE...
MIAKA... HONG-NAN IS NOT A STRONG COUNTRY.
GATHER THE SEVEN CONSTELLATIONS OF SUZAKU QUICKLY!
PLEASE !?!

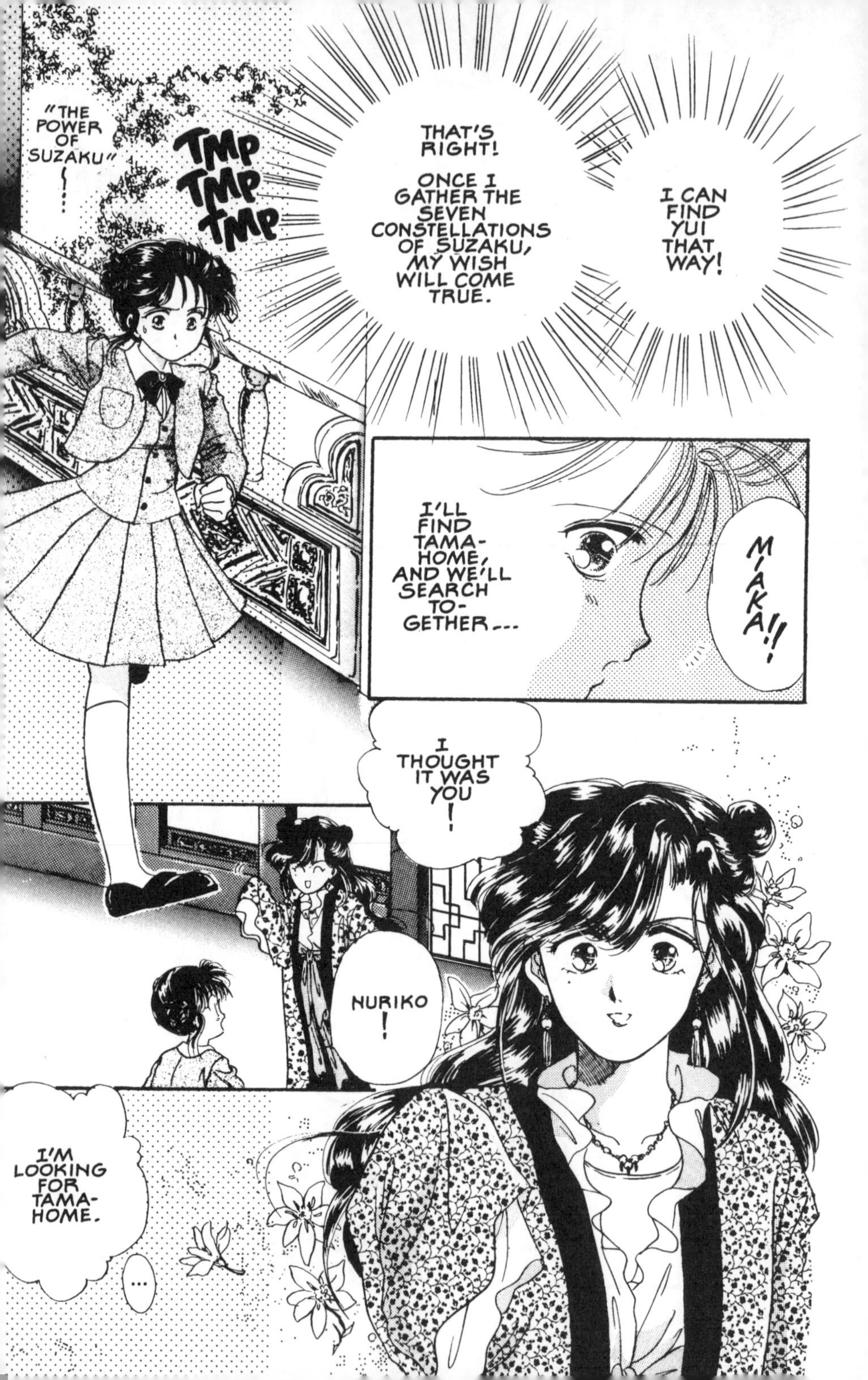
"THE POWER OF SUZAKU"
TMP TMP TMP
THAT'S RIGHT!
ONCE I GATHER THE SEVEN CONSTELLATIONS OF SUZAKU, MY WISH WILL COME TRUE.
I CAN FIND YUI THAT WAY!
I'LL FIND TAMA-HOME, AND WE'LL SEARCH TO-GETHER...
MIAKA!!
I THOUGHT IT WAS YOU!
NURIKO!
I'M LOOKING FOR TAMA-HOME.
...

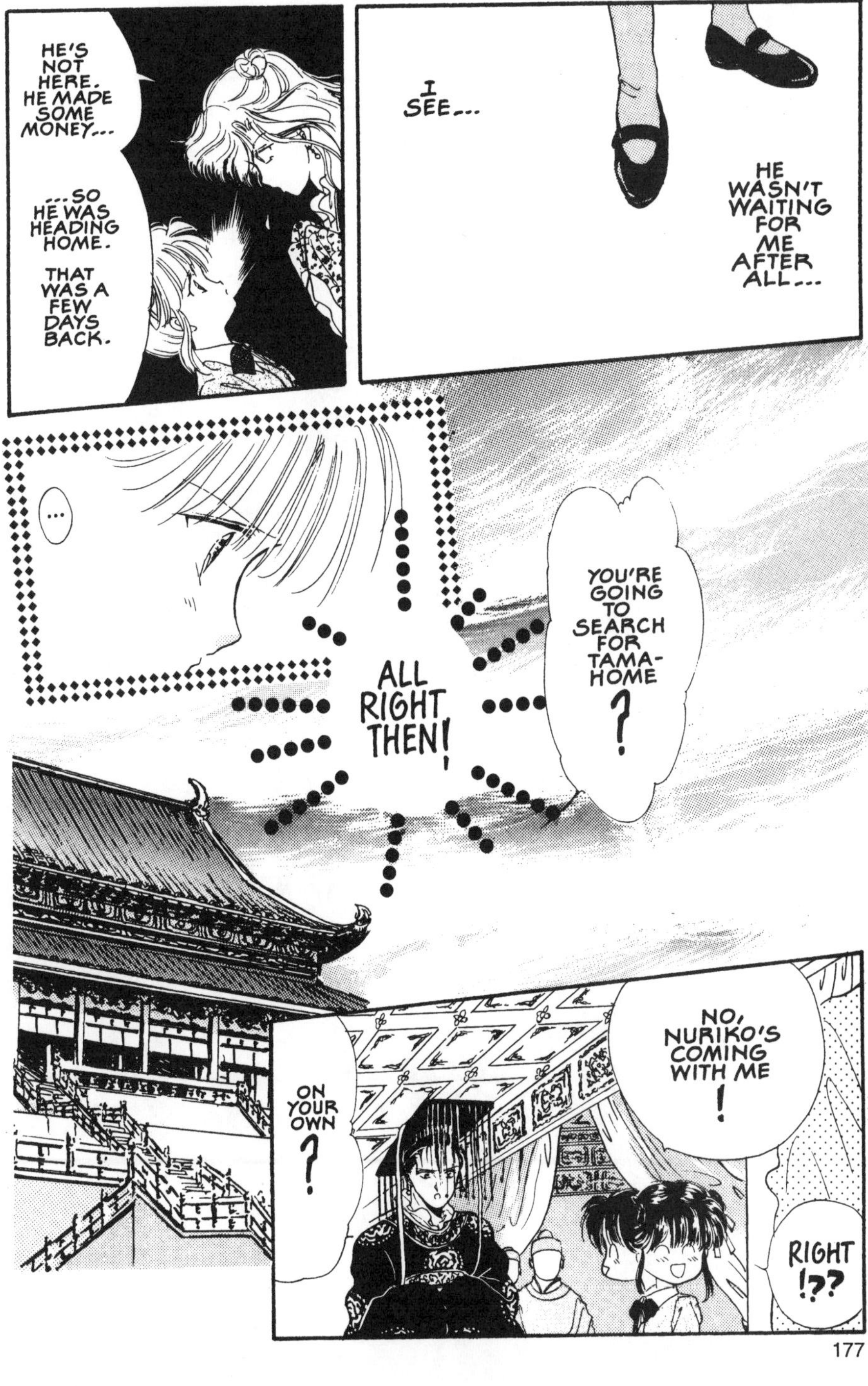
HE'S NOT HERE. HE MADE SOME MONEY...
...SO HE WAS HEADING HOME.
THAT WAS A FEW DAYS BACK.
I SEE...
HE WASN'T WAITING FOR ME AFTER ALL...
...
ALL RIGHT THEN!
YOU'RE GOING TO SEARCH FOR TAMA-HOME?
ON YOUR OWN?
NO, NURIKO'S COMING WITH ME!
RIGHT!??

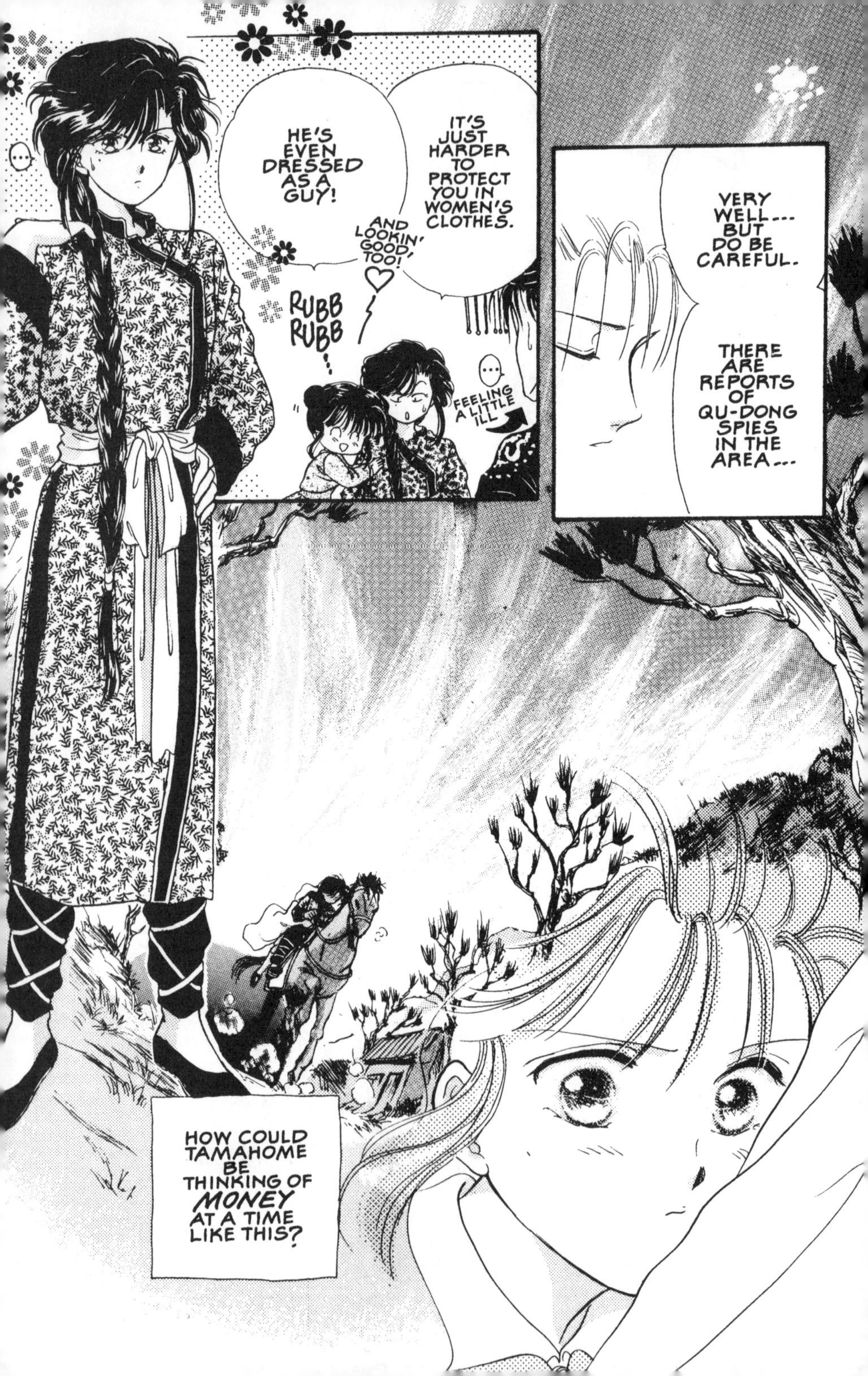
...
HE'S EVEN DRESSED AS A GUY!
IT'S JUST HARDER TO PROTECT YOU IN WOMEN'S CLOTHES.
AND LOOKIN' GOOD, TOO!
RUBB RUBB
...
FEELING A LITTLE ILL
VERY WELL... BUT DO BE CAREFUL.
THERE ARE REPORTS OF QU-DONG SPIES IN THE AREA...
HOW COULD TAMAHOME BE THINKING OF *MONEY* AT A TIME LIKE THIS?

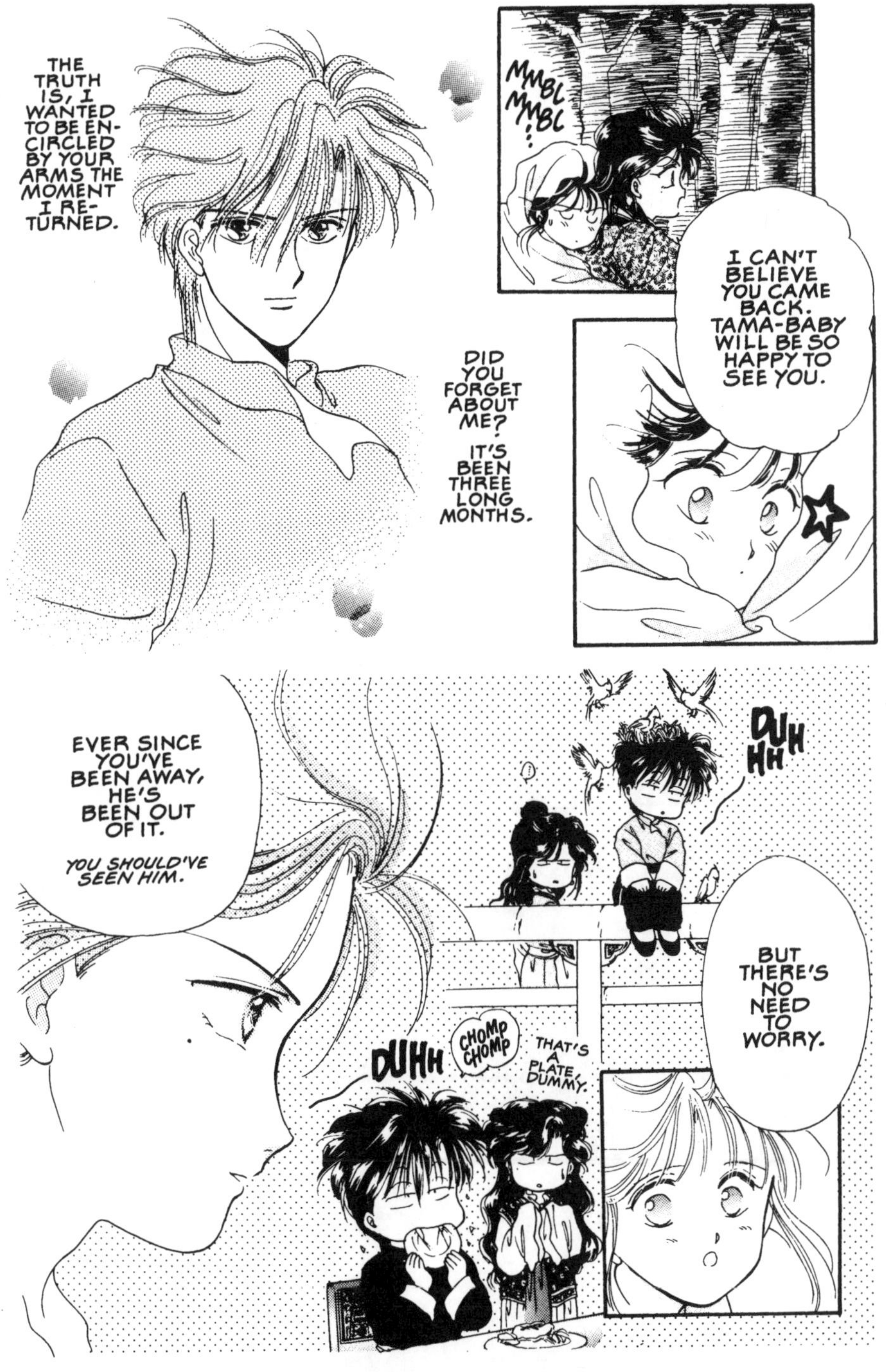

THE TRUTH IS, I WANTED TO BE ENCIRCLED BY YOUR ARMS THE MOMENT I RETURNED.
DID YOU FORGET ABOUT ME?
IT'S BEEN THREE LONG MONTHS.
MMBL MMBL...
I CAN'T BELIEVE YOU CAME BACK. TAMA-BABY WILL BE SO HAPPY TO SEE YOU.
EVER SINCE YOU'VE BEEN AWAY, HE'S BEEN OUT OF IT.
YOU SHOULD'VE SEEN HIM.
DUHHH
DUHH
CHOMP CHOMP
THAT'S A PLATE, DUMMY.
BUT THERE'S NO NEED TO WORRY.

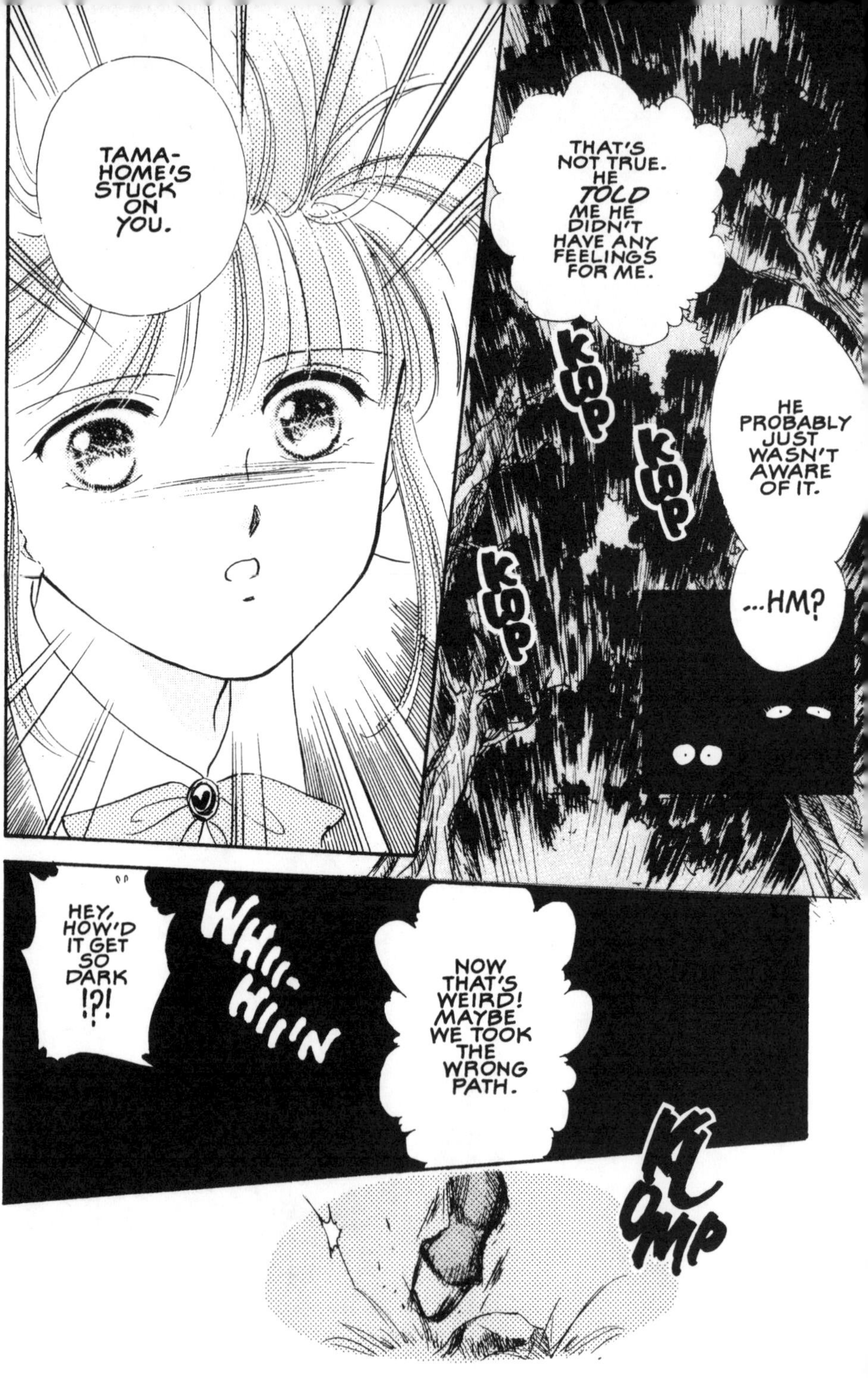
TAMA-HOME'S STUCK ON YOU.
THAT'S NOT TRUE. HE *TOLD* ME HE DIDN'T HAVE ANY FEELINGS FOR ME.
KLOP
KLOP
KLOP
HE PROBABLY JUST WASN'T AWARE OF IT.
...HM?
HEY, HOW'D IT GET SO DARK !?!
WHIII-HIII'N
NOW THAT'S WEIRD! MAYBE WE TOOK THE WRONG PATH.
KLOMP

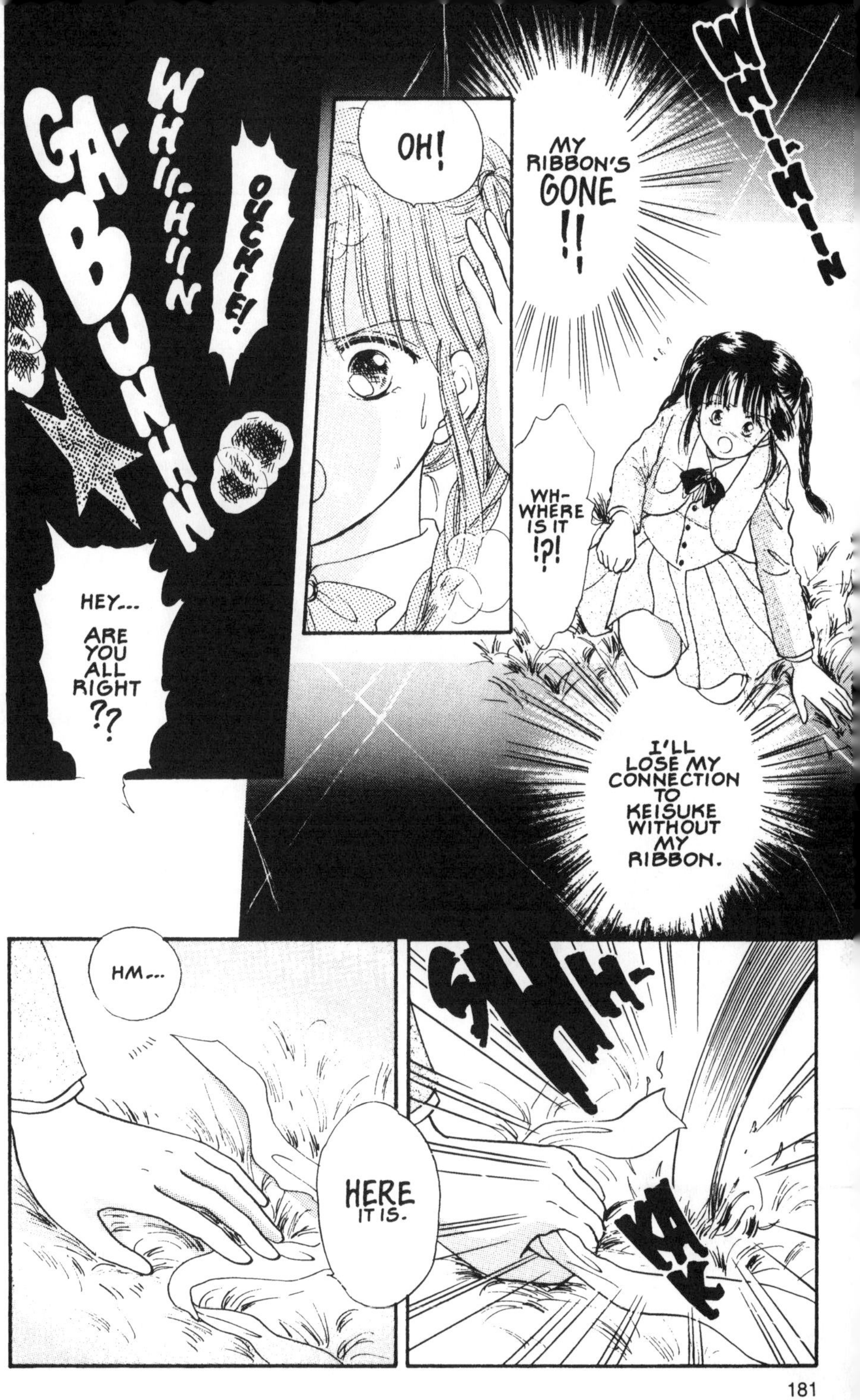
GA-BUNHN
WHIIHIIN
OUCHIE!
HEY... ARE YOU ALL RIGHT??
OH!
MY RIBBON'S GONE!!
WHIIHIIN
WH-WHERE IS IT!?!
I'LL LOSE MY CONNECTION TO KEISUKE WITHOUT MY RIBBON.
HM...
HERE IT IS.
GAHH-
KAK

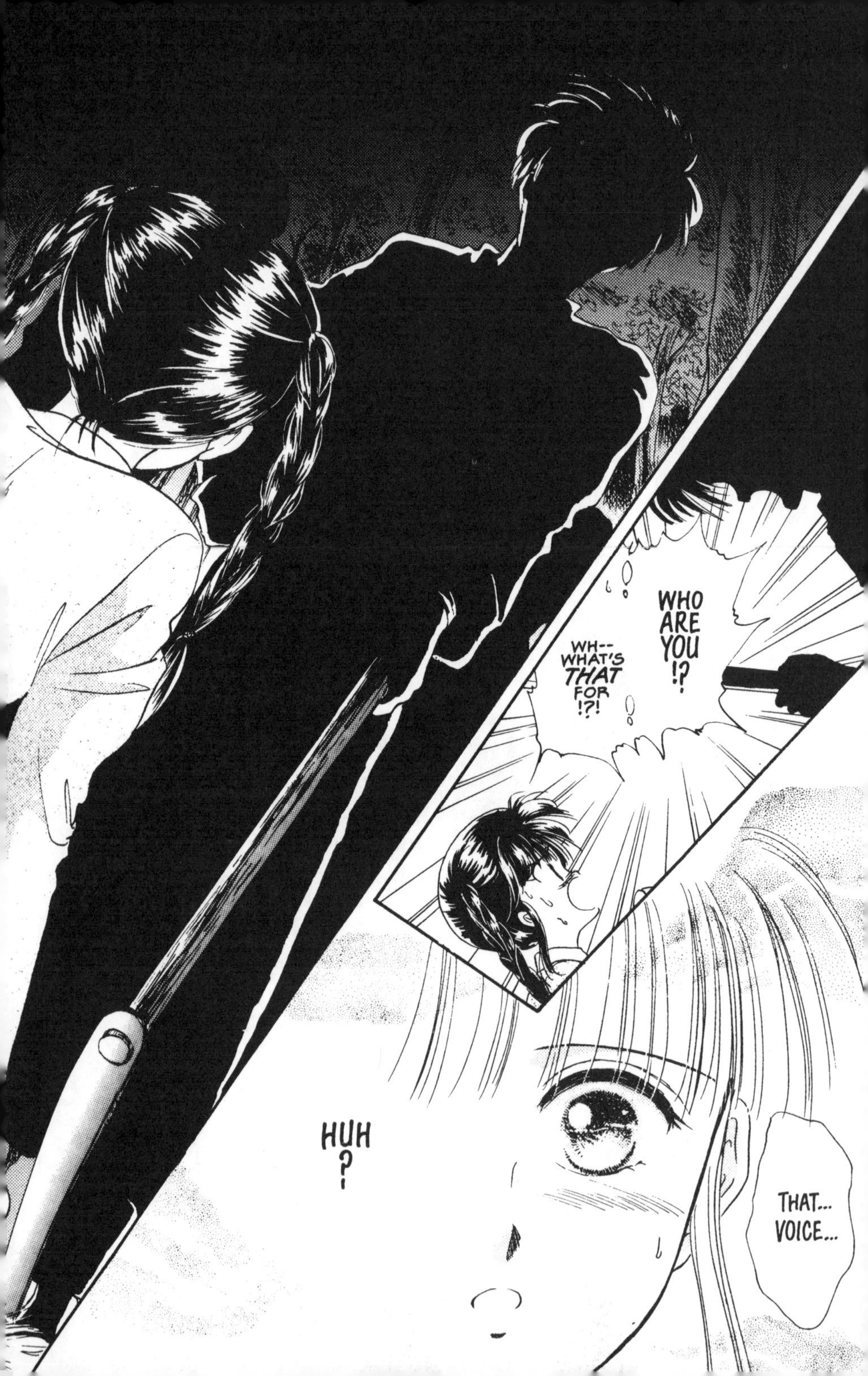
WH-- WHAT'S THAT FOR !?!
WHO ARE YOU !?
HUH ?
THAT... VOICE...

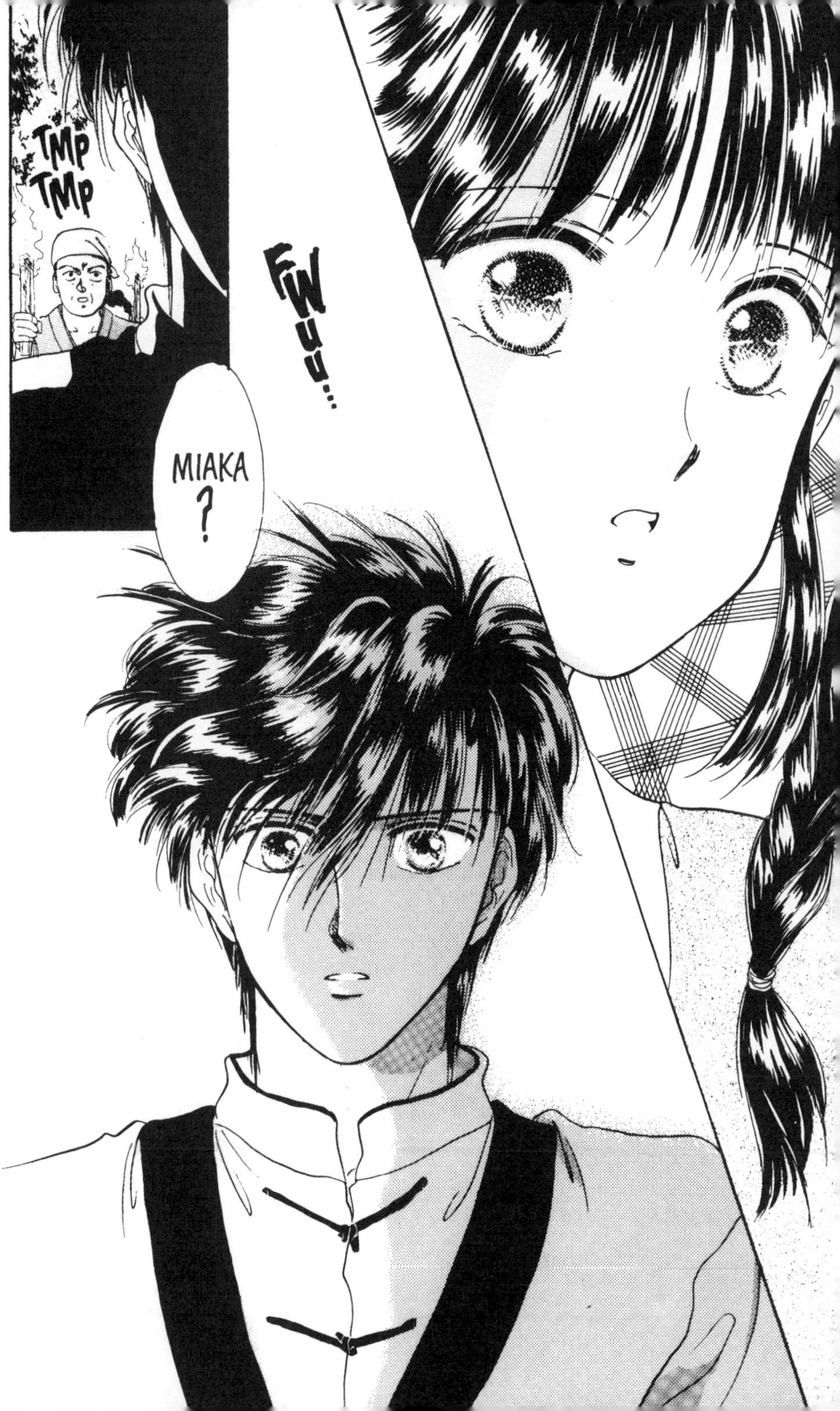
TMP TMP
FWUUU...
MIAKA ?

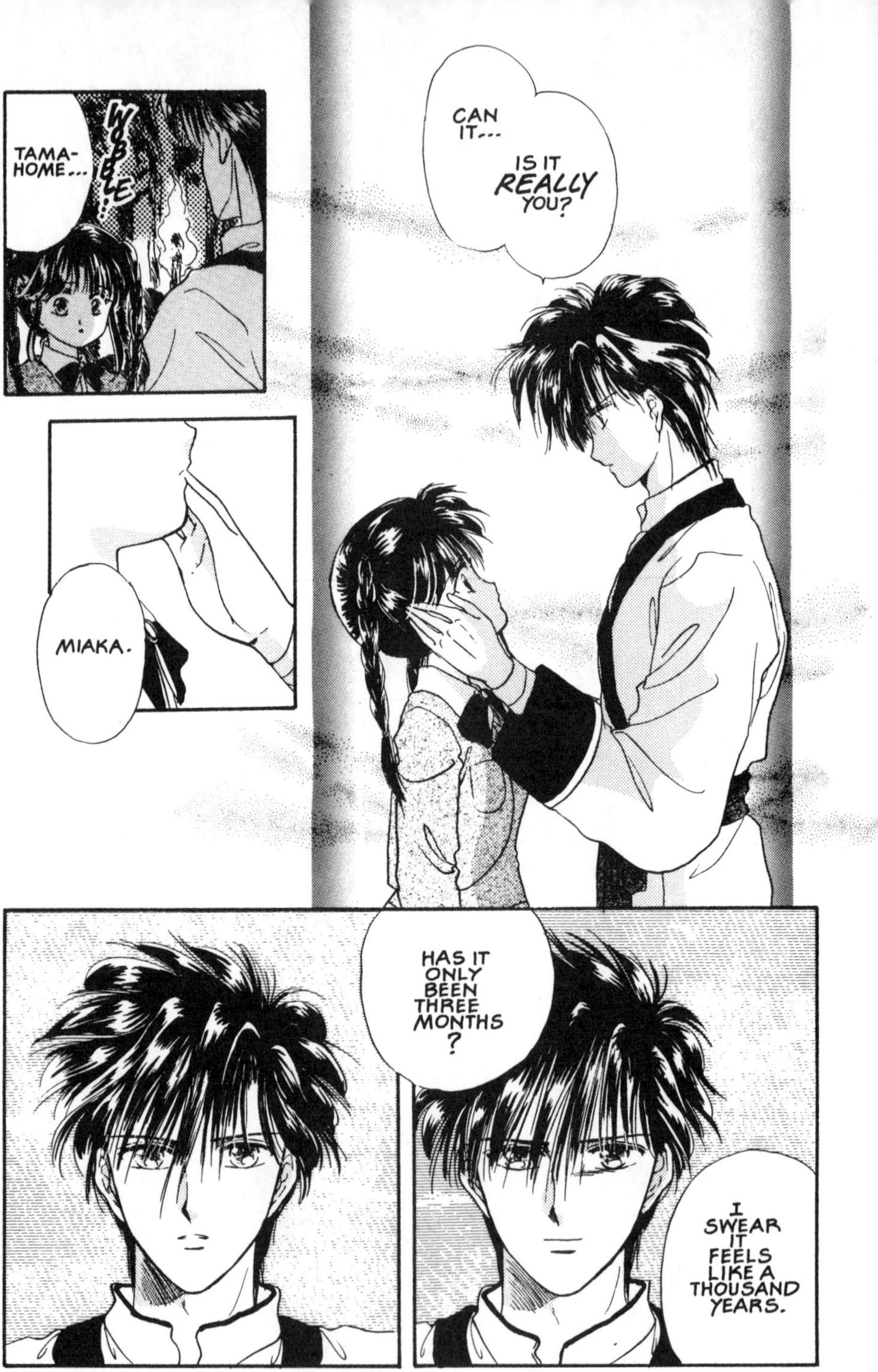
TAMA-HOME...
WOBBLE...
MIAKA.
CAN IT... IS IT REALLY YOU?
HAS IT ONLY BEEN THREE MONTHS?
I SWEAR IT FEELS LIKE A THOUSAND YEARS.

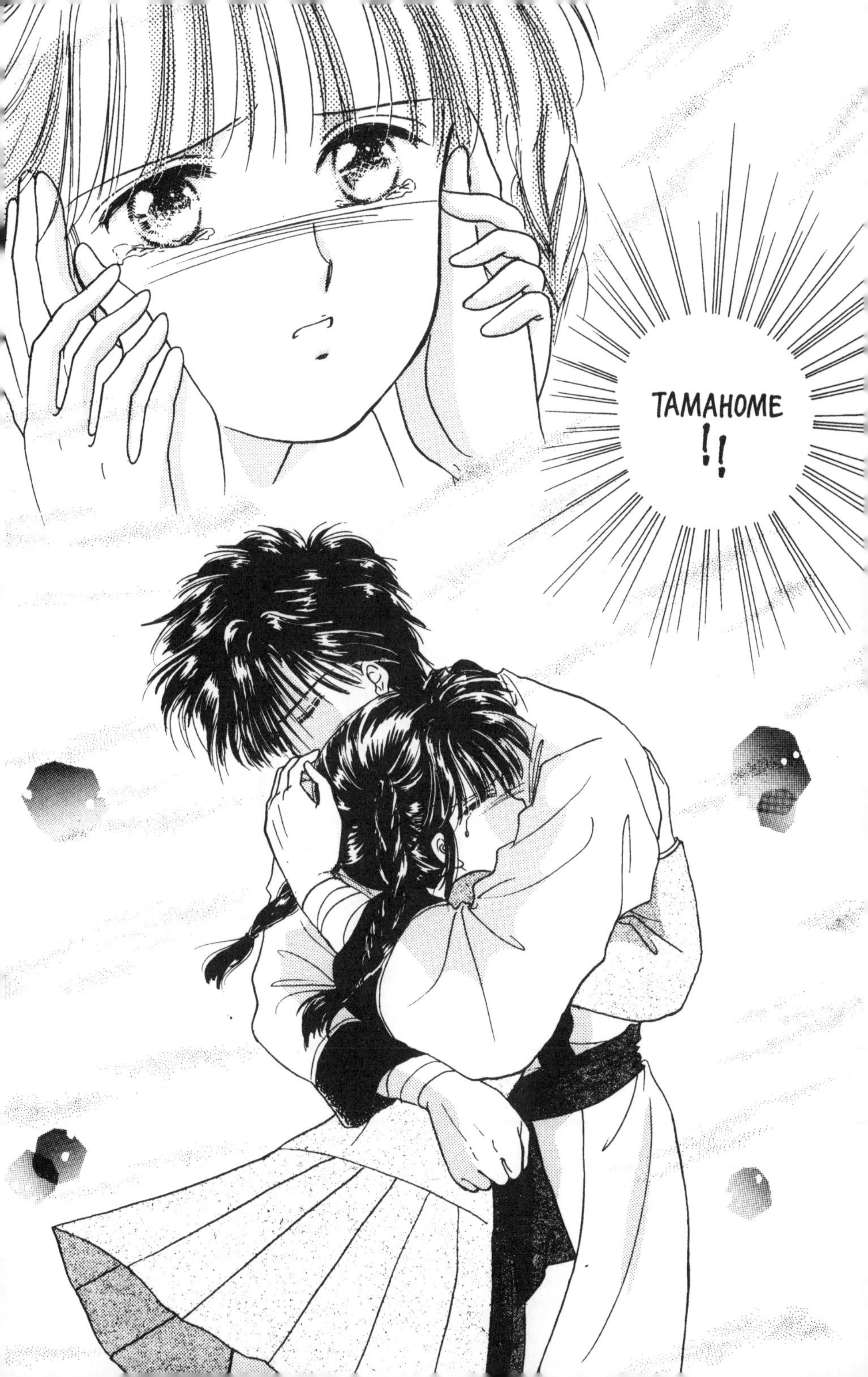
TAMAHOME !!

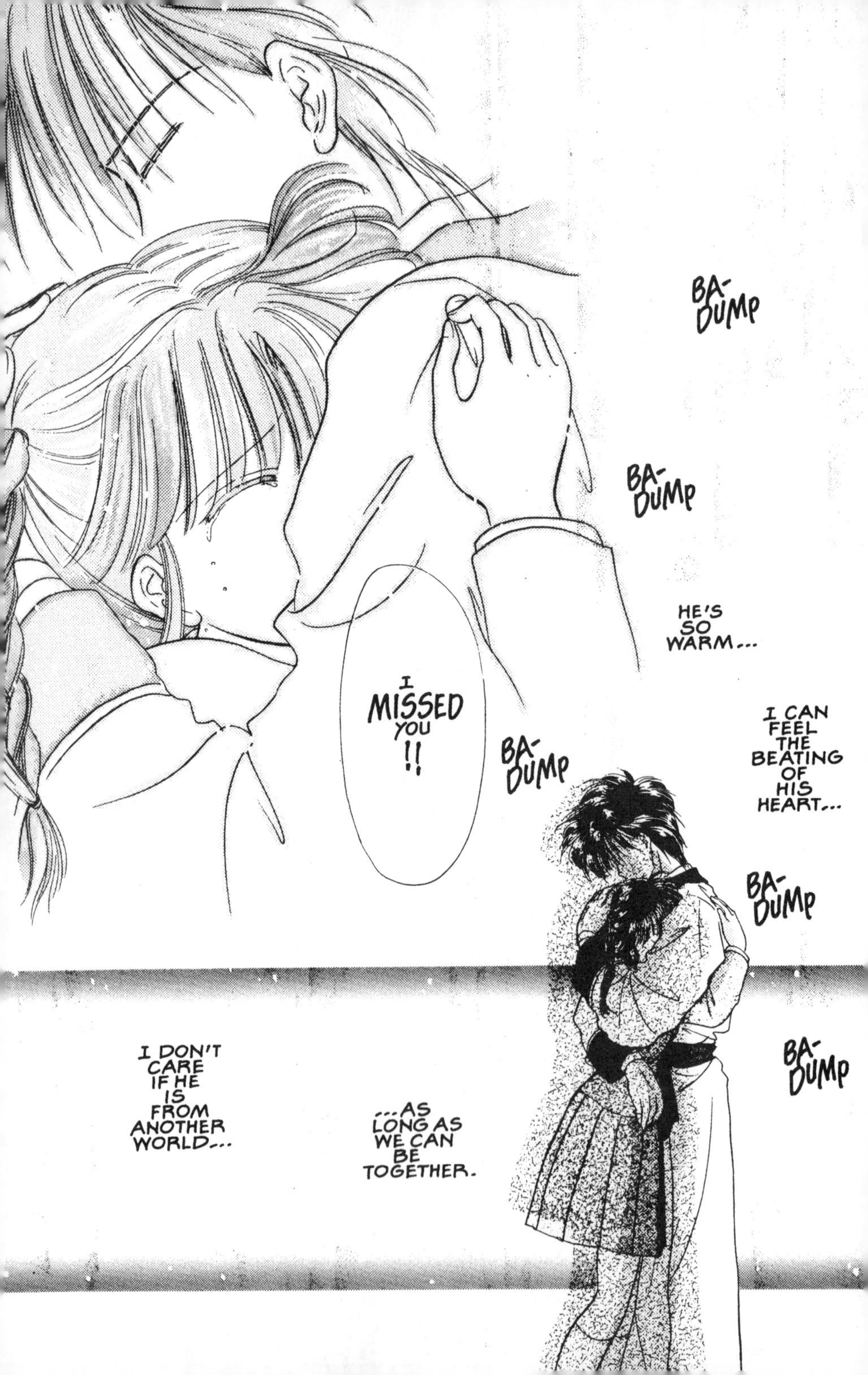
BA-DUMP
BA-DUMP
HE'S SO WARM...
I MISSED YOU!!
BA-DUMP
I CAN FEEL THE BEATING OF HIS HEART...
BA-DUMP
I DON'T CARE IF HE IS FROM ANOTHER WORLD...
...AS LONG AS WE CAN BE TOGETHER.
BA-DUMP

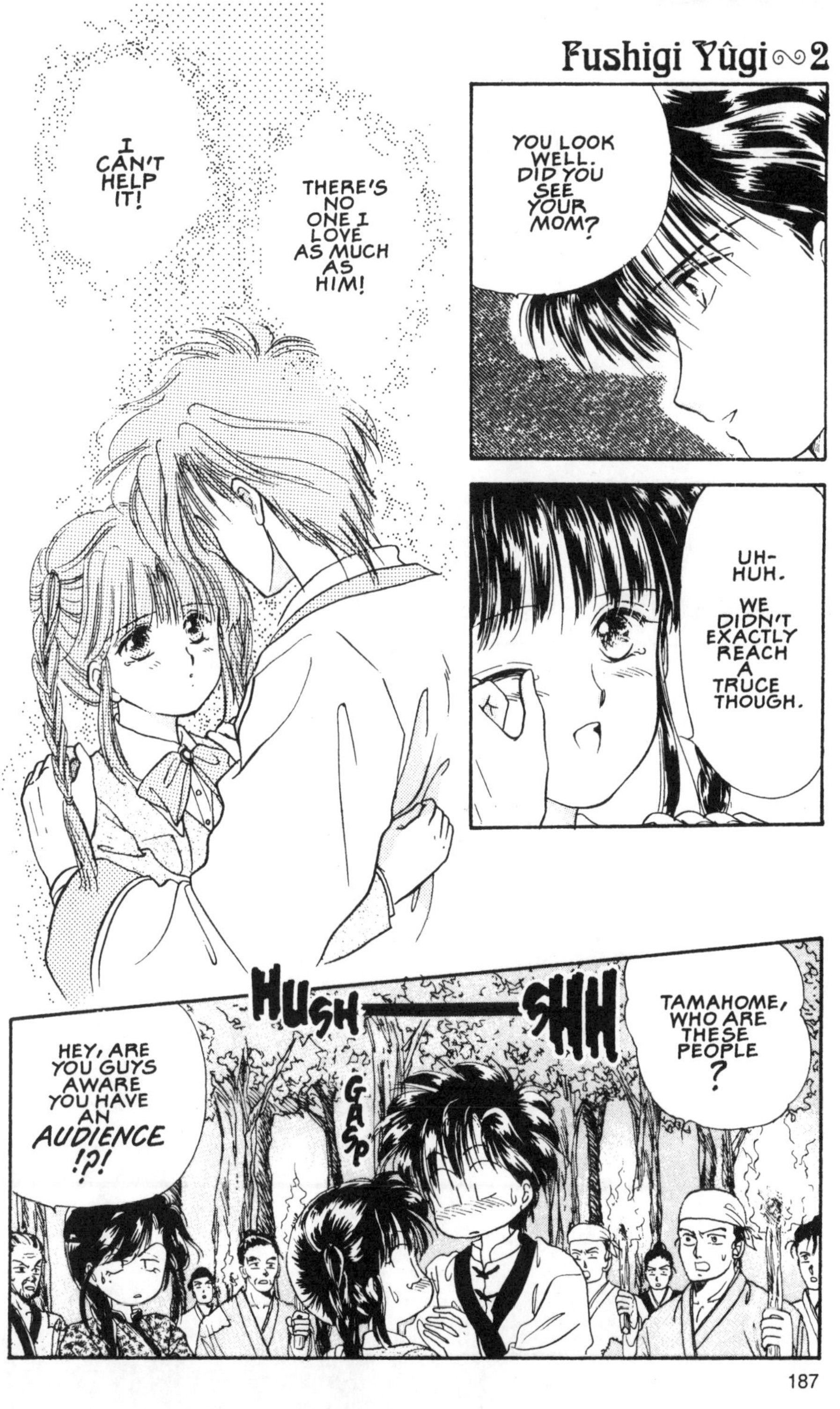
I CAN'T HELP IT!
THERE'S NO ONE I LOVE AS MUCH AS HIM!
YOU LOOK WELL. DID YOU SEE YOUR MOM?
UH-HUH.
WE DIDN'T EXACTLY REACH A TRUCE THOUGH.
HEY, ARE YOU GUYS AWARE YOU HAVE AN AUDIENCE !?!
HUSH
GASP
SHH
TAMAHOME, WHO ARE THESE PEOPLE ?

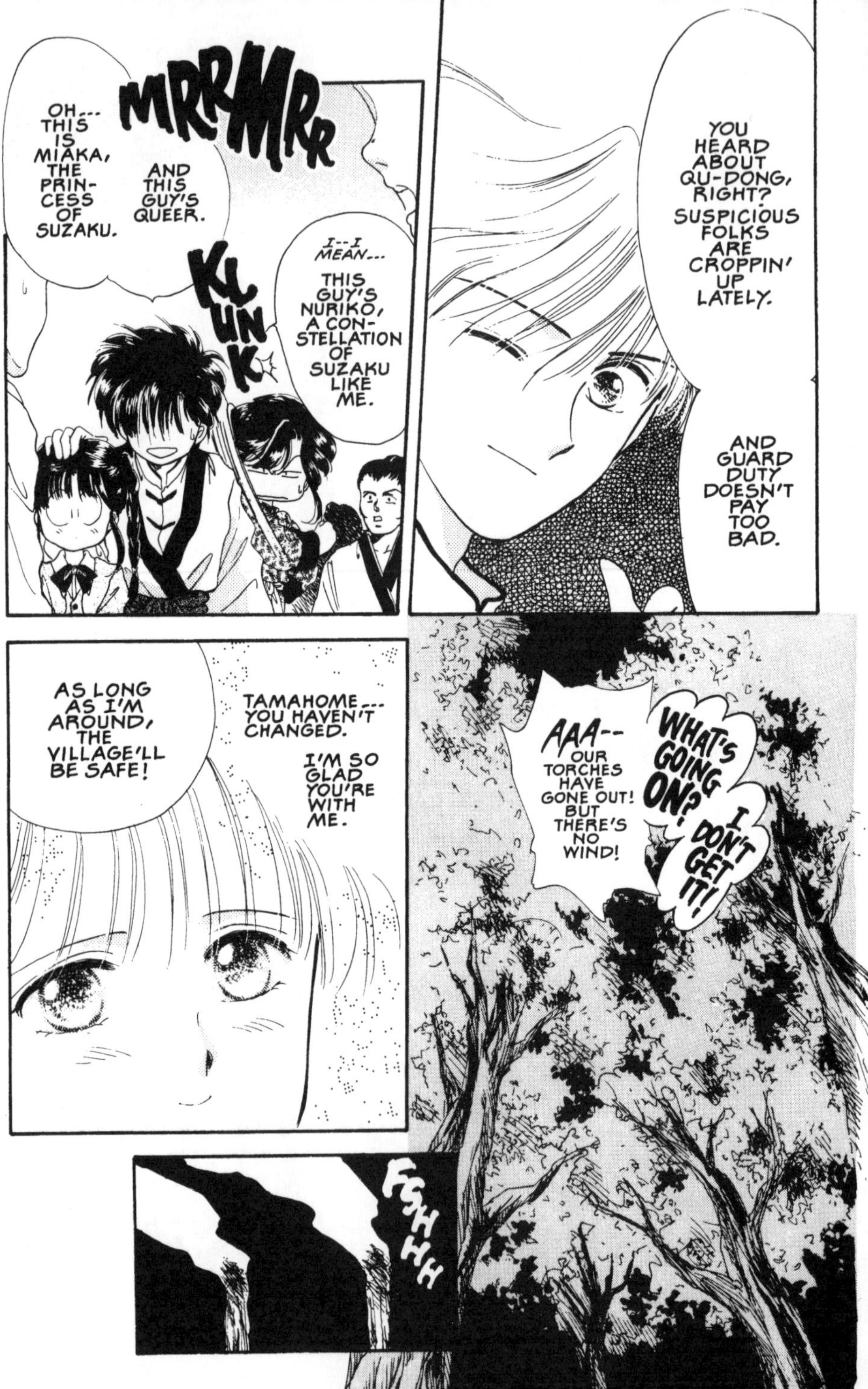
OH... THIS IS MIAKA, THE PRINCESS OF SUZAKU.
MRRMRR
AND THIS GUY'S QUEER.
KLUNK
I--I MEAN... THIS GUY'S NURIKO, A CONSTELLATION OF SUZAKU LIKE ME.
YOU HEARD ABOUT QU-DONG, RIGHT? SUSPICIOUS FOLKS ARE CROPPIN' UP LATELY.
AND GUARD DUTY DOESN'T PAY TOO BAD.
AS LONG AS I'M AROUND, THE VILLAGE'LL BE SAFE!
TAMAHOME... YOU HAVEN'T CHANGED.
I'M SO GLAD YOU'RE WITH ME.
FSHHHH
AAA-- OUR TORCHES HAVE GONE OUT! BUT THERE'S NO WIND!
WHAT'S GOING ON?
I DON'T GET IT!

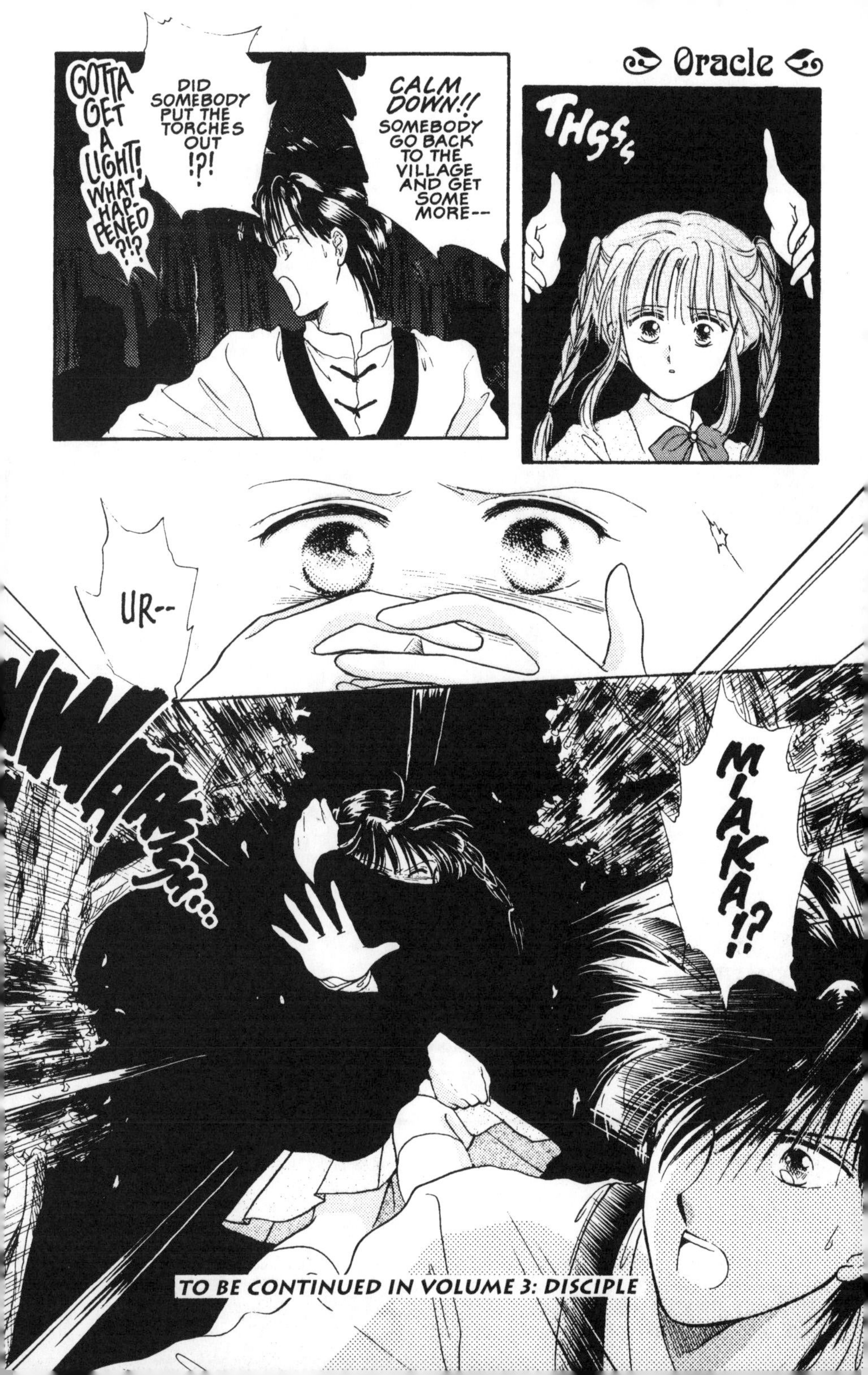

GOTTA GET A LIGHT! WHAT HAPPENED ?!?
DID SOMEBODY PUT THE TORCHES OUT !?!
CALM DOWN!! SOMEBODY GO BACK TO THE VILLAGE AND GET SOME MORE--
THSSS
UR--
MWAAAH...
MIAKA!?
TO BE CONTINUED IN VOLUME 3: DISCIPLE